W9-BCD-777

FLAVIUS JOSEPHUS

FLAVIUS JOSEPHUS

His TIME *and his* CRITICS

By LEON BERNSTEIN

LIVERIGHT PUBLISHING CORPORATION
NEW YORK

Printed in the United States of America

DEDICATED

TO THE MEMORY OF

MY FATHER AND MOTHER

צבי יואל בן אברהם
ושרה בת מרדכי

PREFACE

"And God said, Let there be light."
(Gen., i. 3.)

THE JEWISH ATTITUDE toward Josephus has, due to his description of the Zealot insurrection against the Romans as the work of assassins and robbers, always been one of hate, malice and bitter prejudice. The Gentiles, who for fifteen centuries had regarded Josephus with veneration, and his writings as scarcely less sacred than their Gospels, have, since the recognition of the testimony to their Messiah in Josephus' works as a spurious interpolation, abandoned their high esteem of him and completely repudiated and anathematized him. A Jewish writer said, "To appraise him is fairly difficult." An Anglican author observed, "For a Gentile to write about Josephus requires some courage." Yet, much precious time and talent, which should have been dedicated to a better cause, have been devoted by both Jews and Gentiles to vulgar and abusive tirades against Josephus.

The chief intention of this work is to grant Josephus his undeniable right to state his own case,—to testify in his own defense, if you will,—without the assistance of, or rather hindrance by, his befrocked persecutors who, beginning with Jost a century ago, to serve some one interest or another, have grossly misinterpreted, garbled, distorted, and very often even misunderstood his testimony. The second object here is, to present a detailed description of the Palestinian civilization of the time in which Josephus lived, of the principal causes and events of the revolt against Rome, and of the war with which he was concerned. The third object is, to examine into the fitness of certain holy gentlemen to sit in judgment upon Josephus, the fairness of their adjudications, and the means and methods which, either "for the truth of God"[1] or for the glorification of race, they have used in their attacks on his personal character and his historical integrity; to consider whether these men are justified in their assault upon the ideals and endeavors of an immortal, which are here regarded in the same light as those of the Prophet Jeremiah, who recognized the wisdom of saving Jerusalem by accepting the yoke of Nebuchadnezzar,[2] and those of Jochanan ben Zakkai, the saver of Judaism, who, five hundred years later, during the siege of the Holy City, surrendered to Titus, and both before and after his surrender counseled peace with the Romans as the only salvation.[3]

The idea of an unmuzzled and unenslaved treatment of the subject has for many years interested me. Neither bound to old traditions nor wedded to new opinions, enjoying no lofty distinction and concerned about no rich connections, but with enthusiasm and determination, I decided to enter the arena, setting myself up as a sort of Satan among the Seraphim.[4] And here the question arises as to whether I, so profoundly unlettered in Hebrew, Targum, Greek and Latin, should have engaged in a task where vast learning, great in-

[1] Compare, Roms., iii. 7.

[2] Jeremiah, xxvii. 8, 11.

[3] On this see Moore's "Judaism," ii. p. 116; Jost's "Judenthum," ii. p. 16ff.; Derenbourg, p. 282; and especially Abot de-R. Nathan, iv. 5.

[4] The Seraphim are an order of angels, whom Isaiah (Is., vi. 1-3, 6ff.) beheld in vision standing above Jehovah as He sat upon His throne. Their occupation was to sing "Holy, holy, holy is the Lord of hosts," and to act as a medium of communication between heaven and earth.

geniousness, elegance and magnetism, far more than sincerity and candor, often determine the credibility of a writer.

> "*For he that is but able to express*
> *No sense at all in several languages,*
> *Will pass for reliabler than he that knows*
> *To speak the strongest reason in his own.*"[5]

Not being a professional historian, I am fully aware of the numerous imperfections my work embraces, and of its falling far short of that degree of excellence which another writer might have attained. However, I trust to the broad understanding of those for whom my book was intended, and to the lenity of critics who, while it will be very easy for them to find those faults, will also appreciate the immense disadvantages under which I labored. I am cognizant also of the fact that in various instances, notably in the second chapter, I have drifted beyond my program, which alone may provide abundant ground for unfavorable comment; and so, here again I beg not to be judged harshly. I hope for this extenuation on two grounds: first, because whenever I have thus over-zealously exceeded my outline, I have never knowingly misstated any facts; secondly, because of the rarity, importance and instructiveness of the material, the information contained in such deviations will far more than counterbalance the infraction. One observation I wish to make is this: If the love of a subject can help one to understand it, it will readily be seen that I have not been wanting in that condition. The only other thing I wish to add is that this work, representing ten full years of arduous toil, was written with good intentions, and I hope its readers will peruse it with the same good intentions with which it was written.

And now, I wish to express my sincere gratitude to the learned librarians, Dr. Wm. Rockwell and Dr. D. H. Schroeder, and to Miss Charlotte Maupin of the Union Theo-

[5] Verse by Dr. James Watts Peppercorn, in his "Maimonides' Laws of the Hebrews."

logical Seminary, for the kind assistance and courtesy they have invariably extended to me; and to Professor Foakes-Jackson of the same liberal institution for the many wise ideas he gave me, though by no means agreeing with all of my opinions. I am likewise very grateful to Dr. Michael Higger of the Jewish Theological Seminary for his many learned counsels, and to the assistant librarian, Mrs. Mary Fried, for the especially generous and helpful attention she always gave me. My hearty thanks are also due to Charles Scribner's Sons for their kind permission to use "in any way desired" material from the indispensable work of Emil Schuerer; and to the Macmillan Company for similar liberty to help myself from the great work of Joseph Klausner. My sincerest thanks are further due to Dr. E. F. Newell of the American Numismatic Society for his help in the identification of the coins reproduced here; to the learned Sopher of the East Side, Mr. M. Tausner, for his assistance in the translation of the Hebrew text of Kalman Schulman; to Dr. F. C. Gilbert of Washington for his first-hand sketch of the Temple Area; to Professor William Popper of the University of California for his mailing to me for reproduction his personal photograph of the now demolished tomb of Jochanan ben Zakkai, which may possibly be the only one existing;[6] and last but not least to my daughter Minna for her artistic drawing of the map of Palestine and the plans of Jerusalem and the Temple Mount.

LEON BERNSTEIN

New York, May 1938

[6] According to the information which reached me, this tomb was destroyed in 1929 by Arab vandals.

"If I forget thee, O Jerusalem,
let my right hand fail."

(Ps. cxxxvii. 5.)

CONTENTS

LIST OF ILLUSTRATIONS

FLAVIUS JOSEPHUS

CHAPTER I

The WORKS *of* JOSEPHUS

IN the perilous and mournful life of the Jews after the destruction of the Jewish State by the Romans in the year 70 of the Christian Era, scientific recording of events was of little interest. The eminent teacher, R. Jochanan ben Zakkai, having escaped the hands of the beleaguered bandits at Jerusalem, labored at his refuge in Jabne to retrieve and restore Judaism from its sad degeneracy, and to build the spiritual wall that was to preserve his nation in the Dispersion. The Canon of the Bible had already been completed; but the Mishna was yet to be arranged and perpetuated in writing,[1] and the Jewish laws were yet to be modified to fit new conditions.[2]

[1] Derenbourg (Revue des Études Juives, vi. 41) says, It is well known that from the time of the destruction of the second Temple down to the commencement of the third century of the Christian era, there have been several redactions of the Mishna. The first complete redaction, says Schuerer (Div. I. Vol. i. p. 130, n. 25), seems to have been undertaken by R. Akiba before the war of Hadrian (ab. 135 CE.).

[2] Instances of such new laws are found in Sukka, iii. 12; Rosh Hashana, iv. 1, 3-4; Sota, ix. 9; Menachoth, x. 5; Aboth, ii. 8; etc.

Regarding Jabne, as the chief seat of learning "after the Destruction," see Shekalim, i. 4; Rosh Hashana, ii. 8-9, iv. 1-2; Kethu-

Few Jewish scholars of ancient times devoted themselves to the writing of history; and most of what was written was lost.[3] The historical references in the Talmud show an extraordinary lack of historical sense and leave great gaps in the history of Israel.[4] The New Testament, the Books of the Maccabees and the rest of the Apocrypha, the writings of Philo, the works of the heathen writers Livius, Tacitus, Suetonius, the two Pliniuses, and many others, both Jewish and Gentile, for the preservation of which we are indebted to the Christian Fathers, contribute to our understanding of the Jewish life of their day, but they are restricted to limited periods, limited topics, limited events, and in too many instances even to very limited degrees of veracity, ranging downwards to the most ridiculous and nauseating falsehoods. The works of Josephus alone, for the preservation of which also we are indebted, first, to the Flavian Emperors, who honored them with a place in the imperial library,[5] and later, to the Christian Church, give a full and connected account of the Maccabean and Herodian

both, iv. 6; Sanhedrin, xi. 4; Edujoth, ii. 4; Aboth, iv. 4; Bechoroth, iv. 5, vi. 8; Kelim, xi. 4; and Para, vii. 6.

As the most important teacher in the decade "after the fall of the Holy City," Rabban Jochanan ben Zakkai is mentioned in the Mishna in the following passages:—Shabbath, xvi. 7, xxii. 3; Shekalim, i. 4; Sukka, ii. 5, iii. 12; Rosh Hashana, iv. 1, 3-4; Kethuboth, xiii. 1-2; Sota, v. 2, 5, ix. 9, 15; Edujoth, viii. 3, 7; Aboth, 8-9; Menachoth, x. 5; Kelim, ii. 2, xvii. 16; Jadajim, v. 3, 6; and Sanhedrin, v. 2. For these references I am gratefully indebted to Schuerer.

[3] The "Book of Jashar," mentioned in 2 Samuel, i. 18, and in Joshua, x. 13; the "Book of Chronicles" referred to in I Maccabees, in the very last verse; that of the "Wars of Jehova" in Numb., xxi. 14; the "Writings of Shemaiah the Prophet," and the "History of the Prophet Iddo," in 2 Chronicles, xii. 15, xiii. 22; and "The Scripture which is laid up in the Temple" and the "Books laid up in the Temple," mentioned by Josephus in Antiq., III. i. 7, last verse, and V. i. 7.

[4] "All we get there as history," says Prof. Foakes-Jackson (Josephus and the Jews, p. 159, n. 2), "are isolated tales for legal purposes."

[5] Eusebius, Eccl. Hist., iii. 9.

periods; that is, of the Jewish events during the two centuries between Simon Hasmonai and the fall of the Jewish Commonwealth. And it is these works alone which form the chief and indispensable authority and basis for any essay on this period.

The works of Josephus consist of the following:—

(1) "The Wars of the Jews," in seven books: The first book begins with the time of Antiochus Epiphanes, 175-164 BCE., and reaches down to the death of Herod the Great in the year 4 BCE. The second continues the history down to the outbreak of the Jewish war against Rome in 66 CE., and gives an account of the first year of the war, 66-67 CE. The third treats of the first Roman assault in Galilee in 67, where Josephus commanded the Jewish forces; the fourth, of the continued course of the war down to the complete isolation of Jerusalem; the fifth and sixth describe the siege of Jerusalem, and the seventh relates the events that followed the war down to the revolt and end of the fugitive rebels in Alexandria and Cyrene in the year 73 CE.

In the Preface to "The Wars of the Jews" (sec. 1) we are informed that it was originally written in the Semitic dialect, that is, in Aramaic or Hebrew, "for the Jews who lived among the Upper Barbarians," that is, in Babylonia, Arabia, Parthia, and beyond the Euphrates, as a message of warning of the hopelessness of further revolt against the invincible power of Rome, and to allay the after-war thirst for revenge,[6] which found vent thirty years later in the furious outbreak under Trajan and which was finally suppressed with barbarous cruelty by Hadrian in the year 117 CE.[7] We are also informed that when, after the war, Josephus arrived in Rome and found numerous accounts written by Greek authors underrating the Jewish warriors and stigmatizing them as cowards, he rewrote this Jewish version into Greek as a refutation of their misrep-

[6] Compare, Preface to Wars, secs. 1 and 2.

[7] See "War under Trajan" and "Rebellion under Hadrian," in Schuerer, Div. I., Vol. ii., pp. 281-321.

resentations; [8] for which, he elsewhere says,[9] he availed himself of the assistance of several Greek scholars, because he was deficient in the syntax of that language. This rewritten version, which was published about 75 CE., when Josephus was thirty-eight years of age, is the one that has come down to us.

(2) "The Antiquities of the Jews," in twenty books: The first ten books of this work repeat the facts narrated in the Old Testament from Creation to the end of the Babylonian captivity. The eleventh contains the history from Cyrus to Alexander the Great, an interval of two hundred and fifty-three years; the twelfth, from the death of Alexander the Great to the death of Judah Maccabee, an interval of a hundred and seventy years; the thirteenth covers the interval of the following eighty-two years, carrying the history down to Queen Alexandra's death; the fourteenth book covers the interval of thirty-two years, down to the death of Antigonus; the fifteenth, an interval of eighteen years, down to the finishing of the Temple by Herod; the sixteenth, covering the interval of the next twelve years, carries the history as far as the death of Alexander and Aristobulus; the seventeenth, covering the interval of fourteen years, to the banishment of Archelaus; while the eighteenth, nineteenth and twentieth books, after relating the important events of the following sixty years both in Italy and Judea, bring us down to the Jewish revolt against Rome in the year 66 CE.

For the first ten books, as far as Nehemiah, Josephus had no other authority at his disposal than the Old Testament, especially the LXX translation. Frequently, however, he omits or modifies points, either not to give offense, or in order to

[8] Preface to Wars, secs. 1, 3, and 5-6.

[9] It is the opinion of many scholars that Josephus must have spoken Greek from childhood, and that he must also have received some training in that language during his two years' sojourn in Rome before the war. Josephus nowhere denies this fact; he rather confirms it in the Antiquities (XX. xi. 2) when he says, "I have so long been accustomed to speak our own tongue, that I cannot pronounce Greek with sufficient exactness."

render his history more palatable to the tastes of his heathen audience; at times he also supplements with such rabbinical traditions as were current in his time. For the facts about the Hasmoneans he has made use of the First Book of the Maccabees, Polybius, Strabo, and Nicolas of Damascus. Nicolas is also his chief authority for that portion which relates to the reign of Herod. About Herod's successors, Josephus appears to have known little, with the exception of the two Agrippas; but these belonged to contemporary history, and he could have learned from Agrippa II about the reign of his father Agrippa I. For the history of the last decade he probably relied on his own recollections.

This great work was designed to magnify the antiquity and glorious past of the Jewish people in the eyes of the cultured Greeks and Romans, and also to refute the degrading and malicious accounts, written by a number of pagan authors, of the Jewish origin and religious system. Josephus' object for this work, as described by himself, was "to reconcile other people to us; to remove the cause of that ill-will which unthinking men bear us, . . . and to inform them that they ought not to consider differences of certain institutions as sufficient cause of hatred, but JOIN WITH US in the pursuit of virtue and probity, for this belongs to all men in common, and is in itself alone sufficient for the preservation of life and happiness." [10]

In the Preface (sec. 3), Josephus further tells us that, first, in writing the Antiquities he also wished to imitate the generosity of the high-priest Eleazar who, three centuries earlier, upon request of the Egyptian king Ptolemy Philadelphus, had sent to Alexandria seventy-two learned men, well versed in both Hebrew and Greek, to translate the Pentateuch into the Greek language for the royal library; [11] and, secondly,

[10] Preface to the Antiquities, secs. 2-3; compare also "Against Apion" II. Thackeray's sec. 28, or Whiston's sec. 29.

[11] The very interesting details concerning this transaction are given in the Antiquities, XII. ii. 4-15.

to enlarge upon it, "for the king did not obtain our entire Scripture at that time, but only the Books of the Law, while there was a vast amount of other material in our sacred books containing the history of five thousand years."

The Antiquities was completed and dedicated to his learned friend Epaphroditus, in the thirteenth year of Domitian's reign, or 93 CE., when Joseph was in the fifty-sixth year of his age.[12]

(3) The "Life of Josephus," in seventy-six sections: This work is almost exclusively a defense of his own conduct as governor of Galilee, during the winter of 66-67 CE., preparatory to the arrival of the Roman army. It was called forth by the publication of a history written by a learned Galilean revolutionist, Justus of Tiberias, which represented Josephus as the actual organizer of the Jewish revolt against Rome,[13]—a charge extremely inconvenient to him, who by that time had attained a position of eminence in Italy. It was, therefore, never intended as a complete autobiography, the first six and the last two sections alone being of a biographical nature. A passage at the close of the Antiquities leads to the belief that it was published as an Appendix to that work.

Conspicuously in the center of this treatise (secs. 38-41) appear charges of fraudulent use of public funds against the celebrated Talmudic figure, Simon ben Gamaliel,[14] and of

[12] Antiq., XX. xi. 3.

[13] Vita, 9, 65. Josephus (sec. 65) speaks with astonishment of the impudence of Justus in writing of the proceedings in Galilee and the sieges of Jotapata and Jerusalem, of which he knew nothing at first hand; "indeed," he says, (sec. 9) "he was not unskilled in the learning of the Greeks, and upon that attainment it was that he undertook to write a history of these affairs, hoping by this way of haranguing to disguise the truth."

[14] Graetz, following a late Mishnaic addition, honors Simon ben Gamaliel with the title of President of the Sanhedrin. The fact that the president of the Sanhedrin during the hundred years preceding the burning of the Temple was always the high-priest in office is well known to every student of Jewish history. But Simon ben Gamaliel was neither a Sadducee nor a high priest in or out of office; and the designation of this Talmudic "celebrity" by this high title

bribing and betraying the nation's interests for personal gain and advantage against both Simon ben Gamaliel and Ananus, who was "the oldest and most prominent high-priest" (ex-officio). These, and more charges against traditional favorites, along with his praises of some "unpatriotic" personages, made this work extremely unpopular in some quarters.

(4) "Josephus against Apion," in two books: This is Josephus' greatest Apologia for Judaism. It is not directed solely against Apion, as the name might imply, but rather generally against the venomous attacks and prejudices from which the Jews of those days suffered. Manetho, an Egyptian priest during the time of Ptolemy II Philadelphus (308-247 BCE.), writing in Greek, was the first of a line of literary anti-Semites who delighted in holding up the Jewish people to derision and contempt. In his own time, and during the reign of the entire Ptolemean dynasty, the mischief his writings did was but limited. Ptolemy II, to whom Manetho dedicated his History, was too enlightened and wise a monarch, and too truly alive to his own interests to allow his mind to be influenced against a people whom he always found loyal, industrious and law-abiding. But Manetho's works were later repeated, augmented and embellished by other writers, reaching the climax of virulence with the stories of the most malignant and most scurrilous of all,—Apion, who in the year 40 CE. headed the anti-Semitic deputation of Alexandria before Caligula, when Philo appeared in the defense of the Jews.

The humiliation inflicted on the Egyptians and their gods in Exodus, supplemented by Ezekiel's prediction,[15] "Egypt should be a base kingdom, . . . the basest of kingdoms, it shall never exalt itself again above the nations," and the general prosperity of the Jewish community at Alexandria,

is only one of the many generosities extended by Graetz to rabbinic darlings at the expense of history. A complete and fully documented treatise on this subject is given by Schuerer, Div. II., Vol. i., pp. 180-184.

[15] Ezekiel, xxix. 14-15.

appear, according to Josephus,[16] to have been the chief causes of their bitterness against the Jews. "The great contrast between the two systems of worship," he continues, "created intense animosity, . . . and the sight of so many of their own nation admiring our institutions filled them with envy." And so, to please their people whose pride had been so fearfully humbled, "these authors undertook to distort the facts (as set forth in the Bible), misrepresenting the circumstances of the entry of our ancestors into Egypt . . . and of their departure; . . . some of them being so blinded by their passion as to contradict even their own ancient records."

Of several such perversions quoted by Josephus, the first (I Apion, 26) is that of Manetho. King Amenophis of Egypt, this author says, collected all the lepers of the country, numbering eighty thousand, and sent them to work in the stone-quarries on the east of the Nile. Having continued in that miserable state for a long time, they petitioned the king to assign them to the deserted city of the shepherds called Auris, which wish the king granted them. When they got possession of the town they made it a base for revolt, appointing as their leader one of the priests of Heliopolis, called Osarsiph, and swore to obey all his orders. The first law this leader decreed prohibited the worship of their gods, ordered the killing of all such animals as were held sacred, and prohibited association with anyone outside their number. He then invited the "Hyksos" from Jerusalem to join them as allies. The "Hyksos," delighted with the idea, went off in a body, twenty thousand strong, and soon reached Auris. When the news of the invasion reached the king, he crossed the Nile with three hundred thousand warriors to meet the enemy. Instead of engaging them, however, he turned back, and with all his army went to Ethiopia. There the king made them welcome, assigned to them cities and villages on the Egyptian border and provided them with food. No sooner had they settled, however, than the "Hyksos" came down upon them with the lep-

[16] I Apion, 25.

rous Egyptians, and not only did they treat the inhabitants very cruelly, but also burned their settlements and temples, and mutilated the images of their gods. Having accomplished this, the priest Osarsiph changed his name to Moses.

Following the account of Chaeremon[17] (I Apion, 32-33), who in the main agrees with Manetho, Josephus quotes that of Lysimachus. This writer brings up the same theme as the two Egyptians before him, but surpasses them both in deceitfulness and bitterness. Instead of mixing the Palestinian "Hyksos" with the Egyptian lepers, he takes the more direct course:—In the reign of Bocchoris, the king of Egypt, he says, the Jewish people, who were afflicted with leprosy, scurvy and other diseases, took refuge in the temples and lived a mendicant existence; and that on the advice of "a certain Moses" crossed the desert to the country now called Judea and founded the Hierosyla in which they settled under the name of Hierosolymites (I Apion, 34).[18]

The most virulent enemy of Judaism, however, was Apion, the demon whose name Josephus' Defense mentions in its title. To him belongs the distinction of being the prototype of the modern professional Jew-haters of Germany and eastern Europe. Apion is in perfect agreement with all the other Egyptian writers on the Exodus and the lepers, but improves their stories on the subject, saying that after a six days' march the Jews developed tumors in the groin, and that was why, after safely reaching the country now called Judea, they rested on the seventh day and called that day Sabbaton, preserving the Egyptian terminology; for the disease of the groin in Egypt is called sabbo (II Apion, 2). In addition, he denounces them also for not posting the Emperor's statue in the synagogue; attacks the Jewish claim to Alexandrian citizen-

[17] According to Suidas (10th or 11th century), Chaeremon was the instructor of Nero. He must therefore have lived towards the middle of the first Christian century.

[18] According to Josephus (II Apion, 2), and Cosmas Indicopleustes (ab. the 6th century CE.), Lysimachus was an Alexandrian and seems to have lived in the first century BCE.

ship, and their refusal to worship the city's gods. He also derides them for practicing circumcision, and for abstaining from pork (II Apion, Thack., sec. 13, Whist., 14); and reproaches them for having produced no inventors in the arts and crafts, or eminent sages (II Apion, Thack., sec. 12, Whist., 13).

The outworn accusation of ritual murder which had first been used in Egypt against the Jews, then transferred from Jews to Christians, and later again employed by Christians against the Jews, has also been invented by Apion.[19] As quoted by Josephus, this author says that, "at a fixed time every year the Jews catch a Greek foreigner, fatten him up, lead him to a wood where they kill him; sacrifice his body with their accustomed solemnities, taste his flesh, and take an oath upon the sacrificed victim that they would forever remain at enmity with the Greeks. The remains of the Greek are then thrown into a pit" (II Apion, 8, loosely quoted).

The reputation Apion had in his own day was apparently very low. A contemporary, Gaius Plinius (known as Pliny the Elder), informs us that Emperor Tiberius used to call him, "the player of his own cymbals" (i.e., the blower of his own horn). Apion, boasting about himself, said, "He to whom I present a book becomes thereby immortal" (Pliny, Hist. Natur., Preface, sec. 25). Comparing himself with Socrates and other great men, he congratulated Alexandria for having such a citizen as he was (II Apion, Thack., 12, Whist., 13). Alexandrinus Clemens, who wrote in the reign of Emperor Severus, calls him "The Crab" (Strom., i. 21, 101). Aulus Gellius (died ab. 180 CE.), citing Apion's fifth book, says, "He was notorious for his impudence" (Noetes Atticae, v. 5, Beloe's transl.); while Josephus (II Apion, 1) describes him

[19] "It is a curious and instructive fact," says Prof. Radin ("Jews Among the Greeks and Romans," p. 393), "that Chinese have charged Christian missionaries with precisely the same crime, i.e., of kidnapping and killing children as part of their religious ceremonies."

as "a man of low character and a swindler to the end of his days," and (II Apion, Th. 13, Wh. 14) tells us that his death was caused by an ulcer on his privy against which even circumcision was of no avail.

The two other philosophers with whom Josephus deals are Posidonius and Apollonius Molon. Posidonius' great grievance against the Jews is their "not worshipping the same gods as others do" (II Apion, 7); Apollonius Molon charges them with atheism, misanthropy and fanaticism, and upbraids them for having contributed nothing to general culture (II Apion, Th. 14, Wh. 15), and for having no fellowship with persons who have different ideas than their own about God (II Apion, Th. 36, Wh. 37).

The two books "Against Apion," however, were not aimed alone at these Egyptian Greeks who had long been dead. They were, rather, a renewed effort in his drive against the anti-Jewish sentiment prevalent in some literary quarters, especially after the destruction of Jerusalem. The Antiquities, which had recently been published as a history, message of good-will, and general defense, had evidently not accomplished the anticipated effect upon those readers whose minds had been poisoned by the Apionic literature which was still circulating. Josephus, at the outset of this great work, states, "A number of persons, influenced by the malicious calumnies of those individuals, will not believe what I have written in my Antiquities concerning the extreme ancientness of our people, the purity of our stock, and how we established ourselves in that same country which we still occupy today." Why, they ask, is it that the Jews are not given even a bare mention as a nation in the records of those great Greek writers to whom the world looks for information, whereas the history of the Greeks and others fill the volumes of authors read and admired in every corner of the earth?

Intensely astonished at this sophisticated pretension of the Greeks, Josephus proceeds to repel their alleged priority, and to account for their silence on Jewish history. To these perverted "truth seekers" he demonstrates that, contrary to their claims, everything concerning the Greeks is new; their cities, arts, and the compilation of a code of laws, dating, so to speak, since only yesterday, and that it is admitted even by themselves that the Egyptians, Chaldeans and Babylonians possessed a far older history than their own. Greece, he says, having experienced countless catastrophes obliterating the memory of the past; and as one civilization succeeded another, the people of each epoch believed that the world began with themselves. They were late in learning the alphabet, and even that they learned from the Chaldeans and Cadmus. Throughout the whole Greek literature no undisputed work exists older than that of Homer, and even he did not leave his poems in writing, but only scattered songs transmitted by memory which were not compiled till later. Cadmus and Acusilaus (6th century BCE.) were the first to write history, but they lived only a short time before the Persian invasion of Greece; and the first Greeks to write on astronomy and religion, such as Pherecydes, Pythagoras and Thales, were disciples of Egyptians and Chaldeans. These are the oldest Greek writings, and even the authenticity of these the Greeks themselves are doubting (I Apion, 2). There are discrepancies between Hellanicus and Acusilaus; Acusilaus corrects Hesiod, Ephorus exposes the mendacity of Hellanicus, Timaeus that of Ephorus, that of Timaeus himself is exposed by later writers, and that of Herodotus by everybody. On many points even Thucydides is accused of deceit, notwithstanding his reputation as the most accurate historian of his time (I Apion, 3).

One reason for these inconsistencies among the later writers, he says, is the neglect of the Greeks to keep official records of current events (I Apion, 4); another cause is that the writers did not concern themselves so much with the truth as to display their literary ability and the prospect it offered them of outshining their rivals. Hence, while for eloquence and style of composition one must bow to the Greeks, the Jew has no reason to do so for veracity, especially when the history of a foreign nation is concerned (I Apion, 5). "Because, not only did our forefathers take greater care in recording their chronicles than the Babylonians, Phoenicians, and Egyptians, and committed that task, which has been continued to this very day with most scrupulous accuracy, to men known to be of the highest character, but our ancestors, who set only high-priests over this business, investigated also their pedigrees and appointed none but such as proved by records to be of unbroken and the purest lineage" (I Apion, 6-7).

The galaxy of classical erudition to be seen in the remaining pages of this first book "Against Apion" seems to be beyond anyone's power of description. One may admire Cicero or Demosthenes, the one for talent the other for craft, or perhaps enjoy chuckling over Machiavelli's charlatanism, but to pore over this most remarkable work in defense of Judaism is to revel in a most astonishing and salutary literary performance. Dr. Thackeray, in his Fifth Lecture on Josephus, commenting on this work, says, "We seem to be moving in the literary circles of Apion's own Alexandria, in which antiquarian problems and questions are discussed and the merits of great masters criticized." Prof. Foakes-Jackson (Josephus, p. 20) thinks, "There is something quite modern in the arguments advanced in the first book of Apion and also in the method of reply adopted by Josephus." Prof. Norman Bentwich (Josephus, p. 226), referring to Lysimachus' story, says, "To vary a saying of Dr. Johnson, this section of Josephus must be read for the quotation, for if one reads it for the argument of assailant or apologist, one would shoot himself"; and Rabbi Dr. Morris J. Raphall (Post-Biblical Hist., I. p. 144), evidently short of his usual eloquence, disposes of the matter by simply saying, "For this Defense we must refer our readers to 'Contra Apionem.' "

And now, having thus completely established the antiquity of the Jewish nation and proved that the Jews were neither Egyptians by race nor expelled from Egypt in consequence of contagious diseases, Josephus, entering his second book, turns against Apion and his attack on the Jews of Alexandrian citizenship. "By what authority," Apion asks, "do the Jews of Alexandria call themselves Alexandrian citizens? And if they are citizens why do they not worship the same gods the Alexandrians do, nor erect statues for the Emperor?" In the first place, Josephus' reply to this is that Apion, who was born in the depths of Egypt and who, pretending to be a native of Alexandria, secured his citizenship by fraud,[20]—said citizenship being a privilege which, though granted to all other nations under the Roman sway, not a single emperor had ever conferred upon Egyptians,—is not the sort of a character who could advantageously serve emperors as a defender (II Apion, 6). As for the Jewish title to citizenship, he points out that the Jews owed their occupation and subsequent undisturbed tenure of Alexandria's "quarter-by-the-sea" not only to Alexander the Great, who presented it to them as their residence in recognition of their virtue and valor, but also to all the Macedonian's successors who without exception shared his high opinion of them. Ptolemy I entrusted the fortresses of Egypt into the hands of Jews, feeling that they would keep them for him faithfully and bravely. Ptolemy II not only paid them the highest honors and freed all his Jewish captives, but also paid their ransom money [21] and gave them many presents (II Apion, 4). Ptolemy III, after his conquest of Syria, did not offer thank-offerings to the Egyptian gods, but came to Jerusalem and there "offered many sacrifices to our God and dedicated to Him such gifts as were suitable to such a victory;" and as for Ptolemy Philometor and his wife Cleopatra, they committed their whole kingdom to the Jews, Onias and Dositheus, both of whom were the generals in command of their entire army. "Caesar Julius witnesses the loyal support

[20] On Apion's origin see, II Apion, 3.

[21] For the redemption of 100,000 Jewish slaves at 120 drachmas per person and 20 drachmas for each child, the total sum Ptolemy paid was 460 talents—according to one authority, equal to $460,000, or according to another figure, $1,000,000. For the details on this redemption, see Antiq., XII. ii. 3.

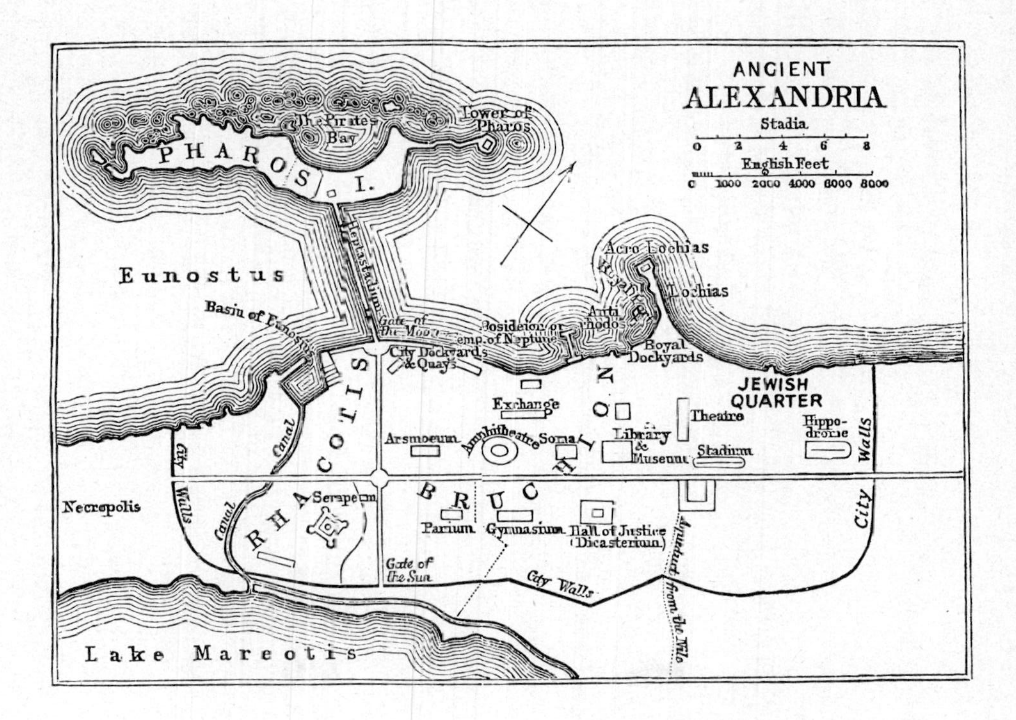
ANCIENT
ALEXANDRIA
Stadia
0 2 4 6 8
English Feet
0 1000 2000 4000 6000 8000
PHAROS I.
The Pirates Bay
Tower of Pharos
Eunostus
Heptastadium
Basin of Eunostus
Gate of the Moon
Posideion or Temp. of Neptune
City Dockyards & Quays
Acro Lochias
Lochias
Antirhodos
Royal Dockyards
JEWISH QUARTER
Exchange
Theatre
Hippo-drome
Arsinoeum
Amphitheatre
Soma
Library & Museum
Stadium
City Walls
RHACOTIS
BRUCHION
Serapeum
Canal
Necropolis
Parium
Gymnasium
Hall of Justice (Dicasterium)
Gate of the Sun
Aqueduct from the Nile
Lake Mareotis

we rendered him, and Caesar Augustus, and Senatorial decrees and letters attest our services (II Apion, 5).... Thus, our position in the city which we owe to Alexander,[22] and the privileges extended to us by the Ptolemies who followed him,[23] have been generously safeguarded by the succeeding Romans for all time" (II Apion, 6).

On the question of veneration of imperial images, Josephus suggests that Apion, instead of denouncing the Jews for such impiety, ought rather to admire the Romans for their magnanimity and moderation in not requiring their subjects to violate the laws of their own countries, and for being content with only such honors as are consistent with their religious ordinances. Reminding him of his personal pettiness and unfitness as an imperial defender, he also directs his attention to the fact that "the emperors are not grateful for honors conferred upon them under compulsion."... "Our legislators did not forbid us to pay honors to worthy men; such honors we confer upon emperors. For them we offer perpetual sacrifices, and not only do we perform these ceremonies daily and at the expense of the entire community, but in paying this respect, which is accorded to Emperors alone, every participant joins in the performance" (II Apion, 6).

But the refutation of such charges was not the main object Josephus had in view in writing this treatise. Owing to their nonconformity and general separatism the Jews appeared as enemies of public regulations and institutions. And, while such peculiarities as the practice of circumcision, abstinence from pork, the lighting of candles, observance of the Sabbath, the eating of matzohs on Passover, and the refusal to intermarry gave occasion rather for derision and reproach, their

[22] In recognition of Alexander's kindness, the Jews decreed that every male child born to the Cohanim in the year of his visit to Jerusalem should, in honor of him, be named Alexander. Thenceforth this name—a truly Greek one—is found in frequent use among the Jews, even to this day.

[23] The chief synagogue of the Jews in Alexandria was respected as much as the temple of Jupiter and that of Isis.

contempt for the national gods was assailed most bitterly. And so, Apion (II Apion, Th. 11, Wh. 12) finds the Jews witless atheists, their laws unjust and their religious ceremonies erroneous, while Lysimachus, Apollonius Molon and the others (II Apion, Th. 14, Wh. 15), adjudge Moses a charlatan and an impostor whose code is a text-book which teaches everything in vice but nothing in virtue. To refute these charges, Josephus begins his actual Apologia, which forms the noblest part of the whole work. And considering that the best defense against all the false accusations is to be found in the Law itself, he proceeds to describe it.

> "*And I will walk around thine altar, O Jehovah,*
> *To publish with the voice of thanksgiving,*
> *And to relate all thy wondrous works.*"
>
> (Psalms, xxvi. 6-7.)

"What are the features of our Law? They are simple and easily known. The first command is concerning God. It confirms that the world is in His hands; perfect and happy, self-sufficient and sufficing for all. He is the beginning, the middle, and the end of all things; He is seen by His works and bounties, and though more conspicuous than any other being, His form and magnitude surpass our power of description. No material, however costly, is fit to make an image of Him, and no art has the skill to fashion His likeness. The like of Him we have never seen, we cannot imagine, and it is impious to surmise. We see His works; the light, the heaven, the earth, the sun and the moon, the waters, the generations of animals, the productions of fruits. These God created, not with hands, not with labor, not with assistants. He decreed it so, and immediately they were made in all their splendor (II Apion, Th. 22, Wh. 23).

"We have but one temple for the one God. This temple is common to all as God is common to all. His priests are continually engaged in His worship, under the leadership of the priest who by birth is the first of the line (of the sons of

Aaron). Their business is to offer sacrifices to God, to see that the laws are observed, to adjudicate cases of dispute, and to punish those who are convicted of crime. He who does not submit to this tribunal shall be subject to the same punishment as for impiety towards God Himself. Our sacrifices are not occasions for bacchanalian revelries, but for orderliness and sobriety. At these sacrifices we pray first for the common welfare of all, and after that for our own; for we are made for fellowship, and he who prefers the welfare of the community before his own is above all acceptable to God. The Law also prescribes several purifications, such as after a funeral, after child-birth, and others. This is our doctrine concerning God and His worship (II Apion, Th. 23, Wh. 24).

"And what are our marriage laws? The Law commands us, in taking a wife, not to be influenced by dowry, not to carry off a woman by violence, not to persuade her by misrepresentation or chicanery, but to demand her of him who is authorized to give her away on account of nearness of kin. The husband must consort with his wife alone. The penalty for assault, rape, or abduction is death. The Law orders all our offspring to be brought up, and a woman convicted of abortion is regarded as an infanticide (II Apion, Th. 24, Wh. 25). Again the Law does not permit us to make the birth of our children occasions for drunkenness, but it ordains that the very beginning of our education should be directed to sobriety. It also commands us to bring our children up in learning, and to familiarize them with the laws and deeds of their forefathers from infancy (II Apion, Th. 25, Wh. 26).

"The rites provided for the dead do not consist of costly funerals or the erection of outstanding monuments. The funeral ceremony is to be performed by the nearest relatives, and all who pass the funeral procession must accompany and share the mourning of the family (II Apion, Th. 26, Wh. 27).

"The Law ordains also that honor to parents should rank second only to honor to God, and a son ungrateful for the benefits he has received from them is to be stoned.[24] The young must pay respect also to their elders, because God is the eldest of all.[25] It allows us to conceal nothing from our friends; and forbids the revelation of secrets even though an enmity arise between them.[26] If a judge takes bribes, his punishment is death; [27] and if he refuses a petition when he has the power to aid he is accountable to justice.[28] He that lends money must not demand usury for his loan [29] (II Apion, Th. 27, Wh. 28).

"We must supply fire, water and food to all who ask for it,[30] point out the road,[31] . . . and not let the dead unburied, not even of declared enemies.[32] We must treat our enemies with consideration; we are forbidden to set their country on fire, or to cut down their fruit trees,[33] or to spoil those who have been slain in war.[34] Our legislator has also provided that prisoners of war may not be outraged, and especially that women may not be abused.[35] In that lesson which teaches us gentleness and humanity, even the care of brute beasts is not overlooked,[36] and if a creature takes refuge in our house, we are forbidden to kill it; nor may we take away the parent bird from its young [37] (II Apion, Th. 29, Wh. 30).

[24] The fifth commandment, Ex., xx. 12; Deut., v. 16, and xxiff.

[25] On respect for elders, see Lev., xix. 32, and perhaps also Daniel, vii. 9.

[26] A current Essene tradition, not in our Bible.

[27] Ex., xxiii. 8; Deut., xvi. 19, xxvii. 25; but in our Bible the capital punishment is omitted.

[28] Deut., xv. 7ff.

[29] Concerning the prohibition of usury, see Ex., xxii. 25; Lev., xxv. 36-37.

[30] Current traditions.

[31] Deut., xxvii. 18:—"Cursed be he that maketh the blind wander."

[32] In regard to burial, see Deut., xxi. 23, and Tobit, 17ff.

[33] Deut., xx. 19.

[34] Not in the Law, but it is taught in the Talmud.

[35] Deut., xxi. 10-11.

[36] Deut., v. 14.

[37] Deut., xxii. 6.

"The penalty for adultery, outraging an unmarried woman,[38] and unnatural vice is death. Fraud in measure or weight, cheating in trade, or embezzling, is punished more severely than among other nations; [39] and the mere intention to do wrong to parents, or of impiety against God is punishable with death (II Apion, Th. 30, Wh. 31). Thus in every particular has our lawgiver had an eye to mercy, though using the laws to enforce the lesson, he ordained penalties for crimes admitting of no excuse" (II Apion, Th. 29, Wh. 30).

Of immense interest also, in addition to the many uncanonized traditions which Josephus has recorded, are his own personal gentleness, his humaneness, and his ultramodernism in having discerned the principle of religious toleration:—"We must not revile the gods recognized by others." [40] or as he elsewhere says, "Every one should be permitted to worship God in accordance with the dictates of his own conscience." [41] . . .

"Yet, in spite of all this, the Lysimachuses, the Molons, and some other writers, probate scoundrels and deceivers of young men, reproach us as the vilest of mankind. Gladly would I have avoided an inquiry into the laws of other nations; for the custom of our country is to keep our own laws and to refrain from criticizing those of others. . . . But since our enemies expect to confute us by a comparison of their religion with ours, it is impossible to keep clear of the question." Accordingly, Josephus proceeds to show the cause wherefore the Jews spurn paganism, and to prove that their uncompromising exclusiveness is not due to unsociability, but to a desire to secure their own laws and customs from corruption:

"The gods which the Greeks have,—'frail images of

[38] Deut., xxii. 23:—"if betrothed."

[39] Compare, Lev., xix, 11-13, 35-36; Deut., xxv. 13ff.

[40] II Apion, Th. 33, Wh. 34; see also, Ex., xxii. 28, where "nor curse the ruler of thy people" is added.

[41] Compare, II Apion, Th. 33, Wh. 34, with Vita, 23.

wood, stone, silver or gold, the work of men's hands, or animals of every kind,'—are condemned and derided even by their own intellectual leaders, who, though ostensibly observing the laws of their own countries, yet, in their conduct and philosophy agreed with the Jews on the conception of God. And who in fact is there among the admired sages of Greece who has not censured the inventors of these deities for spreading such worship among the masses? They represent them to be as numerous as they choose, born of one another and engendered in all manner of ways. They assign them different places and ways of living: some of them under earth, others in the sea, the oldest of them bound in hell; . . . some with beards and others without, one god a smith, the goddess a weaver, that god a warrior or a harper, and the other an archer, a builder, a shepherd, or a chained criminal in a prison of brass (II Apion, Th. 33-34, Wh. 34-35).

"Now, what is the cause of such irregular and erroneous conception of the deity? For my part, I trace it to the ignorance of the true nature of God with which their legislators entered their task, and to their failure to formulate even such correct knowledge of it as they were able to attain and to make the rest of their constitution conform to it. Instead, as if this was the most trifling of details, they allowed the poets to introduce what gods they chose, subject to all passions, and the orators to pass decrees for entering the name of any suitable foreign god on the burgess-roll. Painters and sculptors were given great license in this matter by the Greeks, each designing a figure after his own imagination, one moulding it of clay, another using paints. The artists most admired by all use ivory and gold as the material for the novelties which they are constantly producing. And now the gods who once flourished with honors are grown old, which is the kinder way of putting it; and others, newly introduced, are the objects of worship. Some temples are left to desolation, others are but now being erected, according to individual caprice; whereas they ought, on the contrary, to have preserved immutably their belief in God and the honor which they rendered Him" (II Apion, Th. 34-35, Wh. 35-36).

And further, to prove that exclusiveness was not peculiar to Jews alone, he shows that Plato also insisted that the Greeks prevent foreigners from mixing with them at random, and that they keep the commonwealth pure and restricted to followers of their own laws. The Lacedemonians, likewise, made a practice of expelling foreigners and forbidding their own people to travel abroad for fear that their own laws would be corrupted; and they may justly be reproached also for refusing to foreigners both citizenship and residence among them. "We, however, while we do not wish to imitate the customs of others, yet willingly admit those who wish to share our own, which plainly indicates our humanity and magnanimity" (II Apion, Th. 36, Wh. 37).

"On what account was Socrates put to death? Was it that he betrayed Athens or that he desecrated its temple? No. But because he swore novel oaths and said that he received messages from a spirit, he was condemned to die by drinking hemlock. His prosecutor, Meletus, also accused him of corrupting young men by inducing them to scorn the constitution and laws of their country. Anaxagoras, because he said the sun, which the Athenians worshiped as a god, was a ball of fire, was within a few votes from being condemned to death." They also offered a talent for the head of Diagoras, and put Protagoras to death for a similar offense. Even women were not spared, for the priestess Ninus was put to death for having been accused of initiating people into the worship of foreign gods.... "With us, however, such abuse, even of brute beasts, is a capital crime, and from these laws, no cruel despot can force us to withdraw. We patiently submit to any form of defeat, but for the preservation of our Law we go to war, even under tremendous odds, and bear the greatest calamities to the last extremity" (I Apion, Th. 37, Wh. 38).

Omitting, he says, the many subterfuges which the majority of Greek law-makers have afforded to offenders of adultery , assault, and all manner of corruption; indeed, violation of the laws among them had become a studied art, Josephus adds, "but not so with us; for though we may be deprived of our wealth and of our cities, our Law remains immortal; and there is not a Jew, however far from his country he may be, who has not greater fear of it than of the severest lord. If, then, our affection for it is due to its excellence, let it be granted that it is excellent. If however, it be imagined that the Law to which we are so loyal is bad, what penalty do the Greeks deserve for not observing their own laws which they think are superior? But since Time is always the surest test of merit, I would call Time to attest to the excellence of our lawgiver and of his revelation concerning God which he has transmitted to us (II Apion, Th. 38, Wh. 39).

"I have adequately shown," he here sums up, "that our race goes back to remote antiquity, whereas our accusers assert that it is of late origin. I have produced many ancient writers who mention us in their books, whereas they say there are none. They said we sprung from Egyptians, while I have proved we came from another country into Egypt. They further asserted that we were expelled from that country as lepers; it has been shown that we returned to our country by our own choice, physically sound and strong. They reviled our legislator as a vile person, whereas God and Time bear witness to his sterling merits. . . . A glance at our Law shows that it teaches not vice but the truest piety. It does not make men hate one another, but encourages good fellowship and brotherhood. Our Law is a foe of injustice and a friend of righteousness; it banishes extravagance and idleness, and teaches men to be content with what they have and to work with a will. It expressly forbids men to war for conquest, but makes them courageous defenders of the Law itself; resolute in punishing offenders, not to be deceived by chicanery, but always guided by facts; on which account we have become the teachers of other nations. And what is finer than inviolable piety? What is more beneficial than mutual harmony?

M. Mettius Epaphroditus, who, according to Professor Laquer, was Josephus' publisher.

and this so far that we are neither to be divided by calamities nor to become arrogant in prosperity; in war to contemn death, in peace to devote ourselves to our arts or to the tilling of our grounds, and to be happy that our actions are under God's eye and protection. If these precepts had either been written or kept by others before us, we should owe them our gratitude as their disciples, but if it is evident that their original invention is our own, then let the Apions, the Molons, and the rest of those who delight in lies and abuse stand confuted" (II Apion, Th. 39 to end, Wh. 40 to end).

Dedicating this work to Epaphroditus, "and to all who, like him, may desire to know the truth about our nation," Josephus ends his noble Defense of Judaism.

CHAPTER II

In the TIME *of* JOSEPHUS

THE SOCIAL, ECONOMIC, AND RELIGIOUS CONDITIONS OF PALESTINE:—THE SANHEDRIN AND THE HIGH PRIEST

FLAVIUS JOSEPHUS, or in Hebrew, Yosef ben Mattathias ha-Cohen, was born in Jerusalem in the year 37 of the Christian era, into the most turbulent and tragic period of Jewish history. Regarding his family connections, we have the following details. His forefather Simon the Stammerer belonged to the first of the "twenty-four orders" of priests,[1] therefore to the order of Jehoiarib, which was a great distinction in those days. Simon's son was Mattathias Eplias, who married a daughter of the Maccabean, Jonathan Haphus. Of this marriage was born Mattathias, surnamed Curtus, or "the Hump-back." A son of Mattathias Curtus was Joseph, and Joseph's son was Mattathias, the father of our Josephus. Josephus was therefore not only of the highest priestly aristocracy, but also a descendant of the first Maccabeans who ruled over the Jewish Commonwealth during the period of its greatest glory.[2]

[1] For details on the "twenty-four orders" of priests see, I Chron., xxiv. 7-19, and II Chron., viii. 14.

[2] Vita, sec. 1.

A first century Roman marble head, found in Rome and presumed by Dr. Eisler to be a bust of Josephus. It is now in the Ny Carlsberg Glyptotek, Copenhagen.

The education which Josephus received was the best Judea could afford. As a child he was extremely precocious. At the age of fourteen he was praised by all for his love of learning, and often priests and outstanding men of Jerusalem came to him with questions on difficult points of the Law.[3] At sixteen, having mastered the schools of the Pharisees, Sadducees, and Essenes,—the three sects into which Jewry was divided,—he attached himself to an ascetic philosopher named Banus, who lived in the desert, wearing only such clothing as trees provided, such as leaves or bark, feeding on no other food than what grew of its own accord, and bathing in cold water by day and night to preserve his chastity. Josephus remained with Banus for three years. At nineteen, having thus fulfilled his desire for learning, and having acquainted himself with every Jewish philosophy, he returned to his native city, and, finding the Pharisaic as the best doctrine to live by, he became a member of that sect.[4]

The plight of the Palestinian Jews during this period was the most unhappy of their entire history. The masses of the people were ground under the heel of oppression and they were scarcely able to eke out their existence. The seacoast was infested with Syrian pirates[5] preying on commerce; the country was overrun with bands of Greek highwaymen, looting Roman officials and soldiers, and native and Egyptian marauders, ambuscaders, "Prophets" and "Messiahs,"[6] making life and travel extremely trying and uncertain. Chicanery,

[3] Vita, sec. 2.—This fact is not surprising, since according to the Talmud, Yoma, ch. i., the whole priestly caste during the Herodian period was composed of very ignorant people. The Talmudic account reads: "The High-Priest recited when it was time to recite, sang when it was his duty to sing, offered sacrifices when sacrifices were due; but religious discussions, or the study of the Law and its commentaries, was beyond him."

[4] Vita, sec. 2.

[5] Strabo, xiv. 668-9; I Apion, 12; Appian, de Bell. Mithr., 94-96; Antiq., XIV. iii. 2.

[6] Vita, 26; Antiq., XVII. x. 8-10; XVIII. i. 1, middle of section, XX. viii. 6; Bell. Jud., II. i. 1-3; Tacitus, Annals, xii. 54; Jebamoth, xvi. 7; Berachoth, 29b; Tosefta, iii. 7.

conspiracy and treachery were held as talents of a higher intellectuality; and perjury and lying were the order of the day.[7] Thrones were acquired through murder,[8] and Jewish high-priesthoods were sold by pagan Roman governors to the highest bidders or given out as favors or evidences of political influence.[9]

For the better understanding of this subject, however, a general description of the background underlying these destructive conditions in Palestine during this calamitous period, and of other important influences governing the poor, downtrodden and despairing masses of Judea must be given here. The study first necessary is that of the three prevailing religious systems,—that of the Pharisees, Sadducees, and Essenes:

(1) The Pharisees, the sect to which Josephus belonged, though not the most powerful, formed the most popular of the three religious parties. Their first appearance in history was in the time of the Maccabean conflict with Syria (167-165 BCE.), when they fought on the side of Judah. Having gained their freedom of religion in that contest, they seem to have retired and not to have appeared again till the time of John Hyrcanus (135-106 BCE.), when they fought, not on the side of this Maccabean descendant, but against him.[10] They fought against the Maccabeans under Aristobulus (106-105), and Alexander Jannaeus (105-79), when their religious practices were interfered with.[11] They were not a political party and had no interest in temporal power. They abhorred war,—submission was the basis of their lives. Their chief aim was the strict carrying out of the Law, and as long as this

[7] Documentary proofs for these statements are too voluminous to be given here, but we shall witness all this in the course of our history.

[8] Among the Romans: Nero (forced suicide), Galba, Otho (forced suicide), and Vitellius. Among the Jews: several within the Maccabean descendants; Herod's murder of Antigonus and of Aristobulus III, and others.

[9] Yoma, 8b.

[10] Antiq., XIII. x. 5-6.

[11] Antiq., XIII. xiii. 5.

was not interfered with they were content with any government. It was only when the secular power prevented the practice of the Law in that strict manner which their doctrine demanded that they became in a certain sense a political party and opposed it. According to Josephus, they were "the accurate interpreters of the Torah,"[12] and the "most skilful in the knowledge of the laws."[13] As civil and religious magistrates they were kind and merciful in their punishment and were opposed to the execution of the death penalty for any offense.[14] They had the greatest influence upon the congregation, so that all acts of public worship, prayer, and sacrifices were performed according to their injunctions.[15] The confidence in them was so great, that they could obtain a hearing even when they said something against the king or the high-priest.[16] The Roman yoke over Israel, they held, was the will of God; it was He who had given the heathens power over His people to punish them for their sins; that the harsh Roman government must be borne, and that this punishment of God should be willingly submitted to as long as the Law was not thereby interfered with.[17] The chief Pharisee, Simon ben Gamaliel, who during the revolt and beginning of the war against Rome headed the War Council,[18] joined the insurgents only because he was forced to, though in his heart he opposed the war because it was not in defense of the Law.

From the main body of this sect, however, in the year 6 or 7 CE., a fanatical faction, the members of which called themselves "Zealots," broke away. The Zealots were against submission to Rome under any circumstances. They did not wish to wait till God's decree, the Messianic hope of Israel,

[12] Bell. Jud., II. viii. 14.
[13] Vita, 38.
[14] Antiq., XIII. x. 6; Pirke Aboth, i. 7, ii. 5.
[15] Antiq., XVIII. i. 3.
[16] Antiq., XIII. x. 5.
[17] Antiq., XIV. ix. 4, XV. i. 1.
[18] Bell. Jud., IV. iii. 9.

should be fulfilled, but would rather rush into the conflict with the "pagan enemy" and hasten its realization. From the time of their organization by Judas the Galilean, up to the destruction of Jerusalem in the year 70, they headed the pillagers and outlaws everywhere, at first as a real revolutionary party but later as bandits and highwaymen, and it was to their machinations that Josephus ascribes the unquenched fire of the rebellion which ended with the Jewish national downfall.[19] But from this faction again, during the procuratorship of Felix (52-60 CE.), a still more malignant outgrowth, the "Sicarii," appeared. The Sicarii were the most atrocious and the most vicious outlaws in the country. The assassinations which they committed were so numerous that no one felt safe in Jerusalem. Armed with short daggers they mingled with the crowds and, unobserved in the rush, stabbed their opponents. Feigning sorrow over the misfortune of the victims, they succeeded in deflecting suspicion from themselves. One means of securing the liberation of those of their faction who had been captured was to seize some prominent official and return him in exchange for ten of their own comrades.[20]

(2) The second sect, the Sadducees, was a product of contemporary origin. Considering their remarkable fewness, however, they cannot, strictly speaking, be called a sect. Neither can they be regarded as a religious party, since theirs was not essentially a religion, but only an un-Jewish doctrine or theory. Their membership consisted of a small group of ignorant but wealthy political scoundrels who during the Herodian period (37 BCE.-66 CE.) operated as high-priests under the more ancient and honorable name of "Zaddikim," by which Josephus handed them over to history. And his designation of them as "Aristocrats" he evidently attributed to the fact that they belonged to the high-priesthood, for

[19] Compare generally, Bell. Jud., IV. iii. 9, v. 1, vi. 3, VII. viii. 1, and especially Antiq., XVIII. i. 1, 6; and Bell. Jud., II. viii. 1.
[20] Antiq., XX. viii. 10, ix. 2-3; Bell. Jud., II. xiii. 3, xiv. 1.

since the commencement of the Greek or even the Persian period it was the high-priestly aristocracy which governed the Jewish State, as it was also the priesthood in general that constituted the nobility of the Jewish people. And although "they were able to persuade none but the rich, and had not the populace on their side,"[21] their power—due mainly to the support which they received from the Roman government for their pro-Roman tendencies—vastly exceeded that of the Pharisees.

God, according to their doctrine, is not concerned in our doings; to do right or wrong is men's own choice.[22] They acknowledged the written Torah, but rejected the entire traditions of the Fathers.[23] They refused to believe in the Resurrection and the reward and punishment after death, thereby renouncing the entire Messianic hope. The behavior of the Sadducees towards each other was wild and their conversations with those of their own party as barbarous as if they were strangers to them.[24] As judges they were most severe and merciless.[25] While, for example, the Pharisees would interpret the precept of Deuteronomy, xix. 21, "An eye for an eye, and tooth for tooth," symbolically, and allowed a money compensation to be paid for an atonement, the Sadducees insisted not only upon the verbal fulfilment of this law, but on going beyond its demands, in accordance with the law of Exodus, xxi. 32, 35f.[26] False witnesses were condemned by them to death, even when their evidence had inflicted no injury upon the accused, according to the strictest letter of the law. Or, whereas the Pharisaic conception of Deuteronomy, xix. 21, "life for a life," was to inflict the death penalty upon a false witness only when through his perjury an inno-

[21] Antiq., XIII. x. 6.
[22] Bell. Jud., II. viii. 14; Antiq., XIII. v. 9.
[23] Antiq., XIII. x. 6; compare XVIII. i. 4.
[24] Antiq., XVIII. i. 4; Bell. Jud., II. viii. 14; "The soul dies with the body." Antiq., XVIII. i. 4.
[25] Antiq., XX. ix. 1.
[26] Jadajim, iv. 7b.

cent man had been put to death, the Sadducean use of that law would be in accordance with Deuteronomy, xix. 19, "You shall do to him as he thought to do to his brother."[27] Jesus and Paul were condemned by them. James, the brother of Jesus, was also their victim. In the Mishna, where this priestly Aristocracy is mentioned as "the condemners," there are some trustworthy traditions concerning them, but in the Talmudic period there was but a misty notion of them.[28]

(3) The Essenes. This sect differed essentially in many points from traditional Judaism and exercised no influence upon the development of the people, but deserves attention only as a peculiar monastic order. Their origin is obscure. Josephus first mentions them in the time of Jonathan the Maccabean (about 150 BCE.),[29] and again speaks of one "Judas the Essene" in the time of Aristobulus I (105-104 BCE.).[30] They consisted of two branches; those who entirely condemned marriage,[31] numbering about 4,000 souls,[32] and those who permitted marriage for propagation only, abandoning their wives when with child as a demonstration that they did not marry out of regard to pleasure.[33] The number of those who belonged to this branch is not recorded.

Whoever desired to become a member received a pick-axe, an apron and a white garment. He underwent a year's probation until he was admitted to the lustrations. There was a further probation of two years, and after this period had ended he took a fearful oath and was then allowed to become a full member. In this oath he had to bind himself to absolute openness towards his fellow members, as well as complete

[27] Makkoth, i. 6.

[28] An excellent treatise on the subject of Sadducees is given by Schuerer, Div. II. Vol. ii. pp. 2-43.

[29] Antiq., XIII. v. 9.

[30] Antiq., XIII. xi. 2; Bell. Jud., I. iii. 5.

[31] Bell. Jud., II. viii. 2.

[32] Antiq., XIII. i. 5.

[33] Bell. Jud., II. viii. 13.

secrecy concerning the doctrines of the order to non-members.[34] Only adults were permitted to join, but children were also received (probably orphans) for the purpose of training in the principles of Essenism.[35] They lived chiefly in villages, avoiding towns because of the immorality of the inhabitants, but dwelt in some of the towns of Palestine[36] and even in Jerusalem,[37] where a gate was named after them,[38] probably because the house of their order was near it.

For the sake of living as a community, they had special houses in which they lived together. At the head were directors whom the members were bound unconditionally to obey.[39] "The community," says Josephus, "is wonderful; one does not find one to possess more than another. For it is the law that those who enter deliver up their property to the order, so that there is nowhere to be seen either humiliation of poverty or superfluity of wealth, but on the contrary, one property for all as brethren, formed by the collection of possessions of individuals....[40] None desires to have any kind of property of his own, neither a house, nor a slave, nor an estate, nor flocks, nor anything at all that constitutes wealth.[41] They neither bought nor sold among each other; but while one gave to another what he wanted, he received in return what was useful to himself, and even without giving anything in return they received freely whatever they needed."[42] The managers of the common property were chosen by vote;[43] suitable persons as receivers of revenues and of the produce of the earth, and priests for the preparation of bread and food

[34] Bell. Jud., II. viii. 7.
[35] Bell. Jud., II. viii. 2.
[36] Bell. Jud., II. viii. 4.
[37] Antiq., XIII. xi. 2, XV. x. 5, XVII. xiii. 3; Bell. Jud., II. xx. 4.
[38] Bell. Jud., V. iv. 2.
[39] Bell. Jud., II. viii. 6.
[40] Bell. Jud., II. viii. 3.
[41] Philo (ed. Mangey), ii. 623; Schuerer, Div. II. Vol. ii. p. 196.
[42] Bell. Jud., II. viii. 4.
[43] Bell. Jud., II. viii. 3.

were also selected by all.[44] Transgressions of members of the order were judged by a court of at least one hundred fellow-members,[45] and those found guilty were expelled from the community.[46]

The daily labor of the Essenes began before sunrise with certain prayers, as if they made a supplication for its rising, after which supervisors ordered them to their work in the fields or at their crafts. They reassembled "on the fifth hour" to bathe themselves in cold water and partake of their morning meal. After this they again went to work, to return only for their evening meal.[47]

The wages which they earned (mainly for agricultural work, Antiq., XVIII. i. 5) they gave to their supervisors, who bought and dispensed to them provisions and whatever else they required.[48] Not only had they food and ordinary clothing in common, but heavy cloaks during the winter season and light overalls for the summer were at the disposal of everyone. For what one had was regarded as the property of all, and what all had as that of each individual.[49] The sick needed not fear on account of their inability to earn, because the common purse was in readiness for the care of them. The old enjoyed a happy old age under the tender care of the younger, just as if they had had many good children of their own [50] about them.

Everyone had a right to help the needy from the common purse according to his discretion. Only when relatives were in question had they to obtain consent of the supervisor.[51] Traveling members of the order found hospitality

[44] Antiq., XVIII. i. 5.
[45] Bell. Jud., II. viii. 9.
[46] Bell. Jud., II. viii. 8.
[47] Bell. Jud., II. viii. 5.
[48] Philo (ed. Mangey), ii. 633.
[49] Philo (ed. Mangey), ii. 623.
[50] Philo (ed. Mangey), ii. 458f. with 633.
[51] Bell. Jud., II. viii. 6.

everywhere and a special officer in each town cared for the wants of his traveling brothers.[52]

Swearing was forbidden, for that which did not deserve belief without an appeal to God was held already condemned.[53] Moreover, in their observance of the Sabbath they were stricter than any other Jews. For, while on the other days they dug a hole a foot deep in the ground when satisfying the needs of nature, on the Sabbath, when it is not allowed to dig a hole, they did not satisfy their needs.[54]

Labor and Commerce:—Though the Jews of Palestine in the time of Josephus were not solely an agricultural people, tillage of the soil was generally their occupation. Such was especially the case in the northern part of the country. The land there was so rich and fruitful that even the most indolent was tempted to its cultivation. The towns, owing to the fertility of the land, were close together and so populated that not even the smallest of them contained less than fifteen thousand inhabitants.[55] Even Perea, east of the Jordan, with a soil much inferior, owing to the moisture of the land from torrents descending from the mountains and springs which never dried up, produced all kinds of fruit, olives and grapes.[56] Samaria and Judea, too, although not naturally watered by many streams, but deriving their fertility chiefly from rainfall, were also luxuriously wooded and rich in fruit both cultivated and wild. And owing to the singularly sweet taste of the few running waters which they had, and to the abundance of excellent grass, the cattle of these districts yielded more milk than those of any other.[57]

Aside from the scenery of the country around the Sea of Galilee, which was exceptionally beautiful, its climate was so

[52] Bell. Jud., II. viii. 4.
[53] Bell. Jud., II. viii. 6; comp., Antiq., XV. x. 4.
[54] Bell. Jud., II. viii. 9
[55] Bell. Jud., III. iii. 2.
[56] Bell. Jud., III. iii. 3.
[57] Bell. Jud., III. iii. 4.

wonderful that all sorts of trees could grow there. The walnut which requires the coldest zones flourished there in great plenty. There were palm-trees, which grow best in hot regions, growing side-by-side with fig and olive trees, which require a more temperate clime: "as if it were the ambition of nature to force these plants that are naturally enemies to one another to dwell together." Autumnal fruits grew beyond men's expectation; grapes and figs continued for ten months a year, and the other fruits ripened throughout the whole year. The Lake, too, as if jealous of the great wealth of the soil around it, contained, besides its own rich stock of fish, several of such choice varieties as were found nowhere else.[58]

Under favorable conditions, not counting revolutionary disturbances, spasmodic social upheavals, crime waves or droughts, the corn and hardy legumes produced in Palestine, were enough not only for home consumption but also for exportation. There was constant building,[59] done by laborers hired in the market and paid by the day,[60] and life was boisterous, much occupied and gay. At night, at a distance from the village, the singing and dancing of the holiday-makers could be heard.[61] In the market places the children were wrangling in their sports, and calling to their fellows.[62] The drunken steward storms, beats, or otherwise misuses the maid-servants.[63] One buys a piece of ground and must go to prove it; the other must examine the oxen which have been knocked down to him; the third has other business, a feast, a funeral, or a marriage.[64]

Of foreign food articles and other commodities imported into Palestine, were the following among others:—Babylonian

[58] Bell. Jud., III. x. 7-8.
[59] Luke, xiv. 30, xvii. 28.
[60] Matt., xx. 3, 6, 8; Lev., xix. 13; Deut., xxiv. 15.
[61] Luke, xv. 25.
[62] Matt. xi. 16.
[63] Luke, xii. 45.
[64] Luke, xiv. 18-20.

Copper and silver coins without the Emperor's image, minted in Jerusalem under the Roman Procurators, from Coponius, 6 CE. to Gessius Florus, 66 CE.

Copper coins with Greek inscriptions.

Copper coins inscribed with Hebrew characters.

Silver coin inscribed with Hebrew characters.

sauce, Median and Egyptian beer and mustard, Edomite vinegar, Bythnian cheese, Greek pumpkins and mint, Spanish kolas and Persian nuts; Pelusian and Indian linen and cotton cloth, Cilician haircloth, calico, organdie, handkerchiefs, felt hats and felt socks. Sandals came from Cilicia and Laodicia. From Egypt came also dishes, baskets, ladders and rope. Imported from Italy and Greece were the bench, the arm-chair, curtains, tablecloths, mirrors, wooden dishes, wine-barrels and sacks. Domestic linen was manufactured in Galilee; woolen cloth in Judea.[65]

In the northern part of Jerusalem, "where the narrow streets led obliquely to the wall," there was a special market for woollen and cotton goods, an exchange for iron workers and carpenters,[66] and a timber market.[67] Near the sheep gate [68] there was a sheep market,[69] with goldsmiths and merchants trading nearby.[70] The existence of a fish market, too, is implied in the numerous mentions in the Bible of the fish gate.[71] In the southern section of the city, the part called "the Upper City," there was a "High" or general market or bazaar,[72] a cheese market,[73] and a bakers' street; [74] while still other markets and associated traders which are mentioned in the Talmud are the corn market, the meat and cattle markets, tanners, apothecaries, physicians, barbers, bloodletters, potters, dyers, carpet makers, builders, shoemakers, tentmakers, glaziers, and weavers. Thus, R. Joshua was a gritmiller; [75] R.

[65] Many of the authorities on this are given by Schuerer, Div. II. Vol. i. pp. 41ff.

[66] Bell. Jud., V. viii. 1.

[67] Bell. Jud., II. xix. 4.

[68] Neh., iii. 1, 32, xii. 39.

[69] John, v. 2.

[70] Neh., iii. 32.

[71] II Chron., xxxiii. 14; Neh., iii. 3; Zeph., i. 10.

[72] Bell. Jud., II. xiv. 9, xv. 2.

[73] Bell. Jud., V. iv. 1.

[74] Jer., xxxvii. 21.

[75] Erubin, 21b.

Jochanan, a perfumer;[76] R. Ishmael, a Torah writer;[77] and R. Akiba seems to have been connected with shipping.[78] There was also a non-Jewish laundry to which R. Gamaliel of Jabne gave his linen to wash, as reported by R. Eleazar ben Zadok.[79]

The Population:—Naturally, not only Jews lived in Palestine. Under Roman rule, more than ever before, the country was inhabited by a mixed population. Judea was its only district in which the great mass of the people was purely Jewish. In addition to the intermediate cities of Carmel, Kadesh, Scythopolis, and Caesarea, all northernmost and the majority of Perean communities were almost entirely Gentile.[80] The balance of the populations in those towns where Jews formed only a small minority consisted of Greeks, Syrians, Phoenicians and Arabs.[81] Herod, especially, had besides his Greek court secretaries, writers, lawyers and orators, even a private army of Greek, German and Gallic mercenaries,[82] supplementing his Roman garrisons distributed throughout the country.[83] In all towns along the coast of the Mediterranean, with the exception of Jabne and Joppa, which were partially Judaized by the Maccabeans, a Gentile population preponderated. At no period of their history had the Jews been able to gain a permanent footing on the seacoast; and the settlement of Jewish colonists in the towns of Raphia, Gaza, Anthedon, Ascalon, Azotus, Dora, and Ptolemais, dated from the time of the Greek invasion of the East.[84]

[76] Chullin, 55b.

[77] Sotah, 20a.

[78] Nedar, 50a-b.

[79] Shabbath, i. 9; Baraitha, 19a; Tosefta, i. 22.

[80] Bell. Jud., II. xviii. 1, III. iii. 5; Vita, 6; and other instances.

[81] Matt., iv. 15; Vita, 12, near end.

[82] Antiq., XVI. vii. 2-3, viii. 3, 5, x. 1; XVII. viii. 2-3, ix. 3-5; Bell. Jud., I. xvi. 1-4, xxiv. 2, xxxiii. 8; II. i. 3-4.

[83] Bell. Jud., II. xviii. 6, near end; III. vii. 32; Vita, 24.

[84] On this subject see Schuerer:—"The Hellenistic Towns," Div. II. Vol. i. pp. 57-149.

The Judean Government:—The important question of government among the Jews of Palestine during the Herodian century has been debated with the utmost energy and erudition, and, as with numerous other historical questions, many scholars are still undecided about it. The information on the subject is derived from three sources:—Josephus, the Talmud, and the Gospels. Many pedagogues, due to the unpopularity of Josephus, have ignored him altogether. Some have obtained their information from the Talmud, disregarding both Josephus and the Gospels; while others have derived their facts from the Gospels, likewise placing no faith in either of the other two records. Others again, claiming open-mindedness, have consulted all three of our authorities on the subject, not, however, in diligent search for truth or for the honest comparison of facts, or in the effort to discover in one such details as are deficient in the two others, but that they might in this manner the better qualify to present before their disciples "fully documented" conclusions, which, without variation, in every such instance is in accordance with the writer's individual religious affiliations. But this is not all. Many who have written on the subject think they have surmounted their obstacles by combining or even juggling the narratives contained in all three accounts, as might best suit their convenience. An unbiased examination of the existing records and the facts contained in them concerning the subject, however, will reveal the following:

(1) The Works of Josephus, it will be remembered, were designed for specific purposes. They were written mainly not as histories, but either for the glorification of Judaism, or in refutation of the anti-Jewish literature circulated among the Greek gentry of those days; possibly also for the propagation of the Mosaic faith.[85] Such mentions, therefore, which Josephus makes of the Jewish Home Rule, other than those which he refers to as an "Aristocracy," are in the service of

[85] Antiq., Preface, secs. 2-3; XVI. vi. 8; comp. II Apion, Th. 28, Wh. 29.

that scheme. On one occasion he speaks of the Court of Hyrcanus II, before which Herod (ab. 47 BCE.) was called to account for his decapitation of the robber-leader Hezekiah; [86] on another, of the "Entire Sanhedrin, except one," which Herod, on his accession to the throne (37 BCE.), put to death; [87] of "The Sanhedrin" to which Herod had submitted evidences of Hyrcanus' treasonable dealings with the Arabian king, Malchus (30 BCE.); [88] or, of the Great War Council which was hastily organized at the beginning of the Jewish uprising against Rome in the time of Nero.[89] In addition to such references, however, there are also many other instances in the works of Josephus which, though not quite as direct, offer all the necessary facts concerning our question. Yet, though available to any one who wishes to make use of them, it is remarkable how few have utilized the advantage, as will be seen in the course of this Chapter.

(2) Unlike Josephus, however, who owes his complete familiarity with this period to his nearness to the time, the Mishna, or the basis of the Talmud, was not put into its present form until at least the end of the second century of the present era,—long after the disappearance of the Supreme Judiciary which it describes. In one Tract devoted exclusively to the subject of "Sanhedrin," and in several additional passages,[90] where the question is described more systematically and completely than by Josephus, the arguments of the Talmudists are at best only of a general or idealistic character.

Seeming to have had but a vague acquaintance, not only with the Jewish system of self-government under Herod, but also with the general history of those years, and particularly with that important portion of time in which Christianity had its origin, their discussions are chiefly concerning either

[86] Antiq., XIV. ix. 3, 5.

[87] Antiq., XV. i. 2; comp. XIV. ix. 4, end; Bell. Jud., I. xviii. 4.

[88] Antiq., XV. vi. 2, end.

[89] Bell. Jud., II. xx. 3; Vita, 12.

[90] Fourth Seder, Tracts 4-10.

the ante-Herodian Sanhedrin, or the post-war Court of Justice which Jochanan ben Zakkai had established at Jabne; or else, of how they themselves might have conducted the government had they been the Sanhedrists. Such references as those concerning Christianity or similarly isolated and incomplete facts as are found in some editions of the Talmud and Midrash are only additions of the Amoraic period and consequently of no historical value.[91] The Talmud, in fact, very rarely refers even to events of the period from the return of the Jews from Babylon to the end of the Maccabeans in the year 37 BCE., and does so only in connection with some Rabbinical decision on a Scriptural law; or for the edification of some old tradition or a current belief. "What, for example," remarks Dr. Klausner, "should we have known of the great Maccabean struggle against the kings of Syria if the Apocryphal books, I and II Maccabees, and the writings of Josephus had not survived and we had been compelled to derive all our information about this great event in the history of Israel from the Talmud alone? We should not have known even the very name of Judas Maccabeus!"

But now, in accordance with one of Josephus' descriptions of the Jewish self-government, from the death of Herod the Great, in 4 BCE. (or rather the banishment of his son and successor Archelaus, in 6 CE.), to the end of the Jewish state, its form was that of an "Aristocracy" under the direct supervision of the High-Priest.[92] This Aristocracy which, as the occasion requires, he also refers to as "the Sanhedrin,"[93] "the Sanhedrin of Jerusalem,"[94] "the Sanhedrin of Judges,"[95] "the

[91] A masterly treatise on this subject is given by Klausner in his "Jesus of Nazareth," pp. 18-54. For the Amoraic references to Christianity, see Prof. R. Travers Herford's "Christianity in the Talmud and Midrash" (London, 1905).

[92] Antiq., XX. x.—near end.

[93] Antiq., XIV. ix. 3-5; XX. ix. 6.

[94] Vita, 12.

[95] Antiq., XX. ix. 1.

Council,"[96] or "the People of Jerusalem,"[97] according to himself, consisted of seventy men.[98] But according to one account in the Talmud it was seventy-one,[99] whereas according to another, it consisted of seventy-two members.[100] In smaller towns, according to the Talmud, the number of the members of the governing body amounted to twenty-three,[101] while according to Josephus there were seven men.[102] In such cases, however, where a small local Council could not arrive at a decision, Josephus informs us, the issue was brought before the high-priest and the Sanhedrin at Jerusalem, "to determine as it shall seem good to them."[103]

The function of the Great Sanhedrin of Jerusalem, as a Court of Appeals, is described in the Talmud as follows: "The judgment of the 'Seventy-one' is besought when the affair concerns a whole tribe, or is regarding a false prophet or the high-priest; when it is a question of whether war should be declared or not; when it has for its object the enlargement of Jerusalem or its suburbs; whether tribunals of twenty-three shall supersede smaller ones, or to declare that a town has become defiled, and to place it under excommunication."[104]

"Anyone," says the Mishna, "was qualified to act in civil causes," but in criminal cases "none were eligible but priests, Levites, and Israelites whose daughters it would be lawful for priests to marry"[105] (that is, those who could furnish documentary evidence of their legitimate Israelitish origin). To be elected, however, it was necessary also to be of good birth, to

[96] Vita, 41.
[97] Vita, 42.
[98] Bell. Jud., II. xx. 5, IV. v. 4; Vita, 14.
[99] Sanhedrin, i. 6; Shebuoth, i. 2.
[100] Sebachim, i. 3; Jadajim, iii. 5, iv. 2.
[101] Sanhedrin, i. 6.
[102] Antiq., IV. viii. 14, 38; Vita, 14; Bell. Jud., II. xxii. 5.
[103] Antiq., IV. viii. 14.
[104] Mishna, Sanhedrin, i. 1.
[105] Sanhedrin, iv. 2.

have a physical appearance inspiring reverence, to have children, and to be of not too advanced age.[106]

At the head of the sacerdotal body, Josephus states, stood the high-priest,[107] but according to the Talmud, the presidency was held by "Pairs" of leaders with the title of Nassi and Ab-beth-din, or president and vice-president of the Sanhedrin.[108] But, points out Prof. Schuerer, not only is this tradition of very late origin, but also an only solitary passage in the Mishna in which it occurs, standing there anomalously, and as it were, in perfect isolation.[109] The first senatorial president to whom the title of Nassi is applied, he says, is R. Jehuda, the redactor of the Mishna (Aboth, ii. 2), at the end of the second century CE., and that there is no one known as yet, under the designation of Nassi previous to R. Jehuda.[110] Among the scholars agreeing with Dr. Schuerer are Basnage, Geiger, Keil, Kuenen, Milman, Morrison, Seidel, Smith, Stapfer, Wellhausen and Winer; but while Jost takes a safe middle course, Graetz and Zunz alone accept and follow this late addition in the Talmud.

Sessions of the smaller Councils in towns and villages, the Talmud informs us, were held on Mondays and Thursdays,[111] while at Jerusalem the Sanhedrin sat daily, excepting on festival days, holy days and Saturdays.[112] The location of the Court-House, the Talmud further says, was at the "Lishkath Hagazith,"[113] which was in the inner court of the Temple, whereas according to Josephus, Court was held in the "Council House adjoining the Xistus,"[114] which was outside the

[106] Sifre, ii. 153; Sanhedrin, 17a, 24b et seq., 27 et seq., 36b.
[107] Antiq., IV. viii. 14, near end; XX. x. near end; II Apion, Th. 23, Wh. 24.
[108] Chagiga, ii. 2.
[109] Schuerer, Div. II. Vol. i. p. 183.
[110] Schuerer, Div. II. Vol. i. p. 184, note 505.
[111] Kethuboth, i. 1.
[112] Beza, v. 2.
[113] Sanhedrin, x. 2, xi. 2; Middoth, v. 4.
[114] Bell. Jud., V. iv. 2.

Temple area. The Talmud, however, also states that, "forty years before the destruction of Jerusalem the Sanhedrin had removed from the usual official court-house, and that after that it held its sittings in the 'Chanujoth,'" or merchants' booths in the outer court of the Temple[115] (which probably were those which, in the Gospels of Matthew and John, are mentioned as the booths of the dove merchants and money changers).[116]

Court opened after the morning sacrifices and closed before the evening sacrifices,[117] and never was a trial permitted to continue into the night. Nor was a court allowed to assemble on a day preceding the Sabbath or a holy day.[118]

A criminal case, says the Mishna, resulting in acquittal may terminate the same day on which the trial began, but if a sentence of death is to be pronounced, it cannot be concluded before the following day.[119] On the night intervening, the judges, having retired by twos to their houses, are to consider the evidences of the crime and the arguments made for the defendant. And furthermore, in order to secure a more careful deliberation, the judges are under obligation to abstain from heavy food, wine, and from everything that would have a tendency to incapacitate them from correct thinking. The next day, on their return to the Court of Justice, each judge votes for or against the accused.[120]

When in session, the Sanhedrin sat in the form of a half-circle, with the president in the center.[121] Facing them were three rows of benches on which sat their disciples who were intended in this manner to make themselves acquainted with

[115] Shabboth, xva; Rosh Hash., xxxia; Sanhedrin, xiia; Aboda Zara, viiib.

[116] Matt., xxi. 12; John, ii. 14.

[117] Sanhedrin, x. 88; also Maimon., Sanhedrin, iii. 1.

[118] Mishna, Sanhedrin, iv. 1.

[119] Mishna, Sanhedrin, iv. 1.

[120] Mishna, Sanhedrin, v. 5.

[121] Mishna, Sanhedrin, iv. 3.

the laws.[122] The prisoner at the bar was required to present himself in a submissive manner, dressed in mourning and with his hair disheveled.[123]

Should a man bring an accusation against himself, such confession of guilt was not to be used against him unless properly attested by two other witnesses.[124] Says R. Ashi, "The opening (of a case) should be with an announcement of the Court: 'Everyone who knows of a defense concerning the defendant may come and tell it to the Court.' "[125] In criminal cases, before testifying, the judge addresses each witness as follows: "It is not conjecture, nor anything you may have gathered from public rumor, that we ask of you. Remember that a heavy responsibility rests on you; that it is not a question of money where restitution can be made. If you should cause the accused to be condemned unjustly, his blood, and even the blood of his posterity, shall cry for vengeance against you, and God will hold you accountable."[126] The following seven questions were next asked each witness: "Was it during a year of Jubilee? Was it an ordinary year? In what month? On what day of the month? At what hour? In what place? Do you identify this person?"[127] If one witness contradicted another the testimony was not accepted.[128] For instance, if one witness were to testify to having seen a man in the act of worshipping the sun, and another to having seen the same man in the act of worshipping the moon, yet although each of the two facts proved clearly that the man had committed the horrible crime of idolatry, the discrepancy in the statements of the witnesses

[122] Mishna, Sanhedrin, iv. 4.

[123] Antiq., XIV. ix. 4.

[124] Mishna, Sanhedrin, iv. 2; Kidushin, iii. 9; Sanhedrin, 9b, 25a; Kethuboth, 18a; Yebamoth, 25a.—M. M. Lemann, p. 113; Rabbi Drucker, p. 13.

[125] Gemara, Sanhedrin, iv. 1.

[126] Mishna, Sanhedrin, iv. 5.

[127] Mishna, Sanhedrin, v. 1.

[128] Mishna, Sanhedrin, v. 2.

invalidates the testimony and the accused is to be set free.[129]

In capital trials a majority of one vote is sufficient for acquittal, but for a condemnation a majority of two votes is necessary.[130] For instance, the members of the Sanhedrin being seventy-one in number, if thirty-five condemn the accused he is to be set free immediately. If thirty-six condemn him, he is also to be freed immediately.[131] If, furthermore, the vote for condemnation is unanimous, the whole proceeding is to be annulled in favor of the prisoner, "since in such a case, it is not a trial but a conspiracy."[132]

The ordinary punishments were fines of money, corporal punishment, confiscation of goods, and imprisonment.[133] The capital punishments were becoming rare, and the Tannaim were of the opinion that they should be abolished entirely.[134] The Mishna says, "The Sanhedrin, which as often as once in seven years condemns a man to death, is a slaughter-house." A contemporary of R. Akiba, the eminent and wealthy priest R. Eleazar ben Azariah, goes still further: "Even one which does so once in seventy years," says he, "is a slaughter-house." And both R. Akiba and R. Tarphon say, "If we were among the Sanhedrin a death sentence would never occur."[135]

Such was the nature of the Sanhedrin, and such were its functions, in accordance with the descriptions of it by Josephus and the Talmud.

(3) The problem we meet with in the Gospels, as sources of historical information, however, is of a totally different character. The form in which we have them today few ortho-

[129] Maimon., Sanhedrin, xx.

[130] Mishna, Sanhedrin, iv. 1.

[131] Mishna, Sanhedrin, v. 5.

[132] Talmud, Sanhedrin, 17a; Maimon., Sanhedrin, ix. 1.

[133] Talmud, Baba Kamma, 62b; Mishna, Baba Kamma, vii. 1; Kiddushin, 66a; also, Antiq., XIII. x. 5-6.

[134] Sanhedrin, vii. 1; comp. Antiq., XX. ix. 1; Bell. Jud., I. xxvii. 6, xxxiii. 4; also, Deut., xxii. 18-19, xxv. 1-3; Ezra, vii. 26.

[135] Mishna, Makkoth, i. 10.

dox critics attribute to the Evangelists themselves. There is a superabundance of evidence, not only that they are based on some earlier tradition very unlike their present nature, but also that they are extremely contrary to their original intent. On how these traditions originated no two critics are ever found in agreement. What they were no one knows. Whether they were originally transmitted by word of mouth or in writing, in Aramaic, Hebrew, Latin or Greek, is equally a question. Nor do we precisely know why, if the history of the life of Jesus was faithfully recorded "according to" St. Matthew in the year 60, was it necessary to revise and republish it "according to" St. Mark in the year 80, and again "according to" St. Luke in the year 100, and over again "according to" St. John twenty years later.

The earliest manuscripts of the Gospels in existence today are two of the fourth century and three of a century later,—all written in Greek,—and each of them disagreeing more or less with the others. It is from these, "after much discussion and comparison and with some uncertainties and doubts about words," that the four Gospels as we know them today have been copied. But our oldest manuscripts must also have been copied from other books, and how accurately this was done can be judged only by what is known of the habits of the Church copyists of those early days. Theirs was an age when the meaning of truth was scarcely understood, and piety was held a higher virtue than honesty.[136] To distort and misrepresent facts for God and Church was not only allowable but even a religious duty. Chancellor Mosheim[137] says that, among the early Christians "it was an almost universally adopted maxim that it was an act of virtue to deceive and lie,

[136] Good treatises on this subject are, Max Radin's "Trial of Jesus of Nazareth" (Chicago, 1931); Conrad Henry Moehlman's "The Christian-Jewish Tragedy" (New York, 1933); Giovanni Rosadi's "The Trial of Jesus" (Engl. transl., New York, 1905); and Edward Holton James' "The Trial Before Pilate" (Concord, Mass., 1909).

[137] Johann von Mosheim, "Instit. Hist. Eccl.," Vol. i. p. 198.

when by so doing they could promote the interest of the Church." St. Paul (Rom., iii. 7) furnishes evidence of this when he asks, "If the truth of God hath more abounded through my lie unto His glory, why am I judged a sinner?" And though Paul does not clearly disclose for what purpose this policy was employed, it can easily be inferred. Fraudulence, in those days, grew so common, that Origen (185-254), even in his own lifetime, had to complain of falsification of his works and forgeries under his name.[138] A missionary of the Church of England, the Rev. Thomas Brown, speaking of the early clergy, tells us that, "almost all persons of those days handed down to us as saints and Fathers of the Church were the most infamous villains and murderers that ever lived on God's earth."[139]

The first and third of the Evangelists, Matthew and Luke, give us a genealogy of Jesus, and tell us that he descended from and through a line of kings embracing the house of David. But in presenting the names and the number of generations, to prove his royal distinction, they exhibit a most messy tissue of discrepancies, differing not only with each other but also with the genealogy given in the Old Testament.

Luke names and counts off forty-one generations from David to Joseph, though he had previously represented it as being forty-two.[140] Matthew says that, "from Abraham to David are fourteen generations,"[141] though according to his own showing and according to his own list of names there are only thirteen.[142] He then tells us that from David to the carrying away into Babylon there were only fourteen genera-

[138] Prof. Harnack, in the Encycl. Brit., 9th ed., Vol. XVII. p. 841.

[139] Brown's "Destruction of Jerusalem," p. 113 (Albany, N. Y. 1825).

[140] Luke, iii. 23-31.

[141] Matt., i. 17.

[142] Matt., i. 2-6.

Brit. Mus.—Cod. Alex.—(St. John i. 1-5.)

ΕΝΑΡΧΗΗΝΟΛΟΓΟΣΚΑΙΟΛΟΓΟΣΗ
ΠΡΟΣΤΟΝΘΝ·ΚΑΙΘΣΗΝΟΛΟΓΟΣ·
ΟΥΤΟΣΗΝΕΝΑΡΧΗΠΡΟΣΤΟΝΘΝ
ΠΑΝΤΑΔΙΑΥΤΟΥΕΓΕΝΕΤΟΚΑΙΧΩ
ΡΕΙΣΑΥΤΟΥΕΓΕΝΕΤΟΟΥΔΕΕΝ
ΟΓΕΓΟΝΕΝΕΝΑΥΤΩΖΩΗΗΝ
ΚΑΙΗΖΩΗΗΝΤΟΦΩΣΤΩΝΑΝΩΝ
ΚΑΙΤΟΦΩΣΕΝΤΗΣΚΟΤΙΑΦΑΙ
ΝΕΙΚΑΙΗΣΚΟΤΙΑΑΥΤΟΟΥΚΑΤΕ
ΛΑΒΕΝ·

Brit. Mus.—Add. 17, 211.—(St. Luke xx 9, 10.)

Specimen of early Greek manuscript of the Gospels. The lower portion of the illustration shows the original script partly obliterated by a new version superimposed upon it.

tions,[143] whereas according to the Old Testament there were eighteen.[144] And then the names comprised in the two genealogies are so widely different from those found in Chronicles, as to set all analogy at defiance.

Matthew tells us that the son of David through whom Joseph descended was Solomon, but Luke says it was Nathan. The next name in Matthew's list is that of Roboam, but the corresponding name in Luke's list is Mattatha. Matthew's next name is Abia, but Luke gives it as Menan, whereas in Chronicles it is Abijah. Matthew says Joram begat Ozias, but according to Chronicles Joram had no such son, although he had a great-great-grandson Uzziah. But Luke says, in effect, there was no such person in the family line as either Joram, Ozias or Uzziah. Matthew says again, "Josias begat Jechonias and his brethren about the time they were carried away to Babylon."[145] But according to Chronicles, Jechonias was Jehoiakim's son.[146] And besides the fact that Josiah had no such son, we learn that he was killed at Megiddo eleven years before the exile to Babylon,[147] and naturally could not well beget a son after he had been dead for eleven years.

Matthew, further, after naming twenty-four generations as filling out the line, and making it complete between David and Jacob, concludes by saying, "and Jacob begat Joseph, the husband of Mary."[148] But Luke, before spinning out his list to fourteen generations more than Matthew, declares that "Joseph was the son of Heli."[149] Again Luke says that Salathiel was the son of Neri; but Chronicles says he was the son of Jechonias.[150] And after Chronicles had registered

[143] Matt., i. 17.
[144] I Chronicles, iii. 1-15.
[145] Matt., i. 11.
[146] I Chron., iii. 16.
[147] II Kings, xxiii. 29.
[148] Matt., i. 16.
[149] Luke, iii. 23.
[150] Compare Luke, iii. 23 with I Chronicles, iii. 17.

Jerobabel as the son of Penniah, Matthew and Luke say he was the son of Salathiel. Agreeing here in contradicting Chronicles, it is the only instance but one in which they agree in the whole list of ancestors from David to Joseph.

But in Matthew, following the elaborate genealogy by which he attempts to prove Jesus' descent from David, his Davidic origin is suddenly cut short. The fatherhood of Joseph, "the husband of Mary," is entirely disclaimed, and in a manner incomprehensible to mortal man, Jesus becomes a God, "conceived by the Holy Ghost," who "shall save His people from their sins," in fulfilment of "which was spoken of the Lord by the Prophet."[151]

That Jesus never intended any such doctrine, viz., that he was one of the three persons in the Godhead, is proven by his answer to the Scribe who asked him, "Which is the first commandment of all?" which was, "Hear O Israel, the Lord our God is one Lord."[152] When again, "a certain ruler" hailed him as "Good Master," his reply was, "Why callest thou me good? There is none good but one God."[153] But in addition to these evidences in the New Testament that Jesus never sanctioned the dogma that he was God, are also the testimonies of the Prophets, which utterly preclude any Son or Holy Ghost from participating in the divine essence or claim in the Godhead:—"I am Jehovah, and besides me there is no Savior";[154] "There is no God besides me, a just God and a Savior";[155] "I Jehovah am thy Savior and thy Redeemer";[156] and "I am Jehovah, thy God, thou shalt not acknowledge a God beside me."[157]

Jesus, indeed, believed himself to be a son of God. But

[151] Matt., i. 16-25.
[152] Mark, xii. 28-29.
[153] Mark, x. 18; Luke, xviii. 18-19.
[154] Isaiah, xliii. 11.
[155] Isaiah, xlv. 21.
[156] Isaiah, xlix. 26.
[157] Hosea, xiii. 4.

all men are, or may become so in different degrees.[158] Everyone ought daily to call God his father; all who are raised again will be sons of God.[159] The divine sonship was attributed in the Old Testament to beings whom it by no means pretended were equal with God.[160] The word "Son" has the widest meaning in the Hebrew language, and even in the New Testament we find, "The children of the Kingdom,"[161] "The children of hell,"[162] "The children of this world,"[163] "The children of the Resurrection,"[164] "The children of peace,"[165] etc. Not less among the pagans, Jupiter was "the 'fatherly' ruler of mankind."[166]

Neither did Jesus authorize the claim which the Evangelists have made for him, that he was born in Bethlehem. But to fulfil the prophecy of Micah,[167] which requires the Messiah to be a Bethlehemite and of Davidic descent, they were compelled to show that he whom they called Messiah and a son of David, came from the same city as David. Nor did he know anything of the attempt of his disciples to connect his Bethlehemic origin with the census which had taken place under Quirinius. This census to which Luke attributes the journey to Bethlehem[168] did not occur until a full decade after the year in which Jesus was born. For his birth took place in (the last year of) Herod's reign,[169] whereas the census of Quirinius was not taken until after the deposition of

[158] Matt., v. 9, 45; Luke, iii. 38, vi. 35, xx. 36; John, i. 12-13, x. 34-35, and elsewhere; and in the Old Testament: Deut., xiv. 1; and Wisdom, ii. 13, 18.

[159] Luke, xx. 36.

[160] Gen., vi. 2; Job, i. 6, ii. 1, xxviii. 7; Ps., ii. 7, lxxxii. 6; II Sam., vii. 14.

[161] Matt., viii. 12, xiii. 38.

[162] Matt., xxiii. 15.

[163] Mark, iii. 17; Luke, xvi. 8, xx. 34.

[164] Luke, xx. 6.

[165] Luke, x. 6.

[166] See Encycl. Brit., 9th ed., Vol. XIII. p. 780b.

[167] Micah, v. 2.

[168] Luke, ii. 1-5.

[169] Matt., ii. 1, 19, 22; Luke, i. 5.

Herod's son Archelaus, viz., ten years after the death of Herod, or in the thirty-seventh year of Octavius' victory over Antony at Actium.[170]

A brief review of the Gospels will further show that the intention of Jesus was never a negation of the Law of Moses. According to what evidently is part of the original Gospel of Matthew, Jesus declared he wished "not to destroy the Law or the Prophets, but to fulfil,"—that is to practice the Law: "Till heaven and earth pass away, not one jot or tittle shall pass from the Law.... Whosoever shall break one of the least commandments, or shall teach men so to do, shall receive his due in the Kingdom of Heaven....[171] All things, therefore, whatsoever they (the Scriptures) bid you, those do and observe,[172]... (and) keep the commandments if thou wouldst have eternal life."[173] Nor did he oppose fasting or prayer: he only required that it be done without pride or display;[174] and even rebuked in most scorching language the abuses of the Law and the hypocrisy of the wealthy, trafficking hierarchy with which the nation of that time was afflicted.[175]

That the Jews were in sympathy with the teachings of Jesus is testified by Josephus. For he tells us that (in the year 62) they vigorously protested the stoning of James, the brother of Jesus, and others of his followers, whom the high-priest Ananus, the instigator of the murders, accused as "breakers of the laws." And, indeed, it was on this complaint of the Jews to the procurator Albinus and to King Agrippa, against what they clamored had been "unlawful executions," that the king removed Ananus from office.[176] Even the Gospels themselves, obviously unwittingly, affirm that the mass of the Jewish people were favorable to Jesus. For, it is re-

[170] Compare generally, Antiq., XVII. xiii. 5, XVIII. i. 1, ii. 1.
[171] Matt., v. 17-19.
[172] Matt., xxiii. 3.
[173] Matt., xix. 17.
[174] Matt., vi. 16-18.
[175] Matt., xxiii. 1-34; Mark, vii. 8-13; Luke, 41-44.
[176] Antiq., XX. ix. 1.

corded that, on his arrival near the Gate of Jerusalem, "they strewed branches from trees, and spread their garments in his way, and received him with Hosannas," thereby extending him such honors as would be worthy of no less than one who had come to redeem them from the tyrannical government under which they suffered; and blessed him "that cometh in the name of the Lord";[177] and remained his faithful friends to the end. For when he was led to Golgotha, "there followed him a great company of people, and of women, who bewailed and lamented him."[178]

But Josephus and the older and more genuine Gospel accounts are not alone to testify the friendliness between the Jews and Jesus and his immediate disciples. For even as late as the year 175, the Platonic philosopher, Celsus, in his "True Discourse" against Christianity, distinguished scarcely any difference between the Jews and the primitive members of the new sect. In his opinion, "the controversy between the Jews and the Christians is a most foolish one: ... the discussions which they have with each other regarding Jesus, differ in no respect from what in the proverb is called a fight about the shadow of an ass."[179]

Our knowledge of Celsus and his treatise is derived only from Origen's "Contra Celsum," which he wrote against him. We cannot, therefore, know accurately who Celsus was. A summary description of him by Dr. James Donaldson, in his "Early Christian Literature and Doctrine," is that, "He was a Platonist. He believed in a Supreme God, the Supreme Good, higher than all in existence. This God was everywhere and in everything. Alongside of this God was original uncreated matter, the source of all evil. These two made up the universe, which remained a constant quantity." (It is a strange creed, and yet, a still purer one than that of the both

[177] Matt., xxi. 8-9; John, xii. 12-13.
[178] Luke, xxiii. 27.
[179] Origen, "Contra Celsum," iii. 1.

anti-Jewish and anti-Christian philosopher, Ernest Renan, and was far better understood, and much more adaptable in the second century, than the tri-cult of the French Orientalist was in his own day.)

Origen, on the other hand, was born of Christian parents. When he was eighteen years of age he began to give catechetical instruction,[180] and made and sold copies of old authors. How faithfully these were reproduced, especially when such works dealt with religion, we can easily judge by the attacks made on his character, which, beginning even during his own lifetime, did not cease for centuries. At about the same age he made himself a eunuch, "for the Kingdom of Heaven's sake,"[181] in accordance with Matthew, xix. 12. At some time later he began to study Hebrew, but never became proficient at it. As examples of his pronunciation of Biblical terms are the following: "Bresith," "Walesmoth," "Waikra," "Ammesphekodlin," etc. And "Dibre Hammayim," he gives us for "Dibre Hayammim."[182] During a visit to Palestine, in the year 216, he gave lectures in the Church. When Bishop Demetrius of Alexandria, who knew him well, became informed of the fact, he complained of this course as contrary to Christian dogmas, and summoned him back to Alexandria at once.[183] In 218, on advice and with the financial aid of a rich adventurer, Ambrosius, who held office both in the Alexandrian government and as Confessor in the Church at the same time, he became a publisher. Seven able writers, as many copyists, and several female artists for the ornamental lettering were put at his disposal.[184] About the year 230, however, he went to Greece; but while passing through Palestine, he was there ordained a presbyter. This again aroused Demetrius; and a synod of bishops summoned by him divested Origen

[180] Eusebius, Eccles. Hist., vi. 3.
[181] Eusebius, Eccles. Hist., vi. 8.
[182] Euseb., Eccl. Hist., vi. 16.
[183] Euseb., Eccl. Hist., vi. 19.
[184] Euseb., Eccl. Hist., vi. 23.

of his presbyterial dignity, and communicated its decision to the foreign churches.[185] In the Decian persecution he was finally arrested and tortured, but managed to escape, and in the year 254, at the age of 68, he died a natural death at Tyre, where he was buried.

Judging by Origen's own discussion of his deceased opponent's "True Discourse,"[186] Celsus was, without doubt, the most formidable of the literary assailants of Christianity in the second century. His attacks upon the Christian religion are marked by a spirit of great hostility, and his method of approaching the subject proves that he was a man of keen intellect. Celsus does not speak in his own person, but introduces a Jew as his mouthpiece. And so, speaking through this Jew, he disputes the Christian claim of the divinity of Jesus and the miracles ascribed to him. He attacks the Resurrection, and the Christian belief that Jesus endured sufferings and death for the benefit of mankind. He asks, If Jesus was God, and knew that Judas would betray him, why did he make him his companion? And if Jesus rose again, why did he not confront his judge, his accusers, and the general public, and give indubitable evidence that he was not a malefactor? And finally, while urging the Christists to abandon their cavilous tendency, and calling their attention to the false position which they occupy in separating themselves from the rest of mankind without any good reason, he justifies the Jews for their own separatism on the ground that they at least adhere to their national beliefs.[187]

But during the two hundred years from 175, about which time Celsus wrote his "True Discourse," to the year 375, about which time the Greek originals of our present

[185] Euseb., Eccl. Hist., vi. 8.
[186] Origen, "Contra Celsum," i. 26, 41, 72; ii., first half, 74; iv. 2-30; vi. 72, 74; viii. 12, 14, etc.
[187] Origen, "Contra Celsum," ii. 38, 59, 70; v. 14.

Gospels were written, the already distorted doctrines of Jesus which Celsus had known had evidently undergone many additional corruptions. The Ebionim, or the poor, primitive followers of Jesus, who had accepted only his moral teachings but would not admit or recognize the newly invented dogmas of his miraculous birth and divinity, had disbanded.[188] The old natural enemies of the Jews,[189] the Antiochian Greeks,[190] who were formerly half-Judaized pagans,[191] and universally regarded as "most dishonest and deceitful liars,"[192] now stepped into the dramatic scene of action.[193] Under them, the already great mass of tradition falsely ascribed to Jesus waxed rapidly to enormous proportions. Novel aphorisms and precepts continued to multiply as their generations succeeded one another, until, as St. John said, "If they should be written every one, I suppose that even the world itself could not contain the books that should be written."[194] The essential elements of Jesus' religion, love, was superseded by hate; hu-

[188] Justin Martyr, Dial. c. Trypho, 47; c. Celsum, v. 61. The Ebionites, according to Eusebius (Eccl. Hist., iii. 27, vi. 17), regarded Jesus as "a plain and common man, justified only by his advances in virtue," and that he was born of Joseph and Mary. They lingered in Palestine and in Antioch till the 5th century, but were few and unimportant after the 2nd (New Standard Encycl., Vol. 10, p. 133).

[189] Antiq., XVI. ii. 3-4, vi. 1-8, XVIII. ix. 9, XX. viii. 7; Bell. Jud., II. xiii. 7; I Apion, 1-4; Philo, Leg. ad Cajum; Cicero, Orat. pro Flacco.

[190] Bell. Jud., VII. iii. 2-4, v. 2. Not to be confounded with the Jewish inhabitants of the Antioch in Pisidia, against whom Paul and Barnabas, according to Acts, xiii. 51, "shook off the dust of their feet."

[191] Bell. Jud., VIII. iii. 3.

[192] Cicero, Orat. pro Flacco, 4-5, 15, and in other passages; Epistle to Titus, i. 12; I Apion, 1-4; and numerous other ancient and modern historians who describe the Greeks in similarly unfavorable terms.

[193] Eusebius, Eccl. Hist., ii. 3, tells us, "The Greeks of Antioch were the founders of the Christian name, and the Church of Antioch was the first Church among the Gentiles."

[194] John, xxi. 24-25.

mility, by arrogance; forgiveness, by revenge; and peace, by bloodshed. The form of his ideas became so conflicting and mutilated that his image as it came down to us is steeped in contradiction and blurred beyond all hope of recognition.

> *Both Origen and Eusebius admit what Celsus had contended, that the early Church writers were continually occupied in "correcting" and altering the Gospels:—"Like persons who in a fit of drunkenness," says Origen (c. Celsum, ii. 27), they..."have corrupted the Gospel from its original integrity, to a threefold, and fourfold, and many-fold degree, and have remodelled it, so they might be able to answer objections."*
>
> *Eusebius (Eccl. Hist., iv. 23) tells us, "Apostles of the devil have filled with tares, exchanging some things, and adding others,...to adulterate the sacred writings of the Lord"; and, whereas until the thirteenth bishop of Rome, Victor, "the truth of the Gospel was preserved," in the following section (v. 28) his record says, that since (his successor) Zepherinus (202-217* CE.), *"the truth was mutilated."*

According to what evidently were of the original passages in the Gospel of Matthew, Jesus insisted upon a universal forgiveness of injuries,[195] and forgives an enemy four hundred and ninety times,—that is, "seventy times seven";[196] whereas according to later additions in the Gospel of Luke,[197] he asks God to slay his enemies. He preaches, "Bless them that curse you,"[198] and then curses a fig tree because he found no figs growing on it;[199] though it was during the week preceding Passover—a season when no sane person would expect figs to grow. He teaches, "Love thy neighbor as thyself,[200]...love

195 Matt., v. 23f.
196 Matt., xviii. 22.
197 Luke, xi. 49-50, xix. 27.
198 Matt., v. 44; Luke, 27-28.
199 Matt., xxi. 18-19; Mark, xi. 13-14, 19-20.
200 Matt., xxii. 39.

thy enemies, and do them good that hate thee,"[201] and later tells his followers, "He that cometh to me and hateth not father, mother, brother and sister, cannot be my disciple."[202] He says, "Whosoever shall smite thee on the right cheek, turn to him the other also,"[203] and then drives the cattle-dealers and money changers (single-handed?) out of the temple-court with a whip.[204] He announces the Kingdom of Heaven,[205] but consigns whole communities—Capernaum, Chorazim, and Bethsaida—to hell.[206] He brings, "Peace on earth and good will to men,"[207] and says that "they who take the sword shall perish by the sword,"[208] but later tells us, "Think not I am come to send peace, but a sword:[209] I came to send fire on earth;[210]... there shall be five in one house divided, three against two, and two against three; I am come to set a man at variance against his father, the daughter against her mother, and the daughter-in-law against her mother-in-law; a man's foes shall be they of his own household."[211]

According to the original Gospel traditions Jesus ministered to none but "unto the lost sheep of the house of Israel," and commanded to his Twelve Apostles, "Go not into the way of the Gentiles, and enter not any city of the Samaritans";[212] but on the other hand, he declares himself to be the hope of the Gentiles;[213] orders that the Gospel should be preached in all the world,[214] and more, that the Kingdom of

[201] Matt., v. 44; Luke, vi. 27.
[202] Luke, xiv. 25-26.
[203] Matt., v. 39.
[204] John, ii. 14f.; Mark, xi. 15; Matt., x. 7 xxi. 12; Luke, 45.
[205] Luke, xii. 32; Mark, i. 15; Matt., iii. 2, vi. 13, etc.
[206] Matt., xi. 21-23; Luke, x. 13-15.
[207] Matt., xxvi. 52.
[208] Luke, ii. 14.
[209] Matt., x. 34.
[210] Luke, xii. 49.
[211] Matt., x. 35-36; Luke, xii. 51-53.
[212] Matt., x. 5-6, xv. 24.
[213] Matt., xii. 21; comp. "Savior of the world" of John, iv. 42.
[214] Matt., xxiv. 14; Mark, xiii. 10.

God shall be taken away from the Jews and given to another nation: [215]—"They shall put them out of the synagogues; yea, the time cometh when whosoever killeth them will think that he does God service." [216] And to make such forgeries as these come true, says Renan, "Tortures and death have been inflicted for ages in the name of Jesus, on thinkers as noble as himself. Even at the present time, penalties are pronounced for religious offenses. Jesus is not responsible for this. He could not foresee that people with mistaken imaginations would one day regard him as a frightful Moloch, greedy for burned flesh." [217]

Again, Jesus teaches, Sell and give to the poor: [218] "Give every man that asketh; [219]... he that hath two coats let him share with him that hath none, and he that hath meat let him do likewise." [220] Yet, when the Canaanish woman pleaded with him for mercy on her little daughter who was "grievously vexed with the devil," his answer was, "It is not fit to take bread of the children (of the faith) and cast it to the dogs: [221] —Give not that which is holy unto the dogs, neither cast your pearls before swine." [222] Very truly says Dr. Klausner that, "If any other Jewish teacher of the time had said such things, the Christians would never have forgiven Judaism for it." [223]

According to Paul, Jesus further said, "If any man will not work, neither should he eat." [224] But according to Matthew, Jesus said, "Take no thought (of) ... what ye shall eat, ... consider the lilies of the field how they grow; they toil not,

[215] Matt., viii. 11-12, xxi. 43.
[216] John, xvi. 2.
[217] Renan, "Life of Jesus" (Brentano's ed., N. Y. 1863), p. 282.
[218] Luke, xviii. 22; Matt., xix. 21.
[219] Matt., v. 42; Luke, vi. 30.
[220] Luke, iii. 2.
[221] Matt., xxv. 22-26; comp. Mark, vii. 25-26.
[222] Matt., vii. 6.
[223] Klausner's "Jesus of Nazareth," p. 294.
[224] II Thess., iii. 10.

neither do they spin. Behold the fowls of the air, ... for they sow not, neither do they reap, nor gather into barns."[225] And thus, these two distinct currents of teaching can be traced throughout all four Gospels.

To exemplify true reverence for, and observance of duty towards God, Luke says, that when a man said to Jesus, "I will follow thee, but Lord, let me first go bid them farewell which are at home in my house," Jesus said to him, "No man having put his hand to the plough and looking back is fit for the Kingdom of Heaven."[226] And when another man begged, "Lord, suffer me first to go and bury my father," his answer was, "Let the dead bury the dead, but go thou and preach the Kingdom of God."[227]

When the author of the Gospel of John designates the enemies of John the Baptist or of Jesus, he refers to them always as "the Jews":—"The Jews seek to kill Jesus"; "No man spoke openly to Jesus for fear of the Jews"; "The Jews said among themselves"; "The Jews sought him at the feast";[228] etc. And while in one place he speaks as if all the Jews were seeking the life of Jesus,[229] in another he conveys the idea that the whole Jewish nation were on Jesus' side, seeking to protect him against the Jews.[230] By Matthew and Mark, the persecutors of Jesus are dubbed "the multitudes," and "all the people,"[231] while Luke adds to them also "the chief priests," and "the rulers."[232] Whether Jesus intended to hand down to posterity that all the Jews of Palestine (num-

[225] Matt., vi. 25-34.

[226] Luke, ix. 61-62.

[227] Luke, ix. 59-60

[228] John, iii. 25, v. 10, 15-16, 18, vi. 41, 52, vii. 1, 11, 13, viii. 22. etc.

[229] John, v. 19.

[230] John, xi. 48.—On this see, Edward Holton James' "The Trial Before Pilate," p. 16, and 228.

[231] Matt., xxvii. 24-25; Mark, xv. 8, 11, 15.

[232] Luke, xxiii. 1, 4, 13.

bering four million),[233] or only the people of Jerusalem and the (two and one half million) pilgrims who gathered together from Egypt, Syria, Cyrene, Asia Minor and other foreign countries for Passover,[234] were all involved in this greatest of all tragedies, the Evangelists have not recorded.

Again, according to the accounts given in all four Gospels, the Roman governor, Pontius Pilate, was a straight-forward man and of good intentions. He is represented as having been disposed to do justice and even anxious to save Jesus from crucifixion, but that he was compelled to issue the death warrant by fear of the Jews who would not allow him to exercise his rightful duty.[235] But do these "divinely inspired" representations correspond with the descriptions given of him in the more trustworthy secular writings? The pages of Josephus are filled with hatred of Pilate on account of the avarice and blood-thirstiness which he displayed in Judea.[236] And Philo cannot find words to express his bitterness against him, "in respect to his corruption, and his acts of insolence, and his rapine, and his habits of insulting people, and his cruelty, and his continual murder of persons untried and uncondemned, and his never-ending and gratuitous, and most grieving inhumanity." [237]

Yet again, according to all four Gospels, the "Jews" demanded crucifixion specifically, as the punishment for Jesus.[238] But, had the devisers of this account had sufficient knowledge of the Jewish criminal laws, they would not have presented such inanimate matter for our belief. Crucifixion may have

[233] Jean Juster's "Les Juifs dans l'Empire Romain," Vol. i. p. 209-210.

[234] Bell. Jud., II. xiv. 3; compare also VI. ix. 3.

[235] Matt., xxvii. 22, 24, 26; Mark, xv. 15; Luke, xxiii. 1-2, 5; John, xix. 6-8, 12, 16.

[236] Antiq., XVIII. iii. 1-2, iv. 1-2; Bell. Jud., II. ix. 2-4.

[237] Philo, Leg. ad Cajum, sec. 38 (Mangey's ed. Vol. ii. p. 590).

[238] Matt., xxvii. 22f.; Mark, xv. 13f.; Luke, xxiii. 21, 23; John, xix. 6, 12, 15.

been sanctioned by a Sadducean high-priest like Caiaphas, but could not have been asked for by the Jews, had they considered Jesus guilty of a capital crime, for the Jewish penal code prescribed no such penalty. The extreme punishments in accordance with the Jewish laws were four in number: hanging, beheading, burning, and stoning. Hanging, in the first place, was not essentially a capital punishment, but merely an act of despite done to the body of a criminal who had already been put to death by some other method of execution;[239] this posthumous form of execution was spared to women out of regard to their modesty.[240] Decapitation was inflicted in cases where all the inhabitants of a city were found guilty of apostasy in following polytheistic or idolatrous creeds.[241] Burning was employed only in certain cases of adultery.[242] But the punishment by stoning was the most frequently employed. It was considered the extreme penalty "par excellence," and as that which was to be understood in every case where the law did not indicate any other mode of death. Accordingly, since the charge against Jesus was, in effect, blasphemy,[243] "the Jews," had they found him guilty of such a crime, could not have demanded any other punishment for him but stoning. For the Scriptural law specifically says: "And he that blasphemeth the name of the Lord, he shall surely be put to death; and all the congregation shall certainly stone him."[244] It is true that one of the Maccabean kings, Alexander Jannaeus, crucified 800 of his opponents, but he, who like the high-priest Caiaphas belonged to the Sadducean sect, was severely condemned for this most barbarous action,

[239] Joshua, viii. 23-29, x. 26.

[240] "Mishna, Sanhedrin, 49, 52, 456,"—So given by Rosadi in his "Trial of Jesus," p. 213.

[241] Deut., xiii. 12-17.

[242] Lev. xx. 14, xxi. 9.

[243] Matt. xxvi. 11-14; Mark, xv. 2-5; Luke, xxiii. 2-5; John, xviii. 33-38.

[244] Lev., xxiv. 16; also Deut., xvii. 2-7 with xiii. 6-11.

and the name of "Thracidas," that is, barbarous Thracian, was given him by the Jews.[245]

Again, concerning Pilate, the writer of the Gospel of Matthew tells us: "When he saw he could gain nothing but rather that a tumult was made, he took water and washed his hands before the multitude, saying, I am innocent of this just man's (Jesus') blood."[246] But here too, to wash one's hands to attest one's innocence was a Jewish custom,[247] not Roman. Therefore, that Pilate washed his hands, in the Jewish manner, of the murder which he had committed, is likewise incredible. Again, Matthew says, "When Caiaphas heard Jesus say he was the Christ, he rent his clothes."[248] But rending of garments as a sign of anger was not at all peculiar to Jews, but a strictly Roman custom. It was done in the Roman Senate,[249] when Augustus tore his garments upon hearing of the defeat of Varus in Germany.[250] Moreover, rending of clothes by high-priests especially, on any occasion whatsoever, is twice strictly forbidden in the Scripture:—"And Moses said unto Aaron and unto Eleazar, ... 'Uncover not your head neither rend your clothes lest you die, and lest God's wrath come upon all the people.'"[251] More explicit even is this prohibition:—"And he that is the high-priest among his brethren, upon whose head the anointed oil was poured, and that was consecrated to put on the garments, shall not uncover his head nor rend his clothes."[252]

And here we must not neglect to acquaint ourselves also with Pilate's wife's dream of which the same "Matthew" makes a most dramatic record. He tells us that, "When Pilate

245 Antiq., XIII. xiv. 2; Bell. Jud., I. v. 2-3.
246 Matt., xxvii. 24.
247 Deut., xxi. 6-7; comp. Mishna, Sotah, viii. 6.
248 Matt., xxvi. 63-65.
249 Dion Cassius, "Rome," liv. 14.
250 Dion Cassius, "Rome," lvi. 64.
251 Lev., x. 6.
252 Lev., xxi. 10.

was sitting on the judgment seat, his wife sent unto him, saying, 'Have thou nothing to do with that just man (Jesus), for I have suffered many things this day in a dream because of him.' "[253] Now, while this may have been a strong piece of evidence for an audience of "Matthew's" own mentality, we cannot accept it as such. And besides, we have records showing that Julia's illegitimate sixteen year old daughter, Claudia, whom Pilate had married in Rome immediately before his departure of Judea, did not go along with him,[254] and consequently was not in Palestine during the trial of Jesus. A Roman law prohibited the wives of provincial rulers to accompany their husbands to the seat of their government.[255] As a matter of fact, there is not one record showing a Roman procurator ever having been accompanied by his wife on leaving Rome for his Judean post, excepting two, and these, under special circumstances. The first one was Felix (52-60 CE.); but this official, besides having married King Agrippa's youngest sister, Drusilla, during his term of office in Judea,[256] enjoyed such special privileges with the Emperor as did no other procurator before or after him. For, not only was he related to, and a great favorite of Emperor Claudius himself, which alone entitled him to perpetrate any crime he desired, but also was he at liberty to hire confederates to plunder and massacre his subjects, for either booty or rancor, by sufferance of his superior, the legate of Syria, Quadratus,[257] 50-60 CE.,[258] who feared Felix's brother, Pallas, the Emperor's most intimate secretary.[259] The second man who brought his wife along with him to Judea was Gessius

[253] Matt., xxvii. 19.

[254] Petrucelli della Gatina, "Memorie di Giuda," Vol. i. c. 2.

[255] Transcribed in the Justinian Code, L. iv. 2, D. de off. Procons. et Leg., i. 16.

[256] Antiq., XX. vii. 2; Acts, xxiv. 24.

[257] On the date of his appointment, see Tacitus, Annals, xii. 45; comp. with Schuerer, Div. I., Vol. i., p. 367.

[258] On his death and succession, see Tacitus, Annals, xiv. 26.

[259] On this, see account of Felix, and notes thereto, in our Chapter V.

Florus, 64-66 CE. But this lady, named Cleopatra, was an intimate friend of Nero's wife, Poppea, through whom he obtained his appointment.[260]

And now, concerning Judas Iscariot, of whom so much has been spoken but very little is actually known, Matthew tells us that, after repenting the betrayal of Jesus, "the traitor turned over the thirty pieces of silver to the chief priests and elders."[261] But according to Acts, Judas did not turn over the money but purchased a field for the price of his perfidy.[262] And whereas Acts informs us that the burial ground was "bought by Judas,"[263] Matthew says it was "bought by the chief priests." Again, whereas Matthew says Judas hanged himself,[264] in the Acts he did not hang himself, but "falling headlong, his body burst asunder and all his bowels gushed out."[265] Matthew further says they gave Jesus to drink "vinegar mixed with gall,"[266] but Mark says it was "wine medicated with myrrh."[267] And whereas Matthew says that with Mary Magdalen only one other woman came to the Sepulcher,[268] Mark says there were two other women,[269] Luke says there were more than two other women,[270] while John says that the tomb was visited by Mary Magdalen alone, who found the stone displaced and the body of Jesus missing.[271] (According to Mark, xvi. 9, this Mary had been possessed by seven devils.) Again, while Luke says that the two angels that were seen at the Sepulcher were standing up,[272] Matthew

[260] Antiq., XX. xi. 1.
[261] Matt., xxvii. 3-5.
[262] Acts, i. 18.
[263] Matt., xxvii. 6-7.
[264] Matt., xxvii. 5.
[265] Acts, i. 18.
[266] Matt., xxvii. 34.
[267] Mark, xv. 23.
[268] Matt., xxviii. 1.
[269] Mark, xvi. 1.
[270] Luke, xxiv. 10.
[271] John, xx. 1, 11-12; Luke, viii. 2.
[272] Luke, xxiv. 4.

says that only one angel descended upon the tomb from heaven, and that he was sitting down.[273]

For these reasons, the facts which these religious documents furnish us cannot be accepted as historical. They only prove that those persons who moulded the Gospels into their present rancorous form were as unfamiliar with Jewish life, laws, customs and personalities, as they were ignorant of the meaning of truth and charity, or about the importance of such clean dietary and personal habits as those of the original followers of Jesus, the Ebionim, whom they supplanted. And that they knew no more of what a Sanhedrin meant, or what the Jewish political organization of Jerusalem was, is manifest everywhere in their own writings.

But whether the foregoing accounts in the Gospels "according to" Matthew, Mark, Luke and John, really represent the doings and teachings of the Jewish reformer, Jesus, or whether they are genuine or of divine inspiration, is not essentially part of our program. Indeed, it is not only the carrying of the inquiry so far beyond the aim and outline of this work, but even the very entering into so difficult and extremely delicate a subject is deeply regretted. And the Christian reader will realize the passion which writing on a subject of this kind must irresistibly awaken in a Jewish writer. But to enable one to form an opinion of the historical value of the information each of our sources,—Josephus, the Talmud, and the Gospels,—individually, or possibly in combination, gives us concerning the Jewish system of government in Palestine, and over which many of our critics are so peculiarly undecided,[274] a thorough analysis of every available fact about it, as well as concerning the dependability of our authorities, was unavoidable.

[273] Matt., xxviii. 2-5.

[274] So G. A. Smith, "Jerusalem from Earliest Times," Vol. i. p. 418; Milman, "Jewish History," Vol. ii. p. 115; Morrison, "Jews under Roman Rule," p. 213; Hausrath, "Times of Jesus," p. 80; and many other historians of note.

Now, no one doubts that in the days of Palestinian independence the Sanhedrin was a great and honorable institution. In those days the office of the High-Priest and president of the Sanhedrin was of the highest dignity and power within the gift of the people. The authority of the High-Priest was so absolute that he could declare war unquestioned and unrestrained; he was the Commander of the army.[275] But with the Roman occupation and installation of Herod on the Judean throne, the honor and dignity of this representative government vanished. "Sanhedrin" became an empty name, a false front, an expedient in Rome's political machinery. As his first act on his accession to the throne, Herod slew every member of the Sanhedrin,[276] and an oligarchy of wealthy "hypocrites, liars, and scoundrels, . . . in the last stages of moral rottenness,"[277] appeared on this scene of history. In imitation of the Assembly, which since at least the commencement of the Greek era down to the days of the Romano-Herodian rule was a "Theocracy"[278] under the leadership of the high-priest whose office was hereditary and tenable for life, Herod formed an "Aristocracy" under the leadership of the high-priest who was appointed and deposed by himself and the Romans alike.[279]

Presiding over this hierarchical Camorra from Herod the Great to the destruction of Jerusalem, according to the different notices found in Josephus, were the following twenty-eight high-priests:

(a) Appointed by Herod, 37-4 BCE.

1. Ananel, 37-36 BCE., brought from Babylon, "an old and particular friend of Herod."—Antiq., XV. ii. 4, iii. 1.
2. Aristobulus III, a youth seventeen years of age; the last high-priest of Maccabean lineage; a

[275] Bell. Jud., I. ii. 3.
[276] Antiq., XIV. ix. 4 end.
[277] Thus quoted by Edward Holton James, pp. 164, 166.
[278] Apion, II. Thac., sec. 16, Whist., 17.
[279] Antiq., XX. x., end.

brother of Herod's second wife, Mariamne I.—Antiq., XV. iii. 1; drowned by a servant at the instigation of Herod. Antiq., XV. iii. 3, comp. XX. x., near end.—Ananel, reappointed 34 BCE.—Antiq., XV. iii. 3, end.

3. Joshua the son of Phabi, 34 BCE. When Herod married Mariamne II, he took the high-priesthood away from this man and gave it to his father-in-law, who follows.
4. Simon the son of Boethus, 25 BCE.—Antiq. XV. ix. 3, XVII. iv. 2. After twenty years of office, Herod deposed him for concealing his daughter's conspiracies against him.
5. Matthias the son of Theophilus, 5-4 BCE.—Antiq., XVII. iv. 2, vi. 4.
6. Joseph the son of Ellem, 4 BCE.; officiated only once on the Day of Atonement merely as a substitute for Matthias, who had been prevented from doing duty himself in consequence of some Levitical defilement.—Antiq., XVII. vi. 4.
7. Joazar the son of Boethus, 4 BCE.; he replaced Matthias who had been deposed for instigating sedition.[280]—Antiq., XVII. vi. 4.

(b) Appointed by Archelaus, son and successor of Herod, 4 BCE.—6 CE.

8. Eleazar, son of Boethus, 4 BCE.; he replaced Joazar whom Archelaus accused of sedition.—Antiq., XVII. xiii. 1.
9. Joshua, son of Seth; replaced Eleazar after a short term of office.—Antiq., XVII. xiii. 1.

Joazar for the second time, somewhere before 6 CE.—Antiq., XVIII. i. 1, ii. 1.

[280] In connection with this appointment Josephus reports an eclipse of the moon. This eclipse, in accordance with astronomical calculations occurred on March 13 of the year in which Herod died, i.e. 4 BCE. Therefore, since the birth of Jesus also took place in that year, the Christian chronology is short by four years.

(c) Appointed by Quirinius, the newly appointed Roman Legate to Syria and Censor of Judea, 6 CE.

(At this time the Judean kingdom is reduced to a Roman province, and Caponius becomes the first Roman Procurator of Judea. The duties of the Procurator consisted of maintaining order in the country, and in enforcing the punctual payment of taxes. He had also the power of supervising the Sanhedrin's administration of the criminal law, of pronouncing death sentences, and of appointing and disposing of high-priests according to their friendly or unfriendly inclinations towards Rome.)

10. Ananus, son of Seth, 6-15 CE. Antiq., XVIII. ii. 1-2. He was the well known high-priest who, later, as ex-high-priest figured in the trial of Jesus.—John, xviii. 13f.; Acts, iv. 6.

(d) Appointed by Valerius Gratus, the fourth Procurator, 15-26 CE.

11. Ismael, son of Phabi, 15-16 CE.—Antiq., XVIII. ii. 2.
12. Eleazar, son of Ananus, 16-17 CE.—Antiq., XVIII. ii. 2.
13. Simon, son of Kamith, 17-18 CE.—Antiq., XVIII. ii. 2.
14. Joseph Caiaphas, 18-36 CE., (who presided at the trial of Jesus).—Antiq., XVIII. ii. 2, iv. 3. According to John, xviii. 13, he was the son-in-law of Ananus.

(The fact that Caiaphas retained the high-priesthood for eighteen years, whereas his predecessors under Gratus held the office for barely a year, proves that he was a sly diplomat and knew how to conduct himself towards the people and the Roman procurator alike.)

(e) Appointed by the Roman legate, Vitellius, 35-39 CE.

15. Jonathan, son of Ananus, 36-37 CE.—Antiq., XVIII. iv. 3, v. 3, XIX. vi. 4. He was still active in politics in the time of the procurator Cumanus, 50-52 CE.—Bell. Jud., II. xii. 5-6; and finally assassinated by the Sicarii at the instigation of the procurator Felix.—Bell. Jud., II. xiii. 3; Antiq., XX. viii. 5.

16. Theophilus, son of Ananus, 37 CE.—Antiq., XVIII. v. 3. He was the third of Ananus' four sons who, in addition to his son-in-law, Caiaphas, officiated as high-priests.

(f) Appointed by King Agrippa I, 41-44 CE.

17. Simon Kantheras, son of Boethus, 41 CE.—Antiq., XIX. vi. 2.

18. Matthias, son of Ananus, 42 CE.; replacing Simon whom Agrippa found "less worthy of the dignity of the high-priesthood."—Antiq., XIX. vi. 4.

19. Elionaios, son of Kantheras, 43 CE.—Antiq., XIX. viii. 1. Mishna, Para, iii. 5, identifies him as the son of Caiaphas.

(g) Appointed by Herod of Chalcis, Rome's Supreme Supervisor of the Temple, its treasury and the high-priesthood, 44-48 CE.—Antiq., XX. i. 3.

20. Joseph, son of Kamith, about 45 CE.—Antiq., XX. i. 3, v. 2.

21. Ananias, son of Nebedeus, 47-59 CE; notorious for his wickedness. In consequence of his great wealth he continued to be a power even after his deposition.—Antiq., XX. v. 2, ix. 2-4. Charged with stirring up discontent and riots, and with over-exercising his authority, he was sent by the legate, Quadratus, to Rome to defend his actions before Emperor Claudius.—Bell. Jud., II. xii. 2-6; Antiq. XX. vi. 1-2. In

66, at the beginning of the war, he was put to death by the rebels.—Bell. Jud., II. xvii. 6-9. Of him Josephus says, "He was very rigid in judging offenders."—Antiq., XX. ix. 1.

(h) Appointed by Agrippa, titular king of Judea, 50-70 CE.

22. Ismael, son of Phabi,[281] 59-61 CE.—Antiq., XX. viii. 8. While in Rome as one of a deputation successfully petitioning that a wall erected in the inner court of the Temple against Agrippa's wishes should be allowed to stand, he was detained by Nero as a hostage for the good behavior of the embassage whom the Emperor permitted to return to Jerusalem.—Antiq., XX. viii. 11. With other high-priests who during the war had escaped from Jerusalem, he was finally beheaded in Cyrene for sedition. —Bell. Jud., VI. ii. 2.

23. Joseph Kabi, son of Simon the high-priest, 61-62 CE.—Antiq., XX. viii. 2. After the war he was one of the high-priests who were beheaded in Cyrene for sedition.—Bell. Jud., VI. ii. 2.

24. Ananus, son of Ananus, 62 CE. He was removed from office for instigating the murder of James, the brother of Jesus, having officiated only three months.—Antiq., XX. ix. 1. During the first period of the war, he was one of those who played a leading part, and was put to death by the insurgents. Bell. Jud., II. xx. 3, xxii. 1-2, IV. from iii. 7 to v. 2; Vita, 38-40, 60.

25. Joshua, son of Damnaeus, 62-63 CE. After the

[281] This younger Ismael, son of Phabi (not the high-priest of the same name who stands eleventh in the list), is probably the one referred to in the Mishna, Para, iii. 5; Sota, ix. 15. See in general, Derenbourg's Histoire, pp. 232-235.

war he was also one of the high-priests who were beheaded in Cyrene for sedition.—Bell. Jud., VI. ii. 2; compare Antiq., XX. ix. 1, 4.

26. Joshua, son of Gamaliel, 63-65.—Antiq., XX. ix. 4, 7. In the war he is frequently mentioned with Ananus, whose fate he also shared.—Bell. Jud., IV. iii. 9, v. 2; Vita, 38, 41.

27. Matthias, son of Theophilus, 66-67 CE.—Antiq., XX. ix. 7. In the early stages of the war he was assassinated by one of the rebel leaders. Bell. Jud., VI. ii. 2.

(i) Appointed during the war by the rebels, 67-68 CE.

28. Phannias, son of Samuel of Aphtha, an exceedingly ignorant person and of very humble origin.—Bell. Jud., IV. iii. 8. He was the last high-priest in the entire history of the high-priesthood.

In the bitterest terms Josephus complains of the wickedness of these sacred Moguls, their contemptible selfishness and cowardice, and the shameful jealousies among them, culminating in their throwing stones at each other in street skirmishes. He describes them as hoarders of riches, lording over many servants and living luxurious lives. In the country districts, he bewails, their vicious agents enforced the payment of tithes, even by the very poorest, "and did not refrain from beating with clubs such as would not give these tithes to them; so that some of the (minor) priests, that of old were wont to be supported with those tithes, died for want of food."—Antiq., XX. viii. 8, ix. 2, 4.—Confirmingly the Talmud tells us, that "their table was served with reckless extravagance,"—Pesachim, 57a,—and a late Midrash says that in the Temple they wore silken gloves, in order not to touch the Sacrifices with their "aristocratic" hands.—Echa Rabbathi, i. 16.

A street song popular at the time, composed by one

Abba Saul upon the degradation of the high-priesthood, which has come down to us through the Talmud, runs as follows:—

> "*Woe to the family of Boethus, woe!*
> *because they smite with their rods!*
>
> "*Woe to the family of Ananus, woe!*
> *because of their whisperings!*
>
> "*Woe to the family of Kantheras, woe!*
> *because of their slanderous pens!*
>
> "*Woe to the family of Ismael ben Phabi, woe!*
> *because of their fists!*
>
> "*For they are the high-priests,*
> *their sons the treasurers,*
> *their sons-in-law the Temple-officers,*
> *and their servants smite the people with their rods.*"
>
> —Pesachim, 57a.

Such were the social, economic, religious and political conditions in Palestine, and such was the "Aristocracy" from the accession of Herod and throughout Josephus' early manhood.

And now we turn to the study of Herod, his successors, and the Procurator, or Roman provincial administrator, and their pernicious influences upon the nation which led to the disastrous war with Rome.

CHAPTER III

HEROD *the* GREAT, 40-4 BCE.

AFTER finishing his education in the Judean wilderness under the hermit Banus,[1] and returning to his parents, Josephus found Jerusalem seething with unrest and turmoil. The free Commonwealth created under the leadership of his own ancestors, was then (56 CE.) nothing but a memory. The proud Jewish nation had long been subject to Rome. The descendants of Simon Tharsi did not possess the tact, diplomacy and foresight through which the first Maccabees had gained for Judea her independence and greatness. The last of the Maccabean rulers, Antigonus, was neither a statesman nor a warrior. He was too stupid to avail himself of the many splendid opportunities staring at him. The turbulent conditions in Rome, its war with Parthia, and the violent conflicts and constant shifting of power among its leaders,[2] were most favorable events for him to gain a secure status and to strengthen his wabbling throne. But he did not comprehend how to benefit by these advantages within his reach; and instead, wasted his time and energy on worthless designs and on

[1] On Josephus' childhood and education, see the beginning of Chapter II.

[2] Antiq., XIV. xiv. 2, end of section.

minting coins with his Hebrew and Greek names: "Mattathias, ha-Cohen, ha-Godel," and also "Basileos Antigonon."[3]

His impassionate rival, Herod, possessed all those qualities which Antigonus lacked. He was a born ruler, keen in his judgment, and knew how to win favor when that had to be gained. Blessed with a powerful physique, he was capable of enduring all kinds of hardships. He was a masterful horseman, a feared pugilist, and a daring hunter whose arrow seldom missed its mark.[4]

The founder of Herod's family, Antipas, was an Idumean whom the Maccabean king, Alexander Jannaeus (105-78 BCE.), *made governor of Idumea. The Idumeans, though aliens by race, were Jews in faith, having been conquered and brought over to Judaism by Alexander's father, Hyrcanus I., who ruled for twenty-nine years before him.*[5] *From the time of their conversion, the Idumeans remained constant to their new religion, looking upon Jerusalem as their mother city, and claiming for themselves the name of Jews.*[6] *The founder's successor as governor of Idumea was his son Antipater. In the year* 63 BCE., *when the indolent and easy-minded son and successor of Alexander, Hyrcanus II., was forced by his abler brother, Aristobulus, to renounce his royal claim and the high-priestly office, Antipater succeeded in inducing him to flee to Aretas, the king of Arabia, to assert his rights to the dominion. The close friendship between them continued.*[7] *Together they espoused Pompey's cause in the year* 64, *and, after the battle of Pharsalia on August 9th of* 48 BCE., *that of Julius Caesar also.*[8] *To reward them*

[3] On these coins see, Madden's "History of Jewish Coinage," pp. 76-79; "Numismatic Chronicle," pp. 314-316; and "Coins of the Jews," pp. 99-103.

[4] Bell. Jud., I. xxi. 13.

[5] Antiq., XIII. ix. 1.

[6] Antiq., XX. vii. 1; Bell. Jud., I. iv. 2.

[7] Antiq., XIV. i. 3-4; Bell. Jud., I. viii. 1.

[8] Antiq., XIV. iv. 5; viii. 1-3; Bell. Jud, I. viii. 1.

for their trustworthiness and usefulness, Caesar reinstated Hyrcanus in the political authority and the high-priesthood which he had been forced to give up, making Antipater governor of the whole of Judea,[9] *in addition to bestowing on him the privileges of a Roman citizen, and freedom from all taxes.*[10] *Herod the Great was the second son of this Antipater and his wife Cypros, who was a foreign-born, Arabian woman.*[11]

When Herod was twenty-five years of age, his father gave him the government of Galilee, where he soon displayed his ability by ridding his territory of dangerous bands of robbers,[12] *and shortly that of Coele-Syria also. In the year 41, when Mark Antony came to Syria, he appointed Herod and his older brother Phasaelus as Tetrarchs of Judea.*[13] *In the following year, however, due to an invasion of the Parthians, who supported the claims of Antigonus, Herod was forced to flee from Judea.*[14]

Possessed of an insatiable ambition for power, dominion and glory, and rich in devices, Herod, late in the summer of the year 40 BCE., built a three-decked ship of huge dimensions and set sail for Italy. Passing through many heavy sea storms, and having narrowly escaped shipwreck, he reached Rome by way of Rhodus and Brundusium. On his arrival there, he first went to Antony and related to him all the calamities which had befallen him and his family in Judea. He set forth a long, sad account of the ill-treatment, misery, poverty and persecution they had suffered at the hands of Antigonus and "his Parthian friends, in consequence of the many services he and

[9] Antiq., XIV. viii. 5.

[10] Antiq., XIV. viii. 3; Bell. Jud., I. ix. 5.

[11] Antiq., XIV. vii. 3; Bell. Jud., I. viii. 9.

[12] Antiq., XIV. ix. 2. Herod's age at that time, which is given in the text as fifteen years, is evidently an error of the coypist.

[13] Antiq., XIV. viii. 1.

[14] Antiq., XIV. xiv. 4.

his father had rendered to Rome."[15] He recounted how his brother Phasaelus had been seized by the Parthians and put to death; how "the friend of Rome," Hyrcanus II. (the grandfather of his fiancée Mariamne I.), had been detained captive by them; how for "no less than a thousand talents (about $1,000,000) and five hundred Jewish women, selected from the best families," the Parthians had made Antigonus a king under their guardianship; and how all his immediate relatives as well as his own life were in grave danger; for which reason, he had "sailed through a storm, and contemned all these terrible dangers of it, in order to come as soon as possible to you who are my only hope and succor."[16]

Antony, still cherishing the hospitality he had formerly received from Antipater, was moved by compassion with Herod's reverse of fortune, but above all by the heroic qualities of the man who stood before him; and exceeding Herod's fondest expectations, determined there and then to make him King of Judea. Besides admiration for Herod, he had also a strong incentive in his aversion for Antigonus, whom he regarded as an enemy of Rome. But Octavius (later, the Emperor Augustus), proved an even readier champion of the plan than Antony, as he recalled very freshly the wars and hardships which Antipater had gone through together with his own uncle, Julius Caesar,[17] in the Egyptian campaigns; how he facilitated the march of Mithridates, the king of Pergamus, Caesar's ally, to his relief, and contributed to the reduction of Pelusium; how he conciliated the Egyptian Jews, who had espoused the opposite party, and how also he had greatly distinguished himself in an important battle.

Influenced by all these considerations and recollections, though Herod had intended to advocate only the claims of Hyrcanus before the two heads of the State, Octavius con-

[15] Concerning Antipater's and Herod's services rendered to Rome, see Antiq., XIV. v. 1-2, vi. 2-3, vii. 3, viii. 4; Bell. Jud., I. viii. 1, 3, 7, 9, and x. 1-2.

[16] Antiq., XIV. xiv. 3; Bell. Jud., I. xiv. 1-3.

[17] Octavius later became Caesar's son by adoption.

curred with Antony on the expediency of placing Herod on the throne, and immediately called the Senate together. And when Antony came forward before the Assembly and said that in view of Rome's war with Parthia it would be for their own advantage to proclaim Herod as Judea's king, they all gave their votes for him. Antigonus was accordingly declared an enemy, and, dissolving the meeting, Octavius and Antony left the senate-house with Herod between them, while the Consul and the other magistrates went before them, in order to offer sacrifices, and to lay up the decree in the Capitol.[18]

But Herod was not a man to make the most of the favors of fortune; he wasted no time in the courtly circle, or in the luxuries of Rome. In seven days he dispatched all his business, returned to his ship in Brundusium, and after an absence of scarcely three months, early in the year 39, landed at Ptolemais, on the Galilean sea-coast. From the Senate's proclamation of Herod as king to the actual possession of the throne, however, was a more difficult task; for Judea was still under the authority of Antigonus and the Parthians, and had yet to be subdued. The fortress of Masada,[19] in which Herod's mother, his younger brother Joseph, and his bride, Mariamne, were shut up, was his first object. He quickly raised an army, and, united with some Roman auxiliaries under Ventidius and Silo, took Joppa, overran Galilee, relieved his relatives and some eight hundred supporters from that stronghold, all of whom he transported to Samaria, and very soon after sat down before Jerusalem. But now his troops insisted on taking up winter quarters.[20]

In the spring of 38 BCE., however, the Parthians renewed their attack on Syria, and Ventidius and Silo, instead of resuming operations with Herod against Jerusalem, had to fight against the invaders.[21] On June 9th when the Parthians were

[18] Antiq., XIV. xiv. 4-5; Bell. Jud., I. xiv. 4.

[19] Masada will assume much greater importance as the history proceeds.

[20] Antiq., XIV. xv. 1-3, xvi. 1; Bell. Jud., I. xv. 3-6.

[21] Antiq., XIV. xv. 5; Bell. Jud., I. xvi. 4.

beaten, Ventidius turned his attention against Antiochus of Commagene, till he too surrendered. But during the siege of Antiochus' capital, Somasata, Antony himself arrived from Rome. Herod could not ignore this opportunity of relating to his friend how military assistance had been withheld from him, and proceeded to Samosata at once. Antony received him most affectionately, and as the surrender of Antiochus soon afterwards took place, he ordered Sossius, the successor of Ventidius, to give Herod adequate assistance. Accordingly, Sossius sent two legions ahead into Judea, while he himself followed with a much larger army.[22] The march of the Romans from northern Syria to Jerusalem—700 kilometers—and a few skirmishes, however, consumed the rest of the summer, and the siege was again delayed till the spring of 37 BCE.[23]

As soon as that season permitted, Herod began the attack on Jerusalem. This was the third year since his proclamation as king. Having been engaged for a long time, while the battering-rams were being erected he went to Samaria to celebrate the retarded marriage.[24] When the wedding was over he returned, bringing with him some 30,000 men. Sossius also arriving with a vast army, they met at the northern side of the city. It required fifty-five days for the combined armies to reach the inner court of the Temple. But now Antigonus, fearing lest the enemy should hinder him from offering the daily "Sacrifices to God" (!),—for that was his greatest anxiety at this time of extreme national danger,—sent an embassy to Herod to beg him for permission to bring in the Korbonim. This, Herod granted. The onslaught, however, continued, and soon the "Upper City" was stormed and taken. It was only through the interference of Herod, who strenuously remonstrated with the furious soldiers of Sossius on the indignity of leaving him "King not of a noble city,

[22] Antiq., XIV. xv. 7-9; Bell. Jud., I. xvi. 6-7.
[23] Antiq., XIV. xv. 11-13; Bell. Jud., I. xvii. 3-8.
[24] Antiq., XIV. xv. 14; Bell. Jud., I. xvii. 8.

but a desert," that the whole town escaped destruction. Antigonus, surrendering to Sossius, threw himself at the feet of his conqueror, begging his life in the most abject manner; his conduct was so unmanly and unbecoming, that Sossius called him Antigona, as though he had been a woman. Antigonus, however, was taken in chains to Antioch, where Antony at the time had taken up his residence. The Triumvir at first intended to carry his captive to Rome, but at the request of Herod, Antony ordered him beheaded. "Such," remarks Josephus, who, like Antigonus, was himself of Maccabean lineage, in closing this account, "was the just punishment which Antigonus' 'cowardice' deserved and brought upon him."[25] "And thus," he mournfully resumes, "did the government of the Hasmonean dynasty cease, a hundred and twenty-six years after it was first set up. This family was a splendid and illustrious one, both on account of the nobility of their stock, and of the dignity of the high-priesthood, as also for the glorious actions their ancestors had performed for our nation: but these men lost the government by their dissensions with one another, and it came to Herod, the son of Antipater, who was no more than of a vulgar family, and of no eminent extraction, but one that was subject to other kings."[26] Thus, Herod the Great, now in the thirty-sixth year of his age, became the master of Judea.

The situation in Jerusalem, however, was still difficult and precarious. The mass of the people were still ardently attached to the great Maccabean family, and the faction of Antigonus was still strong. Against the latter Herod proceeded with relentless cruelty. He inaugurated his reign by appropriating Antigonus' possessions and confiscating all his wealth, a great quantity of which, such as silver and gold, he presented to his benefactor Mark Antony. Then, to deliver himself from the powerful enemies of within, who looked upon the rule of a half-Jew Idumean with deep aversion, he ordered

[25] Antiq., XIV. xvi. 1-4, xv. 1-2; Bell. Jud., I. xvii. 9, xviii. 1-3.
[26] Antiq., XIV. xvi., end of last section.

forty-five of the principal men of Antigonus' party put to death, "as supposing he could in no other way bend the minds of these Jews...who had been forced to call him king."[27] As his next step he executed all the members of the Sanhedrin.[28] But to make himself absolute master, Herod found it necessary also to restrict the authority of the high-priest. Accordingly, to fill the pontifical office which had become vacant by the death of the former king, Antigonus, who had also been the high-priest, he sent for an obscure priest from Babylon, whose name was Ananel, and made him the high-priest; thus discontinuing the principle of inheritance and life tenure of the high-priesthood, and avoiding a possible rival who might become a menace to his life and throne.[29] Now, with the government of all Judea under his control, Herod promoted such private citizens as had favored him, "but Pollio, and Sameas (Simon ben Shetach), were honored by him above the rest."[30]

Herod's choice of a high-priest, however, was not so successful. Both his wife Mariamne and his mother-in-law Alexandra regarded the appointment of an obscure Babylonian to the high-priesthood, which by right belonged to Mariamne's young brother Aristobulus, as an affront to the Maccabean dignity. Mariamne began to complain to Herod, while Alexandra, a hot-headed woman, went even further, and wrote her complaint to Cleopatra, the Queen of Egypt. Cleopatra warmly espoused her cause, not from any love of right or especial attachment to the Hasmoneans, but because she craved the possession of Judea, and expected that if Herod were ruined she herself might easily obtain a grant of that country from her lover Antony. But, however secretly the correspondence, which Alexandra entrusted to a house musician, was conducted, Herod's wide-spread espionage obtained for him

[27] Antiq., XV. i. 2; compare, Bell. Jud., I. xviii. 4.
[28] Antiq., XIV. ix. 4 near end.
[29] Antiq., XX. x. —, but especially, XV. ii. 4.
[30] Antiq., XV. i. 1.

some intimation of what was going on, which convinced him that his public safety as well as his domestic peace rendered it necessary for him to restore his priestly inheritance to Aristobulus. Accordingly, Herod, in the beginning of the year 35, dismissed Ananel, who had ministered for over a year, and Aristobulus, now nearing his seventeenth birthday, was appointed in his stead.[31]

The peace, however, was not of long duration. Alexandra's ambition had long been that her grandson should also wear the crown of his Hasmonean ancestors. And Herod, fully aware of this, determined to rid himself of his dangerous rival. Moreover, at the Feast of the Tabernacles, solemnized as usual with great magnificence, the young high-priest appeared at the altar in his pontifical garments and ornaments, and officiated with such grace and dignity that shouts of acclamation rent the air, and the city resounded with the praises and blessings that the people showered on the heir of the Hasmoneans. This outburst sealed the doom of the unfortunate youth, and impelled Herod to the immediate execution of his purpose. Soon an opportunity for doing so presented itself. After the holiday Herod came to Jericho where Alexandra invited him to a banquet. During this visit on a hot afternoon Aristobulus was induced to bathe in one of the fish-ponds about the palace; some of Herod's Gallic mercenaries also entered the water and mixed in the sports of the young man. Taking advantage of the rapid transition from daylight to darkness which prevails in Judea, one of these hirelings, evidently on instructions from Herod, caught hold of the unfortunate high-priest, and forced his head under water until he was suffocated. Ananel was then reappointed.[32]

In the year 34, by instigation of Alexandra, again through Cleopatra, Herod was summoned by Antony to appear before him at Laodicea-by-the-Sea to answer for the murder of Aristobulus. But by the skilful arguments and rich

[31] Antiq., XV. ii. 5-7, iii. 1.
[32] Antiq., XV. iii. 2-3; Bell. Jud., I. xxii. 2.

gifts he soon induced the Triumvir to dismiss the charge and to advise the Queen of Egypt that "it is not proper to watch the affairs of a king, for at that rate he could not be a king at all," and that "it would be best for her also to cease meddling with the acts of Herod's government." Thus Herod, pronounced innocent, returned to Jerusalem.[33]

Before his departure from Jerusalem, however, Herod had placed his aged uncle Joseph, who was also the husband of his sister Salome, in charge of the State's affairs, entrusting to him also the care of his wife, with secret orders that if Antony should execute him, to kill her immediately. Herod had reason to believe that Antony was no stranger to the fame of Mariamne's beauty, and he could not bear to think that after his own death his widow might fall into the power of that debauchee.[34] But while so administering the government of the kingdom and paying frequent respects to Queen Mariamne, one day the old babbler, joining the discourses among the royal women, divulged the secret entrusted to him by Herod.[35] When, then, Herod returned, his sister Salome, of a spirit as intriguing and relentless as his own, and who hated both her husband and Mariamne, made use of this betrayal of confidence in conjunction with her accusation against them of unlawful intimacy. Thereupon Herod, without giving Joseph an opportunity to defend himself, ordered him executed.[36]

In the year 30 he murdered his wife's grandfather, Hyrcanus II, who, through the instigation of Alexandra, had formed a secret league against him with Malchus the king of Arabia.[37] In the year 29, through the instigation of his sister Salome, he killed Mariamne herself;[38] and a year later, Alex-

[33] Antiq., XV. iii. 5, 8-9.
[34] Antiq., XV. iii. 5.
[35] Antiq., XV. iii. 6.
[36] Antiq., XV. iii. 9.
[37] Antiq., XV. vi. 1-4.
[38] Antiq., XV. vii. 4-6.

andra was also executed[39] rather belatedly, for she had far more deserved that fate than the others.

In 25 BCE., he executed Costobar, his sister Salome's second husband, of whom she had tired. With Costobar he also killed the sons of Babas,[40] who were of Maccabean descent and belonged to the Antigonus party. Costobar had had them concealed in his farm for twelve years, during which time Herod had searched for them to bring them to punishment as enemies to his government. With the death of these Maccabeans, there was not one surviving to dispute with him the occupancy of the throne. Palestine was now entirely in Herod's hands.[41]

Thus, having himself firmly established, he renewed the schemes and measures of the high-priest Jason, who a century and a half earlier had labored to effect a Judean-Grecian fusion. As Jason had erected a Greek gymnasium at Jerusalem, Herod built a magnificent theater in that city and a spacious amphitheater in the plain nearby, where he introduced wrestling, charioting, and every kind of musical and poetic art, and even the barbarous Roman gladiatorial and wild beast contests, for which he invited from foreign lands the most famous performers, offering high rewards to the victors.[42]

In the year 24, he built for himself a strongly fortified palace in the "Upper City," with apartments, each of a particular name, and large enough to accommodate large numbers of guests. Those named after Caesar and Agrippa he adorned wtih gold and marble.[43] A tower of this palace is still to be seen, the so-called Tower of Hippicus or Tower of David.

To satisfy the demands of the Greek inhabitants of the non-Jewish cities of his domain, and thereby also please the Emperor and the Romans generally, he built for those com-

[39] Antiq., XV. vii. 8.
[40] Perhaps the Baba ben Buta, mentioned in Baba Bathra, 3b.
[41] Antiq., XV. vii. 10.
[42] Antiq., XV. viii. 1.
[43] Antiq., XV. ix. 3; Bell. Jud., I. xxi. 1, V. iv. 3-4.

munities, and even in the province of Syria, numerous temples, adorning them most lavishly.[44]

In the year 25-24 BCE. a famine and plague broke out, and continued into the year 24-23 ("from Nisan to Nisan"). It involved not only Judea, but neighboring countries also, and carried off thousands of people. The little corn that remained, rotted, so that there was not enough seed to crop the ground. Herod immediately opened his treasures, secured a vast importation of grain from Egypt, and made constant contributions of food and clothing. Fifty thousand persons were maintained at his sole expense; he even furnished corn for seed to the inhabitants of neighboring Syria. In his distribution of food he made special provisions for those who were not able, either by reason of old age or any other infirmity, to provide food for themselves, that the bakers should make their bread ready for them. This kindness and generosity not only caused a great reaction among his subjects, in removing their old hatred of him on account of his violations of some of their customs, but secured him a high degree of popularity with all the bordering states.[45]

But these great expenditures seem by no means to have exhausted the revenues of Herod. He still indulged in his sumptuous passion for building. New cities in large numbers were erected under his direction throughout Judea. The ancient city of Samaria, which some thirty years before had been raised from its ruins and partly rebuilt by the pro-Consul Gabinius, was now (year 23) reconstructed by Herod and named Sebaste (the August).[46]

In the year 22 BCE. he built on the site of the ancient Straton's Tower the large and magnificent maritime city, which in honor of the reigning imperial family and its founder he named Caesarea. In order that large ships might be able to moor and receive their cargoes in safety, a mole or

[44] Antiq., XV. ix. 5; Bell. Jud., I. xxi. 4.
[45] Antiq., XV. ix. 1-2.
[46] Antiq., XV. viii. 5; Bell. Jud., I. xxi. 2.

breakwater, two hundred feet wide, for the construction of which, stones fifty feet long, eighteen wide and nine deep were sunk into a depth of six fathoms, was carried far into the sea. A pier over half the width of the mole, protected by a massive wall and numerous towers, provided accommodation for seamen when in port, while a beautiful promenade, covering the other half and running round the entire haven, served for the entertainment of the public. He also built an underground sanitation system, sloping direct into the sea, which washed itself clean by the flux of every tide. In the center of the city stood a great and handsome temple dedicated to Caesar, and two statues, one representing Rome, the other Julius Caesar. Twelve full years were occupied in the building of the city.[47]

In place of the old city Capharsaba, he founded a city which he named in honor of his father Antipatras. On another spot above Jericho he built a citadel which he named after his mother Cypros. Still further north, in a previously unbuilt but fruitful district, he founded a new city and named it after his brother Phasaelis.[48] Having thus perpetuated the memory of his family, he built in honor of himself two fortresses, both named Herodium, one nine miles south of Jerusalem and the other in the mountains toward Arabia.[49]

At Rhodes he erected a temple to Apollo, and gave the community several hundredweight of silver for the repair of its fishing fleet. He gave liberally to numerous cities of Greece and Syria for the construction of such public works as they needed. He also built most of the public buildings at Nicopolis, near Actium, and caused cloisters to be erected on both sides of its main street, and the open road to be paved with polished

[47] Antiq., XV. ix. 6, XVI. v. 1; Bell. Jud., I. xxi. 5-8; compare also Antiq., XV. viii. 5. The erection of the temple and statues plainly show that Herod had intended Caesarea for a heathen, not a Jewish city.

[48] Antiq., XVI. v. 2; Bell. Jud., I. xxi. 9.

[49] Antiq., XV. ix. 4; Bell. Jud., I. xxi. 10; compare Antiq., XIV. xiii. 9; Bell. Jud., I. xiii. 8.

marble.[50] He then built palatial gymnasiums at Tripoli, Damascus and Ptolemais; a wall, temples, and market places at Berytus and Tyre; theaters for Damascus and Sidon; aqueducts for Laodicia, baths and fountains for Ascalon, in addition to liberal donations which he gave to many other cities.[51]

The most magnificent of all his building operations, however, was the rebuilding of the Temple at Jerusalem. The expense he laid out for this work, and the repairs of the fortress which, in honor of Mark Antony, he named Antonia, was incalculable. The lapse of five hundred years, and the sieges which it had undergone, as it was the great military post of the nation, had much dilapidated the structure of Zerubabbel. Therefore, in the year 20, at the annual festival of Passover, Herod, with his usual eloquence, dwelling on the goodness of God, who not only granted his people peace, and whose blessing had amply compensated them for their losses by famine and pestilence, but who further secured to them a continuation of prosperity through the friendship of the great Emperor of Rome, addressed the assembled multitude. He spoke of his own zeal for the religion of Israel and called their attention to the condition and size of the Temple, so greatly inferior to the sacred structure erected by Solomon; that this inferiority arose, not from want of zeal on the part of those who returned from Babylon and built the Temple, but from want of means and ability on their part. But since he, by the grace of God, possessed both the zeal and means, he declared his determination to rebuild the Temple in all its pristine greatness, as an offering of gratitude to the Lord God of Israel, for the manifold blessings vouchsafed unto him and his kingdom.

The assembly was taken by surprise, and seized with apprehension. All recognized the grandeur of the offer, the importance of the undertaking, and the need and benefit of its being carried out, but they had no confidence in Herod's

[50] Antiq.., XVI. v. 3.
[51] Bell. Jud., I. xxi. 11.

professions of zeal. The difficulty and cost of such a work, and the length of time it would require, alarmed them. The fear became general that after the king had taken down the old Temple he might prove unable or unwilling to build the new one. To calm their fears, Herod solemnly promised that he would not begin to demolish the old Temple until all the materials required for the new one were prepared and collected together on the spot; and on this condition his offer was accepted with satisfaction. Herod faithfully kept his promise to the people.

Two years were devoted to preparations. Ten thousand of the most skilled craftsmen, under the direction of one thousand priests, were taken into the king's pay. One thousand wagons were employed in the transportation of the materials, some of which came from very long distances. And when everything was ready, demolition of the old Temple began. The Holy Place, properly so called, was finished in a year and a half; and legend tells us that, in proof of divine approval, during the whole of this period no rain fell during the day time to interrupt the work, but only at night.[52] It took eight years to complete the structure only so far as to fit it for worship; but the building was carried on for many more years, both by Herod himself and long after his death. Even shortly before the destruction of Jerusalem no less than eighteen thousand men were yet employed and at work on the Temple.

The stones were white marble, each stone twenty-five cubits long, twelve high, and nine broad;[53] all wrought and polished with exquisite beauty. The Temple was only sixty cubits in breadth, but a wing on each side projected twenty cubits more. The entrance was through an open gateway seventy cubits high, and twenty wide, so that the front of the Temple measured one hundred and twenty cubits. This was the tallest part of the whole structure on the summit of the

[52] Antiq., XV. xi. 7.

[53] Cubit equals 18 to 20 inches.

ΜΗΘΕΝΑ ΑΛΛΟΓΕΝΗ ΕΙΣ ΩΟ ΡΕΤΕΣΘΑΙ ΕΝ-ΤΟΣ ΤΟΥ ΩΕ ΡΙ ΤΟ ΙΕΡΟΝ ΤΡΥΘΑΚΤΟΥ ΚΑΙ ΠΕΡΙΒΟΛΡΥ ΟΕ Δ ΑΝ ΛΗ ΦΘΗ ΕΛΥΤΩΙ ΑΙ-ΤΙΟΣ ΕΣ ΤΑΙ ΔΙΑ ΤΟ ΕΞΑΚΟΛΟΥ ΑΕΙΝ ΘΑΝΑ-ΤΟΝ.

Let no foreigner enter within the screen and enclosure surrounding the sanctuary. Whosoever is taken so doing will be the cause that death overtaketh him.

One of the signs put up by the Jews, with the permission of the Roman government, on the stone wall of the inner court of the Temple, intended to be read by Gentiles. It was discovered by Clermont-Ganneau in 1871, and is now at the New Museum in Constantinople.

It is very remarkable that Josephus, who refers to this ordinance in Bell. Jud. VI ii. 4 and in Antiq., XV. xi. 5, does not use the words which are on this tablet, but others. However, there were also other signs with different inscriptions, because in Bell. Jud. V. v. 2 he mentions "Greek and Roman" or Latin inscriptions, and Titus in his speech before John and his party, in Bell. Jud., VI. ii. 4 mentions "in Greek and in your own (Hebrew) letters."

ΜΗΘΕΝΑ ΑΑΛΟΓΕΝΗ ΕΙΣ ΩΟ ΡΕΤΕΣΘΑΙ ΕΝ-ΤΟΣ ΤΟΥ ΩΕ ΡΙ ΤΟ ΙΕΡΟΝ ΤΡΥΘΑΚΤΟΥ ΚΑΙ ΠΕΡΙΒΟΛΡΥ ΟΕ Δ ΑΝ ΛΗ ΦΘΗ ΕΛΥΤΩΙ ΑΙ-ΤΙΟΣ ΕΣ ΤΑΙ ΔΙΑ ΤΟ ΕΞΑΚΟΛΟΥ ΑΕΙΝ ΘΑΝΑ ΤΟΝ.	Let no foreigner enter within the screen and enclosure surrounding the sanctuary. Whosoever is taken so doing will be the cause that death overtaketh him.

One of the signs put up by the Jews, with the permission of the Roman government, on the stone wall of the inner court of the Temple, intended to be read by Gentiles. It was discovered by Clermont-Ganneau in 1871, and is now at the New Museum in Constantinople.

It is very remarkable that Josephus, who refers to this ordinance in Bell. Jud. VI ii. 4 and in Antiq., XV. xi. 5, does not use the words which are on this tablet, but others. However, there were also other signs with different inscriptions, because in Bell. Jud. V. v. 2 he mentions "Greek and Roman" or Latin inscriptions, and Titus in his speech before John and his party, in Bell. Jud., VI. ii. 4 mentions "in Greek and in your own (Hebrew) letters."

ΜΗΘΕΝΑ ΑΛΛΟΓΕΝΗ ΕΙΣ ΩΟ ΡΕΤΕΣΘΑΙ ΕΝ-ΤΟΣ ΤΟΥ ΩΕ ΡΙ ΤΟ ΙΕΡΟΝ ΤΡΥΘΑΚΤΟΥ ΚΑΙ ΠΕΡΙΒΟΛΡΥ ΟΕ Δ ΑΝ ΛΗ ΦΘΗ ΕΛΥΤΩΙ ΑΙ-ΤΙΟΣ ΕΣ ΤΑΙ ΔΙΑ ΤΟ ΕΞΑΚΟΛΟΥ ΑΕΙΝ ΘΑΝΑ-ΤΟΝ.

Let no foreigner enter within the screen and enclosure surrounding the sanctuary. Whosoever is taken so doing will be the cause that death overtaketh him.

One of the signs put up by the Jews, with the permission of the Roman government, on the stone wall of the inner court of the Temple, intended to be read by Gentiles. It was discovered by Clermont-Ganneau in 1871, and is now at the New Museum in Constantinople.

It is very remarkable that Josephus, who refers to this ordinance in Bell. Jud. VI ii. 4 and in Antiq., XV. xi. 5, does not use the words which are on this tablet, but others. However, there were also other signs with different inscriptions, because in Bell. Jud. V. v. 2 he mentions "Greek and Roman" or Latin inscriptions, and Titus in his speech before John and his party, in Bell. Jud., VI. ii. 4 mentions "in Greek and in your own (Hebrew) letters."

marble.[50] He then built palatial gymnasiums at Tripoli, Damascus and Ptolemais; a wall, temples, and market places at Berytus and Tyre; theaters for Damascus and Sidon; aqueducts for Laodicia, baths and fountains for Ascalon, in addition to liberal donations which he gave to many other cities.[51]

The most magnificent of all his building operations, however, was the rebuilding of the Temple at Jerusalem. The expense he laid out for this work, and the repairs of the fortress which, in honor of Mark Antony, he named Antonia, was incalculable. The lapse of five hundred years, and the sieges which it had undergone, as it was the great military post of the nation, had much dilapidated the structure of Zerubabbel. Therefore, in the year 20, at the annual festival of Passover, Herod, with his usual eloquence, dwelling on the goodness of God, who not only granted his people peace, and whose blessing had amply compensated them for their losses by famine and pestilence, but who further secured to them a continuation of prosperity through the friendship of the great Emperor of Rome, addressed the assembled multitude. He spoke of his own zeal for the religion of Israel and called their attention to the condition and size of the Temple, so greatly inferior to the sacred structure erected by Solomon; that this inferiority arose, not from want of zeal on the part of those who returned from Babylon and built the Temple, but from want of means and ability on their part. But since he, by the grace of God, possessed both the zeal and means, he declared his determination to rebuild the Temple in all its pristine greatness, as an offering of gratitude to the Lord God of Israel, for the manifold blessings vouchsafed unto him and his kingdom.

The assembly was taken by surprise, and seized with apprehension. All recognized the grandeur of the offer, the importance of the undertaking, and the need and benefit of its being carried out, but they had no confidence in Herod's

[50] Antiq.., XVI. v. 3.
[51] Bell. Jud., I. xxi. 11.

professions of zeal. The difficulty and cost of such a work, and the length of time it would require, alarmed them. The fear became general that after the king had taken down the old Temple he might prove unable or unwilling to build the new one. To calm their fears, Herod solemnly promised that he would not begin to demolish the old Temple until all the materials required for the new one were prepared and collected together on the spot; and on this condition his offer was accepted with satisfaction. Herod faithfully kept his promise to the people.

Two years were devoted to preparations. Ten thousand of the most skilled craftsmen, under the direction of one thousand priests, were taken into the king's pay. One thousand wagons were employed in the transportation of the materials, some of which came from very long distances. And when everything was ready, demolition of the old Temple began. The Holy Place, properly so called, was finished in a year and a half; and legend tells us that, in proof of divine approval, during the whole of this period no rain fell during the day time to interrupt the work, but only at night.[52] It took eight years to complete the structure only so far as to fit it for worship; but the building was carried on for many more years, both by Herod himself and long after his death. Even shortly before the destruction of Jerusalem no less than eighteen thousand men were yet employed and at work on the Temple.

The stones were white marble, each stone twenty-five cubits long, twelve high, and nine broad;[53] all wrought and polished with exquisite beauty. The Temple was only sixty cubits in breadth, but a wing on each side projected twenty cubits more. The entrance was through an open gateway seventy cubits high, and twenty wide, so that the front of the Temple measured one hundred and twenty cubits. This was the tallest part of the whole structure on the summit of the

[52] Antiq., XV. xi. 7.
[53] Cubit equals 18 to 20 inches.

Temple-Mount, and was on all sides surrounded by a succession of piazzas or porticoes, and terraces, rising above each other, and enclosing a multitude of courts and buildings. The first of these enclosures, nearest to the city, called the Court of the Gentiles, because it was open to all visitors, was surrounded by a strong and lofty wall of large stones well cemented. On the side of this wall, toward the Temple, it had a piazza, supported by columns of such size, that three men with arms extended could barely embrace one, or equal to about twenty-five feet in circumference. Of these columns there were one hundred and sixty-two, supporting a flat cedar ceiling. A flight of five marble steps led into the second enclosure. Stately tablets placed over this partition, at even distances, had inscriptions engraved on them in Greek and Latin, "Non-Jews are forbidden to pass this wall under penalty of death." The third enclosure, raised above the second by fourteen marble steps, formed the court of the Hebrews. It contained the altar of burnt offerings, parted off by a low marble screen from the larger court, which formed the Court of the Priests, the Holy Place, and the Holy of Holies, surrounded by the Temple's treasury vaults. The entrance to this part of the third enclosure was adorned by a magnificent door cast in Corinthian brass, presented by a wealthy and pious Alexandrian, after whom it was named Nicanor's Gate. Within the third enclosure also, were the Court of the Levites, the Hall of the Sanhedrin and the Men's Court, while divided from the men by a low wall or partition, were the court and galleries reserved for women; so that we see the complete separation of the sexes which is kept up in the synagogue to this day.

The whole structure, with its terraces rising in succession, was visible at a great distance, and equally strong and splendid. Its white marble walls, in many places inlaid with gold, towering above the city, reflected the blinding rays of the sun, and, after sunset, gave to the Mount the appearance of perpetual snow on its summit. And so solid was the masonry, that even today, after a lapse of nearly two thousand years, and in spite of the rage of man, which exerted every effort in order that not one stone should be left on the other, the whole of the foundation, and the basement of the Temple, still remain entire and uninjured; while a portion of the western wall, erect, and attesting its strength, is visited by Jewish pilgrims from every part of the world, whose streaming eyes are raised to Heaven with prayers for Israel's restoration.[54]

The inauguration of this Temple was a solemnity for which the presence of his sons was deemed necessary by Herod. His two sons by Mariamne I., Alexander and Aristobulus, had been in Rome for five or six years, receiving their education under the Emperor's guardianship. In order, therefore, to bring them home, and to pay his respects to Augustus and to thank him in person for his kindness to the young princes, Herod repaired to Italy. His reception by the Emperor of Rome was very gracious, his entertainment very lavish, and the presents by which he demonstrated his gratitude, right royal. And so, after a short stay at Rome, he returned with his two sons to Jerusalem.

On their return home, Alexander and Aristobulus, notwithstanding their Roman education, were received by the people with the loudest acclamation. Their majestic bearing, their polite manners, and above all, the blood of the ancient Hasmoneans which flowed in their veins, rendered them objects of the deepest interest to the whole Jewish nation. Alexander soon married Glaphyra, the daughter of Archelaus, King of Cappadocia; and to Aristobulus, Herod gave Berenice, the daughter of his sister Salome.[55] Herod now looked forward to long years of peace and happiness.

But his declining days were soon to be darkened with a domestic tragedy as melancholy and awful as those of his

[54] For the complete description of the Temple, compare Antiq., XV., entire eleventh chapter; Bell. Jud., I. xxi. 1, and V. entire fifth chapter. About the dates on which these transactions took place, see Schuerer, Div. I. Vol. i. p. 410, note 12.

[55] Compare Antiq., XV. x. 1, with XVI. i. 2.

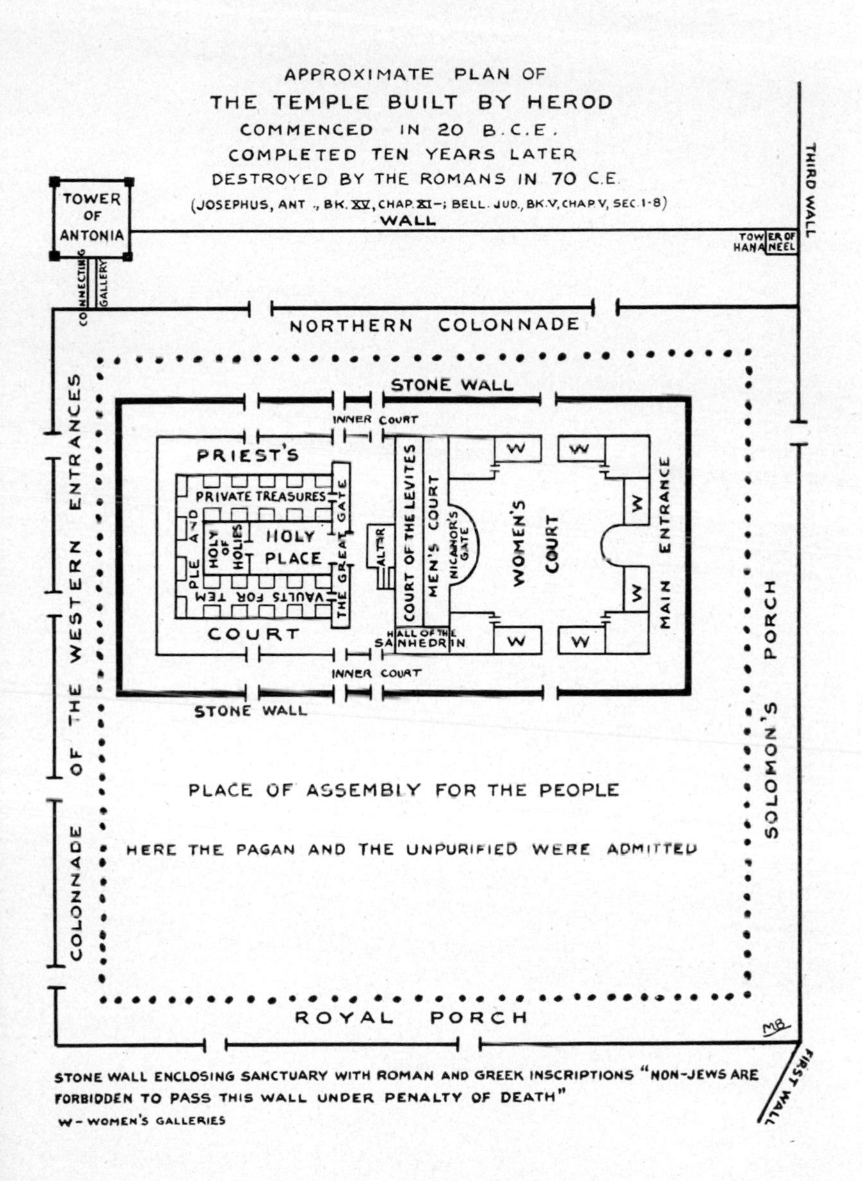
APPROXIMATE PLAN OF
THE TEMPLE BUILT BY HEROD
COMMENCED IN 20 B.C.E.
COMPLETED TEN YEARS LATER
DESTROYED BY THE ROMANS IN 70 C.E.
(JOSEPHUS, ANT., BK. XV, CHAP. XI–; BELL. JUD., BK. V, CHAP. V, SEC. 1-8)
TOWER OF ANTONIA
WALL
TOWER OF HANANEEL
THIRD WALL
CONNECTING GALLERY
NORTHERN COLONNADE
STONE WALL
INNER COURT
PRIEST'S
PRIVATE TREASURES
HOLY OF HOLIES
HOLY PLACE
VAULTS FOR TEMPLE AND
THE GREAT GATE
ALTAR
COURT OF THE LEVITES
MEN'S COURT
NICANOR'S GATE
WOMEN'S COURT
W
MAIN ENTRANCE
COURT
HALL OF THE SANHEDRIN
INNER COURT
STONE WALL
COLONNADE OF THE WESTERN ENTRANCES
SOLOMON'S PORCH
PLACE OF ASSEMBLY FOR THE PEOPLE
HERE THE PAGAN AND THE UNPURIFIED WERE ADMITTED
ROYAL PORCH
MB
FIRST WALL
STONE WALL ENCLOSING SANCTUARY WITH ROMAN AND GREEK INSCRIPTIONS "NON-JEWS ARE FORBIDDEN TO PASS THIS WALL UNDER PENALTY OF DEATH"
W - WOMEN'S GALLERIES

earlier days, and his sumptuous palaces were again to resound with strife, mourning and murder. The two young princes had not forgotten their mother's wrongs. Her innocent blood called for justice, and her sons did not conceal their aversion for the authors of her death. Salome and Pheroras, the sister and brother of Herod, feared that should their brother die and these young men inherit the throne, they would punish those who had been guilty of their mother's death. Thus, not long after their return from Italy, the old feud between the Hasmoneans and the house of Antipater once again began. While the two brothers spoke unwisely about their mother's fate, their enemies, Salome and her party, practiced and experienced in the school of intrigue, knew how to extract venom and accusations even from the most harmless words and gestures. Salome abused her influence over her daughter Berenice, so that the most secret thoughts of Aristobulus, which in the confidence of connubial privacy he had communicated to his wife, were by her betrayed to his bitterest enemies. And in her endeavor that none of Mariamne's posterity should remain alive, she led Herod to believe that his sons were conspiring against his life.[56]

For three years this and similar accusations made no deep impression on Herod, who was justly proud of the popularity of his sons. But while he was absent with Agrippa, in his war near the Bosphorus, during which he obtained for the Jews of Asia Minor a ratification of all their privileges which the Greeks there had endeavored to take away from them,[57] these sinister reports began to obtain much strength and consistency, and consequently more credit with the suspicious father. Salome's hatred of the young Hasmonean descendants became

[56] Antiq., XVI. iii. 1-3; compare also XVI. vii. 3, middle of section.

[57] Antiq., XVI. ii. 3-4; compare also XII. iii. 2. The long oration of Nicolas of Damascus (Antiq., XVI. ii. 3.), who was appointed by Herod to plead in behalf of the Jews of Asia Minor before the tribunal of Agrippa, furnishes curious evidence of the numbers, wealth, and importance of the Jews in those regions.

more and more bitter, and the quarrels in Herod's family which she fomented, more frequent and more severe. Herod became alarmed for his safety, and while Salome was at hand to take advantage of his anxiety she induced him to adopt a most dangerous measure in order to subdue the pride of his sons, and to make them more subservient to his will.

Before his marriage with Mariamne, Herod had espoused a woman of humble birth, named Doris, by whom he had a son, Antipater.[58] This wife of his young affections, Herod had divorced upon his marriage with Mariamne, and Doris with her son had been exiled from the city. He recalled this eldest son to Jerusalem and put him up as a counterbalance to the influences of the Hasmonean princes. Antipater, however, having inherited all the malice, craft and ambitions of his father, found, upon his arrival, a most favorable atmosphere for his talents and joined in all the plots of Salome and Pheroras; and as Herod had permission from Rome to bequeath his crown to whichever of his sons he chose, Antipater lost no time in alienating his father's affections from the sons of Mariamne. Herod, as if to atone for the neglect with which he had so long treated his eldest son, now began to shower him with favors and marks of distinction; he even sent him to Rome to be presented to Augustus by Agrippa, and caused him everywhere to be spoken of as his successor. This determination of Herod served to embitter the sons of Mariamne more than ever, and drove them to the rashest resentment and outbursts against their father.[59] And as Antipater,—fearful lest during his absence in Rome, they should supplant him and regain the favor of their father,—in his letters and by means of his agents in Jerusalem brought heavy charges against them, things continued going from bad to worse till there was no longer any peace or security at the court of Herod. At last, Herod became so exasperated that he directed Alexander and

[58] Antiq., XIV. xii. 1.
[59] Antiq., XVI. iii. 3; Bell. Jud., I. xxii. 1, xxiii. 2.

Aristobulus to accompany him to Rome, that their conduct might be investigated by Augustus himself (12 BCE.).[60]

Herod and his sons appeared before the Emperor at Aquilea. He opened the charge by accusing them as parricides in intention, and guilty of high treason. His langauge was so strong as to render his sons unable to defend themselves without incriminating their father. When he exhausted his long list of grievances, Alexander began to plead his own and his brother's cause with such becoming modesty and such truthful simplicity, as convinced the Emperor and his Council of the innocence of the two princes. Augustus, with that temperance and moderation which distinguished all his actions after he became Emperor, taking upon himself the office of peace-maker, gently reproached Herod for his too rash belief in the criminality of his sons, and exhorted the young men to honor their father and love their brothers and sisters, to which they replied with tears and protestations of duty and affection. Herod at length was prevailed upon to embrace his sons, and, apparently happy, he returned with them to Jerusalem. The diabolical Antipater, having made his debut before the Emperor, returned with them.[61]

Still, however, as Herod could not bring himself to repose full confidence in any of his elder sons, he designed a plan by which they should succeed him in the order of their birth:—first Antipater, then Alexander, and lastly Aristobulus. But this arrangement satisfied no one. Antipater was not contented with the prospect of leaving a barren scepter, in default of any issue. The sons of Mariamne were indignant that they, of royal lineage, should, even for a time, be set aside for the son of a low-born plebeian. The people, again, favored the sons of Mariamne, because of their noble Maccabean origin. Antipater, too cunning and too unscrupulous, sometimes apologizing for his brothers, sometimes accusing them, kept the mind of Herod in a constant fever of sus-

[60] Antiq., XVI. iv. 1.
[61] Antiq., XVI. iv. 2-6; Bell. Jud., I. xxiii. 3-5.

picious excitement. The King's favorite brother, Pheroras, increased his wretchedness. Pheroras had become so infatuated with a slave girl as to refuse the hand of one of Herod's daughters. Not long after, on the offer of another daughter, Pheroras consented to break off his connections with the slave, but before the espousals he changed his mind, and refused to conclude the marriage. Pheroras, however, was a still worse enemy to the peace of Herod. He instilled into the mind of Alexander that his father secretly cherished a passion for his wife Glaphyra, and Alexander boldly questioned Herod about this imputation. Pheroras, to avoid the fury of his offended brother, laid the plot to the instigation of Salome who vindicated herself with great difficulty. For some time both Pheroras and Salome lost their influence in the Court. But Antipater still remained, and the sons of Mariamne were every day accused of new plots. Salome had soon contrived to make her peace with Herod, and now, backed by Antipater, she charged the sons of Mariamne with conspiring to poison their father. The suspicions of Herod against his sons became morbid. His whole life became disturbed. He hated everybody, trusted no one, and finally developed a fear of ghosts. Worked up to a pitch of frenzy, Herod caused Alexander and Aristobulus to be thrown into prison. Alexander, now exasperated at being continually exposed to the groundless suspicions and anger of his father, adopted a strange and desperate measure. He sent four letters ("papers") to his father avowing that the accusation was true and that he was really guilty, but that Salome, Pheroras, and several of the King's most trusted statesmen were his accomplices. Herod, in delirium, seized all persons of rank, and either put them to the torture, or executed them at once, though he hesitated to lay hands on Salome and Pheroras.[62]

When Archelaus, King of Cappadocia, Alexander's father-in-law, heard of this unfortunate state of affairs at the Jewish court, he began to fear for his daughter and son-in-

[62] Antiq., XVI. vii. 2-6, viii. 1-5; Bell. Jud., I. xxiv. 1-8.

law, and went to Jerusalem in order, if possible, to bring about a reconciliation. He appeared before Herod, first very angry over his good-for-nothing son-in-law, threatening to take his daughter back again to his own house; then by arguing dispassionately the improbability of the accusations. By such maneuvre the wily Cappadocian succeeded in reconciling the father and son; Alexander was reinstated in freedom and favor, and Archelaus was able to return to his own country quite satisfied.[63]

The reconciliation, however, was of very short duration. It just so happened that at this time there arrived at Jerusalem a Greek by race, but a Lacedemonean by birth, far superior to Archelaus in slyness, and so corrupt that "Greece could no longer meet his extravagant requirements." He was twice arraigned before the emperor for spreading sedition throughout Achaia, and for fleecing the cities of that province, till he was finally banished from the country. By presents which he brought to Herod as bait to secure his quarry and which he soon found returned with interest, and by flattery, clever talk, and lying encomiums upon the king's merits, he was soon numbered among his most intimate friends. When he had learned everything about the rottenness that was sapping the royal house, he insinuated himself into favor, with each member of the family by a different method, but principally acted as a hireling of Antipater and as a traitor to Alexander. His visit was short, but before it was over he destroyed every hope of peace forever; he enraged the father against his sons, envenomed the sons against their father and embittered each of them against all the others more than they had ever been before.[64] Antipater, Salome and Pheroras followed and developed matters to such a state of subversion, that Herod, by now thoroughly prostrated, put his two sons in irons, and in separate cells, and dispatched a complaint of high treason

[63] Antiq., XVI. viii. 6; Bell. Jud., I. xxv. 1-6.
[64] Antiq., XVI. x. 1; Bell. Jud., I. xxvi. 1-4.

against them to Emperor Augustus.[65] When the officers bearing the accusation reached Rome, they found Augustus in a favorable mood, and he gave Herod complete liberty to deal with his sons in accordance with his own discretion, but advised him to summon to Berytus, in Syria, a judiciary court consisting of Roman judges, and to have the charge investigated by it.[66] The court pronounced the death sentence. Accordingly, the sons of Mariamne were brought back to Judea, and at Sebaste, in the year 7 BCE., together with three hundred men who were, or were suspected of being, their supporters, they were executed on the gallows.[67]

Antipater was now incontestable at court, and enjoying the fullest confidence of his father. But this did not yet satisfy him. As the old king lived too long for his impatience, he conspired with Pheroras to remove him by poison.[68] In order not to be suspected, however, Antipater contrived to have himself sent to Rome, while Pheroras left Jerusalem on some pretense of offense taken, and swore never to return during Herod's life. That Herod, meanwhile, did not entertain any suspicion against Antipater, is shown by his will in which he nominated him as successor to the throne.[69] But while Antipater was in Rome, Pheroras died.[70] This disconcerted the scheme, and Salome, ever true to Herod, discovered the plot, proving the guilt of Antipater and the innocence of Herod's two sons by Mariamne—the victims of false accusations. Herod's third wife, Mariamne II., the daughter of the high-priest Simon ben Boethus, was found implicated in the conspiracy: Herod repudiated her immediately, and dismissed her father from office.[71] Antipater was recalled from Rome, and upon his arrival at Jerusalem was committed to prison in the

[65] Antiq., XVI. x. 5-7; Bell. Jud., I. xxvii. 1.
[66] Antiq., XVI. xi. 1; Bell. Jud., I. xxvii. 1.
[67] Antiq., XVI. xi. 2-7; Bell. Jud., I. xxvii. 2-6.
[68] Antiq., XVII. i. 1, ii. 4; Bell. Jud., I. xxviii. 1, xxix. 1.
[69] Antiq., XVII. iii. 2; Bell. Jud., I. xxix. 2.
[70] Antiq., XVII. iii. 3; Bell. Jud., I. xxix. 4.
[71] Antiq., XVII. iv. 1-2; Bell. Jud., I. xxx. 1-7.

king's palace.[72] On the next day he was tried before Quintilius Varus, the Roman Legate of Syria, who at the time was passing through Palestine. During the opening of the trial Herod fell weeping, and unable to continue, he ordered his attorney Nicolas of Damascus to proceed with the indictment. When the lengthy prosecution ended, Varus called upon the prisoner to make his defense. The proofs and exhibits brought against him, however, that he not only plotted against his father's life and corrupted the morale of his household, but that he was also guilty for the death of his half-brothers, were too numerous and too indisputable, and Antipater could offer no plausible refutation of the charges. Varus, therefore rose, and handing a secret verdict to Herod left for Antioch. Thereupon Herod, evidently requiring the Emperor's approval to punish his son capitally, put Antipater in chains, and reported the matter to Augustus.[73]

Herod was now almost seventy years of age. A disease from which he had long suffered broke out with such violence that no hope was left for his recovery.[74] He had low fever, an intolerable itching, a rabid appetite which he could not gratify on account of ulcers and pains in the colon. His feet were swollen and exuding sores, breeding worms, preyed on the lower region of his abdomen. His breathing was heavy, fast and very offensive, and torturing spasms threw him into convulsions. He went to Callirhoe for its warm asphalt bath, but returned to Jericho without relief.[75] When the news got abroad of his hopeless condition, two eminent Pharisees, Judas ben Tsaripha and Matthias ben Margaloth, urged on their pupils to pull down the offensive eagle which Herod had placed over one of the gates of the Temple. But when the work was accomplished, he was still strong enough to pass sentences of death, and to cause Judas and Matthias and those

[72] Antiq., XVII. iv. 3, v. 1-2; Bell. Jud., I. xxxi. 2-5.

[73] Antiq., XVII. v. 3-7; Bell. Jud., I. xxxii. 1-5.

[74] Antiq., XVII. vi. 1; Bell. Jud., I. xxxiii. 1.

[75] Antiq., XVII. vi. 5, first half of section; Bell. Jud., I. xxxiii. 5.

who were caught with them to be burnt alive.[76] In a new will which he now executed he named his youngest son Antipas, by his fourth wife, as his successor.[77]

Amid all the pains which his disease caused him, however, Herod lived long enough to have the satisfaction of accomplishing the death of his son Antipater. A courier from Rome brought him the authorization for his execution, and it was quickly carried out.[78] As the days of Herod were now ending, he gave orders that the leading men of the nation be thrown into prison and that upon his death they be cut down so that there might be a national mourning as he passed away.[79] He also again remodeled his will. He now named Archelaus, the older son of his fourth wife, Malthace, king; his brother Antipas, as tetrarch of Galilee and Perea; and Philip, the son of his fifth wife, Cleopatra, as tetrarch of Gaulanitis, Trachonitis, Batanea, and Panias. He also made provisions for the rest of his large family; and bequeathed about $2,000,000 in coined money to Emperor Augustus, and his gold and silver vessels, and costly garments to the emperor's wife, Julia; besides about $2,000,000 to others. Having thus dispensed death on one hand, and wealth and kingdoms on the other, Herod, five days after the execution of Antipater, died at Jericho,[80] shortly before Passover,[81] in the year 4 BCE.[82]

From the date of his appointment as King by the Roman Senate, Herod reigned thirty-seven years, or thirty-four years from his conquest of Jerusalem.[83] Of the wives he had,

[76] Antiq., XVII. vi. 1-5; Bell. Jud., xxxiii. 1-4.

[77] Antiq., XVII. vi. 1. For chronology concerning this will, compare Antiq., XVII. vi. 1-2, with Bell. Jud., I. xxxiii. 2-4.

[78] Antiq., XVII. vii.; Bell. Jud., I. xxxiii. 7.

[79] Antiq., XVII. vi. 5; Bell. Jud., I. xxxiii. 6.

[80] Antiq., XVII. viii. 1; Bell. Jud., I. xxxiii. 7-8.

[81] Antiq., XVII. ix. 3; Bell. Jud., II. i. 3.

[82] Concerning the date of Herod's death, see Schuerer, Div. I. Vol. i. p. 465.

[83] Antiq., XVII. viii. 1; Bell. Jud., I. xxxiii. 8.

Josephus enumerates ten:—Doris, Mariamne I, Mariamne II, Malthace, Cleopatra, Pallas, Phaedra, Elpis, and two others—one of whom was his brother's daughter, and another, his sister's daughter.[84]

[84] The list of Herod's wives, and of his children by each wife, are found in Antiq., XVII. i. 3, XVIII. v. 4, and Bell. Jud., I. xxviii. 4.

CHAPTER IV

From the ACCESSION *of* ARCHELAUS *to the* ETHNARCHY *of* JUDEA, SAMARIA *and* IDUMEA, *in* 4 BCE., *to the* DEATH *of* KING AGRIPPA I, *in* 44 CE.

THOUGH the third will of Herod was subject to the approval of the Emperor, Archelaus, immediately after the funeral of his father, assumed the direction of affairs at Jerusalem. Having completed the customary seven days of mourning, he gave a funeral banquet, and, dressed in white holy day garments,[1] entered the Temple; and taking his seat on the golden throne, delivered an address to the people. He spoke to them kindly, thanked them for their loyal reception, alluded to his father's oppressions, and promised them that his chief care should be to make his rulership more easy and happy than his father's had been. He would, however, he said, for the present not take upon himself the authority of a king nor assume the titles of royalty until his right to the succession had been ratified by the Emperor. To confirm his promise he pledged himself to grant them whatever petition they presented to him as soon as the Roman authorities had given him complete title to the kingdom.[2]

[1] White garments were then the raiment of a gentleman, as the black coat is today.

[2] Antiq., XVII. viii. 4; Bell. Jud., II. i. 1.

But the hatred which the Jews had so long nursed and pent up against Herod was not to be overcome by a few smooth words or gracious acts of his son. Scarcely had the cheers ceased with which his promises were received, when a procession in mourning advanced to demand that justice should be done to the families of those men who had been put to death for destroying the golden eagle. Archelaus sent one of his principal officers to order the procession to disperse. The command was answered by a volley of stones. The new king was unwilling to stain the first days of his reign with bloodshed and sent repeated messengers to remonstrate with the rioters, but in vain. In the meantime the festival of Passover brought the pilgrims in vast numbers to Jerusalem, many of whom joined in the clamorous cries for justice raised by the original malcontents; and the tumults became so threatening that Archelaus was induced to send some of his guards to disperse the mob, which, however, stood at bay and attacked and killed most of the soldiers, while the officer in command was dangerously wounded. The outbreak called for immediate suppression and Archelaus promptly sent all his mercenaries against the rioters. After an obstinate conflict between the people and the soldiers, the tumult was put down; but three thousand of the people had been killed, and Archelaus compelled all non-residents to quit Jerusalem at once, so that the Paschal solemnities for that year were abruptly terminated.[3]

Following these rigid measures, Archelaus hastened to Rome, leaving his brother Philip in charge of the palace and his private interests. Sailing with him were Nicolas of Damascus and his brother Ptolemy, who like Nicolas had been an intimate friend of Herod, and many of Archelaus' relations, among whom was Salome, all with the ostensible purpose of supporting his claims to the throne, but in reality to oppose his elevation. Scarcely had they left the port of Caeserea, however, when his younger brother, Antipas, also sailed for Rome in order to press his own claims there. His pretensions

[3] Antiq., XVII. ix. 1-3; Bell. Jud., II. i. 2-3.

were based on the second will of Herod, executed, as his supporters asserted, when his father was in a saner state of mind than shortly before his death, and in which Antipater was named as his successor. The eloquent Nicolas of Damascus appeared on behalf of Archelaus, while Antipater, the son of Salome, the ablest orator among his opponents, represented Antipas. Malthace, the mother of both pretenders, and a lawyer named Ireneus, also espoused the cause of Antipas. When Augustus had heard both sides, not wishing to issue his decision immediately, he dismissed the gathering, in order to be able to give the matter sufficient consideration.[4]

But while Archelaus and Antipas were waiting for the decision, an embassy of fifty of the leading men of Judea also appeared before the Emperor. Taking advantage of the disputes that divided the Herodian family, they came to petition the suppression of this detested dynasty and to plead that the Judeans be permitted to live in accordance with their ancient constitution but under Roman suzeranity. They were supported by eight thousand of the Jews residing in Rome. Before an assembly of leading Roman statesmen, especially convocated by the Emperor for this purpose in the temple of Apollo, they reported Herod's iniquities and the tyranny with which he had exercised his authority over his subjects. They complained that "whereas when he took the kingdom it was in an extraordinary flourishing condition, he had filled the nation with the utmost degree of poverty"; that upon unjust pretenses he had slain many of the nobility, and taken away their estates; that "besides the annual impositions he had laid upon them, they had had to make liberal presents to him, to his domestics and to their friends, and to those of his slaves who were his tax-gatherers, because there was no way of obtaining immunity from violence without giving them either gold or silver for it." In short, the miseries which Herod had inflicted on the people exceeded all their forefathers had suffered since their return from Babylon. Furthermore, they

[4] Antiq., XVII. ix. 3-7; Bell. Jud., II. ii. 1-7.

pointed out, how on his father's death, though a son of such a tyrant, they had promptly acclaimed Archelaus as king, and joined him in his mourning for his father's death, and in his prayers for the prosperity of his own reign. But he, "apparently not to be taken for a bastard son of Herod," had ushered in his reign with the massacre of three thousand citizens, thereby giving a specimen of his future conduct towards his subjects. Wherefore it is but natural that those who had survived such disasters should implore the Romans to take pity on the relics of Judea and not to throw what remained of it to those who so barbarously tore it to pieces.

When they had ended, Nicolas of Damascus arose and spoke in behalf of Archelaus. But at this time, Philip, the third of the beneficiaries to whom Herod had bequeathed territories, also arrived in Rome, both to press his own claims and to support those of his half-brother Archelaus.[5] In view of these conflicting claims, Augustus was obliged to hasten his decision. By it, Archelaus was appointed to the sovereignty of Judea, Samaria and Idumea, under the title of Ethnarch; that of king was promised to him later if he should prove worthy of it. Antipas obtained Galilee and Perea, with the title of Tetrarch; Philip, also as Tetrarch, received Batanea, Trachonitis, Auranitis, and Panea. The annual revenue of Archelaus was fixed at 600 talents (c. $600,000), of Antipas 200 talents, and of Philip 100 talents. Salome received the cities of Jabne, Asdod and Phasaelis, in addition to 500,000 pieces of silver, and the palace at Ascalon.[6]

The description by Josephus of Archelaus' rulership is exceptionally barren. Archelaus, we are told, on taking pos-

[5] Antiq., XVII. xi. 1-3; Bell. Jud., II. vi. 1-2.

[6] Antiq., XVII. xi. 4-5; Bell. Jud., II. vi. 3. According to XVIII. ii. 2, Salome enjoyed these legacies for some fourteen years, having died during the procuratorship of Marcus Ambivius (9-12 CE.), and bequeathing Jabne, Phasaelis, and the city of Archelais, which Archelaus had built and named after himself, to the Empress Julia. (The building and naming of the city of Archelais after himself, is mentioned in XVII. xiii. 1.)

session of his ethnarchy, did not forget his old feuds, but treated not only the Jews but also the Samaritans with great brutality. He also gave great offense by his marriage with Glaphyra, the widow of his half-brother Alexander. This marriage with a deceased brother's wife was within the forbidden degrees of consanguinity, and only permitted where the deceased had left no children. But as Alexander had left two sons,[7] the marriage of his widow with his brother, Archelaus,

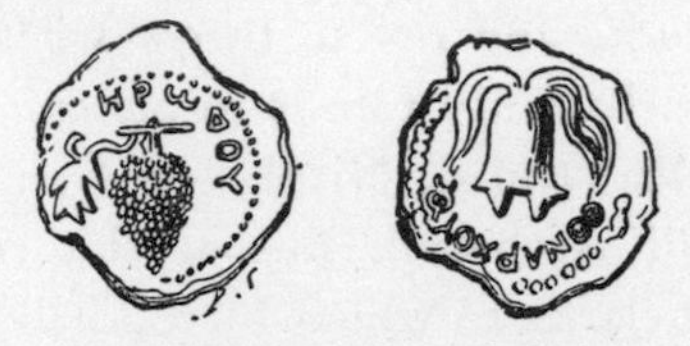

Bronze coin of Archelaus.

was detested by his zealous subjects as a heinous sin against the law of God, and a grievous insult to the memory of the dead. Again, in his rebuilding of the royal palace at Jericho, he diverted half of the water with which the village of Neara used to be watered, and drew it into the plain to water his own palm-trees. But very few incidents of his ethnarchate besides these are recorded by Josephus. In the tenth year of his rule, however, a deputation of Jewish and Samaritan aristocracy set out for Rome to denounce him before Augustus. We are not told what the accusation was, but it must have been very serious; for the emperor hastily summoned Archelaus to Rome, where after a formal hearing he was found guilty of misgovernment, all his estates were confiscated, and he was banished to Vienne, in Gaul, from where he never returned.[8] His territory was now incorporated into the Roman province of Syria, and the subordinate administration of Judea entrusted to an officer by the title of Procurator.

[7] After the death of Alexander, Herod had sent Glaphyra back to her father, with her dowry but without her children.—Bell. Jud., I. xxviii. 1; compare with the beginning of the following section.

[8] Antiq., XVII. xiii. 1-4; Bel. Jud., II. vii. 3.

With the banishment of Archelaus, conditions in Palestine became entirely changed. A Roman senator, Sulpicius P. Quirinius, was appointed to the prefecture of Syria, and the first procurator whom Augustus sent to Judea was Caponius, a man of equestrian rank. The powers of the imperial legate over his province as the direct representative of the Emperor were unlimited. But the authority of the procurator, who was under his supervision, also was very extensive. For in addition to his chief duties of maintaining order in the country and

The Emperor Augustus.

of enforcing the payment of the imperial taxes, he had also the unhindered command of the Roman cohorts and full power of life and death within his territory.

In order to ascertain the exact capabilities of the enlarged province,—the amount of wealth and the number of inhabitants,—it was the first duty of the legate, Quirinius, to take a general census in accordance with the Roman method of taxation. Now, the counting of the people was looked upon by the Jews as contrary to the will of God, for following the census taken in the reign of King David a plague broke out.[9] Therefore, they were ready to rise as one man to resist the numbering. Moreover, they considered the compulsory disclosure of their private affairs and possessions as an introduction to slavery to which they would never submit. Only the eloquence and good judgment of the high-priest Joazar, who well knew that the rebellion would be of no advantage, succeeded in appeasing the people, so that at last the census was carried out.[10]

Following the abatement of this popular opposition, however, the effect resulting thereof was of far more serious moment. Judas the Galilean—the son of the robber leader Ezekiah, whose extermination had been the first fruit of Herod's public life (Antiq., XIV. ix. 2)—formed a political association under the name of "Zealots." They denounced the enrollment and the payment of taxes, and under the cloak of religion incited the people to rebellion against the "pagan Roman power." The infection of their doctrine spread rapidly and widely, especially among young criminals. The robberies, crimes and assassinations committed by them and their offshoot, the Sicarii,[11] sometimes even among themselves, were countless. Their riots, which followed one another, and their devastation of whole cities reduced the nation to the last degree of despair.[12] Right up to the destruction of Jerusalem, and even as late as Hadrian, who finally annihilated them, the Zealots or the Sicarii everywhere led the riots and revolts. But the might of Rome proved irresistible. Judas himself, according to a New Testament record,[13] "perished," and his followers were "dispersed"; while two of his sons, Jacob and Simon, Josephus tells us, were crucified under the procurator-

[9] II Samuel, xxiv.

[10] Antiq., XVII. xiii. 5, XVIII. i. 1; Bell. Jud., II. viii. 1.

[11] In regard to the origin of both the Zealots and the Sicarii, see also the article "The Pharisees," following the beginning of our Chapter II.

[12] Antiq., XVIII. i. 1; Bell. Jud., II. viii. 1.

[13] Acts, v. 37.

ship of Tiberius Alexander (in 47 CE.), "for raising seditions as their father did,"[14] and that a third son, Menahem, was put to death by opposing forces at the beginning of the war (in the year 66 CE.).[15] The last of the family, the leader of the Sicarii, Eleazar ben Jair, destroyed himself in the fortress of Masada,[16] as we shall see in the course of our history.

Of the first three procurators,—Coponius, 6-9 CE., Marcus Ambivius, 9-12 CE., and Annius Rufus, 12-15 CE.,—Josephus gives very little detail. Apparently, under the vigilant eye of Augustus they governed with prudence and moderation. The triennial changing of these officials was evidently a part of his policy. Emperor Tiberius who succeeded him, however, was of a different bent. According to the testimony of Tacitus,[17] Tiberius was averse to the frequent change of either military or civil officers in the provincial administration; and Suetonius[18] tells us that this emperor used to instruct his provincial representatives to be like good shepherds, "who shear their sheep, but do not flay them." The motive for not frequently changing his officials is supplied by Josephus, who relates that Tiberius used to compare the provinces to a wounded man on whose bleeding wound a swarm of flies had settled. "If," said the emperor, "these flies, who have sucked their fill, be driven away from the prostrate and defenseless body, they will infallibly be followed by a second swarm, but far more greedy and tormenting, because impelled by hunger."[19] Therefore, during his reign of twenty-three years, Judea had only two procurators,—Valerius Gratus, 15-26 CE., and Pontius Pilate, 26-36 CE.

The greatest eulogium on the administration of the first of these—Valerius Gratus—is that history records no popular outbreak in Judea while he remained in office. Yet, in spite of

[14] Antiq., XX. v. 2.
[15] Bell. Jud., II. xvii. 9; Vita, 5.
[16] Bell. Jud., VII. ix. 1, compare with II. xvii. 9.
[17] Tacitus, Annals, i. 80.
[18] Suetonius, Tiber, xxxii.
[19] Antiq., XVIII. vi. 5.

his good conduct, when Tiberius' prefect of the praetorian guards, Sejanus, through his unlimited favor with the emperor, rose to power,[20] his unscrupulous policy[21] induced him to place in office throughout the provinces creatures of his own ilk, and altogether dependent on him. Such was Pontius Pilate who had gained for himself a dreadful immortality, and whom Jewish and Christian history alike brand with undying infamy.

The very first act by which Pilate introduced himself into office was to show his contempt for his subjects and for their religious laws. Up to this period care had always been taken by the procurator that Roman garrisons never entered Jerusalem with their flags on which appeared offensive eagles or images of the Emperor. Yet Pilate, although knowing well that the religious feelings of the Judeans had never before been outraged on this subject, ordered the transfer of the winter-quarters of his troops from Samaria to Jerusalem with their standards containing such symbols. For five days the people flocked to Caesarea, where the Procurator officially resided, and appealed to him to remove the obnoxious emblems from the Holy City. Pilate refused: he treated the affair as an insult to the honor of the Emperor; and on the sixth day, when he grew tired of their importunities, he ordered them into the hippodrome, into which at the same time he had placed a detachment of soldiers, expecting from here by threats to disperse them. But when the crowd again began to complain, he gave a signal, whereupon his soldiers surrounded the people on all sides with drawn swords. The Jews, however, remained steadfast. As one man they fell on their faces, bared their necks, and declared that they would rather die than suffer their laws to be broken. At last, realizing that further opposition must lead to wholesale slaughter, which he feared would reach the ear of the Emperor, Pilate ordered

[20] Tacitus, Annals, i. 24, iv. 1, 59, 72, and 74.

[21] Compare Antiq., XVIII. vi. 6, with Suetonius, Calig., xii., Tiber., lxv.

the standards removed from Jerusalem.[22] Such imperial ensigns as appeared in the capital thereafter, had, by orders of Tiberius only his name but not his image.[23]

Some time later Pilate began the building of an aqueduct which was to supply water to the city from a spring at a distance of some twenty-two miles; and in order to meet the necessary expenses, he possessed himself of the rich temple-treasury. But as he himself formed all the estimates and rendered account to no one, the people not only accused him of peculation, but some of them assailed him with bitter execrations. Pilate, expecting some such outbreak, ordered a number of his soldiers, armed, but garbed as civilians, to mix among the crowd. When the multitude began to clamor, he gave the preconcerted signal, whereupon the soldiers drew forth their clubs from under their upper garments and attacked the people with even greater cruelty than Pilate had intended. The innocent were knocked down with the guilty and hundreds of lives were lost.[24] Such scenes seem to have been of frequent occurrence with Pilate. Josephus and the Talmud enumerate several. Luke (xiii. 1-2) speaks of a tumult in which the blood of some Galileans "Pilate had mingled with their sacrifices."

The closing act of Pilate's administration in Judea was in keeping with the whole of his previous conduct. A Samaritan false prophet had promised his followers to show them the sacred vessels which Moses had hidden on Mount Gerizim, and a number of them met with the intention of climbing the mountain to dig for the relics. They had committed no breach of the peace, but as they had assembled without permission, they were arrested by Pilate in the village of Tirathaba. A number were killed, and many were imprisoned. Of those im-

[22] Antiq., XVIII. iii. 1; Bell. Jud., II. ix. 2-3.

[23] Philo, De Leg. ad Cajum, 38.

[24] Antiq., XVIII. iii. 2; Bell. Jud., II. ix. 4.—The length of the aqueduct in the Antiquities is given as two hundred stadia, while in the Bellum, as four hundred. But Eusebius, Eccl. Hist., II. vi. 6, to insure "accuracy," makes it three hundred stadia.

prisoned Pilate selected all men of note and property and had them put to death.[25] But the Samaritans, being convinced that no revolution was intended, complained against Pilate to the legate of Syria, Vitellius (the father of the later emperor). Vitellius examined the complaint, and being convinced of the rapacity and misrule of Pilate, he sent immediate orders to the tyrant to return to Rome, there to answer to the charge which he made against him, and appointed Marcellus to the office of Procurator (36 CE.).[26] During the Passover following this incident, Vitellius himself visited Jerusalem and gained the good will of the people, not only by a remission of taxes, but even by giving up the high-priest's garments, which since the year 6 CE. had been in the keeping of the Roman garrison in the fortress of Antonia. The high-priest Joseph Caiaphas, Pilate's partner in crime, was also dismissed during this visit.[27]

Pilate must have taken about a year on his journey to Rome, because on his arrival in Italy he found the emperor Tiberius dead,[28] and his grand-nephew Caius, surnamed Caligula, seated on the throne. The case against Pilate was never tried publicly, nor are his subsequent fortunes told by Josephus. Christian legends depict him either ending his own life, or being executed by the emperor for his proceedings against Jesus. Eusebius (Eccl. Hist., ii. 7) says that soon afterwards, "wearied with misfortunes," he killed himself;

[25] Antiq., XVIII. iv. 1.

[26] Prof. Foakes-Jackson's interpretation of Pilate's cruelties, in his "Josephus and the Jews," p. 163-4, is most repulsive. His rendition of the facts, which is highly partial and utterly inconsistent with history, is even more remarkable when we note, as he himself wishes us to know, that the object of his book is "to supply a key to the study of the works of Josephus, which upon the whole have been rarely read intelligently (!)." "Perverted learning," he elsewhere (p. 27) remarks, "is the plague of sober scholars of the present time," and yet, he himself perverts our records. Dr. Huidekoper, in his interpretation of Pilate's character ("Judaism in Rome," p. 516, note 44), is another such example.

[27] Antiq., XVIII. iv. 3, comp. XV. xi. 4.

[28] Antiq., XVIII. iv. 2.

but according to the apocryphal Paradosis Pilaton it was Tiberius who caused him to be executed; while according to another legend, Pilate was executed by Nero.[29]

Both the harsh treatment by Pilate of the Jews of Judea, and their persecution at Rome and the deportation of four thousand Jewish youths from that city to Sardinia to fight against the hordes of brigands which infested that island, as reported by Josephus,[30] Suetonius,[31] and Tacitus,[32] is attributed by Philo[33] to the intrigues of Pilate's patron Sejanus, who feared that the attachment of the Jews to the emperor might stand in the way of his secret plottings. However, Philo adds that, when after the execution of Sejanus, Tiberius had discovered this, he issued an edict more favorable to the Jews.

During the reign of Augustus, who preceded Tiberius, the Jews throughout the Roman domain had been treated with extraordinary favor. They were not compelled to appear in a court of law on the Sabbath;[34] he gave them their full share of corn, and when a public contribution took place on a Sabbath, their share was to be delivered to them on the following day;[35] and instead of oil furnished by the Greeks, and which the Jews were forbidden to use, they were to receive its equivalent in money,—a usage which continued even as late as Vespasian and Titus.[36]

The inauguration of Caligula, in the year 37 C.E., after the assassination of Tiberius, was greeted with the greatest

[29] On this see, Smith's Dict. of the Bible, "Pilate"; Schuerer, Div. I., Vol. ii. p. 87-8; also Keim's "Jesus of Nazara," Vol. vi. p. 185.

[30] Antiq., XVIII. iii. 5.

[31] Suetonius, Tiber., xxxvi.

[32] Tacitus, Annals, ii. 85.

[33] Philo, De Leg. ad Cajum, 38.

[34] Antiq., XVI. vi. 1-7.

[35] Philo, De Leg. ad Cajum, 24.

[36] Antiq., XII. iii. 1.

joy throughout the Roman empire, and especially among the Judeans who were the first among the Syrian nationalities who gave the new emperor their oath of allegiance,[37] and offered sacrifices for him.[38] In Rome the joy was so great, that in less than three months after his accession, more than one hundred and sixty thousand animals were sacrificed in the various temples for his prosperity and well-being;[39] and that during the first and second year he well deserved the love of his people is attested by Josephus. But in the process of time his mind became diseased[40] to such an extent that his hallucinations, cruelties and obscenities as recorded by Suetonius[41] and Josephus[42] would be too repelling for publication. In his saner moments, though always aggravated, impatient, suffering from sleeplessness, and occasionally liable to faintness,[43] he was aware of his dementedness, for he regarded his child as inheriting it from himself: "He considered its savage temper as the surest proof that it was his child."[44]

The predominating idea in Caligula's mind was to carry out the new worship introduced by Augustus, that of the reigning emperor, the man-god.[45] Tiberius had modestly rejected his divine honors,[46] but the principle that the emperor had the right to be worshipped as a god was confirmed by him, and he regarded the refusal to worship him as a proof of hostility to his person.[47] To most of the pagan nations a god more or less made no difference, but for the Jews Caligula's claim to divine honors was a question of life and

[37] Antiq., XVIII. v. 3.
[38] Philo, De Leg. ad Cajum, 32.
[39] Suetonius, Calig., xiv.
[40] Antiq., XVIII. iii. 2, near end.
[41] Suetonius, Calig., xxvii-xxxvi, xlix.
[42] Antiq., XIX. ii. 5.
[43] Caligula was unable to sleep more than three hours in a night and then not soundly.—Suetonius, Calig., L.
[44] Suetonius, Calig., xxv.
[45] Antiq., XVIII. vii. 2, end; Bell. Jud., II. x. 1.
[46] Tacitus, Annals, iv. 37-8.
[47] Philo, De Leg. ad Cajum, 11-15; Suetonius, Calig., xxvii.

death. When Caligula's mandate, requiring his statue to be set up in the Temple, reached Jerusalem, Vitellius had already resigned as legate of Syria. The new legate, Petronius, a kind-hearted and clear-headed man, soon perceived how difficult it would be to gain obedience by the Jews, even if force were employed against them.

No sooner had intelligence spread over the country than many thousands of the people, "coming upon him like a cloud," assembled from all quarters. Without distinction of rank, age or sex, unarmed, defenseless and dressed in the deepest mourning, the mass deputation appeared before the Legate. Approaching him, the body of old men leading the van addressed Petronius in the following terms:

> *"We are as you see, without any arms,... even the very weapons of defense with which nature has provided each individual, namely our hands, we have fettered behind where they can do nothing, offering our bodies freely as an easy aim to any one who desires to put us to death. We have brought unto you our wives, and our children, and our families, and in your person we will prostrate ourselves before Caius, having left not a single person home, that you may either preserve us all, or destroy us all together by one general and complete destruction.*
>
> *"Petronius, we are a peaceful nation, both by our natural disposition and by our determined intentions, and the education which has been industriously and carefully instilled into us has taught us this lesson from our very earliest infancy. When Caius assumed the imperial power we were the first people in all Syria to congratulate him. Vitellius, whom you succeeded as governor, was at that time in our city. Writings concerning these matters were sent to him, and the happy news, proceeding onward from here, where it had been received with joy, reached the other cities and found similar acceptance. Ours was*

the first temple which received sacrifices for the happy reign of Caius. Did it do so that it might be the first or the only temple to be deprived of its customary modes of worship?

"We have now left our cities, we have abandoned our houses and our possessions, and we will cheerfully contribute to you all our furniture, all our cattle, and all our treasures, everything in short which belongs to us as a willing booty. We shall think that we are receiving them, not giving them up. We only ask one thing instead of and to counterbalance all of them, namely, that no innovation may take place in respect of our temple, but that it may be kept such as we have received it from our fathers and our forefathers. And if we cannot prevail upon you in this, then we offer ourselves up for destruction, that we may not live to behold a calamity more terrible and grievous than death...."

Petronius, having first sternly rebuked the Jews, and placed before them his own obligation toward his sovereign by pointing out that it was the command of one who was his master, was reluctant to attempt what he was ordered to do. He reasoned with himself what a wicked piece of daring he should be committing, in the first place because of the natural principles of justice and piety by which they were dictated, and secondly because of the danger which threatened any attempt at innovation upon them,—a nation "not infinite in numbers only at home, but also spread over the whole face of the earth, of great courage and spirit, and men who are willing to die in defense of their national customs and laws with unshrinking bravery." Petronius, therefore, hesitated long, attaching great weight to all considerations, and finally resolved to delay the erecting of the statue in the temple for a more deliberate consideration of the matter.[48]

[48] Philo, De Leg. ad Cajum (Bohn's transl.), 30-32; Antiq., XVIII. viii. 2; Bell. Jud., II. x. 1-3.

Different, however, was the case in Alexandria. Already the year before, a deadly conflict had been on the point of breaking out between Greek and Jewish inhabitants of that city. The hatred between the two races was still smouldering. Consequently, knowing that the Jews would not submit to the introduction of the imperial statue into their places of worship, and being equally certain that Caligula would sustain those who upheld his godhead, the Greeks of Alexandria welcomed the opportunity to vent their rage and jealousy against the more prosperous and powerful Jews.[49] The Roman viceroy of Egypt at that time was Avilius Flaccus. During his rulership of five years (32-37 CE.) under the former emperor Tiberius, he had administered his office in a faultless manner.[50] Under Caligula, however, for some uncertain reason, he became careless of business and dilatory in all important duties of his office, and consequently fell out of favor with the emperor. The death of his powerful friends at Rome, young Tiberius, the grandson of the emperor Tiberius, and of Macro, who alone had any influence over Caligula, deprived him of his last support at the court. Flaccus' great anxiety now was to regain the favor which he had lost with the emperor. To accomplish this, he determined to ingratiate himself with the Greeks under his jurisdiction, in order that their good reports to Rome might plead his cause and praise the efficiency of his government.

Accordingly, Flaccus changed everything which had existed before. He relaxed the vigorous discipline of his police; he alienated himself from the Jews who up to then were his dearest friends, and reconciled himself with the Greeks who were his declared enemies and used them as his advisers, "so that the governor became a subject and the subjects became

[49] According to Philo, "Against Flaccus," sec. 6, near end, the Jewish population of Alexandria, together with the scattered settlers throughout Egypt, amounted to, at that time, not less than one million.

[50] Philo, Ag. Flaccus, 3.

the governor."[51] Encouraged by this changed state of affairs, and unhindered, the Greeks proceeded with a general attack on the Jewish quarters.[52] Beginning with the placing of the imperial statues in the synagogues,[53] while at the same time Flaccus himself pronounced the Jews as no longer citizens, the mob proceeded with ransacking and pillaging of over four hundred Jewish shops and warehouses.[54] Jews were slain with the sword or publicly burnt.[55] Flaccus not only permitted this to go on without interfering, but also assisted in the barbarous proceedings. In the boundlessness of his wickedness, he arrested thirty-eight members of the Jewish Council of Elders, marched them through the market-place, some with their hands bound, others in irons, where they were beaten with such severity that some died of their wounds, while others were precipitated into long and severe illness.[56] Under the pretext of searching for arms, a centurion named Castor, with a small band, entered Jewish houses from where the females of each family were dragged to theaters and denuded for public view.[57] A decree of the Jews of Alexandria in which they offered to Caligula all honors compatible with their laws and an explanation of their attitude in reference to the honors demanded by him, and which Flaccus had promised to send to the emperor, was treacherously withheld by him.[58]

But in the scheme of the Infinite Ruler, retribution was bound to come. In the autumn of the year 38 a centurion, Bassus, with a company of soldiers, was sent by Caligula to arrest Flaccus. Having embarked on one of the speediest vessels, and being assisted by most favorable winds, Bassus made a fast crossing, and in a few days arrived at the harbor of

[51] Philo, Ag. Flaccus, 3-4.
[52] Philo, Ag. Flaccus, 6-8.
[53] Philo, Ag. Flaccus, 7.
[54] Philo, Ag. Flaccus, 8 and 11.
[55] Philo, Ag. Flaccus, 9; De Leg. ad Cajum, 19.
[56] Philo, Ag. Flaccus, 10.
[57] Philo, Ag. Flaccus, 11.
[58] Philo, Ag. Flaccus, 12.

Alexandria. He delayed his landing till night, for he intended to debark his soldiers secretly. Flaccus was at the time feasting at a banquet. To explore the banqueting-hall and the conditions therein, before taking any action, Bassus disguised one of his soldiers as a servant and sent him in to mingle with the guests and to gather all the information that was necessary. And when the soldier reported that Flaccus was bodyguarded by only ten slaves, Bassus gave a signal to his soldiers to enter, and he with them surrounded Flaccus before he could realize who was before him. At the sight of Bassus, Flaccus became dumb with amazement and consternation; for even without hearing what Caligula's commands were, he knew that he was enjoying his last banquet. Flaccus was immediately taken as a prisoner to Rome, where upon the accusations of Isidore and Lampson, his properties were confiscated, and he himself banished to the Island of Andros, where soon after he was put to death in a horrible manner by order of Caligula.[59] When the news of the arrest of Flaccus spread abroad the Jews did not rejoice over the ruin of their enemy, for that was forbidden in the Law (Lev., xix. 18; Prov., xx. 22), but praised God, and sang hymns and songs of thanksgiving.[60]

Two years later (40 CE.), in consequence of the continuing conflicts between the Greeks and the Jews of Alexandria, a deputation from each of the parties arrived in Rome to lay the whole history of the late disturbances before the Emperor. At the head of the Jewish party was Philo, the author from whose writings the present account has been extracted; the leader of the other party was the Greek historian, Apion, a determined enemy of the Jews. The records which we possess in connection with these embassies are very scanty. According to the very short account of Josephus, however, the reception which Caligula gave the Jewish envoys

[59] Philo, Ag. Flaccus, 13-14, 19, 21. His departure took place during the Feast of Tabernacles.

[60] Philo, Ag. Flaccus, 14.

was not very flattering: the Emperor hardly permitted them to speak, and "was in such a rage, that it openly appeared he was about to do them some very great harm."[61] In the account of Philo, which is considerably more detailed, the chief substance of the result is that after a lengthy interview, during which the emperor ran from one apartment to another, finding fault with and giving orders to his attendants, while also hurling questions at the constantly following delegates without condescending to listen to their replies, he finally dismissed them with the remark, "These men do not appear so wicked as unfortunate and stupid, in not believing that I have been endowed with the nature of God."[62] And thus, affairs at Alexandria remained in suspense until the death of Caligula.[63]

Again, at Jerusalem, Petronius was still hesitating. The several expedients whereby he sought to persuade the Jews to submit to the command of the Emperor for the installation of his statue in the Temple, "because the army of Syria was all ready, and would soon cover the country with cadavers," were of no avail.[64] Harvest time was now approaching, and the whole land remained unreaped. Finally, Petronius determined to write to the emperor, offering an incorrect explanation for the delay so far in the erection of his statue, and entreating for more time, partly because the preparation required it, and partly because it was then the very height of the wheat harvest, which it would be advisable to see gathered in, since otherwise, in their despair, the Jews might burn the whole corn-bearing district.[65]

When Caligula had read the letter, he became furious at the inactivity of his legate; and unable to muster such wit and courage as he needed for the occasion, he ordered his secretary to write the answer. In the reply, the secretary

[61] Antiq., XVIII. i. 1.
[62] Philo, De Leg. ad Cajum, 25-29, 44-46.
[63] Antiq., XIX. v. 2.
[64] Antiq., XIX. v. 2; Philo, De Leg. ad Cajum, 31.
[65] Philo, De Leg. ad Cajum, 33.

ostensibly praised Petronius for his prudence in the conduct of his office, but advised him to speed up the erection and dedication of the emperor's statue, since by this time the harvesting must also be over.[66]

The humane Petronius shrank from the task of commencing a war of massacre and extermination for such an object, and perplexed as to how he should carry out this mad scheme of Caligula, he once more entered into negotiations with the Jews, urging upon them the power of the Romans, the positive mandate of the emperor, and the uniform obedience of all other nations. But when many thousands of the people again met him with entreaties and supplications not to defile their city with the dedication of the statue, Petronius sent a true statement of the case to Caligula, recommending that upon the grounds of equity and prudence it would be most advisable to recall the mandate. Thus, knowing well the danger to which he exposed himself by his disobedience to the emperor, he dismissed the people, bade them return to their fields, promised to assist them as far as he was able, and wished them, "May God help you." [67]

But before Petronius' letter reached Rome, Agrippa I, who at that time was living in Italy, learned what was happening in Palestine, and addressed a very long and elaborate entreaty to the emperor in the effort to induce him to recall the offensive edict.[68] Agrippa I was the son of Aristobulus, the son of Herod by the Hasmonean Mariamne, and of Berenice the daughter of Salome. The vicissitudes encountered and the changes of fortune experienced by this prince during his early life are so strange and so numerous that the events concerning him recorded by Josephus [69] and Philo [70] would fur-

[66] Philo, De Leg. ad Cajum, 34.

[67] Antiq., XVIII. viii. 3-6; Bell. Jud., II. x. 3-5.

[68] Philo, De Leg. ad Cajum, 35-41.

[69] Antiq., XVIII. vi. 1-7, and 10-11, vii. 1-2, viii. 7-8, XIX. v. 1-4; Bell. Jud., II. ix. 5-6, xi. 16

[70] Philo, Ag. Flaccus, 5-6, 12; De Leg. ad Cajum, 35-41.

nish material sufficient for a separate volume. He was born in the year 10 BCE.[71] After the execution of his father, when Agrippa was six years of age, his grandfather Herod sent him to Rome for his education. The Emperor Tiberius conceived a great affection for the child and placed him as a companion to his son Drusus, whose favor he very soon won. On the untimely death of Drusus, which occurred in 23 CE., however, as Tiberius forbade all friends of his deceased son to come within his sight so they might not revive his grief, Agrippa I was forbidden to come before him; and having thus lost his means of support he was obliged to go back to Palestine, where he shut himself up in an old castle at Malatha, a village south of Hebron, depending on the charity of his family. After a brief seclusion, Antipas the tetrarch, his uncle, made him chief magistrate of Tiberius and presented him with a large sum of money. His uncle, however, soon begrudged the continuance of his support, reproached him for bad economy, and when he could no longer endure the humiliation with which he accompanied his favors, he became a hanger-on of Pomponius Flaccus, the Roman governor of Syria.[72]

Weary of eating the bread of poverty and dependence, Agrippa resolved to try his fortune again in Rome. The Emperor now received him with favor and entrusted him with the supervision of his grandson Claudius, the son of Drusus. But Agrippa, regarding the orphan as an unprofitable acquaintance, chose rather to attach himself to Caius (Caligula), who at that time was universally beloved, and so far won over this prince that he kept him continually about him. Agrippa, however, having one day been overheard by Eutychus, a slave with whom he had made free, to express his wishes for Tiberius' death in order to make room for his friend Caius, was betrayed to the emperor. For this Agrippa

[71] This is evident from Antiq., XIX. viii. 2, according to which he died in 44 CE., at the age of fifty-four.

[72] Antiq., XVIII. vi. 1-2.

was thrown into prison, where he remained for six months, till Tiberius died (37 CE.).[73]

With the death of Tiberius and the coming of Caligula to the throne of Rome began for Agrippa a period of good fortune. The new emperor, even before the funeral was over, delivered his friend from imprisonment, and heaped wealth and favors upon Agrippa. He changed his iron fetters into a chain of gold of equal weight, set a royal diadem upon his head, and gave him the tetrarchy of Batanea, Trachonitis and Auranitis, which Philip the son of Herod had formerly had, and also the district of Lysanias, with the title of king. Agrippa, however, continued to stay in Rome, and it was not until a year and a half later (in the autumn of 38 CE.) that he went back to Palestine to take possession of his kingdom.[74] The imperial favor which Agrippa enjoyed was so great, that even in the year 40, Caligula yet bestowed upon him the tetrarchies of Galilee and Perea which in the previous year, through his own fault, were lost by his uncle Antipas.[75]

But on his departure from Rome, Agrippa had promised the emperor to return after he had set the affairs of his kingdom in order.[76] Accordingly, in the autumn of the same year (40 CE.), after a slow journey,[77] Agrippa was back in Rome, where we still find him in the following January when Caligula was murdered.[78] During this visit Agrippa, by reason of the long-standing friendship and intimacy which had existed between them, on hearing the sad news about the affairs in Palestine, addressed his petition to Caligula for

[73] Antiq., XVIII. vi. 3-7; Bell. Jud., II. ix. 5.

[74] Antiq., XVIII. vi. 10-11; Bell. Jud., II. ix. 6; Philo, Ag. Flaccus, 5.

[75] Antiq., XVIII. vii. 1-2; Bell. Jud., II. ix. 6.

[76] Antiq., XVIII. vi. 2.

[77] That Agrippa had left Palestine in the spring may be deducted from Philo's report in his Leg. ad Cajum, 35, "that he knew absolutely nothing either of what Petronius had written in his letter, or of what Caius had written in his first or second epistle."

[78] Antiq., XIX. iv. 1; Bell. Jud., II. xi. 1-2.

the revocation of his order to Petronius concerning the erection of the imperial statue in the Temple of Jerusalem, showing that none of his predecessors had ever attempted such an innovation in Judea.[79]

The contents of the letter were not entirely pleasing to the emperor. He blamed Agrippa for his excessive desire to please his countrymen, but also praised him for concealing none of his feelings, which conduct, he said, was proof of a liberal and noble disposition. But being appeased, at least as far as appearance went, he condescended to return a favorable answer, granting to Agrippa that highest and greatest of all favors, that the profanation of the Temple should not take place; and commanded a letter to be written to Petronius, instructing him that no change should be made in the Temple at Jerusalem.[80]

At this point, however, a messenger arrived with Petronius' letter relating the difficulties he would encounter were he to attempt to execute the order of his master, advising the emperor also, that in the interest of public tranquillity he must countermand his vicious injunction. This insubordination threw Caligula into such a fury, that, as a punishment for it, he issued an order to Petronius to take his own life. But soon thereafter, as Caligula was passing through a tunnel connecting his palace and the bath-house, he was himself (on January 24th, 41 CE.) murdered;[81] and his Syrian legate, in consequence of storms at sea, did not receive the order for his self-destruction till twenty-seven days after he had already received the news of the emperor's death. So, through God's timely providence, Petronius escaped death.[82] These

[79] Philo, De Leg. ad Cajum, 36-41.

[80] Philo, De Leg. ad Cajum, 42-43.

[81] Concerning the assassination of Caligula, Suetonius (Cal., 58) supplies us with two hearsay accounts, both different. But the single account of Josephus (Antiq., XIX. i. 3-15) is fully detailed and more reliable.

[82] Antiq., XVIII. viii. 7-9; Bell. Jud., II. x. 5.

Private passage between the Palace of Tiberius and the bath-house. It was here that Caligula was killed. (Antiq., XXIX. i. 14.)

tidings reached Jerusalem on the 22nd day of Shebat, which was thereafter celebrated as a day of great rejoicing.[83]

The madman Caius, after a reign of three years and eight months, was succeeded by his uncle Claudius (41-54 CE.). Claudius, born at Lyons in 10 BCE., was the son of Drusus and Antonia, and a grandson of Livia, the wife of Emperor Augustus. His father died when he was an infant, and during the whole of his minority he was afflicted with a variety of physical and mental disorders, to such an extent that after his arrival at years of maturity he was never thought sufficiently qualified for any public or private employment. Paralyzed and lame, and unable to speak with distinctness, he was an object of scorn even to his own mother; and the natural diffidence and timidity of his character were increased by neglect and insult, till he was regarded as little better than an imbecile. His time was spent chiefly in the society of servants, and devoted to the industrious pursuit of literature; and until his accession he took no real part in public affairs, though Caligula had honored him with the dignity of Consul.[84]

Among those who, after the murder of Caligula, were most active in securing the throne to Claudius was Agrippa.

[83] See Jewish traditions in Derenbourg, pp. 207f. (?).

[84] The principal authority for the life of Claudius is the Annals of Tacitus, in whose highly colored picture there is much that gives rise to a suspicion of exaggeration. Suetonius and Dion Cassius are even less trustworthy. The extent of Claudius' literary labors alone seem to preclude the possibility of excessive habitual irregularities as are attributed to him by Suetonius, such as drunkenness, gambling, and addiction to women (Suet., Claud., v.), or of any mental inferiority (Suet., Claud., ii.). When yet a young man, Suetonius in spite of himself tells us that Claudius composed a Roman history in no less than forty-one books; and "A Defense of Cicero against the Books of Assassinius Gallus,"—"which exhibited a considerable degree of learning." He also invented three new letters, and added them to the former alphabet, as highly necessary, and published a book to show their necessity. Even after his elevation to the throne, Claudius wrote twenty books on the Etruscans, and eight on the Carthagenians (Suet., Claud., xli-xlii.). This power of application seems quite inconsistent with the weakness of intellect which his maligners so freely imputed to him.

The Roman senate for a while began to talk of restoring the ancient republic and its form of government; [85] and chiefly through the influence and diplomacy of Agrippa was Claudius recognized as emperor. He persuaded the Senate to abandon their resistance to the infuriated soldiery; reassured them concerning the "weak and unambitious" spirit of Claudius; and at the same time dissuaded him from taking those violent measures against the Senate, to which the army were urging him, and which would have deluged Rome with blood.[86] His services were amply repaid by the grateful emperor. Claudius reconstructed and bestowed upon him the kingdom of Judea with all its dependencies, so that it was as possessed by his grandfather, Herod the Great; he even enlarged it by the tetrarchy of Abilene, the district at the foot of Antilibanus. He entered into a solemn alliance with the new king, issued several decrees in favor of the Jews,[87] and at the request of Agrippa bestowed the principality of Chalcis, in Lebanon, on his brother Herod II. Agrippa I even obtained the honors of consulship, and his brother was appointed Praetor, which entitled both to a seat in the Senate—a dignity which at that time was regarded as the highest on earth, next to the Emperor. The confirmation of these grants was made with the utmost publicity. The edict announcing them contained a high eulogium on Agrippa, and the act was registered on a bronze tablet and placed in the Capitol.[88] In remembrance of these events, coins were also struck, bearing on one side two clasped hands with the inscription, "Friendship of King Agrippa with the Roman Senate and People"; on the other side was the emperor between two figures, and "King Agrippa, friend of the Emperor." [89] Thus laden with honors, Agrippa left for Judea.

[85] Antiq., XIX. ii. 1, 3-4.

[86] Antiq., XIX. iv. 1-5; Bell. Jud., II. xi. 1-5.

[87] For these decrees see, Antiq., XIX. v. 2-3.

[88] Antiq., XIX. v. 1; Bell. Jud., II. xi. 5.

[89] For these coins see Madden's "Numismatic Chronicle" (1875), pp. 69-76; and his "Coins of the Jews" (1881), p. 136f.

Emperor Tiberius. Emperor Caligula. Emperor Claudius.

The first act by which he celebrated his arrival at Jerusalem was indicative of the spirit and disposition with which he was to conduct the government of his kingdom. "He offered all the sacrifices that belonged to him," says Josephus, "and omitted nothing which the the Law required"; and the golden chain which Caligula had bestowed upon him in exchange for the iron one with which he had been bound as a prisoner, he hung over the temple-treasury, as a memorial of the rapid change of human fortune and of the protection of the Almighty Providence.[90] In spite of the contempt and scorn shown to Agrippa by some Christian writers[91] for his alleged execution of James the brother of John and his imprisonment of Peter, as recorded in Acts, xii. 1f., Josephus and the Talmud never weary of praising his humaneness and uprightness. "This king," Josephus again tells us, "was by nature very beneficent and liberal in his gifts, . . . he took delight in giving, and rejoiced in living with a good reputation. He was not at all like Herod, who was cruel and severe . . . and had no mercy on those whom he hated, but was mild and compassionate, and equally generous with all men. He was humane also to foreigners, and made them sensible of his liberality. He loved to live continually at Jerusalem, and was scrupulously careful in the observance of the laws of his country."[92] That the poor idolater be aided with alms, the sick tended and the dead buried, just like Israelites, the Talmud[93] tells us, were among Agrippa's regulations; and when the people carried the first fruits into the Temple, "even King Agrippa himself took his basket upon his shoulders, and went up until he came into the court," etc.[94] When on one occasion some young Greeks carried a statue of the emperor into the synagogue of Dora, Agrippa used his influence with

[90] Antiq., XIX. vi. 1.

[91] Foakes-Jackson, "Josephus and the Jews," pp. 152f., 270f., and many other authors.

[92] Antiq., XIX. vii. 3.

[93] Gittin, 61a.

[94] Mishna, Bikkurim, iii. 4.

the governor of Syria, so that not only was any such future outrage strictly forbidden, but Petronius also ordered the centurion Proculus Vitellius to bring the guilty parties before him for an accounting.[95] And when he betrothed his daughter Drusilla to Epiphanes, Prince of Commagene, it was on the condition that he submit to circumcision; but when Epiphanes later would not fulfil his promise, the marriage was not consummated.[96] He reëstablished an old law (Deut., xxxi. 10ff.) that obliged the king to read the Book of Deuteronomy in the court of the Temple at the end of each Sabbatical year; and when on the eighth day of the Feast of Tabernacles (in 41 CE.), he performed the act and came to the passage, "From among thy brethren shalt thou set a king over thee; thou mayest not set a stranger over thee which is not thy brother" (Deut., xvii. 15), he burst into tears, because he felt himself referred to in it.[97] But the people cried out to him, "Be not grieved, Agrippa! Thou art our brother; thou art our brother."[98]

Unfortunately, however, the happy era of Agrippa's rule was not of long duration. After a reign of little more than three years he died very unexpectedly in the fifty-fourth year

[95] Antiq., XIX. vi. 3.

[96] Antiq., XX. vii. 1.

[97] According to the Law (Deut., xxiii. 7-8), an Idumean was a Jew; for when the Idumeans, about 120 BCE., went over to Judaism, their descendants in the third generation became full members of the faith. But Agrippa, though of Idumean descent and of Maccabean lineage, and in spite of his deep devotion to the Jewish religion and reverence toward God, was in the eyes of the Law not a Jew. For, in the first place, Agrippa's great-grandfather, Antipater, who, about 69 BCE., was counselor to Hyrcanus II and later Caesar's governor of Judea, was not begotten in the third generation, but in the second, when the Law had not yet recognized him as a Jew. Secondly, according to Josephus, Bell. Jud., I. viii. 9, Antipater's wife Cypros, was neither of the Idumean race nor of the Jewish faith but an Arabian woman. Therefore, since Agrippa was a descendant of this unratified and mixed ancestry, his religious status was the same as that to which the Idumeans belonged before their conversion to Judaism by John Hyrcanus I.

[98] Mishna, Sota, vii. 8.

of his age (44 CE.),[99] leaving besides his three daughters, Berenice 16 years, Mariamne 10 years, and Drusilla 6 years old, only one son, then in his seventeenth year, whose name was also Agrippa.[100]

[99] Antiq., XIX. viii. 2.
[100] Antiq., XIX. ix. 1; Bell. Jud., II. xi. 6.

Bronze coin of
King Agrippa I.

CHAPTER V

JUDEA *under the* PROCURATORS,
from CUSPIUS FADUS *to* GESSIUS FLORUS,
44-66 CE.

✻

SINCE Agrippa the Second was yet too young to bear the burden of royalty, the Emperor Claudius decided to restore the system of government which had existed in Judea previous to the reign of Agrippa I, and appointed Cuspius Fadus as Procurator. Out of respect for the memory of the deceased king, Claudius especially selected this man, whom he considered a worthy successor, and made him independent of the Syrian governor, Vibius Marsus, who had always been hostile to Agrippa, and the Judeans.

His very first act after entering office was to clear the country of highwaymen and robbers, who under the easy rule of Agrippa had grown numerous and vicious. But that Fadus was not especially brilliant is proved by his demand that the pontifical robes, which during the period of the earlier procurators (6-36 CE.) had lain under Roman custody and had been given up by Vitellius in 36 CE., should again be committed to the charge of the Romans. The Jews, greatly irritated over this uncalled-for annoyance, sent a deputation to Rome, which through the intercession of young Agrippa obtained a mandate from Claudius that, in the matter of the high-priestly garments, things should remain as they had been.

> *The edict reads:—"Claudius Caesar ... to the Magistrates, Senate and the People, and the whole nation of the Jews sendeth greetings.*
>
> *Upon presentation of your ambassadors to me by Agrippa my friend, whom I have brought up and have now with me, ... who have come to give me thanks for the care I haven taken of your nation, and to entreat me ... that they may have the holy vestments, with the crown belonging to them, in their possession, I grant their request, as that excellent person, Vitellius, who is very dear to me, had done before me. And I have complied with your desire, in the first place, out of regard to that piety which I profess, and because I would have everyone worship God according to the laws of their own country; and this I do also, because I shall hereby highly gratify ... Agrippa, junior, whose sacred regards to me, and earnest good-will to you, I am well acquainted with. ... Now I have written about these affairs to Cuspius Fadus, my procurator. The names of those who brought me your letter are Cornelius the son of Cero, Trypho the son of Theudio, Dorotheus the son of Nathaniel, and John the son of John. This is dated before the fourth of the calends of July, when Rufus and Pompeius Sylvanus are consuls."*[1]

At the same time Herod II, Prince of Chalcis, asked for and obtained the supervision of the Temple and its treasury, and the power to appoint high-priests; whereupon he dismissed Elionaios, son of Kantheras,[2] and appointed Joseph, son of Kamith.[3]

During the short administration of Fadus (44-?), Judea

[1] Antiq., XIX. ix. 2, XX. i. 1-2.
[2] Mishna, Para, iii. 5, identifies him as the son of Caiaphas.
[3] Antiq., XX. i. 3.

was visited with a severe famine, and the sufferings of the people were extreme. They were, however, liberally assisted by Isates, the king of Adiabene, and his mother Helena,[3a] both proselytes to Judaism. This king, a feudatory of Parthia, reigned over the territories situated on the river Tigris, and which contained a numerous Jewish population. He had lately been induced by the teaching of a traveling merchant, Ananias, to embrace Judaism. His mother and his brothers—one of whom, Monobazus II, succeeded him to the throne—had joined him in his new faith.[4]

Before his recall, Fadus was confronted with an unhappy occurrence which led to open war and bloodshed. An impostor, named Theudas, pretending to be a prophet or messiah, persuaded a number of people to follow him to the Jordan, where on his mere word, he asserted, he would divide the river and lead them across it. But when his band of followers approached the river, carrying with them all their possessions, they were met by Fadus' cavalry, who killed many of them, or made them prisoners, and struck off the head of their leader.[5] Shortly after this incident Fadus was recalled and his place was taken by Tiberius Alexander.

Tiberius Alexander (?-48 CE.), though the son of the pious Alexandrian Alabarch, i.e., president of the Jewish community, and a nephew of the philosopher Philo, was himself an apostate Jew. His rule was marked by continuous famine,[6] and the only fact that is recorded about him is that he caused the crucifixion of two bandit leaders Jacob and Simon, the sons of the notorious bandit leader, Judas of Galilee. During his time also, Herod II died, and his dominion of Chalcis,

[3a] Antiq., XX. ii. 5, v. 2.

[4] Antiq., XX. ii. 2-3.

[5] Antiq., XX. v. 1.

[6] In regard to this famine compare besides Antiq., XX. v. 2, also III. xv. 3, XX. ii. 5, and Acts, xi. 28. (Antiq., III. xv. 3, contains an error:—"When Claudius was emperor and Ismael was our high-priest," should read, "and Ananias was our high-priest." Claudius died in 54 CE., and Ismael was not appointed until 59 CE.)

the supervision of the Temple, and the title of King were assigned to young Agrippa,[7] hereafter known as Agrippa II.

Ventidius Cumanus (48-52 CE.) was the third Procurator. During the Passover of his first year in office, a soldier belonging to a detachment customarily stationed at Jerusalem at festival seasons to preserve order, indecently exposed his person towards the Temple. The enraged people demanded immediate satisfaction from the procurator; for they felt it unlikely that a Roman soldier would indulge in such conduct unless he knew it would not be rebuked by his superior. Cumanus, fearing that the matter might reach Rome, and knowing Emperor Claudius' desire to maintain peace, attempted to hush the incident. But when the clamoring people would not be appeased unless he granted them redress, he ordered the entire legion to charge the crowds. In routing them through the narrow streets, two thousand persons were crushed or trampled to death.[8]

Scarcely had this upheaval ended when another followed. On the highway, about twelve miles north-west of Jerusalem, an imperial official named Stephanus, while traveling, was attacked by a band of Sicarii and robbed of all his belongings. As a punishment for this, Cumanus sent a troop of soldiers to pillage the villages in the vicinity where the deed was committed. During this devastation a soldier found a Torah and tore it to pieces. The Jews sent a deputation to Cumanus to demand the punishment of the blasphemer. Cumanus, yielding to the advice of his friends, ordered the soldier to be executed.[9]

A more serious clash with Cumanus cost him his office. A group of Galilean Jews on a pilgrimage to Jerusalem, were, due to the intermediate position of that district, compelled to travel through Samaria. While passing through a village of that section, however, they were waylaid by some of the

[7] Antiq., XX. v. 2.
[8] Antiq., XX. v. 3; Bell. Jud., II. xii. 1.
[9] Antiq., XX. v. 4; Bell. Jud., II. xii. 2.

villagers and murdered. The Jews sought satisfaction from Cumanus, but he, having previously been bribed by the Samaritans, took no action. When it was seen that the guilty would go unpunished, the Zealots, under the leadership of Eleazar and Alexander, took it upon themselves to avenge the crime. Their armed men made a sudden attack upon Samaria, killing men, women and children, and setting some of their villages on fire. Thereupon Cumanus marched against the Zealots, and with the aid of the Samaritans, whom he had armed, and a portion of his forces, killed a number of the insurgents and took many of them prisoners. The principal citizens of Jerusalem, alarmed at the possible consequences of an outbreak against the imperial government, entreated the Zealots to pause and think, lest they should bring disaster on the city. These persuasions prevailed upon them and the Zealots went back to their caves in the mountains, but after this all Judea was subject to their robberies.[10] In the meantime ambassadors, both Jewish and Samaritan, appeared before Ummidius Quadratus, the governor of Syria, with complaints against each other and with additional accusations by the Jews against Cumanus that he had accepted a Samaritan bribe. Quadratus went to Samaria and made a thorough investigation. Having examined the case on the spot, he condemned the Samaritans, but put to death, as seditious persons, all those taken by Cumanus. He then removed his tribunal to Lydda where he heard the Samaritans a second time. There he learned that a Zealot named Dortus and four others were instigating rebellion against the Romans. Quadratus ordered them put to death, and sent Ananias, the high-priest, and Ananus, the captain of the Temple, to Rome to stand trial for their share in the sedition. Cumanus and his tribune Celer were also sent to Rome to answer for their conduct before the Emperor, as also the principal men of both the Samaritans and the Zealots. Having heard all the culprits, Claudius condemned the Samaritans, and ordered three of their ringleaders

[10] Antiq., XX. vi. 1; Bell. Jud., II. xii. 3-5.

put to death. He also ordered Celer returned to Jerusalem to be dragged through the streets and then beheaded in sight of all the people. Cumanus was sent into banishment.[11]

At the request of a former high-priest, Jonathan, the Emperor Claudius appointed Felix (52-60 CE.) as the next procurator of Judea.[12] According to Tacitus,[13] Felix was already in Palestine as an independent governor of Samaria, where he had instigated the bloody conflicts, and should have appeared with Cumanus as a criminal before Quadratus. But Quadratus, knowing Felix's relationship and great influence with the Emperor,[14] passed him over, and even placed him by his side to take part in the trial as judge. Describing Felix's rulership in Samaria, the Roman historian tells us, "Mutual depredations were committed, bands of robbers employed, ambuscades formed, and sometimes battles fought for the spoils and booty obtained therefrom which were given to the governor, . . . while he exercised the authority of a king with the spirit of a slave, relying upon the great power of his brother Pallas at Court, and thinking he might safely be guilty of all kinds of wicked practices."[15] If, therefore, in Jonathan's selection of Felix the Jews had hoped for a just and able official, they were very soon disillusioned.

With Felix began the great drama which ended with the revolt and war against Rome in the year 70. While under Cumanus the uprisings had been sporadic, under Felix rebellion became permanent. First of all, due to his tyranny, the Zealots won a greater sympathy and larger following among the people. Contriving by treachery to lay hands on their

[11] Antiq., XX. vi. 2-3; Bell. Jud., II. xii. 5-7.

[12] Antiq., XX. vii. 1; Bell. Jud., II. xii. 8. For Jonathan, compare Antiq., XX. viii. 5 about middle, with Bell. Jud., II. xii. 6 middle.

[13] Tacitus, Annals, xii. 54.

[14] Felix was three times married. One of his wives was a granddaughter of Mark Antony, who was the grandfather of Claudius (Tacit., Hist., v. 9).

[15] Compare Tacitus' History, v. 9, Annals, xii. 53-54, and Suetonius' Claudius, xxviii.

leader, Eleazar, who for twenty years had ravaged the country, he sent him, together with those of his party whom he had already in prison, to Rome for judgment. But while the country was thus cleared of the Zealots, a still more fanatical faction of bandits was springing up in Jerusalem, the Sicarii, who committed murders in broad daylight in the heart of the city. Carrying short daggers (sicae), from which they received their names,[16] concealed under their clothing, they mixed among the crowds, especially during the festival seasons, and stabbed their enemies, and, pretending deep sorrow, succeeded in avoiding suspicion themselves. The first to be assassinated by them was Jonathan the high-priest, who, as a man of moderate sentiment, was hated by the Sicarii as well as by the procurator Felix, whom he had often admonished to act more worthily in the administration of his office, lest he should be blamed by the people for having recommended him as governor. Felix, weary with Jonathan's importunities, employed a band of Sicarii under the leadership of Doras to put him out of his way.[17]

With the Sicarii there were associated false messiahs, who no less than they themselves, ruined the peace of the country. Under the pretense of divine inspiration fostering revolutionary changes they persuaded the people to follow them into the wilderness in order that they might show them "the tokens foreshadowing deliverance." Against them Felix, who regarded this as the beginning of a revolt, sent a body of horsemen and footmen, who put a great number to the sword.[18] About this time also, an Egyptian impostor appeared in Jerusalem, who said he was a prophet and forerunner of the Messiah. He gathered around him about thirty thousand dupes and persuaded them to follow him to the Mount of Olives where he would perform a miracle. He announced that

[16] In Latin, "Sicarius" is the common designation for a murderer. Thus for example, the law passed under Sulla against murderers is called, "Lex Cornelia de Sicariis."

[17] Antiq., XX. viii. 5; Bell. Jud., II. xiii. 2-3.

[18] Bell. Jud., II. xiii. 4; Antiq., XX. viii. 6.

with one word he would cause the walls of Jerusalem to fall, wrest the government from the hands of the Romans, and re-establish the Jewish nation in all its original glory. Felix did not give the prophet time to perform his miracle, but met him with heavy artillery. Four hundred of his followers were killed; two hundred were taken prisoners, while the remainder dispersed and escaped to their homes. But the Egyptian disappeared.[19]

No sooner were these disorders reduced than the inflammation, as in a diseased body, broke out in another quarter. The Sicarii and the messiahs, banding together, persuaded the masses to revolt, exhorting them to assert their independence, and threatening to kill anyone who submitted to Roman domination. Distributing themselves in companies throughout the country, they looted the houses of the wealthy, murdered their owners, and set the villages on fire.[20] Besides these movements of popular agitators, sedition arose among the high-priests themselves, leading to the increase of confusion. "Each of them formed his own company from among the boldest bandits, and when they struggled together, they did it by casting reproaches and throwing stones at one another." Due to this chaos which prevailed in Palestine under Felix, the high-priests became so audacious that they sent their servants to the threshing-floors to carry away by force the shares of corn that were due to the minor priests, and which were habitually and gladly given to them as tithes, with the result that many of these unfortunates died from hunger.[21]

A conflict arose also between the Jewish and Syrian-Greek inhabitants at Caesarea, over the question of equality in citizen rights. The Jews claimed certain advantages and privileges in that city on the ground that its founder, King Herod, was a Jew. The Greeks admitted the Jewish origin, but maintained that the city itself belonged to the Greeks,

[19] Bell. Jud., II. xiii. 5; Antiq., XX. viii. 6.
[20] Bell. Jud., II. xiii. 6; Antiq., XX. viii. 6, near end.
[21] Antiq., XX. viii. 8; see also ix. 4.

since Herod would never have erected the statues and temples which he placed there had he intended it for Jews. The feud became gradually more fierce, and street rioting and bloodshed an everyday occurrence. At last on one occasion, when the Jews had gained an advantage over the Greeks, Felix stepped in, dispersed the Jews with great loss of life, and permitted his soldiers to plunder some of their houses, "which were full of riches." The disorder continuing, Felix selected the most prominent of both parties and sent them to Rome in order that the matter might be settled by the Emperor.[22] In the year 60 CE., however, even before the question had been determined, Felix, having governed for eight years, was recalled by Nero.[23]

The next procurator (60-62 CE.) was Porcius Festus.[24] Though himself inclined toward kindness and justice, he was unable to undo the mischief done by Felix. The Sicarii grew stronger and bolder, carrying on their work of murder and destruction even more openly than they had under Felix. During his government another false messiah appeared, promising deliverance to all who would follow him. Festus dealt with him in much the same manner as Felix on the earlier occasion.[25] But after two years of vain attempts to quiet the unrest he died. In the absence of any government between the death of Festus and the arrival from Rome of the next procurator, the high-priest Ananus, a son of that Annas, who according to the New Testament[26] figured so largely in the trial of Jesus, "thought it a good opportunity to exercise his

[22] Antiq., XX. viii. 7; Bell. Jud., II. xiii. 7.

[23] According to Josephus (Antiq., XX. viii. 9), when Felix, after his recall, was accused in Rome by the Jews, Pallas secured his acquittal. Pallas must, therefore, by this time have regained his influence at the Court which, according to Tacitus (Annals, xiii. 14), he had clearly lost with the death of Claudius.

[24] On the date of Felix's recall and of Festus' entrance upon office, see Schuerer, Div. I., Vol. ii. p. 182, n. 58.

[25] Antiq., XX. viii. 10; Bell. Jud., II. xiv. 1.

[26] Luke, iii. 2, John, xviii. 13, 24, and Acts, iv. 6.

authority." Accordingly, he put to death James, the brother of Jesus, and others, for preaching the New Doctrine; and also attempted to revive the strict Sadducean penal code, which the Pharisees so abhorred, and to put it into full force. Before the arrival of the new Procurator into Jerusalem, however, he was met on his way by a deputation of Jews with accusations against Ananus for these infringements upon the authority of Rome, and the high-priest was obliged to resign his office after having filled it for only three months.[27]

The successor of Festus was Lucceius Albinus (62-64 CE.). Of this man Josephus says, there was no form of crime that could be named that he did not have a hand in. Not only did he, in his official capacity, steal and plunder private property and burden the nation with exorbitant taxes, but he also permitted the relations of those who were imprisoned for robberies by local councils, or by former procurators, to redeem them for money, so that nobody remained in prison but those who could not pay for their liberty. Nor did the high-priest Ananus behave in a more creditable manner, plundering the peasants without scruple. On one occasion the high-priest Joshua, son of Damnaeus, and his successor Joshua, son of Gamaliel, engaged in fisticuffs in the streets, and in throwing stones at one another, because the former would not give up his office to the latter. The Sicarii, by now too, became a great tribulation to the country. In the open day they seized the secretary of the high-priest, Ananus' son, Eleazar, and in return for the liberation of this scribe secured the release of ten of their own comrades.[28]

Meanwhile, the titular King Agrippa, foreseeing the approaching danger, began to prepare a place of retreat. He enlarged the city of Caesarea-Philippi, and naming it in honor of Nero, Neronias, transferred to it everything that was most valuable in his kingdom. This liberality to a foreign nation

[27] Antiq., XX. ix. 1.
[28] Antiq., XX. ix. 2-3; Bell. Jud., II. xiv. 1.

made him more than ordinarily unpopular among his own subjects.[29]

When Albinus heard of his intended recall, in order to do something pleasing to the people of Jerusalem, and also to make the work of his successor as difficult as possible, he crucified the most notorious criminals and released all others for ransom. "Thus," says Josephus, "the prisons were indeed emptied, but the country was filled with robbers."[30] The completion of the temple-grounds, which occurred at this time, also increased idleness and unemployment, over eighteen thousand wage earners being discharged. The more prudent among the citizens, dreading the roaming about the country of so vast a number of unoccupied and dissatisfied men, proposed to King Agrippa to use the idle money deposited at the temple treasury, and, which only excited the rapacity of the Romans, to reconstruct the eastern cloisters adjoining the Temple with greater magnificence than that with which they had originally been built by King Solomon. But Agrippa, considering the work too gigantic an undertaking, both in time and costliness, refused to consent, but agreed to employ the idle hands on the work of paving Jerusalem with white flagstones.[31] In 64 CE. Albinus was recalled to Rome.

Gessius Florus (64-66 CE.), the last of the procurators, was the most vicious, the most dishonest, most violent, most excessive and most pitiless of all. Josephus seems at a loss for words strong or bad enough to describe the horrid character and monstrous proceedings of this ruffian, upon whom the Jews looked as a robber and assassin who had come to plunder and butcher, rather than a magistrate sent to govern them. To rob single individuals was beneath him. He stripped whole cities, ruined entire populations and almost proclaimed throughout the country that all were at liberty to rob so long as he received his share of the spoils; so that many, un-

[29] Antiq., XX. ix. 4.
[30] Antiq., XX. ix. 5.
[31] Antiq., XX. ix. 7.

able any longer to bear the devastations, were forced to leave their homes and seek refuge in foreign provinces.[32]

At Caesarea, during a wave of anti-Jewish feeling, a Greek, owning land near the entrance to the synagogue, raised small shops on it, leaving only a very narrow approach. The Jews, after offering the landowner a sum equal to many times the value of his property, which he refused, and having no other expedient, offered Florus eight talents (ab. $8000 if silver, or above $120,000 if gold) to hinder the work. Florus accepted the money and promised assistance, but immediately quitted the city as though he had sold the Jews a license to fight the matter out.[33]

Not content with the ravages, outrages and miseries which he had inflicted upon the nation, Florus laid his hands also on the treasury of the Temple and abstracted from it seventeen talents, which action he pretended was necessary in the service of the Emperor. The people's patience was now tried beyond endurance. They rushed to the Temple and with piercing cries invoked the name of Nero, imploring him to liberate them from the tyranny of Florus. Some of the malcontents cast insults upon the procurator and carried a basket around begging coppers for him as for an unfortunate destitute, or as a sort of contempt for his greediness. When Florus heard of this he immediately resolved to take bloody vengeance upon those who insulted him. Accordingly, instead of going to Caesarea, as he should have done, to extinguish the flame of war which was there already assuming enormous proportions,[34] and for which he had received from the Jews eight talents, he marched with an army against Jerusalem, in order to bring the people into subjection, and at the same time, by means of terror and threat, to fleece the city.[35]

But the people, anxious to forestall his intention, went

[32] Antiq., XX. xi. 1; Bell. Jud., II. xiv. 2.
[33] Bell. Jud., II. xiv. 4.
[34] For the continuance of the conflict, see Bell. Jud., II. xiv. 5.
[35] Bell. Jud., II. xiv. 6.

to meet the troops with acclamations, and prepared to give Florus a courteous reception. He, however, sent ahead a centurion, Capito, to order the Jews to go back and not make a show now of receiving submissively him whom they had so foully insulted before, and to tell them that if they were courageous persons they should come out and jeer at him in his presence and show their love of liberty not only in words but also with their weapons. Amazed at this message and dismayed by Capito's cavalrymen charging into their ranks, the crowds retired overnight into their houses before they had a chance of saluting the procurator or of giving his troops proof of their obedience.[36]

The next morning Florus, summoning the principal citizens before him, demanded the surrender of all those who had insulted his name, and threatened that if they refused or delayed he should proceed against them as responsible for the offense. As representatives of the general peaceable disposition of the city, they entreated his forbearance, for the reason that those who had spoken so amiss were a few young rascals whom it would be impossible to detect. If, then, Florus cared for the peace of the nation, he should pardon the few who were guilty rather than victimize the many innocent.[37] At these words Florus broke out into the most violent fury. He called out his soldiers to plunder the "Upper Market Place," a quarter inhabited by the wealthy, and to put to death everyone they met there. The soldiers, whose lust for booty was thus backed by their general's order, not only sacked the district which they had been sent to attack, but forcing themselves into every house about it they slaughtered the inmates. Many of those who fled along the narrow streets were trampled to death or carried away by the soldiers to be first scourged and then crucified. Of men, women and children, for neither age

[36] Bell. Jud., II. xiv. 7.
[37] Bell. Jud., II. xiv. 8.

Copper coins of the Maccabean dynasty, minted under Simon Tharsi (139 BCE.) and John Hyrcanus (109 BCE.)

Silver shekel and half shekel, still in circulation before the war.

nor sex was spared, the number that fell that day amounted to about three thousand and six hundred.[38]

Agrippa, at this moment, was absent, having gone to Alexandria to congratulate Tiberius (the former procurator of Judea) who had recently been elevated by Nero as his viceroy of Egypt; but his sister Berenice was in Jerusalem, where she had come to perform a religious vow.[39] As she witnessed the outrages of the soldiers, she repeatedly sent messages to Florus imploring him to stop the carnage, and even came herself in her penitential attire, with her hair shorn, and barefoot, to supplicate before his tribunal. But her lamentations only increased his audacity, and she had to flee for her life.[40] These events took place on the sixteenth day of the month of Iyar[41]—May (66 C.E.).

On the following day Florus, troubled that these profitable disturbances were over, determined to revive them, if possible, by a new method. He sent for the leading citizens and demanded, as proof of their present peaceful intentions, that the people go forth in a body to meet and salute two Roman detachments which were arriving from Caesarea. Although not inclined to submit to this indignity, the priests exhorted the people to obedience, and they went out to welcome the troops with greetings and apparent gladness. But the soldiers, having beforehand been instructed by Florus, refused to return their salutations. At this some hotheads among the people broke out into audible imprecations against Florus. The troops turned upon the whole assembly and struck them with their swords, forcing them back to the city, while their horses trampled them down, bruising and wounding many.

At the city gates, however, there was a violent rush for entrance, and forcing their way through, numbers were suffocated or trampled to death under the hoofs of the pursuing

[38] Bell. Jud., II. xiv. 9.

[39] Perhaps a traditional law of this age, similar to that prescribed in Numb., vi., relating to Nazarites.

[40] Bell. Jud., II. xv. 1.

[41] Bell. Jud., II. xv. 2.

horses; their bodies were so disfigured that their relatives could not recognize them to give them burial. The troops continued advancing, mercilessly striking the fleeing people before them until they came to the suburb of Bezetha (also called the "New City"), trying to make their way to and occupy the fortified temple area and at the same time also gain possession of the rich temple treasury. In the turmoil, however, the people succeeded in securing a safe position on the temple mount, and in cutting off the connecting galleries between it and the fortess of Antonia. Florus, now realizing that the forces at his disposal were not strong enough to cope with the unexpected situation, and being too cowardly to confront the tempest he had raised, withdrew back to Caesarea, leaving behind him in a most perilous position only one cohort, announcing that he would hold the priests and the Sanhedrin responsible for the quiet and order of the community. As a further inducement to the Jews, now that he had overstepped himself and seeing that his designs had failed, he even permitted them to choose the garrison which had taken the least part in the butchery.[42] The cohort which they selected was that serving under Metilius.[43]

But not content with this arrangement, Florus now devised a plan by which he attempted to embroil the province into hostilities against the imperial government. On his return to Caesarea he dispatched to his superior, the legate of Syria, Cestus Gallus, a report falsely accusing the Jews of revolting, and charging them with atrocities which, in fact, they themselves had suffered. The Jews on their side, however, were not lagging, but also wrote to Gallus, as did Berenice too, of the crimes perpetrated by Florus upon Jerusalem. Gallus, having read both accounts, summoned a council, in which it was resolved that he should go in person to Jerusalem to examine into the cause of the disturbances. The legate, however, decided to send one of his staff beforehand to in-

[42] Bell. Jud., II. xv. 3-6.
[43] Bell. Jud., II. xvii. 10.

vestigate the state of affairs and to present a faithful report to him of the conditions generally, and accordingly dispatched one of his tribunes whose name was Neapolitanus. But while passing through Jabne, this officer met King Agrippa as he was returning from Alexandria and informed him who he was and the object of his mission.[44]

To Jabne also came the leading citizens of Jerusalem and the Sanhedrin to congratulate the king on his safe return. After paying their respects to him, they lamented their own calamities and related to him the barbarous treatment they had met with under Florus. Agrippa artfully concealed his compassion and even pretended to reprove the turbulent conduct of his countrymen. He wished to humiliate them in order to dissuade them from avenging themselves, but these men of position and property understood that this rebuke was intended only for their own good. But as they were nearing Jerusalem, about seven or eight miles from the city, Neapolitanus and Agrippa were met by a more mournful procession; the widows of the slain came running with wild shrieks and outcries, calling on Agrippa for protection and recounting to Neapolitanus all the miseries which they had suffered from Florus. When they entered the city, the Jews showed them the market place, a scene of desolation, and the houses plundered. They also persuaded Neapolitanus to traverse the city to its opposite end, as far as Siloam, with a single attendant so as not to attract attention, to see the orderliness of the people. Having toured the city and satisfied himself as to the people's geniality, he called the multitude together, highly commended them for their loyalty to the Romans and ardently importuned them to continue the peace. He then went to the Temple, "paid his adoration to the Sanctuary of God" from the permitted area,[45] and returned to report to Gallus.[46]

[44] Bell. Jud., II. xvi. 1.

[45] Without passing the stone wall forbidden to Gentiles "under pain of death."—Bell. Jud., V. v. 2.

[46] Bell. Jud., II. xvi. 2.

And now the people turned to Agrippa, pressing him to send an embassy to Rome to explain the events under Florus, and not by his silence to afford the emperor a suspicion that they as rebels had been the originators of the disturbances. Agrippa regarded it as dangerous to appoint men to denounce Florus, but also realized his responsibility should the flames now smouldering break out into open rebellion. He therefore summoned the people to the Xystus, and, taking his place in a lofty part of his palace with Berenice by his side, spoke to them as follows: [47]

"Had I found that you were all disposed to go to war with the Romans,...I should not have come...to give you counsel; for any discourse in support of the right policy would be wasted when the audience unanimously favors the opposite. But because the desire for war in some of you is because some are young and unfamiliar with the miseries it brings, and because some are for it out of unreasonable expectation of regaining independence, and yet others perhaps because of their avarice and the prospect of enriching themselves at the expense of the weak in the event of a general confusion, I have thought it proper to call you together and tell you what I think to be for your advantage. If, however, what I say is not to the liking of any of the audience, pray let him not cause a disturbance, because those who are determined upon rebellion can still retain their sentiments after my exhortation is over, for my words will only be lost to those who are anxious to hear me, unless you will all keep silence.

"Now, I know that there are many who grow tragical on the impudence of the procurators, and deliver magnificent encomiums on the advantages of liberty. But before examining who you are and who the nation is whom you are going to fight, I shall first separate those

[47] Bell. Jud., II. xvi. 3.

two distinct pretenses that are by some connected together. For if your object is to avenge yourselves on those who have done you injustices, why do you make this an issue for recovering your liberty? But if, on the other hand, you consider all servitude intolerable, why do you complain against any particular governor? For if he treated you with moderation, servitude will still remain a source of irritation. Consider then these arguments apart, and see how weak your reasons are for going to war.... Let us take it for granted that the Roman representatives are intolerably severe, yet, not all Romans against whom you would make war are unjust to you alike. It is not by their command that an oppressive governor comes from them to us, nor can they see in the west what their officers do in the east.... Such wrongs as we complain of may speedily be corrected; for the same procurator will not remain for ever,... but war once started can not easily be broken off or carried through without risk of disaster."

He urged that their hopes for independence were in vain; for since they failed to resist a small army under Pompey, they surely could not force the Romans out now when their power extended over the "whole universe." He adduced the example of the Dalmatians, Gauls, Germans, Greeks, Macedonians, and "myriads of other nations,—all brave, powerful, and resourceful,"—who were held in submission by but a few Roman troops, whereas they (the Jews) had no army, no fleet, and no means adequate to fight or meet the cost of a campaign. "If, therefore," he cautioned them, "you will follow my advice, you will enjoy with me the blessings of peace, but if you will let yourselves be carried away by your passion, you will face, without me, this tremendous peril." [48] Having spoken thus, both he and his sister broke into tears, which much restrained the passion of the people.

[48] Bell. Jud., II. xvi. 4.

Still they began to cry out that, while they would not take up arms against the Romans, they would do so against Florus, on account of what they had suffered under him. To this Agrippa replied, that they had already committed acts of war against the Romans: "You have not paid your tribute to the Emperor, and you have cut off the cloisters of the Temple from joining the Tower of Antonia"; and that if they wished to clear themselves of the charge of insurrection, to repair the porticoes and pay up their taxes, "for surely the fortress does not belong to Florus, nor does your tribute-money go to him." [49]

The people obeyed. With the king and Berenice they began to rebuild the galleries; collectors were sent to gather the taxes, and forty talents were speedily brought in. The menace of war seemed at an end. Soon after, however, Agrippa attempted to persuade the people to render the usual allegiance to Florus until the emperor should send another procurator in his place. But the mere suggestion of allegiance to this tyrant, even for a short time, counteracted the favorable effect of the rest of Agrippa's proposals. It was rejected with howls of derision and insults, and some of the bolder men threw stones at the king. Seeing that the passion of those who were for war could not be restrained, and highly indignant at the insults which he had received, Agrippa sent several Jewish leaders to Florus that he might nominate some of them to collect the rest of the unpaid taxes, and then withdrew to his own dominions.[50]

And now some of the rebels made an assault on the important fortress of Masada; [51] and having gained possession of it, they killed the Roman guards and put a garrison of their own in it. At the same time another incident occurred in

[49] Bell. Jud., II. xvi. 5.

[50] Bell. Jud., II. xvii. 1.

[51] This place, some forty miles south of Jerusalem, was of great strength. It was originally built by Josephus' Maccabean ancestor, Jonathan, and fortified at great expense by Herod (Bell. Jud., II. viii. 3).

Jerusalem. At the instigation of Eleazar, a son of the former high-priest Ananias, then holding the position of captain of the temple force, it was resolved to discontinue the daily sacrifices for the emperor, and no longer to accept donations from non-Jews. The cessation of offerings for the emperor was equivalent to an open declaration of war. The leading citizens and the most distinguished of the Pharisees urged that it was not only inhospitable, but also sinful to shut out strangers from offering sacrifices and kneeling in worship before God.[52]

[52] Bell. Jud., II. xvii. 2-3. From time immemorial it had been the custom to receive donations and sacrifices of foreign potentates in the Temple, and since the time of Julius Caesar, according to the policy of Rome, offerings had been regularly made in the name of the emperor. That the Jews had always received the sacrifices from foreign nations is testified by Josephus (Bell. Jud., II. xvii. 4). Alexander the Great once sacrificed in Jerusalem (Antiq., XI. viii. 5). Ptolemy III (Apion, ii. 5) and Antioch VII (Antiq., XIII. viii. 2) have offered sacrifices at the Temple. Marcus Agrippa, when in the year 15 BCE. he returned his visit to Herod, "offered a hecatomb of sacrifices to God" (Antiq., XVI. ii. 1), and gifts "for the embellishment of the Temple" (Philo, Leg. ad Cajum, xxxvii). During the Passover of 37 CE., the Syrian legate, Vitellius, came to Jerusalem for the purpose of "offering sacrifices to God" (Antiq., XVIII. v. 3). "The altar is adored by the whole world, and honored as far as the ends of the earth" (Bel. Jud., IV. iv. 3, middle of second half of section). In like manner Cyrus had given orders that sacrifices and prayers should be offered "unto the God of Heaven" for the life of the king and his sons (Ezra, vi. 10); so that by this and the testimony of I Maccabees, vii. 33, we may suppose that the offering of sacrifices on behalf of Gentile authorities was founded by the Syrian kings themselves. Augustus, according to Philo (Leg. ad Cajum, xxiii.), ordained that one ox and two lambs be sacrificed at the Emperor's expense for all time, or according to Josephus (II Apion, 6, near end), paid for by the Jewish nation. This continued to be regularly offered until the rebellion in the year 66 CE. Besides these offerings, Ptolemy II, on the occasion of the translation of the Pentateuch into Greek, presented to the Temple twenty golden and thirty silver cups, five goblets, and a table of exquisite workmanship (Pseudo-Aristeas, in Havercamp's Josephus, ii. 108-111; also Merx's Archiv., i. 266-269). Apart from this we find that other Ptolemies also gave presents to the Temple (Antiq., XIII. iii. 4; II Apion, 5 beginning, and in II Maccabees, iii. 2 v. 16). Sossius presented a golden crown (Antiq., XIV. xvi. 4); and among

In the course of this argument they brought forward men, most learned in the Law and most acquainted with the precedents and customs of temple worship, who unanimously declared that it was an ancient usage to receive offerings from strangers. But not one of the revolutionary party paid any attention to them. Thereupon, the peace party, to which, as might be expected, all discerning and judicious men belonged, perceiving that it was beyond their power to suppress the insurrection and that they would be the first victims of the vengeance of Rome, resolved to have recourse to violent measures. They sent one deputation headed by Simon, son of Ananias, to Florus, and another to Agrippa headed by the king's own relatives, Saul, Antipas, and Costobar, entreating them to march instantly on Jerusalem, or all would be lost. To Florus the news was a wonderful godsend; determined as he was to kindle the war, he gave the deputation no reply whatever. But Agrippa, still anxious to save Jerusalem and the Temple, sent immediately 3,000 horsemen from Auranitis, Batanea, and Trachonitis, under the command of Darius and Philip.[53]

Under the protection of these troops, the leading citizens and all who were desirous of peace occupied the "Upper City"; for the Mount on which the Temple stood and the "Lower City" were already in possession of the Zealots. A bitter strife now arose between the two factions. They assailed each other with stones or slings, and there was a continuous volley of darts from both quarters. Occasionally hand-to-hand combats took place between groups rushing forth from their camps at one another. The objective of Agrippa's troops was to capture the Temple, while Eleazar and the insurgents strove to gain the "Upper City," besides what they already held. This fighting continued for seven days, with neither

the golden vessels of the Temple which the Zealots caused to be melted during the Roman siege of Jerusalem were the wine goblets that had been presented by Emperor Augustus and his wife (Bell. Jud., V. xiii. 6; compare Philo, Leg. ad Cajum, xxiii).

[53] Bell. Jud., II. xvii. 4.

party obtaining any positive advantage. On the eighth day, however, which was Ab 15th (July-August), the situation changed. On this date it was customary for every individual to bring a supply of wood for the fire of the Temple, which was never allowed to go out.[54] When the members of the peace party appeared with their contributions to the Temple, the insurgents refused their admittance. But with the meaner people who came along with them and were permitted to enter, there also came many of the Sicarii who stole their way in, enlisting their services with the Zealots. Strengthened by these ruffians, the Zealots made a vigorous attack on their opponents, who were obliged to evacuate the Upper City. And in order to avenge themselves on their adversaries, they also set fire to the house of the high-priest Ananias, to the palace of Agrippa and Berenice, and to the archives in which the bonds belonging to their creditors were registered. And now, flushed with their victory, the insurgents retired for the day.[55]

On the next day the Zealots attacked the fortress of Antonia, and after a siege of two days captured and put to death its garrison. They then turned against Herod's palace where the combined troops commanded by Metilius and Philip had taken refuge. Meanwhile a new leader arose among the insurgents. He was Menahem, a son of that Judas the Galilean who in olden days, under Quirinius, had upbraided the Jews for paying taxes to the emperor and for recognizing the Romans as their masters. With his band of Sicarii, Menahem suddenly appeared at the already conquered fortress of Masada,[56] where he broke into the armory and provided arms not only for his own followers, but also for many other outlaws. With these armed men as his bodyguard he returned to Jerusalem, and became the leader of the revolutionary party.

[54] For the law of keeping the fire on the altar constantly, see Leviticus, vi. 12f; for date of festival, Mishna, Taanith, iv. 5.

[55] Bell. Jud., II. xvii. 5-6.

[56] Bell. Jud., II. xvii. 2.

But when finally Metilius and Philip, who had taken refuge in Herod's palace, could offer no effectual resistance, they sent to Menahem a request for permission to quit the city. This, Menahem granted, but only to the troops of Agrippa, and to natives of the country. The Roman soldiers under Metilius, now left in a most desperate situation, deserted their camp and retreated to the three strong towers, named Hyppicus, Phasaelis and Mariamne, while Menahem and his men plundered the baggage that was left by the soldiers in Herod's palace, killed all of those who were not able to save themselves by flight, and set fire to the building. These events took place on the sixth day of the month of Elul (August).[57] On the following morning, Ananias was discovered in an aqueduct leading to the palace where he was hiding, and with his brother Ezekiah, was also put to death by the rebels, while the Zealots under Eleazar surrounded the towers to prevent the Romans from escaping.

Now, the reduction of the strongholds and the murder of the high-priest Ananias so puffed up and brutalized Menahem, that he believed himself without a rival who could dispute the dictatorship with him. Eleazar and his partisans, on the other hand, could not patiently bear that the supreme authority for which they had so cunningly schemed and obstinately imperiled their lives should thus unwarrantably be taken away from them by one socially so "far inferior to themselves." Especially galling did this jealousy become to them one day when Menahem came to the Temple attired in royal garments and surrounded by his bandits in their armor which they had carried off at Masada. Consequently, Eleazar and his companions, assisted by the people, rushed upon him and began to stone him. His followers fled; many were killed during their flight, and many others in their places of concealment. A few of them escaped to Masada, among whom was Eleazar ben Jair, a relative of Menahem. Menahem himself, who had taken refuge in the district of

[57] Bell. Jud., II. xvii. 7-8.

Ophel, was caught, dragged into the open, and put to death.[58]

The people had taken part against Menahem in the hope that by his death the rebellion would be suppressed. In fact, this hope was entertained not by the Jews alone, but by the besieged Romans also. Metilius, their general, unable to resist the Zealots any longer, even sent envoys to Eleazar begging that his garrison be permitted to depart, agreeing to surrender all their arms and personal belongings, for no more than assurance that their lives would be spared. But to their sorrow, while Menahem was a self-admiring brute and a murderer, the Jews found Eleazar to be not only these, but also a treacherous perjurer. He delegated the most despicable three of his followers, Judas, Ananias and Gorion, to treat with Metilius, and to offer him their oaths as a pledge that his conditions would be accepted and executed, but no sooner had the Romans surrendered their swords and bucklers and begun their departure than the Zealots under Eleazar surrounded and butchered all of them except Metilius, who saved his life by promising to become a Jew, and even to submit to circumcision. To the Romans the loss of a few men was but a slight injury, but to the people of Jerusalem this treacherous action appeared as the beginning of their own ruination. The whole city became a scene of mourning; among the moderates there was not one who was not tormented with fear that he himself would have to suffer for the crime of the rebels, even should he escape revenge from the Romans, for this heinous massacre was perpetrated on the Sabbath, a day on which the Jews abstained even from the most innocent acts.[59]

Indeed, while the Zealots thus triumphed in Jerusalem, bloody retaliations took place in other cities. When news of Eleazar's perfidious massacre of the Romans in Jerusalem reached Caesarea, the Syrians and Greeks of that city, perhaps under secret instructions from Florus, rose to a man and within one hour slaughtered over twenty thousand Jews. The

[58] Bell. Jud., II. xvii. 9.
[59] Bell. Jud., II. xvii. 10.

news of the disaster at Caesarea infuriated the whole population of Judea. Everywhere companies formed themselves into free troops who sacked or burned numbers of Greek-inhabited cities and villages wtih immense slaughter.[60] And as these onslaughts again called for revenge, the heathen population of the country killed no less a number of Jews. Even such pagans and Jews who had long been on the friendliest of terms became robbers and murderers of each other. The streets were choked with unburied bodies, aged men and infants lying side by side, and women stripped of their last covering of modesty.[61] Thirteen thousand Jews perished at Scythopolis,[62] fifty thousand lost their lives at Alexandria, twenty-five hundred in Ascalon, and two thousand in Ptolemais, besides many who were put in irons. The Tyrians put a considerable number to death, in addition to the great many who were chained and imprisoned. Hippos and Gadara made away with the young and strong and threw the others into prison; and so on with the rest of the Syro-Greek cities, in accordance with their hatred or fear of their Jewish neighbors. Only the Antiochians, Sidonians and Apamians spared the Jews who dwelt with them, and refused to kill a single one. The people of Gerasa not only refused to maltreat the Jews who lived with them, but also offered to conduct to the borders any of them who wished to emigrate.[63] Such was the catastrophe which Eleazar and his followers brought upon the nation.

At last, however, Cestius Gallus, the Roman governor of Syria, determined to quell the disturbances in Judea. He started from Antioch with the entire Twelfth Legion, two thousand selected men from each of the other legions, six extra detachments of infantry and four squadrons of cavalry, besides some thirteen thousand auxiliary troops which the

[60] Bell. Jud., II. xviii. 1.
[61] Bell. Jud., II. xviii. 2.
[62] Bell. Jud., II. xviii. 3.
[63] Bell. Jud., II. xviii. 5, 7-8.

friendly neighboring kings, including Agrippa, had placed at his disposal. With this army, accompanied by Agrippa as his lieutenant, Cestius advanced to Ptolemais, adding to his forces from each of the Grecian cities as he passed them by. His first exploit was Chabolo, a fortified village on the frontier between Ptolemais and the Jewish district of Upper Galilee. He found it deserted, but well stocked with all kinds of goods and provisions. These he allowed his soldiers to plunder. The village itself, although he admired its beauty, "owing to the resemblance of its houses to those of Berytus, Sidon and Tyre," was burned to the ground. He then overran the whole district, and, having plundered and burned everything in his path, marched back to Ptolemais. But while a part of the army which Cestius left behind as sentry were still plundering, the Jews fell upon them and killed about two hundred.[64]

Leaving Ptolemais again, Cestius advanced to Caesarea. From here he sent part of his forces to Joppa, with orders, if they succeeded in taking the city, to garrison it, but if the inhabitants offered resistance, to wait for him with the rest of his army. Part of these troops advanced by land, part by sea. They found the city open, the people, not having expected the Romans, prepared for neither fight nor flight. The troops put them all to the sword, and pillaged and burned the town. The number of the victims was eight thousand and four hundred. With the same cruelty a strong force of cavalry wasted the toparchy of Narbata, a short distance from Caesarea, killing a great number of its people, and plundering and burning its villages.[65]

To Galilee, Cestius Gallus sent his namesake, Caesennius Gallus, the commander of the Twelfth Legion, with sufficient forces to reduce that province. Sepphoris, the strongest city in Galilee, opened its gates and received him with open arms. The surrounding cities followed the example of their metropolis. The insurgents in the district fled to the mountains which

[64] Bell. Jud., II. xviii. 9.
[65] Bell. Jud., II. xviii. 10.

lie in the very middle of Galilee and facing Sepphoris. Against these Caesennius led his troops, and, at the expense of some two hundred of his own men, killed over two thousand of the rebels.[66] Having thus subdued the province, the general returned with his troops to Caesarea.

With his army again completed, Cestius himself resumed his march on Jerusalem. His first stop was Antipatras, where he dispersed a small body of rebels and burned the city together with its surrounding villages. From Antipatras he marched to Lydda, called also Diospolis, which was deserted, its people having gone to Jerusalem for the Feast of Tabernacles. Some fifty men who came to meet him he put to the sword, and burned the city. And so he marched forward, ascending through the hills of Beth-Horon, to Gibeon, about seven miles northwest of Jerusalem, where he pitched camp,[67] apparently expecting a message of repentant submission.

Differently, however, did Cestius fare on encountering the Zealots of Jerusalem. Unlike the childlike and peaceful peasants he had met with in crossing the hundred-mile stretch from Ptolemais to this point, were these inflexible villains. Their craving for bloodshed, their baseness and perfidiousness, on which account the Romans mistrusted the whole nation, was so rabid, that on neither Feast of Tabernacles nor Sabbath, which the people regarded with special reverence, were they able to abstain from their thuggery.

When the Romans arrived at Gibeon, the Zealots, though it was on a Sabbath, attacked them with such cunning and avidity, that before the Romans could array themselves for action the Zealots broke through their front ranks and killed over five hundred. At the same time a bandit leader, Simon bar Giora, who subsequently became a most outstanding figure, with his following, cut off a large part of their rearguard, put a number of them to the sword, and carried away several wagonloads of baggage and munitions. So perplexed

[66] Bell. Jud., II. xviii. 11.
[67] Bell. Jud., II. xix. 1.

did Cestius Gallus become, that, unable to decide whether to advance or retreat, he remained for three days at his quarters.[68]

At this juncture, Agrippa, still anxious to avert the war, which he saw approaching in reality, dispatched two of his principal officers, Phoebus and Borceus, who were both well known and popular in Jerusalem, to address the people and to offer them, in the name of Cestius, entire forgiveness for all they had done in the past, if they would lay down their arms and return to their allegiance. But the Zealots, fearing lest the amnesty should be extended to the people only, but not to themselves, made a murderous assault upon the emissaries, killing Phoebus and seriously wounding Borceus. And when the people were indignant at this inhuman procedure they were assailed with stones and clubs, and driven back into the city.[69]

Cestius, taking advantage of the violent dissensions which broke out in the city as a result of the murder of Phoebus, brought his legions up nearer to Jerusalem. Having encamped at Mount Scopus, less than a mile northwest of the city wall, he made no assault for three days, in hope of receiving an offer of surrender. It was only on the fourth day, which was the thirteenth of the month of Tishre, when there was no sign of yielding, that he led his forces into the suburb of Bezetha, or the "New City." The insurgents, however, having not only to repel the Romans without, but also to watch the people within the city who were against them, fled from the suburb where they had no adequate protection into the Temple and other fortified city places. To this abandoned portion of Jerusalem, including the "Timber Market," Cestius set fire and encamped further south, opposite Herod's old palace. Had he then forced his way through the second wall he would have captured the city and the rebellion would have been over, but his general, Tyrannius Priscus, and several of his cavalry commanders who were

[68] Bell. Jud., II. xix. 2.
[69] Bell. Jud., II. xix. 3.

bribed by Florus, dissuaded him from the attempt. "Thus," deplores Josephus, "it came about that the war lasted so very long, and the Jews drained the cup of irretrievable disaster."[70]

With the Romans now within the city walls, many of the leading citizens, persuaded by Ananus, the son of Jonathan,[71] invited Cestius into the city, promising to open the gates for him. However, partly because of his anger at the Jews, and partly because he mistrusted them, he refused their offer. When the conspiracy was discovered by the insurgents, Ananus and his adherents were pulled down from the wall, pelted with stones, and driven to their houses. Then, posting themselves on the towers, they fired darts at the Romans who were attempting to approach the wall. For six days the Romans pressed their attack against the wall without success. On the seventh day they formed a Testudo (i.e., a protective covering, similar to the back of a tortoise), so that the darts thrown from above slid off harmlessly, from under which the soldiers attempted to undermine the wall in order to set fire to the gate of the Temple.[72] It was only now that a panic seized the Zealots, so that many ran away from the city. The people, taking advantage of the situation, advanced to open the gates and admit Cestius as their deliverer; "but God, I suppose," bewails Josephus, "because of those scoundrels, had already turned away even from His own sanctuary and would not permit the war to end so easy."[73] At this point, however, Cestius, unaware of the state of affairs within the city, either of the horror and cowardice of the Zealots or the earnest intentions of the people, evidently finding his forces and his provisions inadequate for the situation, suddenly recalled his army and retired from the city. On this unexpected retreat the Zealots at once rose from the deepest depression to the

[70] Bell. Jud., II. xix. 4.

[71] This Jonathan, the high-priest, was the first revolutionary victim of the Sicarii (Bell. Jud., II. xiii. 3).

[72] Bell. Jud., II. xix. 5.

[73] Bell. Jud., II. xix. 6.

wildest courage, and sprang out upon his rear, killing a considerable number of both cavalry and infantry.

Cestius passed that night at his former camp at Mount Scopus. On the following day, as he continued his retreat, the Zealots, still hanging upon his heels, harassed his rear, and, enclosing his troops on both sides, fired their darts at them, disordering their ranks and killing many. He could not venture to beat off the insurgents, his troops being heavily armed and afraid to open their ranks, while their pursuers were light-armed and ready to dash in among them. Among the dead were Priscus, the commander of the Sixth Legion, the tribune Longinus, and the commander of a troop of cavalry, Emilius Secundus. With great difficulty the Romans came back to Gibeon, having further lost part of their baggage. Here Cestius stopped for two days, unable to decide what course to take. But, on the third day, seeing the Zealots greatly gaining in numbers, swarming all the surrounding heights, he decided that his delay had been to his own detriment, and determined on a fast retreat.[74]

That he might retire with greater rapidity, Gallus gave orders to his soldiers to reduce all encumbrances. All the mules and beasts of burden were killed excepting those that carried arrows and military engines. These they saved for future use, and still more for fear that they might fall into the hands of the insurgents and be used against themselves. The Romans then marched to Beth-Horon. In the open plain they were not much harassed by their pursuers. But in a ravine near that city, through which they were passing, they were attacked on all sides with such ferocity that they would have been completely wiped out had not night come on, which enabled them to make their way to their destination.[75]

Cestius, now despairing of being able to free himself openly, determined to sacrifice a portion of his forces in order to save the remainder. Selecting four hundred of his bravest

[74] Bell. Jud., II. xix. 7.
[75] Bell. Jud., II. xix. 8.

men, he posted them about the camp with orders ostentatiously and loudly to repeat their watchwords, while he, taking advantage of the dense obscurity of the night, retreated silently through the difficult and dangerous defiles of Beth-Horon. With the return of daylight, when the Zealots discovered the camp was deserted, they killed the four hundred to a man, and pursued Cestius with the utmost rapidity. Cestius meanwhile had gained upon them by several hours, having thrown off all his war implements as he rushed along. The rebels continued their pursuit as far as Antipatras, and, failing to overtake the army, turned back to Jerusalem, having slain in all six thousand five hundred Romans,[76] with inconsiderable losses to themselves. On their return they also collected all the abandoned machines and plundered the four hundred corpses. This defeat took place on the eighth day of Heshvan (Nov. 66 CE.).[77]

Due to this victory over Cestius, the Zealots quickly gained the upper hand over the nation. Many of the influential citizens fled Jerusalem as "from a sinking ship." The two brothers, Costobar and Saul, and Philip, who had been commander of King Agrippa's forces, deserted to Cestius. Cestius, at their own request, dispatched them to Nero to inform him of the catastrophe which had befallen his army, and to accuse Florus of kindling the war.[78] In the meantime, the Greeks of Damascus, on learning of the disaster which Cestius' army had suffered, avenged themselves by slaughtering ten thousand of their Jewish fellow-residents, even though most of their own wives had been habituated to Jewish practices.[79] All talk of peace was now forbidden. All those who remained in Jerusalem were forced to join the insurgents. Those Pharisees who were anxious for spiritual rather than

[76] Suetonius, Vesp., iv., tells us that a Roman standard also was captured.

[77] Bell. Jud., II. xix. 9.

[78] Bell. Jud., II. xx. 1.

[79] Bell. Jud., II. xx. 2.

political independence were also forced to join the Zealots.[80]

At this time a great political upheaval had, very strangely, taken place in Jerusalem. Josephus does not give us the details of the crisis, but, only very indirectly, he informs us that the Sanhedrin had changed into a Supreme Council, with Simon ben Gamaliel, the chief of the Pharisees, as its president. Neither does he account for the sudden change from a revolutionary government of Zealots and Sicarii,[81] to a government of peaceful Pharisees and leading citizens. Nor is there any way of knowing why the Pharisee, Simon ben Gamaliel, had become the head of the "Aristocracy," over which throughout the Herodian period a Sadducean high-priest had presided.

Thus confusedly continuing, Josephus informs us that "an assembly of the people was held in the Temple," and that by it the following divisional generals were appointed to conduct the war against Rome: Joseph ben Gorion and the high-priest Ananus, both of the Moderate Party, were chosen as governors of all affairs within Jerusalem. Eleazar ben Ananias, that ultra-Zealot who, by ordering the discontinuance of the daily sacrifices for the Emperor, brought about the rupture with Rome, and Joshua ben Sapphias,—two military men and bitter anti-Romanists,—were sent to the most unimportant province, Idumea; and to make these two generals feel dignified, the then governor of Idumea, Niger, was instructed to obey their orders. Another red-handed Zealot leader, Eleazar ben Simon, who defeated Cestius with his great army, was ignored altogether, "because they saw he was of a tyrannical nature." And to the youthful Josephus, a well-known pacifist, —who was destined to describe the war in the record which has come down to us,—was given the most difficult and most responsible province of all, Galilee, where the first onslaught of the Romans was expected.[82] Two priests, Joazar and Judas,

[80] Bell. Jud., II. xx. 3.
[81] Compare, Vita, 7, 12, 13, 38, 39, 49, 52, 60, 65, 70.
[82] Bell. Jud., II. xx. 3-4.

who later proved a blot on Jewish history, were sent along with him as his assistants.[83]

Meanwhile, the Emperor Nero, who at this time was in Achaia, Greece, displaying his talents on the stage as a poet, harpist and chariot driver, "to give the people the benefit of his accomplishments," received the news of the rising in Judea and the failure of Cestius Gallus.[84] The report of these reverses filled him with alarm, since the rebellion in Judea might be the forerunner of revolt in its neighboring nations, which were already showing signs of contagion. And as it would have been impossible to entrust further military operations to the defeated general, Gallus,[85] Nero delegated the stamping out of the Jewish insurrection to his most experienced general, Flavius Vespasian. Vespasian, who had not applauded the Emperor "in measured time and according to a set form of clapping" as the rest of the audience "from one end of the circus to the other," but "sat with his eyes closed as if sleeping," was not in the emperor's favor at the time,[86] and Nero would far rather have given the assignment to some other general; but the Emperor had no choice, for "he found no one but Vespasian equal to the task and capable of undertaking so mighty a war." And so, in the winter of 66-67 CE., Nero dispatched this general to commence his preparations for the campaign.[87]

Flavius Vespasian, the younger son of Flavius Sabinus, a tax-gatherer and usurer, was born on November the 27th, 9 CE. *Beginning his career as a tribune, or commander of a legion, in Thrace, where he became distinguished for his bravery and military ability, he*

[83] Vita, 7.

[84] Bell. Jud., II. xx. 1; comp. Tacitus, Annals, xvi. 4; Suetonius Nero, xxiii-xxiv.

[85] Tacitus (Hist., v. 10) indeed reports his death to have taken place, "probably from disappointment and vexation," soon after his retreat from Beth-Horon.

[86] Tacitus, Annals, xvi. 4-5; compare Suetonius, Vesp., iv.

[87] Bell. Jud., III. i. 1-3; compare Suetonius, Vesp., iv.

speedily rose to the rank of questor, or receiver and paymaster-general, which office he held successively in the Island of Crete and in the province of Cyrene. On his return from Cyrene, Caligula made him aedile, or police-magistrate of the city of Rome, and later, praetor, or superior judge.[88] *In the reign of Claudius, Nero's step-father, Vespasian was sent to a superior command in Germany, and later to Britain, both of which nations he brought into subjection to the Roman Empire. For his valor in Britain he received triumphal honors and two priesthoods, and then was sent as governor to the large and wealthy province of Africa, which he governed with great success, excepting that once, during an insurrection at Adrumetum, he was pelted with turnips. From here, contrary to the general practice of Roman governors, who after administering the affairs of a province for a few years came back with immense wealth, Vespasian returned so poor that he was obliged to mortgage his whole property to his older brother, and for his subsistence he was forced to deal in mules, for which reason he was nicknamed "the Muleteer."*[89]

[88] Suetonius, Vesp., i-ii.
[89] Bell. Jud., III. i. 2; compare Suetonius, Vesp., iv.

CHAPTER VI

JOSEPHUS *in* GALILEE,
from the AUTUMN *of* 66 CE.. *to the* SPRING *of* 67 CE.

OF Josephus' doings or whereabouts between the year 56 CE., and the year 64, we have no account. At this latter date, however, his history reopens as follows:

"When I was in the twenty-sixth year of my age, it happened that I took a voyage to Rome, for the reason which I will now describe. At the time when Felix was procurator of Judea, there were certain priests of my acquaintance, very fine men, whom on a trifling charge he had put in chains and sent to Rome to plead before Nero. I was anxious to procure their deliverance, more especially because I was informed that even under their afflictions they were not forgetful of the dietary laws, but supported themselves on figs and nuts. Accordingly I came to Rome, though it was through many hazards, by sea, for our ship went down in the Adriatic and we who were in it, some six hundred in number, swam for our lives all that night; when upon the first appearance of the day we sighted a ship of Cyrene, and I and others, some eighty in all, who by God's providence outswam the rest, were taken on board. And when I landed at Dicearchia, which the

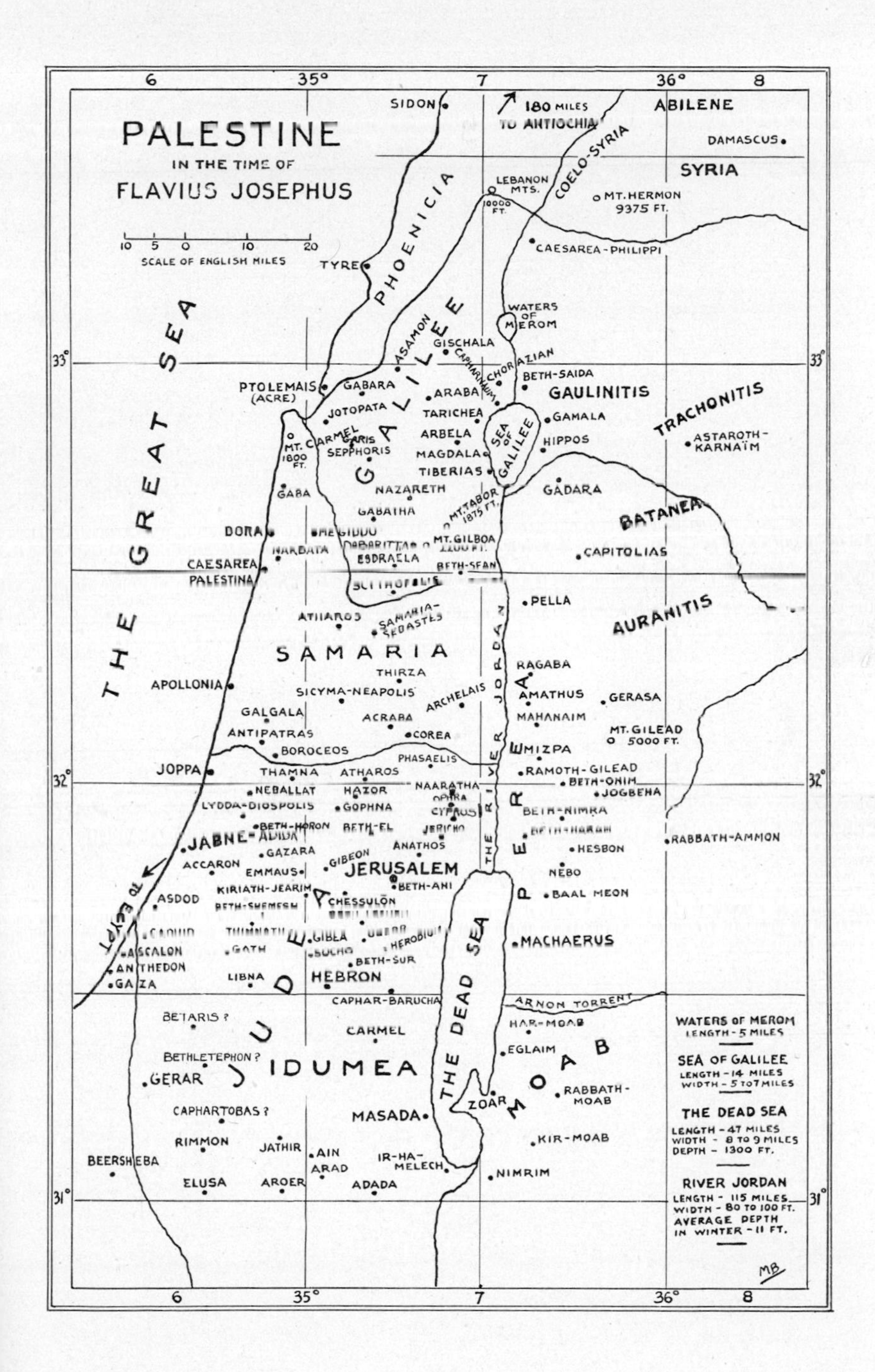

PALESTINE
IN THE TIME OF
FLAVIUS JOSEPHUS
10 5 0 10 20
SCALE OF ENGLISH MILES
6
35°
7
36°
8
33°
32°
31°
SIDON
180 MILES TO ANTIOCHIA
ABILENE
DAMASCUS
SYRIA
COELO-SYRIA
LEBANON MTS.
10000 FT.
MT. HERMON 9375 FT.
PHOENICIA
TYRE
CAESAREA-PHILIPPI
WATERS OF MEROM
GALILEE
ASAMON
GISCHALA
CAPHARNAUM
CHORAZIAN
BETH-SAIDA
GAULINITIS
TRACHONITIS
ASTAROTH-KARNAÏM
THE GREAT SEA
PTOLEMAIS (ACRE)
GABARA
ARABA
JOTOPATA
TARICHEA
GAMALA
MT. CARMEL 1800 FT.
GARIS
SEPPHORIS
ARBELA
MAGDALA
SEA OF GALILEE
HIPPOS
TIBERIAS
GABA
NAZARETH
GADARA
MT. TABOR 1875 FT.
GABATHA
BATANEA
DORA
MEGIDDO
NARBATA
DABARITTA
MT. GILBOA 2200 FT.
ESDRAELA
CAESAREA PALESTINA
CAPITOLIAS
BETH-SEAN
PELLA
SAMARIA-SEBASTES
AURANITIS
SAMARIA
THIRZA
RAGABA
APOLLONIA
SICYMA-NEAPOLIS
ARCHELAIS
AMATHUS
GERASA
GALGALA
ACRABA
MAHANAIM
ANTIPATRAS
COREA
MT. GILEAD 5000 FT.
BOROCEOS
MIZPA
PHASAELIS
JOPPA
THAMNA
ATHAROS
RAMOTH-GILEAD
BETH-ONIM
JOGBEHA
NAARATHA
NEBALLAT
HAZOR
OPHRA
LYDDA-DIOSPOLIS
GOPHNA
CYPROS
BETH-NIMRA
BETH-HORON
BETH-EL
JERICHO
BETH-HARAN
RABBATH-AMMON
JABNE-ADIDA
THE RIVER JORDAN
GAZARA
ANATHOS
HESBON
ACCARON
GIBEON
JERUSALEM
EMMAUS
NEBO
PEREA
KIRIATH-JEARIM
BETH-ANI
BAAL MEON
ASDOD
BETH-SHEMESH
CHESSULON
TO EGYPT
THIMNATH
GIBEA
HERODIUM
MACHAERUS
ASCALON
GATH
SOCHO
ANTHEDON
BETH-SUR
LIBNA
HEBRON
GAZA
JUDEA
CAPHAR-BARUCHA
ARNON TORRENT
BETARIS ?
CARMEL
HAR-MOAB
THE DEAD SEA
BETHLETEPHON ?
EGLAIM
IDUMEA
GERAR
MOAB
RABBATH-MOAB
ZOAR
CAPHARTOBAS ?
MASADA
RIMMON
KIR-MOAB
JATHIR
AIN ARAD
IR-HA-MELECH
BEERSHEBA
NIMRIM
ELUSA
AROER
ADADA
WATERS OF MEROM LENGTH - 5 MILES
SEA OF GALILEE LENGTH - 14 MILES WIDTH - 5 TO 7 MILES
THE DEAD SEA LENGTH - 47 MILES WIDTH - 8 TO 9 MILES DEPTH - 1300 FT.
RIVER JORDAN LENGTH - 115 MILES WIDTH - 80 TO 100 FT. AVERAGE DEPTH IN WINTER - 11 FT.
MB

Italians call Puteoli (in the Bay of Naples), I became acquainted with Aliturius, an actor who was a special favorite of Nero and a Jew by birth, through whom I became known to Poppea, Nero's wife. At the earliest opportunity I entreated her to secure the liberation of the priests, in addition to which favor I also received from the Empress large gifts, and returned to my country."[1]

Empress Poppea.

On his arrival at Jerusalem, he continues, he found his country in the utmost confusion, and the Zealots very elatedly organizing for war. He therefore endeavored to restrain them from their course of action, and to bring them over to a better frame of mind. He related to them the great power, the enormous wealth, and the elaborate system of government he had encountered during his two years' journey in Rome; reminded them of the invincibility of the nation they were about to fight; warned them of their inferiority to the Romans, not only in military skill but also in financial and political resources, and counseled them not to be so hasty in bringing upon their country, their families and themselves that disaster in which such a war must end. But all his efforts were of no avail, for the determination of these men was far too great for him to bring them to reason.[2] Soon, however, he became afraid that his persistence with these unpopular

[1] Vita, sec. 3, slightly changed.
[2] Vita, 4.

warnings might have brought him into suspicion of siding with the Romans. He therefore took refuge in the inner court of the Temple, since the fortress of Antonia was already in the hands of the Sicarii. Not till after the murder of Menahem and many of his followers, by the Zealots, did Josephus venture to come out from concealment and join the leading citizens who secretly formed the peace faction. With the death of Menahem, however, the danger was not entirely over. The revolutionaries were still in arms, and the moderates, powerless to check their proceedings, were at a loss how to manage the situation. Therefore, pretending to be of the same view as the Zealots, Josephus, with his political associates, advised them to make no further move for the present except in self-defense, while really expecting that Cestius would not be long in coming with a large army which would easily suppress the revolution.[3]

(Owing to dissimilarities between the two accounts which Josephus gives us of this period, "it is extremely difficult," some so-called historians say, "to reconstruct the history." The present writer is not inclined to fill in, nor is he qualified to place theories of his own before his readers, in order to bridge over this gap in the narrative. One of these accounts is in the history of the Jewish War, which was written immediately after the war (75 CE.); *the other is in the Autobiography, which was published by Josephus some twenty years later* (93-95 CE.), *neither as a biography nor as a history, but mainly in self-defense, when Justus of Tiberias and others had endangered his life by treasonable charges. If, however, we do not slavishly or deliberately set out to vilify Josephus, but independently and without design eliminate such passages in the Autobiography as are easily identified as being associated with or functioning in his Defense before the Romans, no comparison of this*

[3] Vita, 5; compare Bell. Jud., II. xvii. 8-9.

polemic with the accounts given in the Jewish War will reveal those inconsistencies which were so "long observed by many scholars.")

In the autumn of the year 66 CE., Josephus arrived in Galilee. As his first act, to gain the confidence of the people, he appointed as his lieutenants the representatives of the principal communities; for by receiving his commands through their own leaders he hoped they would follow him more readily. He then selected from the nation "seventy of the most prudent men and elders of age" (resembling the Sanhedrin at Jerusalem) as an advisory board for the administration of the province. In every city he appointed seven judges to hear minor cases. Matters of major importance and those of life and death were to be brought before the seventy elders, with himself presiding.[4]

Having thus formed a government he proceeded with the strengthening of his territory. To meet the threatened invasion of the Romans he built walls about Jotapata, Tarichea, Tiberias, Itabyrion, on Mount Tabor, Gamala, and many smaller towns. To the wealthy inhabitants of Sepphoris, who seemed zealous to enter the cause, he permitted the building of their own fortifications, and granted to John, the son of Levy,—later the notorious John of Gischala,—the right to strengthen that city at his own expense. Many of the fortresses were built under the personal supervision of Josephus, who both assisted and directed the operations. When this task was completed, he enlisted a militia of over a hundred thousand men, all of whom he equipped with old arms which were collected from all quarters and repaired for the purpose.[5]

And knowing that the Romans owed their strength chiefly to discipline and constant instruction in the use of arms, he despaired of providing similar instruction which could be acquired only by continual practice over long

[4] Bell. Jud., II. xx. 5.
[5] Bell. Jud., II. xx. 6.

periods; but observing that their discipline was due to the great number of officers, he proceeded to fashion his army in accordance with that of the Romans. He instituted various ranks of soldiers, whom he put under decurions, these under centurions, and these in turn under tribunes, above whom were the generals in command of the more extensive divisions. He taught this force how to give and understand signals; how to expand and turn the wings of an army; how to come to the relief of those who were hard pressed, and how to act as reserves for those in distress. He instructed them in personal courage and bodily endurance; and above all, he instructed his men to observe the laws of war, and warned them to abstain from the crimes in which they had formerly indulged, such as "theft, robbery, and rapine, for wars are best managed when the warriors preserve a good conscience."[6] Out of this army he now mustered 60,000 infantry and 250 cavalry[7] who were ready for action, besides some 4,500 mercenaries, in whom he placed his chief reliance, and also a bodyguard of 600 selected men for his own person. The troops, excepting the mercenaries, were easily maintained by the cities, for each town sent one half of their men to their army and retained the other half to provide them with supplies, so that those who sent out their corn were paid for it by that protection which they received from the men who were in arms.[8]

While thus engaged in organizing his province, however, he was continually hindered, partly by internal dissensions, but chiefly by the machinations of a local chieftain, John of Gischala, who claimed that the allegiance of the people of Galilee belonged to him and not to a representative

[6] Bell. Jud., II. xx. 7.

[7] Since an army of sixty thousand infantry should require more than two hundred and fifty horsemen, and since we find, in his future history, that Josephus had more horsemen under his command than the number here given, it is evident that one number has dropped in the copying.

[8] Bell. Jud., II. xx. 8.

of the priesthood of Jerusalem. He could not bear to have others over him; least of all could he tolerate Josephus, whose methods of preparing for war seemed too tame for him. Describing this individual, Josephus tells us, "he was a very crafty and unscrupulous rogue, outdoing all villains," and that for wicked practices there was no equal to him. "He was a ready liar,... he thought it a virtue to delude people, and would deceive even those nearest to him. He had a peculiar knack for thieving, and would not stop at shedding blood where he had hopes of even the slightest gain.... A poor brigand at the beginning of his career and hindered by his poverty in his malicious designs, he practiced alone. As he proceeded, however, he found accomplices, few at first, but increasing with his success to four hundred, with whose help he plundered the whole of Galilee and harassed the masses."[9]

And though the cities of Galilee had generally submitted to the administration of Josephus, and had permitted their walls to be put in a state of defense, each had its independent interests and leanings. Sepphoris, though entrusted with the erection of its own fortifications, and apparently eager to enter the cause, was in fact leaning towards the Romans. Its inhabitants were in great distress because their neighboring towns had determined to pillage them on account of this allegiance to Rome and their pledge of loyalty which they had given to Cestius Gallus. But using his influence in their behalf with those neighbors, Josephus averted this danger; he even permitted the Sepphorites to communicate with their fellow-citizens who were held as hostages by Cestius at Dora, in Phoenicia, as often as they pleased.[10] Tiberias, on the other hand, was torn among three factions. The first consisted of peaceful and law-abiding citizens, counseling allegiance to Nero and to King Agrippa. The second faction, led by Jesus ben Sapphias,[11] was composed of pirates and burden carriers

[9] Bell. Jud., II. xxi. 1-2.
[10] Vita, sec. 8.
[11] His name is mentioned in Vita, sec. 12.

who were bent on war. The third faction was led by Justus of Tiberias, who considered his personal interests only. Pretending to hesitate on the subject of war, he was really eager for the revolution, figuring that a change of government would bring him into power.[12]

When Josephus had learned of this state of affairs, he wrote to the Sanhedrin at Jerusalem and asked what he should do about it. They instructed him to remain at his post and take care of Galilee, and if his two assistants, Joazar and Judas, were willing, they too should remain with him until he had put his province in order. His colleagues, however, had in the short time since their arrival in Galilee become so rich from the priestly tithes (and graft) which they had collected that they preferred to return to their homes. But when Josephus pleaded with them to remain a while longer, they consented (since the possibilities for personal profit had not yet been exhausted). All three then removed from Sephoris to a village called Bethmaus, a short distance from Tiberias.

In Bethmaus, Josephus proceeded to carry out the prime order given him by the Sanhedrin before his departure for Galilee, to demolish the palace built by Herod the Tetrarch in Tiberias, which had been decorated with figures of animals in direct defiance of the Law (Ex., xx. 4). While discussing this matter with Julius Capellus and other leading men of that city, however, Jesus ben Sapphias with his following of sailors and destitute men looted the palace, stripped its roof of the gold with which it was covered and set it on fire; and, having divided the loot among themselves, slaughtered all the Greek residents of their city.[13] On hearing of these proceedings Josephus immediately hastened to Tiberias and devoted all his energies to recovering from the plunderers whatever could be recovered. This consisted of candlesticks made of Corinthian brass, royal tables, and a great quantity

[12] Vita, secs. 8 end, and 9.
[13] Vita, 12.

of uncoined silver which the marauders had overlooked, all of which he handed over to King Agrippa's officers.

From Tiberias, Josephus with his two assistants went to Gischala, for the native chief, John, had demanded authority to carry off the corn which the Romans had received as taxes and stored away in the villages of Upper Galilee. This, Josephus would not permit, as he intended to reserve the corn either for the Romans (in the event that some accommodation would be arrived at), or to keep it for his own use (should war with them be unavoidable).[14] But when unsuccessful with Josephus, John turned to his assistants, the priests Joazar and Judas. For a bribe which John had offered them, they delivered the corn.

In another proposal John stated that the Jews of Caesarea-Philippi, having by King Agrippa's order been shut up there, and having no kosher oil for their needs, had sent a request to him to see that they were provided with this commodity, lest they should be forced to violate the dietary law by resorting to oil which came from Greeks. But though Josephus knew that John's new proposal was not actuated by his regard for religion but a desire for gain, he granted the demand, "only out of fear," for, had he not given the permission, he knew he would have been stoned to death. And so it happened that John, by buying this oil at Gischala at the rate of eighty sextaries (sextary=20 ounces) for two drachmae (drachma=20 cents), and selling two sextaries for one drachma, soon accumulated a vast fortune, which he immediately used against him who gave him that privilege.[15]

Josephus now dismissed his disloyal assistants, and sent them back to Jerusalem. He then sent for the most notorious vagabonds in his province, and seeing that it was not within

[14] To Dean Milman ("Jew. Hist.," Vol. ii. p. 234) this appears as "a suspicious answer." The logical facts inserted here in the parentheses, and which the text does not literally express, are evidently beyond the Dean's vision.

[15] Vita, 13; Bell. Jud., II. xxi. 2.

his power to disarm them, persuaded the people to pay them allowances, advising them that it would be to their own advantage to give them small sums voluntarily, rather than suffer their raids upon their properties. He then bound them by oaths to get out of and not re-enter his province, unless they were invited to come, or else when they had not received their pay, and dismissed them with the injunction not to annoy the Romans or disturb their neighbors, "for my first concern is to keep Galilee in peace." Then, to see that justice was dispensed justly and kept clear of bribery, he journeyed along with his seventy elders to supervise their sentences.[16]

Josephus was now in the thirtieth year of his age, a time of life when, even if one restrains himself from satisfying any unlawful desires, it is difficult, especially when one is in a position of authority, to escape the calumnies of the envious. Yet he protected women from injury; he scorned all presents which were offered him, and even refused to accept such tithes as were duly brought to him as a priest, which fact he modestly explains, "as not being in need of them."[17]

The popularity of Josephus by this time extended over the entire province. Observing this, John, overcome with envy, wrote Josephus for permission to come to Tiberias for the hot baths which, he pretended, he needed to cure an ailment. Unsuspicious of any malicious intention on John's part, Josephus wrote those to whom he committed the administration of that city, to provide lodging for him and for any who might come along with him, and to supply them with whatsoever they should be in need of. Josephus at this time resided in a village named Cana.[18] However, no sooner had John arrived at Tiberias than he began to incite the people against Josephus in an attempt to divert their allegiance from his benefactor to himself. Many of them, always craving

[16] Vita, 14.
[17] Vita, 15.
[18] Vita, 16; compare, Bell. Jud., II. xxi. 6.

for change and discord, gladly responded to his projects. Particularly so were Justus of Tiberias and his father Pistus, who immediately deserted Josephus and attached themselves to John; and only by laborious measures and speedy action was Tiberias saved from passing into John's hands.[19]

When the Taricheans heard of the treachery of the Tiberians their fury became so great that, up in arms, and reenforced by other Galileans and many who had escaped from Tiberias, they came to Josephus, offering to take that hotbed by storm, "raze it to the ground and make slaves of its inhabitants." Horrified at the idea of commencing a civil war, Josephus pleaded with them to desist and carry their contentions no further than words, thus appeasing the anger of his loyal subjects.[20] Terrorized by the failure of his scheme, John took his armed men and removed from Tiberias to his native city, Gischala. From here he wrote to Josephus an apology, offering the most horrible oaths and curses upon himself to witness his innocence of the entire sedition which had taken place in Tiberias.[21] When another multitude of armed Galileans, who knew John as a perjurer and the lowest of villains, presented themselves to Josephus, eager to destroy both him and Gischala, Josephus likewise entreated them to be patient, as being "anxious to quell these disturbances without bloodshed."[22]

About this time, two Gentile noblemen from Tranchonitis arrived at Sepphoris, bringing with them their cattle, their arms and their money, which they had salvaged out of their country. The dogmatists of the city would have forced them to be circumcised if they were to remain among them. This, Josephus refused to allow, declaring that "every one should worship God in accordance with the dictates of his own conscience and not under compulsion."..."These men who had

[19] Vita, 17-18.
[20] Vita, 19.
[21] Vita, 20.
[22] Vita, 21.

fled to them for protection," said he, "ought not to be made to regret their having done so." Moreover, Josephus liberally provided the two men with everything they needed in accordance with their own manner of living.[23]

And now, while Josephus was in Tarichea, an incident of far-reaching results came to his attention. Some young bandits of a village called Dabaritta, near Mount Tabor, had waylaid and robbed the wife of one of King Agrippa's officials as she was traveling through the Great Plains en route from the royal territory to the Roman dominion, taking from her six hundred pieces of gold, a number of silver cups, costly garments and other valuable belongings. Josephus, always sincere in his desire to bring about better relations between the Jews and the Romans and deeply concerned for the consequences of this robbery, took possession of the booty and deposited it with Dassion and Jannaeus, who were special friends of the king, to dispatch it to the owner at their first opportunity. The furious youths, having received no share of the plunder, ran through the neighboring cities and villages denouncing Josephus as a betrayer of his people and charging him with planning to turn over Galilee to the Romans. Inflamed at what the people conceded to be his real intention, as John of Gischala and Jesus ben Sapphias had long insinuated, they broke out against him in open rebellion, some demanding the deposition of "the traitor," while others clamored for his life. The principal instigator of the mob was Jesus ben Sapphias, the unrivaled fomenter of sedition and revolution. With a Torah in his hands he stepped into the midst of the crowd, addressing them, "Fellow-citizens! If you are not disposed to hate Josephus on your own account, fix your eyes on these laws of your country which your commander-in-chief is going to betray, and for their sakes bring the man to his deserved punishment." It was only by out-arguing and out-maneuvering them and stooping to their

[23] Vita, 23.

own wretched level that Josephus was twice thereafter able to ward off the threatened danger.[24]

Before long, the feelings of the people were again aroused against Josephus. A band of instigators asserted that if the two men from Tranchonitis who had settled among them would not abandon their own religion and become Jews, they should be exterminated. They also accused these foreigners of being wizards, plying their profession for the advantage of the Romans. To save their lives, Josephus conducted them beyond their reach, over the borders of his district.[25] Again, some time later, a certain Joseph, the son of a female physician, induced a great number of young men to join him and force the leading citizens of Gamala to take up arms against their sovereign, King Agrippa. Those of the Gamalians who refused to do their bidding were put to death. Among those whom they slew were Chares, and Jesus, the brother of Justus of Tiberias. Of Josephus they asked for workmen to repair their town walls, which request was not refused. In addition, Josephus also erected more walls and fortifications for such cities and villages throughout his territory as still needed them.[26] At Tarichea, however, when it became "imperatively necessary" to inflict extreme punishment on an utterly obstinate and reckless organizer of sedition, one named Cleitus, Josephus ordered the man to act as his own executioner and to cut off his left hand.[27]

[24] Vita, 26-30. The events as narrated here are quoted after the Autobiography, which, as should be remembered, is throughout the story of a man advanced in years relating the deeds of his youth from memory. But by comparing these accounts with their parallels, where there are such, in his history of the War, which, properly speaking, is the history of Josephus' own time, we are enabled to arrive at a more complete and correct appreciation of this period.

[25] Vita, 31.

[26] Vita, 37.

[27] Vita, 32-34. Many modern writers have severely criticized Josephus for this act of barbarism. But considering the actualities and usages of the time, and the civilization in which he lived, this inhuman punishment will not appear more ruthless than the penalties inflicted for similar offenses in our own day.

Meanwhile John, whose jealousy at Josephus' increasing popularity grew more intense and more bitter, determined to procure his removal at any cost. Accordingly, having fortified his native city, Gischala, to provide himself with a place of safety, he dispatched his brother Simon, and Jonathan, the son of Sisenna, escorted by a hundred armed men, to Jerusalem, to Simon ben Gamaliel, to persuade him to induce the Sanhedrin to take the command of Galilee away from Josephus and give it to him. Simon ben Gamaliel, being an intimate and old friend of John and at the same time also on unfriendly relations with Josephus, readily gave his support to the delegation. He exerted himself in persuading the high-priest Ananus, Jeshua ben Gamala, and some others who were in charge of the defense forces of Jerusalem, to clip the sprouting wings of Josephus, who, "having reached the height of glory, threatens to make an assault upon Jerusalem at the head of a great army." However, he found it not quite so easy to persuade Ananus by honeyed words alone. Ananus demonstrated that Josephus was held in too high regard among the influential priesthood and city leaders to be disposed of so easily. Moreover, he added, to accuse a man against whom no just charge could be made would be a scandalous proceeding. But Simon ben Gamaliel, Josephus says, "was a man of great wisdom, and able to retrieve an unfortunate situation in affairs of state," and when by his eloquence he found it impossible to secure the co-operation of Ananus, who had command of the soldiery, he, having control over the public funds, resorted to bribery. He called for Simon, the brother of John, and instructed him to send "presents" to Ananus and his friends, as a means of persuading them to change their minds. By this method Simon achieved his purpose, for as a result of bribes, Ananus and his party agreed to expel Josephus from Galilee.[28]

[28] (a) This is reminiscent of a law propounded by the Spanish theologian, Molina (1536-1600 CE.), which says, "It is lawful for a judge to accept secret gifts, to encourage him to give a just ver-

A commission of five men,—Jonathan, Ananias, Joazar, and Jonathan's two sons, Simon and Judas, "all very able speakers,"—was immediately sent off to incite and prejudice the Galileans against the governor. Forty thousand drachmae ($8,000) was taken from the public treasury and placed at the commission's disposal for the campaign. Six hundred Galilean pirates under Jesus ben Sapphias, "that then sojourned at Jerusalem," were given three months' pay "to follow Jona-

Coin of Ananus.

than and obey his orders." They further engaged three hundred local "citizens" (!) to hang on to the rest and "make themselves useful." When all were ready for the march, Simon, John's brother, with his hundred armed men led the way. The specific orders given this army of outlaws were to bring back Josephus dead or alive. A letter was meanwhile sent to John by a runner, advising him to "make ready for

diet." (b) In the Talmud (Sota, ix. 15; Aboth, i. 17-18; and Kerithoth, i. 7), Simon ben Gamaliel is glorified as one of the most celebrated Fathers. In the New Testament he is represented as having sat with Apostle Paul at the feet of his father, Gamaliel II (Acts, xxii. 3), who counseled in the Sanhedrin to release the accused Apostles, "since their work, if it were of man, would come to naught, while if it were of God, it is in vain to oppose it" (Acts, v. 34-39). In consequence of that counsel, Christian tradition represents him as having been a Christian (Clementine "Recognitions," i. 65 seq.). According to the narrative of the presbyter Lucianus of Jerusalem, derived from Laurentius Surius' "Vitae Sanctorum," iv. 502 seq.; also from Confessor Baronius' "Annal. Eccl.," 415; as well as the Benedictine, Paris edition of Augustine, Vol. vii. Appendix, on the finding of the bones of the martyr Stephen, the bones of Nicodemus, Gamaliel and his son Abiba, who all here figure as Christians, were found at the same time as those of the martyr.

fighting Josephus," and ordering the inhabitants of Sepphoris, Gabara and Tiberias to provide him with auxiliaries.[29]

Meanwhile, however, Jeshua ben Gamala, who had been present at the conference, being an intimate friend of Josephus' family, reported the whole plot to Josephus' father, Mattathias, who in turn wrote to his son about it. Deeply distressed, both over the rascality of his fellow-citizens who had given the order to put him to death, and also by the pleadings in his father's letter to come home, as he longed to see him before he died, Josephus, then living in the plain of Asochi, felt that he should withdraw, and notified his friends that such was his intention. But when they spread word throughout the surrounding country, thousands of men, women and children came beseeching him not to abandon them to ruin at the mercy of the brigands; also casting reproaches upon the scoundrels of Jerusalem for not allowing their country to remain in peace.[30] Moved with compassion at the sight of such a mass of sorrowing humanity, Josephus gave up his intention of submitting to the mandate and consented to remain. But, dismissing them to their homes, he ordered five thousand of the men to return to him armed and provisioned. When the five thousand came back he joined them to the three thousand infantry and eighty horse which he had with him, and marched to Chabolo, a village in the confines of Ptolemais, pretending to get ready to fight two cohorts of footmen and one troop of horsemen under Placidus who had been sent there by Cestius Gallus to burn the village in the neighborhood of Ptolemais.[31]

At this time Jonathan and his fellow-emissaries who had been sent by Simon ben Gamaliel and Ananus arrived in Galilee. Not possessing the courage to attack Josephus openly Jonathan sent him the following letter:—"Jonathan and his fellow ambassadors who are sent by the people of Jerusalem

[29] Vita, 38-40; compare Bell. Jud., II. xxi. 7.
[30] Vita, 41-42.
[31] Vita, 43.

to Josephus send greeting. We are commissioned by the leaders of Jerusalem, who have heard that John of Gischala had frequently plotted against thee to rebuke him and instruct him to be subject to thee hereafter. We are also desirous to consult with thee about our common concerns, and to decide on a suitable course of action. Therefore, come to us quickly, and with only a few attendants, for this village cannot accommodate a great number of soldiers."

This letter was brought by a Jewish horseman, in the second hour of the night (7-8 P.M.), when Josephus was dining with his friends and some Galilean worthies. Having been announced and shown in by Josephus' orders, the trooper entered, and with no salute whatever reached out the letter and said: "This letter is sent thee by those who have come from Jerusalem. Write the answer to it quickly, as I must return to them very soon." The guests were astonished at the man's audacity, but Josephus invited him to sit down and join him at dinner. The soldier refused. Then, holding the letter in his hands as he received it, he resumed his conversation with his friends on other subjects. Not long after, dismissing the others to their rest, he motioned to four of his most intimate friends to remain and ordered a servant to bring some wine to the table. He then secretly opened the letter, acquainted himself with its contents, and sealed it up again as if he had not yet read it. Josephus then presented to the messenger twenty drachmae for the cost of his journey, which he accepted thankfully. Noting that he loved money and that he could be entrapped by that means most easily, Josephus offered him a drachma for every cup of wine if he would consent to drink with him. The man embraced the proposal and drank till he betrayed the whole plot. And so, without being questioned he divulged the whole conspiracy against Josephus, and that he was doomed to die by those who sent him.

When Josephus heard this, he wrote the following answer:—"Josephus to Jonathan and those who are with him, sendeth greeting. Upon the information that you have reached Galilee in good health, I am delighted; more especially because I can now resign the care of public affairs here into your hands and return home, as I have for a long time desired to do. And I confess that I ought not only to come to you as far as Xaloth, but even further, and this without your invitation. But I must request your excuse for my inability to do so now, since I am watching the movements of Placidus who is meditating to march into Galilee. Do you, therefore, on receipt of this letter, come to me. Fare you well."[32]

Handing this letter to the messenger, he sent him off with thirty Galileans of the best character, whom he instructed to salute the delegates, but to say nothing else to them. To each of the thirty men he attached a soldier, whom he esteemed trustworthy, to watch that no conversation passed between those whom he had sent and those of Jonathan's party; and so they started off. But when Jonathan on receiving the answer, saw his first attempt had failed, he sent Josephus another letter, the contents of which were as follows: "Jonathan, and those with him, to Josephus send greeting. We require thee within three days' time to come to us to the village of Gabara, without any armed men, that we may hear what thy charges are against John."

Without, however, waiting for Josephus' arrival, Jonathan with his colleagues left his camp at Gabara to begin, in accordance with his original instructions, to antagonize the Galileans against him. His first stop was at Japha. There the inhabitants in abusive language ordered him out. Not daring to reply or show his displeasure, he proceeded to other villages. But everywhere he was greeted with threats and denunciations, the people protesting that they did not want any other governor than Josephus. Unsuccessful in the villages, Jonathan and his companions went to Sepphoris, the largest city in Galilee. Here the inhabitants, whose sentiments were pro-Roman, went to hear them, but neither praised nor reproached

[32] Vita, 44.

Josephus. But when they came to Asochis, the people gave them the same reception they had met with at Japha. No longer able to control his wrath, Jonathan ordered his armed men to beat the Asochians with their cudgels.

They now returned to Gabara, where they met John with three thousand armed men. But as Josephus understood from his last letter that he was determined to assault him, he set out from Chabolo with three thousand men also and came to Jotapata, where he could be near him, and from here wrote Jonathan the following letter: "If you are really desirous to have me come to you, you know there are two hundred and forty cities and villages in Galilee; I will come to any of them which you may select, excepting Gischala and Gabara, the one which is John's native city and the other in confederacy with him." [33]

On receipt of this letter, Jonathan called for a council with John as his principal consultant, to consider by what means they might attack Josephus. John recommended that letters be written to every community in Galilee, "for surely there must be at least one or two men in each of them adverse to Josephus and willing to attest against him. By then presenting a copy of this resolution to the people of Jerusalem as the referendum of Galilee, it would not only bring their own consent to his removal, but their influence would also lead the whole of Galilee to a similar decision, and consequently desert him." John's idea was highly agreeable to the council and accepted with great approval.

In the evening, however, one Saccheus, who had listened to these proceedings, deserting them, came to Josephus and reported what they were about to do, adding that no time was to be lost. Josephus immediately commanded one Jacob, a faithful soldier of his bodyguard, to take two hundred men to the roads leading southwards of Gabara, and Jeremiah, another trusted friend, to go with six hundred men to the southern border of Galilee, where the roads extend towards

[33] Vita, 45.

Jerusalem, charging both of these men to arrest all who were found traveling with letters and to hold them in bonds on the spot, but take the letters from them and send them to him.[34]

Having given these orders, Josephus separated his soldiers that were with him into four divisions, each under a commander, and appointing a number of the most loyal of his men as a bodyguard, he departed from Jotapata to Gabara, where he arrived about noon of the following day. Reaching Gabara he found the whole plain before the village swarmed with armed men who, in obedience to his orders, had come from all parts of Galilee to join him, with great numbers still pouring in from the villages; and when he took his stand to speak to them, they all greeted him with acclamations, hailing him as a benefactor and the savior of their country. Thanking them for their affection, he instructed them to pitch their tents and remain on hand, advising them also, that meantime they should attack no one, nor spoil the country, wishing "to quell the disturbances without shedding blood." On that day also, Josephus received a number of letters from Jeremiah, which he had taken from Jonathan's messengers who were on their way to Jerusalem. Seeing these letters filled with slander and lies, Josephus, without saying a word to anyone, decided to meet his enemies.[35]

When Jonathan heard Josephus was coming, he retired with all his men and with John to ben Sapphias' large and massive castle, locking all its doors except one, within which he placed an armed ambuscade to await his arrival. Their orders were to admit Josephus, but exclude everyone else. Josephus, having betimes discovered their plot, took up his quarters at a short distance from the castle, pretending to sleep, fatigued from his march. Jonathan and his friends, imagining that he was really sleeping, hastened to the nearby villages to persuade the people to come and attack him. But

[34] Vita, 46.
[35] Vita, 47.

upon their appearance at the villages, the popular cries of loyalty to Josephus and reproaches against themselves for coming to throw the province into disorder were the same as those with which the Galileans everywhere greeted them on former occasions. The villagers ordered Jonathan and his bandit armies to be on their way, declaring that their minds were fixed never to have anyone rule over them but Josephus.[36]

When Jonathan and his companions saw this demonstration of devotion to Josephus, they became terror-stricken, lest the Galileans should assault them, and began to consider a way of escape. As they were thus deliberating, Josephus reassuringly bade them to stay and spoke to them. He reminded them of their first letter wherein they had written him that they had been sent by the people of Jerusalem to adjust the differences between him and John, and desired him to visit them, ostensibly for that purpose. He then admonished them for not having examined into the prevailing difficulties between the two enemies and the consequences thereof; and even yet proposed to undergo such an inquiry if in that endeavor they came to Galilee.[37] Josephus then read two of those letters that had been forwarded to him by Jeremiah, containing abuse and falsehoods of every variety.[38] He reasoned with them, and pointed out to them the injustice of their efforts; and forgiving them for their past actions, he appealed to them to go back to Jerusalem and make a truthful report of the conditions in Galilee. Thus advising them to go back to their homes, he jumped on his saddle, ordering the Galileans whom he had assembled to follow him to the village of Sogane, some three miles distant.[39]

On his arrival at Sogane he directed a hundred of the leading men, well advanced in years, to make themselves ready to go to Jerusalem, in order to complain before the

[36] Vita, 48.
[37] Vita, 49.
[38] Vita, 50.
[39] Vita, 51.

people against the emissaries who had come to raise sedition in Galilee. Their orders were that, if the citizenry became impressed with their representations, to induce them to request the Sanhedrin to send him written instructions directing him to continue in Galilee and to order Jonathan and his companions to move out of it.[40]

In the meantime Jonathan and his colleagues, instead of returning to Jerusalem, proceeded to Tiberias, for Jesus ben Sapphias had written to them promising to induce the people to submit to them. Information of this communication, however, reached Josephus in a letter from Silas, whom he had left in charge of that city, advising him to go there immediately. Arriving there unexpectedly, the envoys received him with hypocritical courtesy, explaining their desire to deliver up John,—whom they had beforehand sent away to Gischala,—into their hands, though they were anxious, they said, to return to their homes. Corroborating these assertions with the most awe-inspiring oaths, they requested Josephus to take up his lodging elsewhere temporarily, because of the approaching Sabbath, on which day they claimed, he might inconvenience the city by his presence.[41] Suspecting nothing, he retired to nearby Tarichea.

New excitements and tumults, however, following one upon the other, compelled Josephus to return to Tiberias. The four deputies, with Jesus ben Sapphias and Justus of that city, endeavored to arouse the community against him. They first accused him of misappropriating twenty gold pieces which, they claimed, he realized from the sale of some of the silver bullion which he had recovered from the ruins of Herod's palace. But this money, Josephus proved by Jonathan himself, and by his friends who stood present, he gave them to defray their traveling expenses homewards. Unsuccessful with this, they attempted to murder him for "tyrannizing and deceiving the people of Galilee with his speeches," when

[40] Vita, 52.
[41] Vita, 53.

his loyal Galileans lifted him up and hurried him away out of the reach of his enemies.[42]

Indignant at this treatment, the people pressed on Josephus to delay no longer, but to open war against the trouble-makers. Enraged as they were, however, he restrained them, advising them to tarry a while longer, until he had heard the report of the hundred men he had sent to Jerusalem.[43]

A few days later this deputation came back, reporting the popular indignation at Simon ben Gamaliel and Ananus for having, without their knowledge or consent, sent ambassadors to Galilee to expel Josephus from the province, adding that so great was their indignation that they were ready to burn Simon's and Ananus' houses. They also brought letters whereby the principal citizens of Jerusalem, at the request of the people, confirmed him in the government of Galilee, and ordered Jonathan and his colleagues to return to Jerusalem at once.

Encouraged by these instructions, Josephus began to act with more vigor; and dispensing with all further delay or formality he set out to rid himself of the peace-breakers.[44] Entrapping Jonathan and Ananias as they were journeying from Tiberias to Dabaritta on a mischievous mission,[45] and then Simon, by inviting him to come out a short distance from the city of Tiberias "for a conference on dividing the command of Galilee with him,"[46] and some time later Joazar, by intimidating the Tiberians to give him up, he handed the four over to five hundred armed soldiers, who escorted them back to Jerusalem. The Tiberians now begged forgiveness, promising to make amends for their errors of the past by their fidelity in the future. They also requested Josephus to see to it that those who had plundered their city gave up their plunder. He accordingly ordered the possessors of such prop-

[42] Vita, 54-58.
[43] Vita, 59.
[44] Vita, 60-61.
[45] Vita, 62.
[46] Vita, 63.

erty to return it to the owners. A great quantity of spoils was thus brought together and restored to them.[47]

About this time, however, after seven months of continuous disturbances, and with the entire reconciliatory program which Josephus had in mind thrown into the background, and with both his army and the people unprepared for war, Vespasian and his army appeared in Galilee.

[47] Vita, 64.

CHAPTER VII

The WAR *in* GALILEE, 67 CE.

DURING the winter of 66-67 CE., while Josephus was thus occupied with his enemies, Vespasian pushed forward his preparations for the campaign. Leaving Nero at Achaia, he himself sailed for Antioch, the capital of Syria, to concentrate the Roman army that was there, while he sent his older son Titus to Alexandria to take command of the Fifth and Tenth Legions,[1] with which he was to join him at Ptolemais on the coast of Palestine.

In the early spring, as soon as the weather permitted, Vespasian marched to Ptolemais, there to await Titus with his legions. But shortly after he had reached Ptolemais and before his son's arrival, a deputation from Sepphoris appeared before him, offering their allegiance and requesting that a Roman garrison be installed in their city.[2] Vespasian immediately dispatched six thousand horsemen under the command of Placidus to protect that metropolis. Thus, even before the Roman army had reached its full fighting strength, Josephus lost possession of the most important and strongest fortress in Galilee.[3]

With the arrival of Titus and his two legions, the army

[1] Bell. Jud., III. i. 3.
[2] Bell. Jud., III. ii. 4.
[3] Bell. Jud., III. ii. 4, iv. 1; Vita, 74.

of Vespasian consisted of three distinct legions,—the Fifth, Tenth and Fifteenth,—and eighteen cohorts;[4] five more cohorts and one troop of cavalry enlisted from Caesarea, and five troops from Syria, in addition to two thousand bowmen and a thousand cavalry from each of the subject kings,—Agrippa of Chalcis, Antiochus of Commagene and Sohemus of Emesa,—and one thousand cavalry and five thousand infantry, mainly bowmen from Malchus of Arabia: in all about sixty thousand men, not counting the servants who followed in vast numbers, and who were "inferior to none of the soldiers in either bravery, courage or skill."[5]

Having put his army in order, Vespasian advanced a short distance from Ptolemais, and pitched his camp near Garis, where Josephus had his encampment. But at the approach of Vespasian's disciplined and orderly regiments, the ill-organized, ill-equipped and untrained soldiers of Josephus became so overwhelmed with fear, that even before coming face to face with the Romans they fled in all directions, and Josephus with a few remaining companions was obliged to take refuge in the fortress of Tiberias. Thus without drawing a sword Vespasian became master of all the Galilean lowlands.[6] So Vespasian marched to the city of Gadara, which, owing to the absence there of a sufficient Jewish garrison, he carried upon the first assault. Entering it, he slew all men who were of age, showing no mercy to old or young, so bitter was his hatred of the nation because of the iniquity the Zealots had been guilty of in the affair of Cestius. And not content with setting fire to Gadara, he also burnt all the neighboring towns and villages and carried their inhabitants into captivity.[7]

Deserted by his men, and foreseeing the final catastrophe for which the fortunes of his nation were heading, and recognizing the fact that the only hope of its salvation lay in

[4] A cohort was a tenth of a legion, or about six hundred men.
[5] Bell. Jud., III. iv. 2.
[6] Bell. Jud., III. iv. 2-3.
[7] Bell. Jud., III. vii. 1.

submission, Josephus wrote to the Sanhedrin an exact account of the conditions of his province, demanding instructions as to whether he should enter into negotiations of peace, or if they wanted him to continue the war they should send him an army of sufficient strength to fight the Romans.[8] When these were not forthcoming, Josephus with his few men, on the twenty-first day of Iyar (May-June), took refuge in the fortress of Jotapata, which he himself had made the strongest of all Galilean fortresses.

(What transpired within the Supreme Council at Jerusalem during the present crisis is not known. For, as we proceed, we find the existing government of Moderates superseded by a fusion of all factions. Neither does Josephus tell us why, in default of a response from the Sanhedrin, he resolved to plunge into war, rather than sue for peace, which for him, as a confirmed pacifist, would have been the more natural procedure. We cannot, therefore, but surmise that Josephus' decision, at this crucial moment, to submit to a siege at Jotapata, was the result of despair that Vespasian would any longer entertain moderation, since so much of Galilee was already in his possession.)

When Vespasian was informed that Josephus was in that stronghold, he turned his attention in that direction. For the capture of Josephus, who was reputed to be the most sagacious of his enemies, it appeared to him, would be equal to the capture of all Judea. Accordingly, he immediately sent his general Placidus with a thousand cavalry to surround the city so that Josephus might not in the meantime escape,[9] till the next day when he himself could bring up his entire army and gain possession of him by assault.[10]

On Iyar the 22nd, Vespasian with his army arrived be-

[8] Bell. Jud., III. vii. 2.
[9] Bell. Jud., III. vii. 3.
[10] Bell. Jud., III. vii. 4.

fore Jotapata. But as he came too late in the evening, he meanwhile surrounded the city with two rows of infantry and a third one of cavalry, to prevent every possible escape, and postponed the assault till the following day.[11] In the morning when the attack was made, Josephus and the inhabitants, greatly alarmed for the fate of the city, threw themselves upon the Romans and succeeded in driving them away from the walls. They wounded a great many of them and killed thirteen, but at a cost of seventeen fatalities and six hundred wounded among their own ranks for that single day.[12] Similar attacks and counter attacks with very heavy losses on both sides continued for five days longer.[13]

To overcome the natural strength of the town, its almost impregnable fortifications, and the stubborn resistance of its war-yearning inhabitants, Vespasian summoned an assembly of his generals to deliberate with him on the future course of action. At this council it was decided to raise a bank against the only accessible wall to approximately its own height, for which it was necessary to send the whole army to strip mountains and forests to bring the enormous masses of stone and timber together.[14] On these earthworks Vespasian brought up his war engines to the number of a hundred and sixty, and ordered his artillerymen to fire on the Jewish defenders. One form of the engines shooting lances, another sending firebrands or arrows, and others throwing stones of great weight quickly made the ramparts too dangerous for the Jews to stand on, and finally entirely untenable.[15]

Josephus, thinking it disgraceful not to be able to contrive something in opposition to the Roman earthworks, ordered his masons to increase the height of his walls to the level of their towers and to raise other towers over these structures. And when the workmen protested that it was

[11] Bell. Jud., III. vii. 4.
[12] Bell. Jud., III. vii. 5.
[13] Bell. Jud., III. vii. 6.
[14] Bell. Jud., III. vii. 7-8.
[15] Bell. Jud., III. vii. 9.

impossible to do this work under such a hail of missiles, he devised the following protection for them: he ordered tall stakes to be fixed on top of the walls upon which he suspended fresh hides from newly killed oxen, that these hides by yielding when stones were thrown at them might receive them in their folds, while their moisture would quench the firebrands. Behind these screens the masons were able to work day and night, raising the walls to a height of thirty feet and surmounting them with a greater number of towers than they had before. This ingenuity of Josephus and the perseverance of the inhabitants greatly discouraged the Romans who considered themselves already masters of the town.[16] Deeply irritated at this crafty piece of maneuvering of Josephus and the audacity of the people of Jotapata, Vespasian decided to blockade the city and starve the defenders into surrender. Through great privations, he hoped, they would either sue for mercy or perish of hunger.[17]

The city of Jotapata was well supplied with corn and all other necessaries, excepting salt, but there was a great shortage of water, the people being usually dependent on rain water. Josephus, anticipating this water famine, had from the beginning ordered that the people be given their drink by measure. This condition soon became known to the Romans, for from where they stood they could see over the city wall the Jews flocking to one place and at a fixed hour to receive their water rations, and, directing their quick-firers against them as they passed, they struck down a great many of them.[18] Vespasian hoped that before long their reservoir would be emptied, but Josephus' store of schemes was not exhausted: he ordered a number of his men to soak their clothes and hang them dripping over the battlements, till all the walls were dripping with water. The Romans were confounded, for since they could waste so much water, they

[16] Bell. Jud., III. vii. 10.
[17] Bell. Jud., III. vii. 11.
[18] Bell. Jud., III. vii. 12.

could not possibly be in that miserable state of privation they had expected. Despairing, therefore, of reducing the city by famine, Vespasian returned to armed measures, the mode of attack to which the people of Jotapata wished to drive him.[19]

To provide the city with as many comforts as he could, Josephus devised another scheme. There was a narrow and rugged path, on the west side of the city, leading down to the bed of a dry creek, so rough and dangerous to walk over that the Romans found it unnecessary to guard it. By this path he sent messengers with letters to Jews outside of the city with whom they wished to communicate, and to bring back such necessaries as the people had not been supplied with. These messengers were instructed to creep past the sentries on all fours, covered with sheep-skins, so that in the moonlight they might look like dogs. This was done for a long time till the men were detected, and the ravine was closed up.[20]

But Josephus soon saw that Jotapata could not hold out much longer, and that his own life, since his capture was held by the Romans of such great importance, would be endangered if he remained there. He therefore entered into a consultation with the leading men of the city on how he could flee with them out of it.[21] For by his presence there, he argued, he could not be of any material benefit to them, but on the contrary, only render the Romans more persistent, whereas from the outside of the city he could be of far greater service, for he would immediately raise all Galilee, and, by so diverting their attention elsewhere, would draw the Romans away from it. But such words were inconceivable to the people. Children, men, and women with infants in their arms, threw themselves weeping at his feet, imploring him to share with them their fortunes, not because they begrudged him his own chance of safety, but because they

[19] Bell. Jud., III. vii. 13.
[20] Bell. Jud., III. vii. 14.
[21] Bell. Jud., III. vii. 15.

thought that with him among them no evil could befall them.[22] And so, partly moved by compassion, and partly feeling that if he did not yield to their supplications he might be held by force, he determined to remain; and seizing upon the moment of excitement he led his forces to a desperate attack. Summoning the most ambitious of his men, they suddenly rushed forth, drove away the Roman guards, and, penetrating their camp, tore up their tents and set fire to their lines in many places. Similar attacks continued for several days.[23]

The Romans suffered from these sallies, for in their heavy armor they could not pursue the light-armored Jews who within the instant had done their mischief and disappeared behind their walls. Vespasian, therefore, ordered his troops to avoid the assaults of "these men who were bent on death," and thereafter depended mainly on his Arabian archers, Syrian slingers, and stone throwers, to repel their attacks. Now the Jews suffered greatly by these long-range engines, but also fought desperately, continually refilling for those who were exhausted or slain.[24] Vespasian began to feel as if he were himself besieged by these take-offs of the Jews; but by now, as the earthworks were approaching the walls, he ordered his battering-rams brought up for action. The battering-ram was an immense beam of wood, like the mast of a ship, capped with a huge thumper of iron, shaped like the head of a ram, from which the machine took its name. This beam was suspended to another beam which was supported by strong posts fastened in the ground. It was pulled back by a large body of men and then pushed forwards with so tremendous a crash that no tower or wall ever resisted more than its first few batteries.[25]

When Josephus saw that under the repeated blows of

[22] Bell. Jud., III. vii. 16.
[23] Bell. Jud., III. vii. 17.
[24] Bell. Jud., III. vii. 18.
[25] Bell. Jud., III. vii. 19.

this engine, constantly directed at the same place, the wall began to crumble and was about to topple over, he devised a new expedient. He ordered that sacks be filled with chaff and let down by ropes from the walls to catch the blows of the ram. This seriously delayed the Romans until they invented a counter-device; attaching blades of scythes to the ends of long poles, they cut the ropes which held the sacks. When the battering-ram had thus recovered its force, Josephus resorted to fire; in three sallies, his men, with lighted combustibles in their hands, rushed out and ignited the engines, shelters, and the wooden props which supported the enemy's embankments. The timbers of the earthworks having been cemented with bitumen, pitch, and sulphur, blazed up with such fierceness and rapidity, that the works which cost the Romans many days of severe labor, were destroyed in one single hour.[26]

An act worthy of admiration and recounting, exploited by a certain Eleazar, son of Sameas, a native of Saab, in Galilee, is recorded by Josephus at this juncture. This man, lifting an immense stone from the wall, threw it at the battering-ram with such force and steady aim that its head broke off; then leaping down he secured his prize, and, though pelted with darts and arrows by the enemy, carried it back as a trophy to the top of the wall, where, as he stood among his comrades who admired him for his bravery, he succumbed to his bleeding wounds, and fell in a heap with the ram's head in his hands. Two other Galileans who greatly distinguished themselves, were the brothers Netiras and Philip of Ruma. Jumping upon the front guards of the tenth legion, they charged them with such force and fury, that they broke up their lines and put to flight all who opposed them.[27]

Spurred on by these heroic examples, Josephus and his men again sallied out and set fire to the machines, and the

[26] Bell. Jud., III. vii. 20.

[27] Bell. Jud., III. vii. 21. Netiras and Philip probably had a small company of volunteers under them.

works belonging to the fifth and tenth legions; the other units quickly buried their war materials and combustibles. However, by evening the Romans had re-erected the battering-ram, and brought it up to that part of the wall which had been battered before. But while Vespasian was directing the work, one of the defenders on the wall struck him with a javelin in the foot. The wound was small, but the news of the attack caused the greatest disorder among the Romans, who abandoned the siege and came running to their bleeding chief. Vespasian speedily allayed their fears, and to avenge their commander, the whole army rushed to fight the Jews more energetically than ever.[28]

Josephus and his men did not abandon their walls, but continued firing at the wicker shelters which protected those who worked the battering-ram. However, they fought at a great disadvantage, for the light of their own fires made them as visible a target for the Romans as in broad daylight, while they themselves could not take as steady an aim at the enemy in the distance, whom in the darkness of the night they were unable to see. Consequently, whole files of their own men fell under the constant hail of missiles which came from the Roman quick-firers and stone-throwers with such force as to shatter the capstones of the walls and sweep away the corners of the towers. A man standing near Josephus had his head blown away by one of these stones to a distance of three furlongs. A woman with child was struck so violently that her unborn infant was cast to a distance of half a furlong. It was a night of terror and confusion. The clatter of the engines, the calls of the army, the deafening sounds of the stones from the battering-ram as they struck the ramparts, re-echoing from the surrounding mountains, mingled with the shrieks of the women and children within the city and the moans of the dying defenders on the wall. The ground around the firing lines ran red with blood, and men could ascend to the top of the wall over the piled corpses of their

[28] Bell. Jud., III. vii. 22.

comrades who had fallen in Jotapata in that single dreadful night alone.[29]

In the morning, Vespasian, having allowed his army a short rest, summoned his lieutenants before him to prepare them for the final storming of the city. To prevent any of the besieged from escaping in the meantime, he ordered the bravest of his horsemen to dismount, and stationed them three deep opposite that section of the wall which during the night had been demolished. They were completely encased in armor and armed with lances, to be ready to charge the moment the appliances for entering the breach were appended, for they were to lead the troops into the fortress. Behind these he placed the flower of his infantry. The rest of the cavalry he distributed along the heights encircling the city, to prevent the flight of a single man when the stronghold was taken. In their rear were the archers, arranged in a half circle, the slingers, the engineers, and others with ladders which were to be planted against such parts of the wall as had not yet been touched by the catapults, in order to divert the attention of the besieged and induce them to abandon the opening whereby the Romans were to enter.[30]

When Josephus, with his usual sagacity, perceived Vespasian's cunning movements, he selected the old men, together with the crippled and wounded, to garrison those parts of the wall which were in perfect condition, while the strongest of his men he posted at the breach, six, led by himself, forming the first line. He instructed his men not to become alarmed when the legions trumpeted their war-signals, but when the enemy's darts began to shower, to crouch down and cover their heads with their shields until the archers had exhausted their quivers; then, the moment the gangplanks were fastened, to leap upon them and fight, not for their own safety, for this hope had long passed, but as avengers

[29] Bell. Jud., III. vii. 23.
[30] Bell. Jud., III. vii. 24.

of their fallen comrades and their wives and children whose bitter fate was momentarily impending.[31]

And now the trumpets sounded their signals, and the arrows, "like a cloud darkening the sun," began to pour from all directions; and as the planks were connected, the Jews, obedient to Josephus' injunctions, rushed out upon the enemy before even those who had laid them could set their feet upon them. The effect of the siege on Josephus' forces, however, began to manifest itself with dreadful consequences. Their ranks were diminishing with such pernicious rapidity, that while the Romans could continually replenish their exhausted lines with fresh men, the Jews had none any longer to re-enforce them.[32]

In this critical situation, Josephus resorted to the following expedients. He ordered boiling oil to be poured on the ascending phalanx, dispersing them from the bridges in excruciating agony; for the fat, which heats quickly and cools slowly, seeped into their armor and fed upon their flesh like fire.[33] Hot fenugreek was poured upon the gangplanks, which made the Romans slip and stumble whether attempting to ascend or retreat. Some of them fell on their faces and were crushed under foot by those who followed, while many rolled off from the bridgework, where they were struck down by the darts and stones of the Jews. At last, towards evening, Vespasian called off his soldiers. The Romans had many slain and many more wounded, while the Jews had only six killed, but over three hundred were carried back to the city. This battle took place on the twentieth day of Sivan (June-July, 67 CE.).[34]

To meet this obstinate resistance, Vespasian ordered his troops to raise the height of his embankments still higher, and to erect upon them three towers, each fifty feet high and

[31] Bell. Jud., III. vii. 25.
[32] Bell. Jud., III. vii. 27.
[33] Bell. Jud., III. vii. 28.
[34] Bell. Jud., III. vii. 29.

entirely encased in iron, to be both indestructible and fireproof. In these towers he placed the archers, slingers, and lighter stone-throwers, who thus hidden by the height of the earthworks and the three superstructures renewed their assault upon those on the wall underneath them. Unable to avoid the projectiles which came from the unseen enemy above, and seeing that the towers in their iron casings could not be set on fire, the defenders abandoned the wall and resorted to their only remaining and desperate means of defense, that of repelling those who attempted to enter the city. The cost of life among themselves, during several days of such encounters, was enormous, while the losses among the Romans were very slight.[35]

During this time, too, the seditionary center, Japhia,[36] emboldened by the vigorous defense of Jotapata, revolted against the Romans. Consequently, Vespasian dispatched Trajan,[37] the commander of the tenth legion, with two thousand foot and a thousand horse to reduce that city. Besides the natural strength of the locality, the town was also surrounded by a double wall. But when Trajan arrived there he found the hotheads among its inhabitants impatiently awaiting him outside the walls and ready for action. He joined them in battle, and after a short resistance, chased them back into their enclosure. But when after bursting through the first wall, with the Romans following close at their heels, they endeavored to pass through the second wall, the more judicious residents of Japhia, who were in the majority, closed the gates on the scoundrels. Thus cooped up between the two walls, they were butchered to the last man. This battle took place on the twenty-fifth day of Sivan.[38] To Samaria, where similar outbreaks occurred, Vespasian sent Cerealis, the commander of the fifth legion, with six hundred horsemen and

[35] Bell. Jud., III. vii. 30.

[36] This Japhia, a few miles south of Jotapata, is mentioned in Joshua, xix. 12.

[37] He was the father of the future emperor of that name.

[38] Bell. Jud., III. vii. 31.

three thousand footmen to suppress the insurrections. It was now the height of the summer, and the Samaritans who had not yet laid in provisions were also in great want of water, to the extent that many died from thirst. Therefore when Cerealis concluded that the revolutionists had sufficiently suffered, he demanded that they throw down their arms, promising them a general amnesty. When these overtures were refused, he slew every one of them, eleven thousand and six hundred in all. This massacre took place on the twenty-seventh day of Sivan.[39]

Meanwhile the end of Jotapata was drawing near. For forty-seven days the enemy was kept at bay. But by the end of this time, Josephus' ranks had become weak and worn out from continued fighting by day and watching by night, and greatly thinned down in numbers. A deserter reported to Vespasian how few there were left in the city and how enfeebled these were from hardships which they had suffered, confiding to him that "during the last watch of the night, when the sentries are thoroughly weary, and the morning sleep comes upon them, the city could easily be taken."[40]

At that hour Titus, assisted by one of his tribunes, Domitius Sabinus, with a few men of the fifteenth legion, followed by Sextus Cerealis and Placidus with the troops under his command, mounted the wall, and killing the sleeping sentinels made themselves masters of Jotapata. Remembering well what they had suffered throughout the siege, the Romans spared none, nor pitied any, but drove the people from the city and down the deep slope in a general massacre. Many of the men who had been overlooked in the fortress, foreseeing a similar death at the hands of the Romans, put an end to their own lives by their swords.[41]

Well might the Romans have boasted of concluding this siege with not a single loss of life, had not a centurion, named

[39] Bell. Jud., III. vii. 32.
[40] Bell. Jud., III. vii. 33.
[41] Bell. Jud., III. vii. 34.

Antonius, been treacherously slain when the fortress was captured. One of the defenders who had fled into a cavern entreated the officer to extend his hand to him, to assist him to climb up and surrender. But when the centurion reached him his hand, the fugitive from below stabbed him and killed him instantly.[42] On the next day all who appeared in the streets or were found in the houses were put to the sword. On the same day the Romans searched all caverns and underground passages and wreaked vengeance on all men, sparing none but women and children, whom they made captives to the number of twelve hundred. Of those who were slain during the entire siege, there were forty thousand. Vespasian gave orders that the city should be demolished and the fortifications burned to the ground. Thus was Galilee's most powerful stronghold taken by the Romans on the new moon of Tamuz (July, 67 CE.).[43]

A search for Josephus was now instituted by the Romans, who in vain had sought for his body among the dead and in the most concealed recesses of the city. Vespasian was very anxious for his capture, for he considered that if that wily general were once taken, the rest of the war would be an easy matter. During the final massacre, however, Josephus had taken refuge in a large cave, accessible through a deep pit, which could not be seen from above ground. There he unexpectedly found forty deserters who during the siege had abandoned their withering kin to be mercilessly slaughtered, and provisioning themselves luxuriously, made this cavern their hiding place. In the daytime, when the garrison was strolling about, he remained hidden, while at night he crept out and looked for some way of escape from the city. But even then the Romans were present in every quarter, and he was obliged to descend again into the den. For two days he thus remained undetected. On the third day, however, a

[42] Bell. Jud., III. vii. 35.

[43] Bell. Jud., III. vii. 36. According to Niese, Jotapata was taken on July 20th.

woman who had been with the fugitives in the cavern, on ascending was captured, and she disclosed his whereabouts. Thereupon Vespasian immediately dispatched two tribunes, Paulinus and Gallicanus, with orders to guarantee him his life and to induce him to come up.[44]

These envoys, however, failed to convince Josephus. Not that he doubted their own integrity or kindliness, but being conscious of all the suffering he had inflicted upon the Romans, and fearing that he was summoned to punishment, which in accordance with their laws of war meant death, he declined to give himself up. Vespasian, therefore, sent him in addition to these, a third tribune, Nicanor, an old friend of Josephus, having formed a comradeship with him during his two years' sojourn in Rome. On his arrival, having first enlarged upon the mildness of the Romans towards those whom they had conquered, Nicanor assured the suspicious Josephus that Vespasian had no intention against his life, but rather admired him for his valor and self-devotion, for which reason mainly the commander was anxious to have him brought to him. Moreover, he added, had Vespasian intended to be deceitful he would never have sent one friend to betray another, "thus painting in the fairest of colors the vilest of crimes."[45] On this friendly plea of Nicanor, Josephus finally consented to surrender, however, "not as a traitor to the Jews, but as a priest in the service of God."[46]

[44] Bell. Jud., III. viii. 1.

[45] Bell. Jud., III. viii. 2.

[46] Bell. Jud., III. viii. 3. Whether those dreams which Josephus mentions in the text of this section, as having occurred to him and inspired him to surrender, are intended to replace such events as appeared to him impracticable to reveal to the Romans, or were actual facts we cannot tell. But that his time was one of omens, oracles, prophecies, miracles, messiahs of every brand, and dreams of all descriptions, such as fill the books of Tacitus, Suetonius, and many other ancient writers, is well known to all who are familiar with the literature of his period. If, therefore, Josephus really availed himself of such auguries as might have appeared before him during his sleep, the fact should not surprise nor disturb us.

But as Josephus was about to give himself up, his forty cave-companions suddenly surrounded him in a body, and with drawn swords cried out, "Never indeed shall the glory of our forefathers be tarnished by our surrender.... Die with us by thy own hand as becomes a general of the Jews, or be murdered by us as a traitor to them"; and pointing their blades at him, they threatened to put him to death if he attempted to yield to the Romans.[47] Observing the sanguinary state of mind of his assailants and thinking that self-murder would be a betrayal of God's commandment (Ex., xx. 13), Josephus began to rationalize with them:

> *"Why, my comrades, should we be so eager to kill ourselves? Why should we separate such dear friends as soul and body? One may say it is noble to die in war: yes, but according to the laws of war, by the hands of the conqueror. Were we now flinching from the sword of the Romans, we should surely deserve death by our own hands; but since they admit of lenity and offer to spare us, how much more ought we to be merciful and save ourselves. It may also be said that it is honorable to die for liberty, but that, only on condition that one dies in battle; but at present our enemies do neither meet us in battle, nor try to kill us:—It is equally cowardly to fear to die when dying is necessary, and to choose to die when there is no necessity for it. Why do we refuse to surrender? Is it because of our fear of death? If so, shall we therefore inflict upon ourselves certain death in order to evade a doubtful death at the hands of our enemies? That we are in fear of slavery it may be said; as if much liberty we enjoy at present. It may also be said, It is manly to kill oneself. Certainly not, but a most dastardly act; as I should esteem a pilot an arrant coward who out of fear of danger sinks his ship, even before the approach of storm.*

[47] Bell. Jud., III. viii. 4.

"Now, self-murder is a crime most remote from the common nature of all animals, and an act of impiety against God our Creator: nor indeed is there a creature that dies by its own means, for the desire of life is a law engraven in all of them. That is why we deem as enemies those who would take it away from us openly, and punish as assassins those who deprive us of it by treachery. Our bodies are mortal, but the soul lives forever: it is a part of the Divinity living within us. If then, since a man who misapplies what is entrusted to him by a fellow-man is esteemed a base villain, how much more so is he who casts out of his body the Depositum which God has confided to him?... Know you not that those who depart this life in accordance with the law of nature, and repay the loan when it is demanded by God, obtain everlasting glory; that their houses and families prosper; that their souls, remaining pure and obedient, obtain the most holy places in heaven, whence, in the revolution of ages they are again set in pure bodies? But as for those who have madly lifted their hand upon themselves, the darkest pit of hell receives their souls, and God avenges their outrages upon their children and children's children. That is why suicide, which is so hateful to God, brings such severe punishment. According to our laws, the bodies of those who kill themselves could not be buried till after sunset, although even our enemies slain in war are allowed to be buried sooner.[48] *Even the laws of other nations require that a suicide's right hand be cut off before burial,*[49] *as an homologous retribution for disjoining the soul from the body.*

"Therefore, my comrades, let us reason justly, and

[48] There is no such Jewish law on the subject of suicide; and the laws in Deuteronomy, xxi. 22f., concerning the burial of hanged criminals, and in Joshua, viii. 29, x. 27, of slain enemies, differ with the above. Josephus, therefore, apparently follows here some tradition current in his day, which has not come down to us.

[49] Bell. Jud., III. viii. 5.

not add to our calamities impiety towards our Creator. If our lives are spared let us live; if they intend to kill us, there is nothing dishonorable in a death at the hand of our conquerors whom we have shown so many proofs of our bravery. For my part, however, I heartily wish the Romans may prove treacherous in this matter; for if, after pledging their word, they put me to death, I shall die gladly, carrying away with me, as a consolation greater than victory itself, the sense of their perfidiousness."

Unfortunately, however, all these delicate arguments, noble doctrines and lofty sentiments failed to dissuade these Galileans from suicide. Having long before determined to die, they only became more infuriated at Josephus. They encircled him with their swords in hand, and, reproaching him with cowardice, each of them was ready to plunge his sword into him. But he, calling one by name, fixing a stern eye at another, taking a third by the hand, shaming a fourth by supplication, and turning like a wild beast surrounded by a whole troop of hunters to face each assailant in succession, succeeded for the moment in warding off the blades of all.[50]

And now, to gratify their inextinguishable suicidal mania, Josephus availed himself of the following stratagem:— "Since we must die," he proposed to them, "let us not die by our own, but by each other's hands. Let us commit the order in which we are to kill ourselves to the decision of the lot.[51] He who draws the first lot shall fall by the hand of him who draws the next lot, and so on shall fortune take her course to the last man." The plan was accepted with great

[50] Bell. Jud., III. viii. 6.

[51] In Old Testament times, casting of lots equaled the bringing of a cause before God. If a dispute arose in which no evidence could be obtained, the two parties came before the priest, who decided the question by throwing lots.—See, Prov., xvi. 33, xviii. 18; Exod., xxii. 8-9. Among all vices which the Prophets blame, and against which the Proverbs give warning, we never read of gambling.

acclamation and the drawing began at once. He who drew the first lot presented his throat to him who drew next, in the happy expectation that Josephus would follow in his rear; for sweeter to him than life itself was the hope that his general's immediate succession would crown his own death with glory. By this process, Josephus and one other man remained to the last.[52] And since he himself cared for neither lot nor death, he persuaded the other survivor to accept the Roman terms; and both came out together, leaving the dead heroes in the cavern.[53] Such was the end of these blood-crazed swine, who, rather than die in defense of their homes, robbed their unfortunate families of their last means of sustenance, and, like rats in a trap gone mad, devoured each other.

Nicanor immediately led Josephus to Vespasian. The Romans all flocked to see the dreadful Jewish general. Some were rejoicing at his capture, others threatened him with vengeance, while still others pressed forward to get a good view of him. Those who were at a distance clamored for his life, but those nearest to him were seized with admiration, recalling his courageous actions. Among the Roman generals, however, regardless of their former fury against him, there was not one who at the sight of him did not relent, especially Titus, who was touched by his dignified fortitude and vigor of manhood. The influence of Titus was of great weight in persuading his father to be lenient with the prisoner. Vespasian, however, ordered him kept under strict supervision, intending in a short time to send him to Nero at Rome. Josephus was now thirty years old;[54] Titus, one year younger.

[52] The Greek text here continues, "Should we say by fortune or by the providence of God," whereas in the Slavonic edition it says, "Josephus counted the numbers with cunning, and thereby misled them all." This difference between the two editions is but one proof of the abuses the works of Josephus have undergone. But since the latter fact seems to be the most probable, and most logical procedure under the circumstances, the present writer agrees with that version.

[53] Bell. Jud., III. viii. 7.

[54] Bell. Jud., III. viii. 8.

When Josephus heard this, he immediately demanded a private interview with Vespasian. Accordingly, retaining his son Titus and two friends, the commander ordered all others to withdraw. Josephus then addressed him as follows: "You imagine, O Vespasian, that in the person of Josephus you have taken an ordinary prisoner; but I came to you as a messenger of God with tidings that you will soon assume imperial dignity. Send me to Nero? For what? Do you think that Nero and those who will succeed him will long continue? Bind me in chains and keep me as your prisoner; for you, Vespasian, and your son here, will soon be master, not only over me, but over the entire earth and sea, and the whole race of man." [55] Vespasian naturally mistrusted the flatterer, supposing this prophecy to be a trick of Josephus in order to save his life. Before long, however, he was led to believe it, "for God was already rousing in him thoughts of empire," and by other tokens foreshadowing the throne. Vespasian had also other proofs of Josephus' veracious prophecy. For when one of his two friends who were present at the interview asked Josephus, "Why, if your predictions here are not nonsensical inventions were you not able to foretell the fall of Jotapata to its

[55] It is noteworthy that the Mishna, Aboth de R. Nathan, iv. 5, attributes the same prophecy to Jochanan ben Zakkai, as quoted by Moore, "Judaism," ii. p. 116; and Derenbourg, p. 282.

Extremely remarkable are also the observations of Tacitus (Hist., i. 10) that, "The sovereign power was marked out by secret counsels of heaven, by portents and responses, for Vespasian and his sons"; (Hist., ii. 1), of "prophetic responses, and even unusual circumstances, which are regarded as omens of an event which the mind is previously inclined to believe." By Suetonius (Titus, 2) we are told that a fortune teller, being introduced to examine into the destiny of young Britannicus (he was the son of Emperor Claudius and Messalina), positively affirmed that he would never become emperor, but that Titus, who stood by, would. Other omens and oracles predicting the accession of Vespasian and Titus are mentioned by Tacitus (Hist., ii. 4, and 78), Suetonius (Vesp., 5, and Titus, 5), and Dio Cassius (Epitome, lxvi. 1). An oracle predicting that "the rulers of the world will come from Judea," referring to Vespasian and Titus, is recorded by Tacitus (Hist., v. 13) and Suetonius (Vesp., 4).

people, nor your own capture?" His reply was, "I did foretell to its inhabitants that their city would be taken and that I would be captured at the end of forty-seven days." Vespasian questioned the captives on these statements, and they readily confirmed the story.[56] And now, though still keeping Josephus in chains, Vespasian, in consequence of these oracles and verifications, presented him with precious gifts and several outfits of clothing, and treated him with great kindness and solicitude, Titus joining his father in these courtesies.[57]

On the first day of Tamuz,[58] Vespasian returned to Ptolemais, and from there marched along the coast to Caesarea. Here the Greeks, having massacred their Jewish co-inhabitants, and having their city and the whole surrounding region under their own control, went forth to meet the Romans with loudest acclamations and felicitations; for their vengeance against the Jews was not yet satiated. This feeling showed itself in their request to Vespasian that Josephus be executed. Vespasian, however, not only ignored them, but did not even answer their petition, as emanating from an "injudicious people." He only took possession of the city as salubrious winter quarters for two of his legions, the fifth and tenth, and, in order not to overburden Caesarea with too many troops, established the fifteenth at Scythopolis.[59]

Meanwhile a great number of Samaritan outlaws, who had been driven from their towns and whose homes had been destroyed, united themselves and took possession of the seatown of Joppa, which had recently been destroyed by Cestius. Here they built a number of ships with which they made piratical raids upon the merchant-vessels trading between Syria and Egypt, rendering the sea unnavigable. On learning of this, Vespasian dispatched a large force of infantry and cavalry against that city. The troops arrived at Joppa by

[56] It will be remembered that these ready witnesses were all women and children, as all men of Jotapata had been put to death.
[57] Bell. Jud., III. viii. 9.
[58] According to Niese, this was the twenty-third day of July.
[59] Bell. Jud., III. ix. 1.

night, and as the walls were unguarded, they made an immediate entry. The pirates thus caught unaware, made no resistance, but fled to their ships, and lay at sea for the night, out of the reach of the Roman darts and arrows.[60]

Joppa, however, does not possess a good harbor. Its whole shore, rocky, steep and rugged, runs in a semi-circle, so that in the event of strong northern winds, the waves, dashing full against the cliffs, render the port more dangerous than the open water. Towards dawn one of these gales, called by those who sail these waters the "Black Norther," began to blow with terrific fury. The pirates, dreading both the enemy and the rock-strewn breakers, remained at sea, where with neither possibility of flight nor hope of safety, some were engulfed in the waves and many crushed by their own wreckage, while the rest of them, in order to escape from drowning, threw themselves on their own swords.[61] Thus emptied of its inhabitants, the Romans razed the city to the ground, but established a camp there, lest it should again become a nest of pirates.[62]

But by now, when the news of the fall of Jotapata and the capture of Josephus reached Jerusalem, it was received with general skepticism, both because of the vastness of the calamity and the lack of eyewitnesses to confirm the report; for not a single man survived to run the message. However, as the rumor persisted, Jerusalem became filled with sorrow. There was scarcely a family that did not bewail some private affliction; the loss of a friend, a relation or a brother, but the mourning for Josephus was general; insomuch that the lamentations did not cease for thirty days, and many hired professionals to perform their funeral dirges.[63] In due time, however, when the truth came out that Josephus was not only alive, but was being treated by Vespasian, not as a

[60] Bell. Jud., III. ix. 2.
[61] Bell. Jud., III. ix. 3.
[62] Bell. Jud., III. ix. 4.
[63] Bell. Jud., III. ix. 5.

prisoner but with unheard-of kindness and distinction, sorrow gave way to the fiercest indignation. Some called him a coward, others a traitor, and curses were heaped upon the "renegade." The animus against the Romans became more bitter, and the ardor for revenge intenser than ever, since in having their revenge against them, his now bitter enemies would also avenge themselves on Josephus.[64]

At this time,—whether to give his overstrained army a much needed rest, or, as is possible, to tide over the intense heat of the season,—Vespasian turned aside from his Judean campaign, and accepted an invitation from Agrippa to visit his kingdom. The object of the king was both to entertain the general and his troops most lavishly, and that by the terror of the Roman arms he might quell the seditions within his own dominion. Accordingly, Vespasian left Caesarea-by-the-Sea, and marched to Caesarea-Philippi, the king's capital. But after three weeks of merry-making and fire-works, when Vespasian was informed that some agitators of Tiberias were inciting rebellion against Agrippa, and that Tarichea had already revolted,[65] he proceeded to quell those disturbances. Arriving, however, at some short distance before Tiberias, Vespasian first sent the decurion Valerianus with fifty horsemen to make peaceful proposals to the citizens, for he had heard that the people were anxious for peace, but were forced by a few individuals to join them in arms. Accordingly, Valerianus, leaving his commander, advanced nearer the city, dismounting as he approached the walls, in order to prevent any suspicion that he had come to skirmish. But before he could speak with the people, the most daring of the seditionaries, led by Jesus ben Sapphias, dashed through the city gates in full war array to meet him. Valerianus, though he might easily have dispersed them, but being under orders not to fight and surprised at the daring of these bandits, fled on foot with five of his companions. Thereupon Jesus carried

[64] Bell. Jud., III. ix. 6.
[65] Both cities were parts of Agrippa's kingdom.

off their horses to the city, as triumphantly as if he had captured them in battle.[66]

Greatly alarmed at the consequences of this occurrence, the senate and the more respected of the citizens fled to Vespasian, and throwing themselves at his feet, entreated him not to visit the crimes of a few desperate insurgents, under whose power they had always been subjected, on a people entirely devoted to peace and order. Vespasian, though he had already given orders for the demolition of the city, nevertheless, partly in compliance with their supplications and partly in deference to Agrippa, yielded to their entreaties. Thereupon the insurgents, feeling themselves no longer safe in Tiberias, fled to Tarichea.[67]

Vespasian then continued his march to Tarichea. Anticipating here a long war, he encamped at a considerable distance from the city, and fortified his camp with more than ordinary care; for at Tarichea he expected not only native revolutionaries, but also many others who had flocked to that city, relying on its strong fortifications and nearness of the lake by which, if necessary, they might escape to the opposite shore. But while the Romans were building a wall around their camp, Jesus ben Sapphias and his followers suddenly rushed out from the city, dispersed the builders and demolished a part of the structure. At the appearance of real soldiers, however, Jesus' troops were not so courageous; for when they saw the legionaries mustering, they fled back before sustaining any loss.

And now, Vespasian heard that the main body of the Galilean insurgents had assembled in the open country before Tarichea. He therefore sent his son Titus with six hundred horsemen to disperse them.[68] Their numbers, however, were so great that Titus sent word to his father demanding more

[66] Bell. Jud., III. ix. 7.
[67] Bell. Jud., III. ix. 8.
[68] Bell. Jud., III. x. 1.

forces. Accordingly, Trajan came up with an additional four hundred horsemen, while Antonius Silo was sent with two thousand archers to seize the hill opposite the city, in order to prevent any possible attempt from those who occupied the wall to assist the outlaws outside. Titus now led the attack; the insurgents attempted some resistance, but overpowered by the long spears and overthrown by the cavalry, they fled towards Tarichea. The cavalry pursued, causing so many of them to be trampled under foot or pierced to death by the lances that the field was covered with their bodies. A number of them succeeded in forcing their way into the city.[69]

But no sooner than they entered, great strife began among the people. The native residents who had property in the city were always averse to war, and now even more so than ever. But the invaders, a numerous body, habitually lazy to work and always ready to stir up mutiny, attempted to force their participation in warfare. Titus, who was not far off, heard this commotion; saw the two parties come to blows, and decided to strike at once.[70] Accordingly, he leaped on his horse, rode down to the lake, and, followed by his men, unexpectedly entered the city. Terror-stricken at this audacity, those who were upon the wall left their posts and fled, Jesus ben Sapphias towards the country, and the others towards the lake and into the arms of the Romans. Many were killed as they tried to reach the shore or while endeavoring to swim to their companions who had already reached the open water.[71] In the town itself there was also great slaughter between some of the insurgents who had not fled and the native inhabitants. But Titus, by mauling down the disturbers, quickly stopped the massacre; he also placed a garrison in the city. Those who had taken refuge on the lake,

[69] Bell. Jud., III. x. 2-3. This incident is recorded in Suetonius, Tit., 4.

[70] Bell. Jud., III. x. 4.

[71] The dimensions of the Lake, or Sea of Galilee, are about fourteen by six miles.

upon seeing the city taken, sailed further off, out of the range of the Romans.[72]

Titus now dispatched a horseman to his father to inform him of this signal victory, and on the following day gave orders that vessels be fitted up to pursue the fugitives. These vessels, owing to the abundance of wood in this region and of good ship-builders, were soon ready.[73]

On the completion of the fleet, Vespasian embarked as many of his forces as he thought sufficient to round up the runaways, and rowed off towards the center of the lake to meet them. The rebels in their small pirating boats could not bear up against the heavy craft of the enemy. They therefore hovered at a distance, and from there threw stones at the Romans, which when thrown caused no damage, but only splashed the water; if, on the other hand, they came nearer, they would be pierced by their arrows. If a drowning man rose to the surface of the water, an arrow quickly sent him to the bottom; or if in his despair he attempted to board the enemy's ship, his head or hands would be chopped off. A few who succeeded in reaching the shore met with no more mercy. The whole lake was tinged with blood and covered with bodies, for not a single man escaped. For several days its surface threw off a fetid steam, which stench reached far into the country. The shores were strewn with wreckage and swollen bodies which rotted in the sun, polluting the atmosphere so that it not only plunged the Jews into mourning, but filled even the authors of this misery with disgust. The number of the slain, including those who were killed in the city, was six thousand and five hundred.[74]

A considerable part of the Taricheans consisted of immigrants, upon whom Vespasian looked with suspicion. Therefore, when this battle was over, he called his lieutenants

[72] Bell. Jud., III. x. 5.
[73] Bell. Jud., III. x. 6.
[74] Bell. Jud., III. x. 9.

The Lake of Galilee.

together to consult with them on whether or not they should be expelled from the city. All unanimously declared that their expulsion would be to his own disadvantage, because once made homeless they would never be at rest, but, retreating to other cities, would force into revolt those among whom they found asylum. Vespasian's own conclusion was to put them to death. The only remaining question in his mind was in what manner they should be slain; for if he killed them in the city he might alienate the native residents who would not tolerate the massacre of so many whom only a short time before he had promised life and protection, and who had been loyal to him. But his friends insisted that propriety must give way to expediency where both could not work together. Accordingly, Vespasian gave the foreigners an ambiguous assurance of amnesty, but ordered them to leave Tarichea, and to go by no other road than that which led to Tiberias. Unsuspicious of the general's perfidious intentions, the unfortunate wretches collected their belongings, and departed in the prescribed direction; with Vespasian stealthily following in their rear. Meanwhile, the Romans seized and blockaded that highway to prevent any deviation from it. Arriving at Tiberias, Vespasian had them shut up in the stadium, and ordered twelve hundred of the old and helpless to be instantly slain. Of the most able-bodied he selected six thousand and sent them to Nero, to be employed on the digging of the Isthmus of Corinth canal, which had long been a favorite project of the Caesars.[75] The remainder, being thirty thousand and four hundred, he sold into slavery, excepting such as had formerly been subjects of Agrippa, whom he returned to him as a present with permission to do with them as he pleased. A number of these were seditious ruffians, fugitives from Trachonitis, Gaulanitis, Hippos, and Gadara, whom the king sold into slavery. These prisoners were taken on the

[75] The building of this canal is mentioned in Suetonius' Caes., xliv, Calig., xxi., and Nero, xix.

eighth day of Elul (September the 26th, 67 CE.—Niese).[76]

In consequence of this shocking example of barbarity, most of the towns at once surrendered their fortresses to the Romans. Of all Galilee, only Gischala, Itabryrion and Gamala, on the western border of Agrippa's territory, remained in the hands of the rebels.[77] To the last named city, Vespasian, after breaking up his camp at Tiberias, turned his first attention.[78] But only on the twenty-third of Tishre,[79] after a full month of desperate fighting, and heavy losses on both sides, were the town and fortress reduced by the Romans. During this siege Itabyrion was also taken.[80]

In all Galilee, Gischala alone now remained in arms. The inhabitants of this city were desirous of peace, being a people whose entire attention was devoted to the cultivation of the soil, but John with his band of followers whom he had brought into this, his native town, were craving for war. Against them Vespasian dispatched Titus with a thousand horsemen, while he himself led the fifth and fifteenth legions to Caesarea and sent the tenth to Scythopolis into winter quarters.[81]

When Titus arrived at Gischala, he found it could easily be overpowered. But he knew that if he took the fortress by storm, a general massacre by his troops would follow, in which the innocent would perish together with the guilty. Therefore, to avoid unnecessary bloodshed, he sought to induce John to surrender on terms. Finding the wall manned by his adherents, he asked them what it was they depended

[76] Bell. Jud., III. x. 10. The cruel treatment of these innocent prisoners is the most barbarous and treacherous deed Vespasian ever committed during his whole campaign. Nor does his compliance with the resolution of his officers, that "advantage must prevail over justice where the two could not be made consistent," do any honor to his memory.

[77] Bell. Jud., IV. i. 1.

[78] Bell. Jud., IV. i. 3.

[79] About November 10th.—Thackeray.

[80] Bell. Jud., IV. i. 4-10.

[81] Bell. Jud., IV. ii. 1.

upon, knowing that mightier forces than they had fallen before the Roman arms. They had seen, he reminded them, cities far stronger than theirs, overthrown by a single assault; while those who had entrusted themselves to the pledges offered by the Romans of security of life and possessions, such as were now extended to them, enjoyed their freedom and happiness. He therefore warned them to accept the proposal which he tendered them without any feeling of malice or intention of revenge for their insolence, rather than see their walls crumple like mere playthings before the Roman war-engines which would soon commence to batter.[82] Pretending acceptance of these generous terms, John replied: "Titus ought to have regard to the Jewish law and grant me leave to celebrate the Sabbath on which day it is unlawful not only to remove arms but even to treat of peace also." Seeing no harm in the short delay and considering John's request quite reasonable, and moreover, "feeling it would be becoming a dispenser of peace to honor his beneficiaries," Titus not only conceded this delay, but removed his army some distance away, to Cydessa, an inland village in Tyre.[83]

During the night, however, when John saw there were no Romans about the city, he gathered his armed men with a considerable number of families and fled for Jerusalem. For about two and a half miles the women and children bore on steadily, but after that point their strength began to fail. By degrees, as the men pressed on, they dropped out, and pitiful was their affliction as they sat down thus deserted, wailing by the wayside. Some of the women took courage to call their husbands, or implored them with the bitterest shrieks to wait for them. But the unfeeling John ordered the men to save themselves, and to "fly where they would be revenged on the Romans for those whom they left behind."[84]

[82] Bell. Jud., IV. ii. 2.

[83] Bell. Jud., IV. ii. 3.

[84] Bell. Jud., IV. ii. 4. By most modern historians this episode is completely passed over; and the few who disclose some of these facts about their "hero," curtail the voluminous text thereof to the

On the next morning when Titus appeared before the city to conclude negotiations, the people received him very joyfully, and informed him of John's departure. And as they threw their gates open, they invited him to enter and besought him to remove and punish some agitators who still remained among them. But Titus, considering their request of lesser importance, at once sent a troop of horsemen in pursuit of John. They failed, however, to reach him, for he had already made his escape to Jerusalem. But of his rear lines, which were still lagging on, they killed six thousand men and brought back three thousand women and children.[85]

Greatly disappointed at his inability to visit John's trickery with deserved punishment, Titus entered Gischala, where he was received with general acclamation. His conduct was very lenient, only threatening the seditionaries against future disturbances; fearing, if he attempted to distinguish the guilty from the innocent, that the guilty, out of their private animosities and quarrels, might accuse the innocent and thereby enmesh them in their own destruction. However, he placed a garrison in the city, both to keep the rebels in check and to instill a feeling of security among the citizens on his departure. Thus, in the autumn of 67 CE., all of Galilee was in the hands of the Romans.[86]

utmost minimum. Dr. Raphall (Vol. ii. p. 434), as one instance, apes the record as follows:—"Summoned to surrender, he (John) deceived Titus into a suspension of hostilities, profiting by which he himself, his troops, and his partisans, escaped to Jerusalem, though a number of his followers were overtaken and cut down by the Romans." Professor Graetz (Vol. ii. p. 240), though profusely wordy elsewhere, in order to shield this demon whom he shamefully holds up as a great Jewish hero, reduces the incident thus:—"Upon the approach of Titus, John begged for a twenty-four hours' truce before the capitulation of his fortress, ostensibly to preserve the sanctity of the Sabbath. Upon the acquiescence of the Roman general he made his escape from the city, followed by many thousands of his people."

[85] These numbers seem excessive; an error evidently was made by an early copyist.

[86] Bell. Jud., IV. ii. 5.

CHAPTER VIII

From the CONQUEST *of* GALILEE *to the* SIEGE *of* JERUSALEM, 68-69 CE.

WHEN John arrived at Jerusalem, the people became terror-stricken, wondering what had happened outside. Thousands poured out to meet him and to receive authentic tidings of the disasters in Galilee. His men, though short of breath, hot, and trembling, which showed plainly that they had ridden fast and long, yet, assuming a lofty demeanor, reported that they had not run away from the Romans, but only withdrew from Galilee in order to be able to fight them more advantageously in the unassailable metropolis. But John, little concerned about the fate of those whom he had deserted, went about among the crowds, instigating them to go to war by the hopes he gave them. Bragging about his own exceptional cleverness and marvelous skill, he jested upon the ignorance and clumsiness of the Romans who, he declared, "even had they wings would they never surmount the walls of Jerusalem after having found such great difficulties in taking the villages of Galilee and broken their war-engines against their walls."[1] By such harangues he seduced many more young men into his service, but of the more

[1] Bell. Jud., IV. iii. 1.

discerning older men there was not one who could not see through his puffing that he was lying, and did not foresee the city's future and weep for it as if it had already been destroyed.

Conditions in Judea now became most deplorable. Besides the disorders and civil war which raged in every city, the conflicts between the Peace Party and War Party in Jerusalem became most virulent; the intolerance between these factions grew so intense that even those dearest to one another broke off their relations to join those of their own opinion. Owing, also, to the subjugation of Galilee and the following Roman skirmishes at Caesarea, Jabne and Azdod, the metropolis had become overriden by young criminals who had flown in from those northern sections, plundering and murdering without restriction. Supplies which were needed by the native residents were used up by these unprofitable and useless mobs which, besides being the direct cause of the war, were also the occasioners of indescribable miseries, sedition and famine. The Roman garrisons in the neighboring cities, either considering it not worth the investment, or out of hatred, which, due to these brigands, they bore against the entire nation, afforded little or no protection to the sufferers.

Amidst these conditions John set himself to overthrow those who had been in command, and to obtain for himself absolute control of the government; and within a short time after his arrival he succeeded in uniting all immigrated marauders, including his own Galilean followers, with the city's war faction and in bringing them all under his banner as "the men of the people," or the "Zealots."[2] With fresh bandits continually pouring into the city and joining their ranks they abstained from no form of barbarity. For, restricted no longer to their old calling, such as raids and robberies, they proceeded to murder, and this not in the night time and of ordinary people, but in broad daylight and of the most distinguished citizens in Jerusalem. Their first vic-

[2] Bell. Jud., IV. iii. 2-3.

tims was Antipas, a man of royal lineage and a citizen of such high character as to be intrusted by the king with the charge of the public treasury. Him they seized and dragged to prison. The next were Levias and Sapphias, the son of Raguel, both of the Herodian family, besides other distinguished persons of Jerusalem. The people looked on with terrible apprehension, contenting themselves with the safety of their own persons.[3]

The Zealots, however, did not consider it safe to keep for long these influential citizens in prison. They feared their families, who were both numerous and powerful, and also dreaded a general insurrection. They therefore decided to execute their prisoners and commissioned a certain John, the son of Dorcas, a ruffian ready for the worst atrocities, with ten others of his kind, to kill them. The explanation they gave the people for this monstrous crime was that their victims had conspired the surrender of Jerusalem to the Romans.[4]

Their next move was the appointment of a high-priest. Since the officiating pontiff, Matthias ben Theophilos, belonged to the aristocratic party, to whom they could not look forward for co-operation, they dismissed him and elected a low-born individual for the office, who, being raised to his dignity, would be compelled to obey those who bestowed it on him. Accordingly, they sent for an obscure man named Pinnehas ben Samuel, of the village of Aphtha, who was of priestly ancestry, and made him high-priest. But such a fool was he, and so ignorant, that even the meaning of the high-priesthood was unknown to him. Yet, they haled this man, even without his consent, out of the country, dressed him up as for the stage, adorned him with a counterfeit face, put the sacred robes upon him, and instructed him from a distance what to do on every occasion.[5]

Alarmed at the chaos into which they had sunk, the people rose to a man to overthrow the Zealots' despotism.

[3] Bell. Jud., IV. iii. 4.
[4] Bell. Jud., IV. iii. 5.
[5] Bell. Jud., IV. iii. 6-8.

Joseph ben Gorion, Simon ben Gamaliel, and two influential ex-high-priests, Jeshua ben Gamala and Ananus ben Ananus, sought on their part, both by public speeches and private visits, to exhort the masses to put a stop to the robberies, murders, and sacrileges of the Zealots.[6] A sermon which Ananus delivered at the Temple with this object in view,[7] had, as a matter of fact, enticed a part of the people to declare open hostilities against the bandits who, being in the minority, were obliged to take refuge in the inner court of the Temple.[8]

Meanwhile John, pretending to side with the people, gave them his oath against the Zealots. He thereby gained the confidence of the peace party; watched their most intimate conferences, accompanied Ananus on his rounds, visited the sentries by night, and divulged his secrets to the Zealots; so that everything the people had deliberated was by his means known to their enemies.[9] And now that he might particularly incense the feelings of his Zealots, John, with his characteristic cunning, reported to them that Ananus was negotiating for the surrender of the city to the Romans, warning them to seek for succor from some external quarter, or trust themselves to the mercy of the people by whom they were designated for revenge.

On hearing of these menaces they immediately dispatched two men, both named Ananias, to the Idumeans with a short letter to the effect that Ananus and his friends were betraying the metropolis to the Romans in order to secure supreme power for themselves; that they themselves, having revolted in the cause of freedom, were imprisoned in the Temple; that there was but a short time left wherein they might hope for their deliverance, and that unless they sent prompt assistance, they would soon be in the power of Ananus and the city in the possession of the Romans. Further details the

[6] Bell. Jud., IV. iii. 9.
[7] Bell. Jud., IV. iii. 10.
[8] Bell. Jud., IV. iii. 12.
[9] Bell. Jud., IV. iii. 13-14.

messengers were instructed to communicate by mouth. For the Zealots knew that by a little flattery the Idumeans would comply immediately, as being a fierce and intractable nation who loved adventure and thronged to war as to a festivity.[10]

The Idumeans were astounded at the contents of the letter; and no sooner was the invitation received than they caught up their arms, and even before the appointed time for the proclamation no less than twenty thousand, under four generals,—John, Jacob, son of Sosas, Simon, son of Cathlas, and Pinnehas, son of Clusoth,—had joined the ranks and marched to Jerusalem.[11] But though the departure of the messengers had escaped the vigilance of Ananus, the approach of the Idumeans was not unexpected; for even before their arrival the gates were shut and the walls heavily guarded. Unwilling, however, to make enemies of them, Ananus determined to reason and plead with the formidable invaders. Accordingly, Jeshua, the ex-high-priest, mounted the wall and endeavored to persuade them to follow one of three lines of conduct: either to join them in the extirpation of John and his adherents, or enter the city unarmed and assume the role of arbitrators, or else leave both parties to settle their own affairs. If, however, none of these proposals should appear to them reasonable or fair, he informed them, the gates would remain barred, so long as they remained in arms.[12]

Enraged at their repulsion, and ashamed, thus frustrated, to return home, they tarried before the wall, unable to decide what to do. They thought the Zealots were strong, but saw not one to support them; they were in doubt about the whole matter, and many repented their coming altogether. But, while so deliberating, the night came on, and with it a violent storm of thunder, and lightning and drenching rain broke out over the city.[13] The night became darker, the horror of

[10] Bell. Jud., IV. iv. 1.
[11] Bell. Jud., IV. iv. 2.
[12] Bell. Jud., IV. iv. 3.
[13] Bell. Jud., IV. iv. 5.

the tempest greater; the sentinels on the wall ran off for shelter, and the Zealots, thus without any opposition, succeeded in opening the gates to their confederates. The Idumeans at first drew back, imagining it to be a trick of Ananus, but reassured by the Zealots they entered the city.[14]

Scarcely had they joined the Zealots when plunder and massacre began to reign in Jerusalem. Their rage, at the beginning, was directed mainly against the leaders of the moderate party. Among them were Ananus and his older son Joshua, whose bodies were thrown naked to the dogs.[15] They then fell upon the people, "as upon a flock of porks, ... and there were twelve thousand of the better class who perished in this manner."[16] Having by now satiated themselves with blood and plunder, and besides noticed that what had been imputed as reason was in fact a fraud, the Idumeans decided to sever their connections with the "scoundrel Zealots," and to return to their own province. Accordingly, instituting mock trials, they released from prison about two thousand people and went back to Idumea.[17] The peace party was now so reduced in numbers that they could no longer resist the Zealots. The single surviving peace leader, Joseph ben Gorion, was now put to death by the rebels, and John of Gischala became supreme potentate in Jerusalem.[18] But better, as we shall see, had it been if he had perished in his native city, or been cut down in his contemptible flight from it by the Romans.

Vespasian's generals, wishing to take advantage of these dissensions among the Jewish leaders, urged him to press the attack on the city immediately. But Vespasian regarded it as more prudent to allow the various factions to waste their

[14] Bell. Jud., IV. iv. 6-7.

[15] Bell. Jud., IV. v. 1-2. At this time Simon ben Gamaliel also disappears from history; though we find no record of his death.

[16] Bell. Jud., IV. v. 3.

[17] Bell. Jud., IV. v. 4-5.

[18] Bell. Jud., IV. vi. 1.

energies and destroy one another.[19] Accordingly, that the inhabitants of the capital might have more time to carry on their self-destruction, he directed his attention to Perea, beyond the Jordan, and, on the fourth day of Adar (March, 68 CE.), marched to Perea's capital, Gadara, where at its own request he left a garrison to protect it from robber incursions. Also leaving there Placidus with three thousand footmen and five hundred horsemen to subjugate the entire trans-Jordanian district to as far south as Machaerus, Vespasian returned to his base at Caesarea to prepare for his spring campaign.[20]

Meanwhile, however, news came that the Gallic governor, Julius Vindex, had revolted from Nero, and that Italy was threatened with civil war and danger to its very government. Vespasian was therefore anxious to finish the war in Palestine, that his army might be at liberty for any future service. Accordingly, while the winter still hindered him from going into the field, he put garrisons into the villages and smaller cities, and rebuilt many cities which had been destroyed.

When the spring came round, he marched from Caesarea to Antipatris, where he spent three days restoring order and in burning all its surrounding villages. He then advanced to Lydda and Jabne, placing there a number of destitute families, and reached Emmaus where he stationed his fifth legion, whereupon he raided Bethletephon, and fortified and garrisoned Betaris and Kephartoba, all three in the Idumean district. He then turned back north to Sicyma—Neapolis, and back again to Corea, where he pitched camp on the second day of Sivan, or June, 68 CE. On the following day he came to Jericho, where his general, Trajan (the father of the later emperor of that name), met him with the forces which he brought back from Perea after the subjugation of that province.[21] Having thus subdued and fortified all places round-

[19] Bell. Jud., IV. vi. 2-3.
[20] Bell. Jud., IV. vii. 4-6.
[21] Bell. Jud., IV. viii. 1.

about Jerusalem, Vespasian also garrisoned Adida, and sent a detachment under Lucius Annius to take and destroy the bandit settlement of Gerasa. With Jerusalem completely surrounded, Vespasian was ready for the Zealots.[22]

But as he returned to Caesarea to assemble his army for the assault on the capital, news reached him of the death of Nero.[23] Vespasian therefore decided to suspend all military operations and to await orders from the new emperor. By the middle of winter (68-69 CE.) news came that Galba had been proclaimed emperor. Vespasian then sent Titus to greet him and receive his commands. As Titus, however, was sailing along the coast of Greece, accompanied by King Agrippa, information reached him that Galba had been murdered.[24] So, while Agrippa continued to Rome, Titus decided to go back to his father at Caesarea.[25] Sedition and civil war prevailed at this time not only over Judea, but over the whole of Italy also. Otho who succeeded Galba was compelled to stab himself,[26] and his supporters, who after many weeks of warfare had defeated Otho's adherents, made Vitellius emperor of Rome.[27]

New events in Judea, however, forced Vespasian to take immediate action. A certain Simon bar Giora, hailing from Gerasa's bandit settlement, a procurer by profession,[28] taking advantage of the inactivity of the Romans and the generally prevailing anarchy, had gathered around himself a horde of

[22] Bell. Jud., IV. ix. 1.

[23] He stabbed himself on June 9th, 68 CE.

[24] On January 15th, 69 CE.

[25] Bell. Jud., IV. ix. 2; Tacitus, Hist., ii. 1-4.

[26] On April 16th, 69 CE.

[27] Bell. Jud., IV. ix. 9, first part, and x. 1-2. The description of these seditions and the civil war in Italy is given by Suetonius in Otho, viii-xi, and Vitellius, vii-viii; and by Tacitus, in History, Bk. ii. secs. xliii-l. The entry of Vitellius into Rome is described by Tacitus in Hist., ii., sec. lxxxix, and by Suetonius in Vitellius, xi.

[28] Bell. Jud., IV. ix. 3. The Sicarii, occupying the fortress of Masada, "permitted him and his 'following of women' access only to the lower part of the stronghold" (Thackeray's translation).

bandits, with whom he overran Idumea, plundering, ravaging, and destroying every city and village in his course, including the prosperous city of Hebron.[29]

Infuriated at this perilous eruption, Vespasian, on the fifth day of the month of Sivan, again advanced from Caesarea, where he had camped for over a year, and mowing his way through Acraba, Gophna, Beth-El, and Ephraem, arrived in the vicinity of Jerusalem, only to find that the bandits had abandoned their lair. For even before his arrival they had gained refuge within the walls of Jerusalem.[30] The people who had long been suffering from the tyranny of John had invited

Coins of Emperors Galba, Vitellius and Otho.

Simon, hoping to gain his assistance in putting down the lawlessness and violence which prevailed in the city. Pillage and license had by now so thoroughly degenerated the Zealots, that they plaited their hair, dressed themselves in women's garments, besmeared themselves with perfumed ointments, and painted their eyelids to enhance their beauty; and imitated not only the garments, but also the lust of women... (!). Yet, while wearing women's faces, they carried daggers under their dresses and stabbed whomever they pleased. Thus, those who stayed in the city were tyrannized by John, and those who fled, massacred by Simon.[31]

[29] Bell. Jud., IV. ix. 3-8.
[30] Bell. Jud., IV. ix. 9.
[31] Bell. Jud., IV. ix. 10.

In time, however, mutiny broke out among John's adherents. A considerable number of Idumeans, who of their original large army had remained in the city, grew jealous and hateful of his power and cruelty. They drove the Zealots into Grapte's palace, which John had made his residence and the repository for his plunder; then followed them there, whence they drove them into the Temple, and pillaged John's treasures. But meanwhile the many Zealots who were scattered about the city also came running to the Temple. Thus greatly re-enforced, they threatened to pour down on the Idumeans and the people. The Idumeans being the better soldiers, did not fear the bravery of the Zealots, but dreaded lest in their despair they should steal out of the Temple by night and set the whole city on fire. They therefore called an assembly of the chief priests to deliberate on what action to take. "But God," says Josephus, "perverted their judgment, and they decided on a remedy more disastrous than the disease"; or rather, in order to overthrow John, they determined to admit Simon into the city. Accordingly, they commissioned the ex-high-priest Matthias, a weak but influential man, to invite Simon, of whom they had so long been afraid, to come into the city to deliver it from the Zealots. Proudly consenting to be their lord and protector, Simon bar Giora entered amid joyful greetings of the people, and took possession of the entire Upper City.[32] His entry took place in the third year of the war, in the month of Nisan (April-May, 69 CE).

But the hopes of the people that he would free them from the tyranny of John were doomed to bitter disappointment. For instead of one tyrant there were now two, each battling the other for supremacy, and both regarding the people as their common enemy.[33]

Vespasian was not disposed at this time to undertake the long and difficult siege of Jerusalem, but rather impatient and anxious to watch how the crisis would turn out in Rome.

[32] Bell. Jud., IV. ix. 11.

[33] Bell. Jud., IV. ix. 12; compare V. xiii. 1.

He therefore decided to decamp, and go back to his base at Caesarea. As he arrived at Caesarea, however, the notion took possession of his legions that there was a much juster reason for Vespasian to be emperor than for that "lascivious, childless tyrant Vitellius."[34] Indignantly they cried out against "those soldiers in Rome who live in luxury," questioning their right "to ordain whom they pleased as ruler over us who have undergone so many arduous labors and grown old under our helmets." They refused to recognize the selection of Vitellius and proclaimed their own general as Roman emperor.[35] On the first of July, 69 CE.,[36] Vespasian was proclaimed Emperor by the Roman legions in Egypt also, and a few days later the Roman troops of Syria, under the command of the governor Mucianus, likewise tendered their allegiance to Vespasian.[37]

And now that fortune had everywhere conspired in his favor, Vespasian recalled the prediction which Josephus had made to him at Jotapata. In thankful remembrance of that prophecy, he declared him free from bondage, restored him to the honor and rank he had held before his capture, and at the request of Titus, severed his chains with an axe, in accordance with the Roman custom, as if they should never have been on him.[38]

[34] The Roman authors say Vitellius had children; whereas Josephus says he had none.

[35] Bell. Jud., IV. v. 2-4.

[36] According to Tacitus (Hist., ii. 79), "on the fifth of the nones" of that month; according to Suetonius (Vesp., 6), "on the fifth of the ides of July," or the 28th.

[37] Bell. Jud., IV. x. 6.

[38] Bell. Jud., IV. x. 7. Several such instances are recorded both in the Scriptures and other histories:—Daniel was favored by Darius and Cyrus for having foretold the destruction of the Babylonian monarchy by their means, and the consequent exaltation of the Medes and Persians (Daniel, v. 6ff.). Jeremiah was set at liberty and treated honorably by Nebuzaradan, at the command of Nebuchadnezzar, for having foretold the destruction of Jerusalem by the Babylonians (Jeremiah, xl. 1-7). Similar are the cases of Joseph in Egypt (Gen., xli. 1-45), of Jaddua, the high-priest, in the time of Alexander the Great (Antiq., XI. viii. 5), and others.

With Vespasian, the prosecution of the war in Judea was now of lesser importance. Looking upon himself as already entrusted with the Roman government, he left Caesarea and proceeded to Berytus where embassies from Syria and other Roman and foreign provinces were awaiting him with congratulations of the people. Having responded to the embassies, and having distributed the local offices on a basis of justice and merit, he departed for Syria's capital, Antioch. Here, after some deliberation, he decided to send the Syrian governor, Mucianus, with a considerable army to Italy to put down the disorders meanwhile created by Vitellius. Thus, arranging his affairs delayed Vespasian till late in autumn, when, accompanied by his son Titus, and also by Josephus, he went to Alexandria for the winter.

During his residence there, however, news reached him that on December 20th (69 CE.), Vitellius had been decapitated and that his enemies had also declared themselves in favor of the new Emperor. Vespasian therefore committed the continuation of the war in Palestine to his son Titus while he himself remained in Alexandria till spring, awaiting the summer winds when he could commence his journey to Rome. Among the retinue accompanying Titus on his return to Palestine was also Josephus.[39]

In Jerusalem, in the meantime, the internal strife had reached a new climax. Instead of two factions, those of Simon and John, there were now four distinct parties, each at war with the others for absolute mastery: There were two thousand and four hundred local Zealots under Eleazar ben Simon, six thousand Galilean Zealots under John of Gischala, ten thousand Sicarii and Perean bandits under Simon bar Giora, and five thousand Idumean savages under Jacob ben Sosa. John held the Temple Mount, Eleazar occupied the inner

[39] Bell. Jud., IV. xi. 4-5. For Josephus' going to Alexandria with Vespasian and his returning to Jerusalem with Titus, see Vita, 75. For Vespasian's waiting at Alexandria for the summer winds, see Tacitus' History, iv. 81.

court of the Temple, Simon and Jacob had the entire Upper and part of the Lower City. These twenty-four thousand men might have put their courage to some account had they at this opportune hour acted in harmony against the external enemy. But not one of them was capable of relinquishing his own ambition for the good of all. Eleazar's party claimed pre-eminence on the grounds of being natives of Jerusalem. John demanded supremacy because, as Dr. Graetz graciously says, "he was a born leader and excelled all others in penetration and fertility of invention." Simon and Jacob aimed to avenge themselves on John; the one because he had formerly antagonized him, the other for no special reason other than his desire to be of assistance to Simon. And so, in their mutual hatred of one another they became so deprived of reason that they set fire to the immense warehouse of foods which had been stored up, lest their rival should gain by it, thus robbing themselves of the means of sustaining the siege.

Dreadful was the misery of the deeply afflicted citizenry; they dared not even utter their grief, for watch was kept everywhere, and any in favor of peace with the Romans or suspected of an intention to desert the city were immediately put to death. Old men and women in their distress prayed for the coming of the Romans and eagerly hoped for the external war to liberate them from their internal miseries.[40]

[40] Bell. Jud., V. i. 1-5; comp. vi. 1. The Talmud relates that Jochanan ben Zakkai, induced by either fear of the Zealots or desire of obtaining a place of safety for the Law, formed the idea of taking refuge in the camp of Titus. To escape from Jerusalem, however, was impossible, as all the exits were watched; Jochanan, therefore disguised himself as a corpse and, assisted by three friends, Ben Betiach, Eleazar, and Joshua, had himself placed in a coffin and carried out at sunset through the gates of the city ostensibly for burial. Titus having known through his spies in Jerusalem of Jochanan's peaceful sentiments, received him in very friendly fashion and gave him permission to make some request. His request was that he be permitted to establish a school at Jabne for the purpose of "giving lectures to his pupils." Titus, seeing nothing objectionable in the wish of Jochanan, for he could not foresee that

Such were the conditions in Jerusalem when Titus was carrying on his preparations for his assault upon it.

by this unimportant concession he was enabling Judaism, feeble as it then was, to outlive Rome by thousands of years, readily granted the request. Thus, even before Jerusalem was besieged, the study of the Law had found refuge in a new center from which a better Judaism was to flourish. Subsequently R. Jochanan was blamed for not at once having requested safety and protection for Jerusalem and the Temple; but the rabbi was defended by the remark that if he had asked too much, he would probably have obtained nothing (Gittin, 56a-b; Lamentations Rabboth, i. 5; Aboth de R. Nathan, iv.—Quoted by Prof. Moore, "Judaism," i. p. 83.).

Traditional Tomb of Jochanan ben Zakkai, near Tiberias, with the grave of Maimonides to the right. (Reproduced from a photograph by Professor William Popper of the University of California.)

CHAPTER IX

The SIEGE *and* DESTRUCTION *of* JERUSALEM, 70 CE.

WHEN Titus was appointed to complete the subjugation of Judea, he had at his disposal six legions and numerous auxiliaries. In addition to the three legions, the Fifth, Tenth, and Fifteenth, which had served under his father, he had the Twelfth from Syria, which had formerly been defeated under Cestius Gallus, and the Third and Twenty-second legions from Alexandria. In addition, he had also twenty cohorts of foot and eight squadrons of horse from Agrippa of Chalcis and Sohemus of Emesa, auxiliaries from Antiochus of Commagene, and a band of Arabs. In all he had about eighty thousand men. Sextus Cerealis commanded the fifth legion, Larcius Lepidus commanded the tenth, Tittius Frigius commanded the fifteenth, and Fronto Eternus was the leader of the two legions which came from Egypt.[1] Second in command and principal adviser to Titus, was an apostate Jew, a nephew of Philo, Tiberius Julius Alexander.[2]

[1] The commander of the twelfth legion is not mentioned.

[2] Compare generally, Bell. Jud., V. i. 6, VI. iv. 3, and Tacitus, Hist., v. 1.

Having assembled his forces at Caesarea, Titus ordered the fifth legion to advance by way of Emmaus, and the tenth by way of Jericho, and to meet him before the Holy City. He himself marched with the main body of his army and arrived at Gabaoth Saul, nearly four miles north of Jerusalem, on the fourteenth of the month of Nisan (March-April, 70 CE.).[3] From here Titus, with six hundred picked horsemen, went forward to reconnoiter the ground and also to see whether the insurgents, when they saw him, would surrender before coming to any actual battle; for he had been informed that the people who were under their power were anxious for peace, but remained inactive merely from fear and inability to resist.[4]

But as he rode along the road leading to the city, and descending towards the Tower of Psephinus, an immense number of Zealots suddenly dashed out through the gates facing Queen Helena's monuments, and, throwing themselves among the galloping horses, cut him off with only a few of his men. To advance was impossible; the ground was covered with orchards and gardens, and intersected with irrigation ditches which reached to the city walls. To retreat was almost as difficult, for masses of the enemy were at his rear. Titus saw that no moment was to be lost; he wheeled his horse round, and shouting to his companions to follow him, charged fiercely through. Constantly clearing his way with his sword, and trampling down those who attempted to withstand him, he succeeded in reaching his camp in safety. His comrades, who were in the same danger, kept close to him, for each man's hope of escape lay in pushing through with their commander. Two who were further behind lost their lives: one was surrounded and speared together with his horse, the other who dismounted was killed and his horse led away to the city.[5]

On the arrival of the fifth legion which came by way

[3] As it appears from Bell. Jud., V. iii. 1, with xiii. 7.
[4] Bell. Jud., V. i. 6, ii. 1.
[5] Bell. Jud., V. ii. 2.

Emperor Nero.

Emperor Vespasian.

Emperor Titus.

of Emmaus, Titus moved his camp to Mount Scopus, within a mile north of the city, from which all its extent could be surveyed. The tenth legion which soon after came also, he ordered to encamp on the Mount of Olives which is over on the east.[6]

In Jerusalem, however, even now when the entire Roman army was before the city, the carnage had not abated. It was now the Passover season, a period during which, since time immemorial, multitudes of Jews from distant countries assembled to celebrate the festival in their mother country. From Parthia, Mesopotamia, and the shores of the Euphrates, from Antioch and all Syria, from Asia Minor and the Isles of Crete and Cyprus, myriads of Jews flocked to Jerusalem to commemorate the Passover.[7] Yet, even this festival John made use of as a cloak for treachery and bloodshed. When Eleazar and his men opened the gates to admit the worshippers, some of John's most desperate adherents, armed with concealed weapons, stole in among the rest to take prior possession of the Temple. But no sooner were they in than the holy house became a scene of disorder and confusion. The people who had no connection with the sedition were aghast at the sudden eruption; they regarded it as an assault upon all and even feared a general massacre. Eleazar's Zealots, how-

[6] Bell. Jud., V. ii. 3.

[7] According to a computation made by order of Cestius Gallus from the number of paschal lambs offered, there were present in Jerusalem on the Passover of the year 66 not less than two million five hundred and sixty-six thousand persons (Bell. Jud., II. xiv. 3; comp. also VI. ix. 3). The computation assumes ten partakers to each lamb; but as those who had contracted any defilement could not join in the offering, and as it frequently happened that twenty guests sat down to one lamb, while there were never less than ten, Josephus insists that the number must have been larger and probably approached three millions. The Passover of the year 66 was in no wise distinguished from any other Passover and it may therefore be considered as a fair criterion of the numbers that attended on the present occasion. When Tacitus (Hist., v. 13.) estimates the number of the besieged as only 600,000, he is probably confounding the number of the regular inhabitants of Jerusalem at that time.

ever, knowing well against whom the attack was directed, leaped down from the battlements and took refuge in the subterranean caverns of the Temple. Of the multitude who stood trembling round the altar, some were slain wantonly, others from animosity, while many were trampled to death by the Galileans. And now, having glutted their vengeance upon innocent people, John's party came to terms with Eleazar's faction, permitting them not only to come up from their underground hiding-places, but even to take up arms with them. Being in possession of the inner court of the Temple with all its ammunition, and having reabsorbed Eleazar's party, which originally had been part of his own, John was able to devote his entire attention to Simon and Jacob. Thus the sedition which had been divided into three factions was now reduced to two.[8]

In the meantime, while these chiefs were eagerly preparing to renew their fighting, Titus was cautiously making ready his approach to the city. The whole area between Mount Scopus and the city walls was reduced to a dead level. All fences and hedges with which the inhabitants had enclosed their groves and gardens were ruthlessly swept away. The fruit trees, now in their spring flower, fell before the axe, and the bubbling water courses became repositories for stray and protuberant rocks. A broad and level road led from Scopus to Serpent's Pool.[9]

When this work, which took four days to accomplish, was finished, Titus was ready for action. The Romans took up positions along the north and west of the outermost wall. They were drawn up in lines seven deep: three lines of infantry followed by one of archers and three rows of cavalry behind them. Titus himself encamped about a quarter of a mile from the ramparts, near the Tower of Psephinus; another division of the army entrenched itself near the Tower of

[8] Bell. Jud., V. iii. 1.
[9] Bell. Jud., V. iii. 2.

Hippicus; the tenth legion remained on the Mount of Olives.[10]

Jerusalem was situated on four hills; to the north, that of Bezetha, covered by the suburb of the same name, and the quarter called the New City which had been built by King Agrippa I. To the east was Mount Moriah, with the Temple; and below it the hill and suburb of Ophel. To the south was Mount Zion, or the Upper City, formerly called the City of David; and above it the Acra, or Lower City. The circumference of the city was thirty-five stadia, or about three and a half miles, or according to another instance where Josephus uses a different authority,[11] fifty stadia or five miles. Its fortifications were strong, both by nature and art. Three walls succeeded one another in all those parts where the city was not surrounded by impassable ravines; beyond that, owing to its inaccessibility, a single rampart was sufficient. In addition to these regular defenses, there were several detached citadels or castles of great strength, of which the fortress of Antonia was the strongest. Towering above the city was the Temple, a fortress in itself and equal in strength to any known at that time.[12] (See Plan of Jerusalem.)

Beholding all this, Titus, escorted by a strong guard of cavalry, rode slowly round the city, to select the best point against which to direct his attack. At the same time, however, besides not being excessively eager to destroy Jerusalem, he was also very anxious to return to Rome, where all the felicities and honors belonging to his great position were awaiting him. Therefore, before commencing the assault, he deputed Josephus and his friend, the tribune Nicanor, to parley with the insurgents about terms of peace. But as soon as they attempted such overtures, Nicanor, who ventured too near the wall, was seriously wounded in the left shoulder by an arrow. Titus, infuriated at this vicious assault even on one who approached them for their own welfare, at once ordered

[10] Bell. Jud., V. iii. 5.
[11] I Apion, 22.
[12] Bell. Jud., V. iv. 1ff; compare Tacitus, Hist., v. 11-12.

his troops to clear the suburbs by fire and to bring in timber for the erection of embankments. The spot which he selected for the attack was a place near the sepulcher of John Hyrcanus II, because there the outermost wall was lower and there was no second wall behind it, the builders having considered it unnecessary to fortify that sparsely populated portion of the New City.[13] "Such," says Tacitus, "was the city, such the people against whom Titus determined to act."[14]

Having completed the earthworks and posted his artillery at convenient distances, Titus gave orders to charge. As the situation of the city demanded, he directed his first attack against the northeastern side of the outer or third wall. A terrific sound echoed round the city as the projectiles boomed forward simultaneously from three different directions; a cry went up from the people, and no less terror fell upon the rebels themselves. John and Simon, now finding themselves exposed to the same danger, quickly laid aside their mutual hatred and private quarrels and united themselves against the common enemy.[15] But too late; for on the seventh day of the month of Iyar (May 25th, 70 CE.), being the fifteenth day of the siege, after much hard fighting and heavy losses on both sides, the most powerful of the battering-rams broke the wall through and the Romans became masters of the entire "New City."[16]

To attack the second wall, Titus shifted his camp to the so-called Camp of the Assyrians,[17] occupying all the ground as far as the brook of Kedron. John defended the Antonia; Simon guarded the wall extending from it to the tower of Hippicus. For nine days the conflict between the two parties was more terrific than ever, for after fighting fiercely all day, the night was also spent in armor,—the rebels fearing

[13] Bell. Jud., V. vi. 2; compare also V. iii. 3 middle of section.

[14] Tacitus, Hist., v. 13.

[15] Bell. Jud., V. vi. 3-5.

[16] Bell. Jud., V. vii. 2.

[17] The traditional site of the camp of Sennacherib's army; see 2 Kings, xviii. 17, xix. 35.

the capture of their walls, the Romans dreading an invasion of their camps. On the ninth day after the first wall was taken, however, Titus, with a thousand picked men, stormed the second wall and became master of the Lower City also.[18]

At this point Titus determined to suspend the siege for a few days, in order to afford the rebels an interval for reflection and to see if the demolition of their second wall or dread of famine would bring them to surrender; and as the day appointed for the distribution of salary had also arrived, he commanded his officers to parade the troops in full uniform and to pay each man his money in view of the whole city, intending thereby to terrify the insurgents and to let them see that the Romans had plenty of everything while they themselves were already threatened with starvation. For four days this procession continued filing before the wall. On the fifth day, however, when no overtures for capitulation were coming, Titus gave orders for the resumption of the siege. Separating his army into two divisions, he employed one part in the erection of the embankments against Antonia, where John and his Zealots fought, with the view of taking the Temple; the other against the wall which Simon and his followers defended, as the place from which to take the Upper City. Conscious, however, that the preservation of the city would be of greater advantage to him than its destruction, since Jerusalem intact yielded enormous revenues, whereas if desolated it could contribute none, Titus omitted no expedient to induce the insurgents to surrender. Therefore, while the work was proceeding, he delegated Josephus to exhort them in their own language to seek their salvation by submission.[19]

Accordingly, having found a place from where he might be heard, and yet be out of the range of arrows, Josephus implored them to spare themselves and the people, to spare

[18] Bell. Jud., V. ii. 3-4, viii. 1-2.
[19] Bell. Jud., V. ix. 1-2.

their country and the Temple, describing the rebels as being less concerned about these matters than aliens. The Romans, he urged, though being without a share in them, yet reverenced the sacred rites and places, although they belonged to their enemies, and had thus far kept their hands from them; whereas they who had been brought up in them and would be alone, were they preserved, to enjoy them, hasten their destruction.... Be it granted that it is noble to fight for freedom, but since this is so, they should have done it at the proper time; after having once succumbed and submitted for so long, to seek then to shake off the yoke is the part of men madly courting death, not of lovers of liberty.... What did they depend on, he demanded, when the greatest part of the city had already been taken, and when those within the last wall were afflicted with all sorts of miseries, and famine and disease even worse than capture? They would do well, he warned them, to repent before irretrievable disaster befell them, and to embrace such counsel as might save them while the opportunity was still open to them. The Romans, he assured them, would bear no malice for their past actions, unless they persevered in their insolent behavior to the end; because they were naturally lenient in their conquests, and would consider what was profitable before what their passion dictated to them, which lay not in leaving the city depopulated or the country devastated. That was why, even at this late hour, Titus was ready to grant them terms; whereas, if he took the city by force, he would not spare any of them, especially after they rejected his offer in this, their utmost distress.[20]

Then, turning back to the ancient history of the nation, he pointed out that the Jews never yet had relied on the force of arms, but always on their God:

> "*Such was the trust of Abraham, who did not avenge himself against Nechao, the Pharaoh of Egypt,*

[20] Bell. Jud., V. ix. 3.

who came with an amazing army and carried off Sarah;[21] *although he had three hundred and eighteen captains under him, and a large army under each of them! Indeed, he deemed them to be no number at all without God's assistance, and only spread out his hands towards this Holy Place which you have now polluted by shedding thereon the blood of your own countrymen, and depended upon Him as his Defender. And was not Sarah sent back undefiled to her husband the very next evening, while the Egyptian, fear-stricken at his visions of the night, fled, bestowing silver and gold upon those whom God loved?"*

Other such instances, he here adduced, were the great deliverances from Egypt and Babylon, the overthrow of Sennacherib's army, and the recovery of the holy ark from the Philistines. On the other hand were the examples of the demolition of Jerusalem and the Temple, and the imprisonment and blinding of King Zedekiah when, contrary to the prophetic warning of Jeremiah, he gave battle to Nebuchadnezzar.

"What is it that brought the Romans into our country? How did our servitude begin? Has it not originated from party strife among our forefathers, when the quarrels between Aristobulus and Hyrcanus brought Pompey against our city?... And do we not know what end Antigonus came to when Herod brought Sossius, and Sossius brought upon us the Roman army, by whom our people were besieged for six months?[22]*... Thus without exception have arms been forbidden to our nation, and*

[21] Josephus here follows a reversed version, evidently an Haggadic treatment of the stories in Genesis, xii. 10-20, and xx. 1ff. Furthermore, Nechao was not the monarch of Egypt in Abraham's time, but was, at a much later date, the conqueror of Joshua (2 Chronicles, xxxv. 20ff.).

[22] Bell. Jud., I. xvii. 9ff; Antiq., XIV. xvi. 1ff.

warfare has been the sure signal for defeat. For it is the duty of those who inhabit this holy ground to commit everything to the disposal of God.

"But as for you, what have you done of those things that are recommended by our Law, and what have you left undone of what God has condemned?... You have not even screened such sins as are usually committed in secret;... and while you complain of rapine and murder you, yourselves, vie with each other in inventing and introducing new and unheard-of vices. Yes, the Temple itself has become desecrated; though it has been reverenced even by the Romans, who deferred many of their own religious customs to give place to our laws. And after all this you expect God whom you have so abused to support you? Can you with such sinful hands appear before Him as petitioners and call upon Him to protect you?

"Did King Hezekiah lift up such hands in prayer to God against Sennacherib when He destroyed his mighty army in one night? And do the Romans commit such wickedness as did this king of Assyria, that we may have reason to hope for like vengeance upon them? Did not that king accept money from our king on condition that he would not destroy the city, and yet, contrary to his oath, he came down to burn the Temple, whereas the Romans demand no more than that customary tribute which our fathers paid to their fathers? Once they receive this, they neither aim to destroy the city, nor touch the Temple, but grant you everything else, the freedom of your posterity, the security of your possessions, and the protection of your sacred laws.

"It is plain madness to expect God to appear as well disposed towards the wicked as towards the righteous. He knows at once when to inflict punishment, as when He broke the power of the Assyrians the very first night

they pitched camp hard by the city.[23] *Wherefore, had He judged our generation worthy of freedom, or the Romans deserving of punishment, He would, as He did with the Assyrian, have forthwith inflicted it on Pompey when he fell upon our nation, on Sossius when after him he came, upon Vespasian when he ravaged Galilee, and finally on Titus when he first approached the city. But Magnus (Pompey "the Great") and Sossius, far from suffering any injury, took the city by force,*[24] *as did Vespasian go forth from this war to mount the throne of the Empire; while as for Titus, those springs that were formerly almost dry for you, ran more plentifully for him than ever before. For before his coming, Siloam and all other springs outside the city were failing insomuch that water was sold by distinct measure; whereas now they stream so copiously for your enemies as to suffice not only for drink for both themselves and their cattle, but even for watering their gardens.*[25]*...Therefore I cannot but be-*

[23] As related in 2 Kings, xix. 35; see also Psalms, lxxvi. 2-3, where this is only indirectly hinted at.

[24] For the campaign of Pompey, see Bell. Jud., I. vi. 4-6, vii. 1-7; for that of Sossius, see Bell. Jud., I. xvii. 8-9, xviii. 1ff.

[25] (a) The evidences here are clear enough that the destiny of Judea had already been fixed when Pompey in 63 BCE. invaded it, and the doom of the Jewish Commonwealth sealed when Herod and Sossius in 37 BCE. conquered it; and not in the year 33 CE., when the Jews refused to accept Jesus as a deity, as some Christian disseminators would wish them to suppose. (b) Dean Milman (Vol. ii. p. 353, n. 1.), following Strabo (Bk. xvi.) and Tacitus (Hist., v. 12.), asserts that the supply of water in Jerusalem during the great siege never failed for either the Jews or the Romans. As his "more explicit" witness to the fact he also adduces Dion Cassius (Vesp., lxvi. 3.), who says, "Not only had the Jews plenty of water, but at times they issued out through the subterranean aqueducts, attacked the Romans when seeking water, and cut off stragglers." But since Dion, who was born in 155 CE., wrote over a hundred years after Josephus' Jewish Wars was published, and had never even seen Palestine, does not substantiate his statement by any authority, we can accept it only with that much credence which we give to most other historians of his time. As for Strabo who died in 21 CE., how could his description of certain facts, even if

lieve that God has repudiated this Sanctuary and stands on the side of those with whom you are now at war.[26]

"However, there is a way left for your salvation, should you be willing to accept it; and God is easily reconciled to those who confess and relent. Oh, iron-hearted wretches! Cast away your arms, and take pity on your country now going to ruin. Return from your wicked ways and behold the beauty of that city which you are now betraying, and of that Temple with the gifts of so many nations in it. Who could bear to be the first to set that Temple on fire? Who could be willing that these things should be no more? And if you cannot look at these things with genuine affection, at least have pity on your kin, and set before your eyes your children, and wives, and parents, who before long will be consumed by either famine or war. I am sensible that this danger will extend to my mother, and wife,[27] *and to that noble family of mine, which indeed has been very eminent in olden time; and perhaps you may imagine that it is on their account that I give you this advice; if that be all, kill them; nay, take my own blood as reward if it may but*

they were similar in character, possibly be applied to events which occurred fifty years after his death? Tacitus, again, who was a contemporary of Josephus, though saying that, "A perennial spring and reservoirs of rainwater supplied the city with water," he says so only as a part of his description of Jerusalem, and not that so was the fact during the siege's period.

[26] Rabbi Akiba a half century later also stated, "Since the destruction of the Temple, God is to be sought in the great city of Rome." Yer Taanit, 69a.

[27] The mention of his wife here is evidently an error of an early copyist. His father, though not spoken of here was still alive, his imprisonment being referred to in Bell. Jud., V. xiii. 1; whereas the wife who is mentioned in this oration, and whom the vilifiers of Josephus count as one of his "four wives," never even existed, for his first marriage is nowhere mentioned before that with the girl whom he took from among the captives at Caesarea, by command of Vespasian, and whom he divorced on his liberation from bonds as being against the laws of Moses for a priest to marry a slave or a captive.—Vita, 75. For his entire domestic life see also Vita, 76.

procure your salvation; for I am ready to die, in case you will but return to a sound mind after my death." [28]

Yet, though Josephus tearfully thus appealed to them, these admonitions made no impression on the insurgents. Of the people, however, many, in spite of the constant danger of being slain by the guards, sold their properties for trifling sums, and swallowing the gold pieces to prevent their detection, should they be caught while deserting, fled to the Romans. Titus received them with kindness and permitted them to settle wherever they pleased. Observing this, Simon and John ordered a closer watch of the outlets, and anyone affording even the merest suspicion of an intention to escape was immediately executed.[29] Meanwhile corn was becoming scarce in the city. A house to house search was instituted by the insurgents; if any grain was found, they punished the owners for not passing it over, and if none was discovered they were tortured for concealing it so carefully.[30] Life itself became unbearable; demoralization, general and complete. Thus, wives would snatch the very morsel out of the mouths of their husbands, children from their fathers', mothers from their childrens', while their dearest ones were pining in their arms for a few life-giving drops.[31] Such were the sufferings to which the people were subjected by Simon and John, that to describe them in detail, Josephus finds impossible. "But to put it briefly, no other city ever endured such miseries, nor since the world began has there been a generation more prolific in crime. Indeed they ended by actually disparaging their own race, in order to appear less impious in so treating aliens, and owned themselves, what indeed they were, slaves, the dregs of Jewish society and the bastard scum of their nation. It was they who overthrew the city, and compelled the reluctant Romans to register so melancholy a triumph,

[28] Bell. Jud., V. ix. 4.
[29] Bell. Jud., V. x. 1.
[30] Bell. Jud., V. x. 2.
[31] Bell. Jud., V. x. 3.

and all but attracted that fire upon the Temple, which they seemed to think came too slowly."[32]

Meanwhile, as the embankments of Titus were progressing, he ordered a detachment of horsemen to lie in wait for those who stole out from the city into its surrounding valleys in search of herbs or whatever might serve for food. Some of these were combatants who were no longer contented with their plunder, but the greater part were citizens of the poorer class, who were deterred from deserting by fear for their families; for they could neither hope to escape with them, nor endure to leave them to be slaughtered by the insurgents on their account. Of these, those who were caught by the Romans were first subjected to torture, and then crucified before the wall, in the hope that the spectacle would induce the Zealots to surrender. The Roman soldiers, out of rage and hatred which on their account they bore against all, amused themselves by nailing their prisoners in various ways; and so great was their number, that "room was wanting for the crosses, and crosses for the bodies."[33] On the Zealots, however, these executions had a contrary effect, for they dragged the relatives of those whom Titus had crucified up to the wall, together with a number of others whom they suspected as inclined towards peace, and showed them those examples of Roman mercy. The sight of this checked further excursions, excepting with those who regarded instant death at the hands of the Romans better than to die slowly of hunger. In answer to this, Titus sent some of his prisoners back to John and Simon, with their hands cut off, exhorting them to capitulate, and not to force him to destroy the city. To this message they replied with curses and insults on Titus and his

[32] Bell. Jud., V. x. 5.—Thackeray's translation with some changes. (The awkwardness of the arrangement of these extremely interesting texts of Bell. Jud., V. x. 1-3, and 5, evidently caused by some meddling early transcriber, renders them rather incomplete and at times inexplicable.)

[33] Bell. Jud., V. xi. 1.

father, deriding all his efforts to conquer them so long as "they had God as their ally." [34]

And now, after seventeen days of unremitting labor, on the twenty-ninth of the month of Iyar [35] (70 CE.), the Romans succeeded in raising their embankments. No sooner, however, were these works completed than John, creeping through a subterranean passage, ignited those opposite the Tower of Antonia,[36] while two days later Simon, with the assistance of a certain Galilean, called Tephtheus, an ex-servant of King Agrippa named Megassarus, and an Adiabene by the name of Chagiras, or "the lame man," set fire to those set up against the wall which he defended.[37] Dispirited by the loss of his battering engines, and with little hope of taking the city with the ordinary fighting machines which remained, Titus summoned a council of war to think out a plan which, though it would greatly prolong the siege and immeasurably increase the sufferings of the besieged, promised a proportionally greater certainty of success. The rashest of his adjutants were of the opinion that he should assemble his entire army and storm the city at once. Of the more cautious, some were for the raising of embankments again; while others advised a blockade by surrounding the whole city with a continuous stone wall, in order to cut off every possibility of escape and thus, either force it to surrender or reduce it by famine.[38] The last was preferred, and the whole army set to work. Beginning at the Camp of the Assyrians, where Titus had his camp, he directed the wall towards the lower part of the New City, along the valley of Kedron; then to a rock called Peristereon which overhanged the Siloam, and on towards the sepulcher of the high-priest Ananias, and round the mountain where Pompey had once had

[34] Bell. Jud., V. xi. 2.

[35] According to Thackeray this was about the 16th of June; but Dean Milman gives the date as "the 27th or 29th of May."

[36] Bell. Jud., V. xi. 4.

[37] Bell. Jud., V. xi. 5.

[38] Bell. Jud., V. xii. 1.

his camp, and so continuing northwards joined the beginning of the wall at Titus' camp. The whole work, which was within a furlong of five miles, and might well have taken months to do, was completed in three days.[39]

With every means of egress thus thwarted, the famine soon reached a terrible climax. "It devoured the people by whole houses and families. The roofs were thronged with women and infants completely exhausted. The lanes were full of dead bodies of the aged; children wandered about the market-places like shadows, all swollen from inanition, till they fell dead—where they remained unburied. Many died while burying others, and many hastened their own end before the fatal hour had arrived,—each victim with his eyes fixed on the Temple. A deep silence and a deadly night seized Jerusalem." At first the rebels ordered the bodies buried at public expense, finding the stench unendurable; but when they could no longer continue this, they threw them from their ramparts into the valleys beneath.[40] When Titus, in going his rounds along those valleys, saw the bodies rotting, and the ground under his feet reeking with clammy matter, he groaned and, lifting up his hands to heaven, called to God to witness that this was not his work.

However, as the bandits still showed no inclination to surrender, Titus, out of commiseration of the people and out of his desire at least to rescue those of them who still survived, hurriedly began again to raise earthworks; this time only opposite Antonia, in four sections, and much larger than the former embankments.[41] While these earthworks were going up, Matthias ben Boethus, of high-priestly ancestry, and his three sons, a priest named Ananias ben Masbalus, Aristeus, the secretary of the former Sanhedrin, and fifteen other eminent citizens,—all of whom were suspected of favoring the

[39] Bell. Jud., V. xii. 2.
[40] Bell. Jud., V. xii. 3.
[41] Bell. Jud., V. xii. 4.

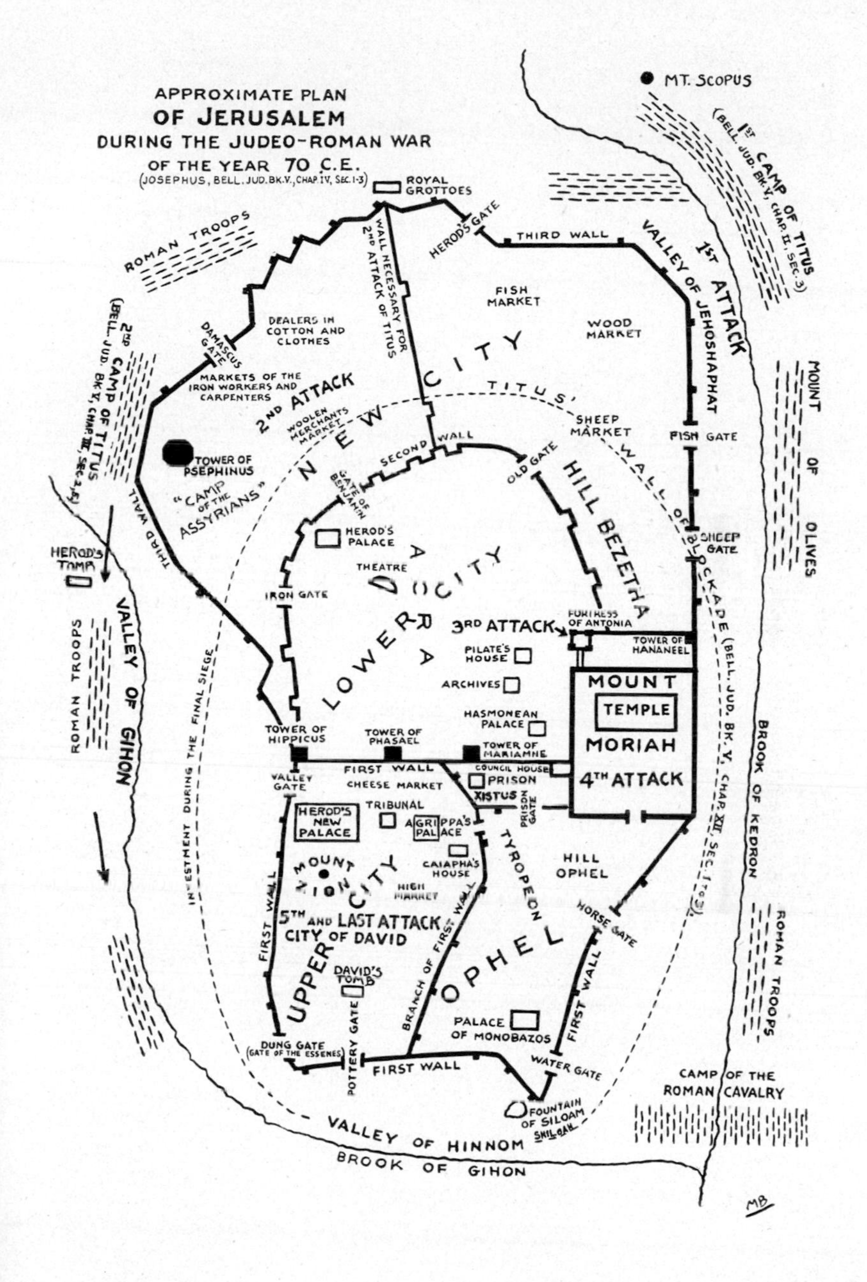
APPROXIMATE PLAN
OF JERUSALEM
DURING THE JUDEO-ROMAN WAR
OF THE YEAR 70 C.E.
(JOSEPHUS, BELL. JUD. BK.V., CHAP. IV, SEC. 1-3)
MT. SCOPUS
1ST CAMP OF TITUS (BELL. JUD. BK. V, CHAP. II, SEC. 3)
ROYAL GROTTOES
ROMAN TROOPS
WALL NECESSARY FOR 2ND ATTACK OF TITUS
HEROD'S GATE
THIRD WALL
VALLEY OF JEHOSHAPHAT
1ST ATTACK
FISH MARKET
WOOD MARKET
DEALERS IN COTTON AND CLOTHES
DAMASCUS GATE
2ND CAMP OF TITUS (BELL. JUD. BK. V, CHAP. III, SEC. 2, 5)
MARKETS OF THE IRON WORKERS AND CARPENTERS
2ND ATTACK
NEW CITY
TITUS' WALL OF BLOCKADE (BELL. JUD. BK. V, CHAP. XII, SEC. 1 TO 3)
WOOLEN MERCHANTS MARKET
SECOND WALL
SHEEP MARKET
MOUNT OF OLIVES
FISH GATE
TOWER OF PSEPHINUS
"CAMP OF THE ASSYRIANS"
GATE OF BENJAMIN
OLD GATE
HILL BEZETHA
THIRD WALL
HEROD'S TOMB
HEROD'S PALACE
ACRA
LOWER CITY
THEATRE
SHEEP GATE
IRON GATE
FORTRESS OF ANTONIA
3RD ATTACK
TOWER OF HANANEEL
PILATE'S HOUSE
VALLEY OF GIHON
ROMAN TROOPS
ARCHIVES
MOUNT
TEMPLE
MORIAH
4TH ATTACK
HASMONEAN PALACE
INVESTMENT DURING THE FINAL SIEGE
TOWER OF HIPPICUS
TOWER OF PHASAEL
TOWER OF MARIAMNE
BROOK OF KEDRON
FIRST WALL
COUNCIL HOUSE
VALLEY GATE
CHEESE MARKET
PRISON
XISTUS
PRISON GATE
TRIBUNAL
HEROD'S NEW PALACE
AGRIPPA'S PALACE
TYROPEON
HILL OPHEL
CAIAPHA'S HOUSE
MOUNT ZION
HIGH MARKET
UPPER CITY
5TH AND LAST ATTACK
CITY OF DAVID
BRANCH OF FIRST WALL
HORSE GATE
OPHEL
ROMAN TROOPS
FIRST WALL
DAVID'S TOMB
POTTERY GATE
PALACE OF MONOBAZOS
DUNG GATE (GATE OF THE ESSENES)
FIRST WALL
WATER GATE
CAMP OF THE ROMAN CAVALRY
FOUNTAIN OF SILOAM
SHILOAH
VALLEY OF HINNOM
BROOK OF GIHON
MB

Romans,—were put to death by Simon.[42] When one of Simon's lieutenants, Judas ben Judas, in charge of one of the towers, saw this butchery, he called for ten of his men, whom he considered most trustworthy, and with them conspired to surrender his tower to the Romans. But as Titus was approaching with a body of men to take possession, Simon, having received advance information, averted the surrender by personal occupation of the tower; and slaying the plotters in full view of the Romans, threw their mutilated bodies before his feet.[43] About this time, too, as Josephus was going his rounds,—for he never ceased his appeals to the bandits,—he was shot in the head with a stone, rendering him unconscious for a short while. They made a rush for his body and would have hurried him into the city, had not Titus immediately sent a rescue party to save him. The rumor of his death spread through the city and reached his mother in prison, but his speedy reappearance reassured his friends and was quickly imparted to his parents.[44]

And here, Josephus adds, "I cannot refrain from saying, that had the Romans delayed their coming against these reprobates any longer, the city would either have been swallowed up by the ground opening upon it, or been overflowed by water, or else been destroyed by such thunderbolts as the land of Sodom perished by."[45] For indeed, no fewer than a hundred and fifteen thousand eight hundred and eighty bodies were reported by Manneus when he fled to Titus as having been entrusted to him in the interval between the fourteenth of Nisan, when the Romans pitched their camp by the city, and the first of the month of Tamuz. But that was not all, for others in addition to Manneus told Titus that the entire number of the dead that were thrown out through the gates into the valleys, together with the corpses that were laid in

[42] Bell. Jud., V. xiii. 1.
[43] Bell. Jud., V. xiii. 2.
[44] Bell. Jud., V. xiii. 3.
[45] Bell. Jud., V. xiii. 6.

heaps and shut up in the large mansions, amounted to six hundred thousand.[46]

The miseries in Jerusalem continued to grow worse and worse. As the famine had by now extended its ravages from the people to the rebels themselves, they became more furious. The piles of corpses that lay in heaps throughout the city was a horrible sight and produced a pestilential stench. Finally, after twenty-one days of incessant labor the embankments were completed.[47]

Scarcely had these earthworks been finished, when the Roman artillery began its deadly work. At first the battering-rams made no considerable progress, but continued blowing against the tower so shattered its foundation that during the night one of its walls suddenly collapsed.[48] But the storming of the city still remained a difficult task, for John had meantime raised a second one behind it.[49] During the night of the fifth day of Tamuz,[50] however, some twenty soldiers of the guard with a standard bearer of the fifth legion, two horsemen and a trumpeter scaled noiselessly up this wall, surprised and killed the sentinels and took possession of the fortress of Antonia.[51] Titus then ordered the troops to raze the foundation of the tower, and to make an easy passage for his army.

On that same day, however, Titus had been informed that for want of men the daily sacrifices had ceased to be offered, and that the people were terribly troubled over it. He therefore sent Josephus to tell John that if he was obsessed by a criminal passion for battle he was at liberty to come out with as many men as he pleased, without involving the city and the Temple in his own ruin; and that he might offer the sacrifices, which were now interrupted, by any of the men he might select. Accordingly, standing in such a place

[46] Bell. Jud., V. xiii. 7.
[47] Bell. Jud., VI. i. 1.
[48] Bell. Jud., VI. i. 2-3.
[49] Bell. Jud., VI. i. 4.
[50] About July 24th,—Thackeray.
[51] Bell. Jud., VI. i. 7.

where he might be heard not only by John, but also by the people, he delivered the message in the Hebrew language:

"*. . . John! It is never dishonorable to repent and amend, even at this late hour. And if you desire to save the city, you have a noble instance before you in King Jechoniah who, when by his conduct he had brought the Babylonian army upon him, of his own accord left the city before it was taken, and with his family underwent a voluntary captivity, rather than deliver up these holy places to the enemy and see the house of God on fire; on which account he is celebrated among all the Jews in their sacred memorials, and his memory has become immortal, and will be conveyed fresh down to our posterity through all ages.*[52] *This, John, is an excellent example, even were it dangerous to follow; and I dare venture to promise that the Romans shall still pardon you. And take notice that I, who make this appeal to you, am one of your own nation; I, who am a Jew, make this promise to you; and it will become you to consider who your counselor is, and the ancestry he comes from.*

"*. . . You are indignant and reproach me, and indeed I deserve even worse treatment for making this appeal in opposition to fate, and for endeavoring to save those whom God has condemned. And who is there who does not know the records of the ancient prophets and that oracle threatening this poor city right now coming true. For they foretold that the city should be taken when*

[52] Our present copies of the Old Testament do not contain this encomium upon King Jechoniah or Jehoiachim. It must, however, have been in the Pentateuch at the time, or else Josephus could not have offered the example to his listeners who were no strangers to its contents.—On this see, 2 Kings, xxiv. 12; comp. Antiq., X. xi. 2. Neither is the following prediction that Jerusalem would be taken and the Sanctuary burnt, etc. to be found in the Scriptures, unless, as suggested by Dr. Thackeray, Josephus followed the Sibylline Oracles, iv. 115ff, which, however, do not date earlier than 80 CE.

one should begin the slaughter of his own countrymen! And are not both the city and the Temple filled with the bodies of your own countrymen? It is God therefore, God himself, who with the Romans is bringing this fire to purge His Temple and to pluck up a city so laden with pollution." [53]

As Josephus spoke these words, his voice broke down with sobs. The Romans could not but pity him, and admire his sincerity and determination. John and his followers remained impenitent, but the people were so moved by his discourse that many of the upper class, disregarding all the dangers surrounding them, fled to the Romans. Among them were the high-priests Joseph and Jeshua, the three sons of the high-priest Ishmael, who was later beheaded in Cyrene, the four sons of Matthias, one son of the other Matthias who was assassinated by Simon, and many others of the nobility. Titus not only received these men very kindly, but knowing that they would not willingly live after the customs of other nations, he sent them to Gophna, advising them to remain there till after the war, when he would restore every man to his possessions. And so they happily retired to that small city. But on their disappearance the rebels, in order to deter others from attempting to escape, sent out a report that the deserters had been crucified by the Romans. This ruse succeeded for but a short while,[54] for Titus recalled these men and together with Josephus sent them round the wall to show themselves to the people; whereupon many more fled to the Romans.[55]

Exasperated over the general state of affairs in Jerusalem, Titus reproached John and his Zealots:

"Was it not you, most abominable wretches, who by our permission put up this wall before your Sanctu-

[53] Bell. Jud., VI. ii. 1.
[54] Bell. Jud., VI. ii. 2.
[55] Bell. Jud., VI. ii. 3.

ary, and were allowed to set upon it those stone signs engraved in both Greek and in your own langauge the prohibition to foreigners from going beyond it? Have we not given you leave to kill such as trespass it, even if they were Romans? And what do you now want, you pernicious villains? Why do you trample on dead bodies in this Temple? And why do you pollute this holy house with the blood of both foreigners and Jews? I appeal to the gods of my own country and to my own army, and to those Jews who are here with me, and even to yourselves, that I do not force you to defile your Sanctuary; and if you will but change the arena of battle, no Roman shall either come near your holy places, or offer any insult to them; nay, I will endeavor to preserve for you your holy house, whether you will or not."

But as Josephus interpreted these words from the mouth of Titus,[56] the insurgents, attributing his exhortations to cowardice rather than to good will, became more insolent than ever. Seeing that these men were neither to be moved by compassion towards themselves, nor that they had any regard for the Temple, Titus again resumed hostilities. As he could not bring up his entire force into action, owing to the narrowness of the ground, he selected thirty of the best soldiers out of every hundred, committed each thousand of these to a tribune, and making Cerealis their commander he gave orders to attack the guards of the Temple about the ninth hour of the night (3 A.M.). He himself was in armor and prepared to go with them, but was restrained by his officers who remarked that he would achieve more by sitting still in the Tower of Antonia as a dispenser of rewards to those soldiers who signalized themselves in the battle than by exposing himself in the forefront; for they would fight more bravely knowing that the eyes of their Caesar looked upon them. To this persuasion Titus yielded and at the hour ap-

[56] Bell. Jud., VI. ii. 4.

pointed he dispatched them upon their enterprise, while he himself went to a spot from which he could see all below, anxiously awaiting the issue.[57]

In the meantime the rest of his army had, in seven days, overthrown the foundation of Antonia and prepared a broad road to the Temple. The legions now approaching the First Court[58] began to erect their embankments: one facing the northwest corner of the outer wall, a second on the north between the two gates, a third against the uppermost of the western entrances, and one against the entrance formerly leading through the connecting gallery of the fortress of Antonia.[59]

The famine meanwhile continued its fearful ravages. The men would fight even their dearest relatives for the most miserable supports of life. Even the robbers began to suffer severely. Gaping with hunger, they went prowling about like mad dogs, or reeling like drunken men, from weakness, battering upon the doors and in their perplexity bursting into the same house twice and thrice during the same hour. Their hunger was so intolerable that even such objects as the filthiest animals would not touch they used as food. They gnawed their belts and shoes and even the very leather of their bucklers; chopped hay and shoots of trees sold a small weight for four Attic drachmas.[60] There was a woman who dwelt beyond the Jordan, named Mary bath Eleazar, of the village of Beth-Hyssop, eminent for her family and riches, who with the rest of the villagers took refuge in Jerusalem. The wealth which she brought to the city had been plundered by the tyrants, while the relics of her treasures, with whatever food she had contrived to bring with her, were carried off by their satellites; the unfortunate woman lost her reason. Her infant was vainly endeavoring to suck off some moisture from her dry bosom,—she seized it, roasted it, ate some of it and cov-

[57] Bell. Jud., VI. ii. 5.
[58] First Court, or the place of assembly for non-Jews.
[59] Bell. Jud., VI. iii. 4.
[60] Bell. Jud., VI. iii. 3.

ered up and stored away the remainder. The smell of the roast reached the rapacious villains; they came and threateningly commanded her to give up what she had been feasting on; she uncovered the body of her child and invited them to eat of it. The savage men turned pale and speechless and, trembling with horror, departed.[61] The sad news was rapidly told to the Romans. Some of them would not believe it, while others were moved with compassion at the distress the people were in. Titus declared himself innocent in the matter, protesting that he had offered peace, liberty and an amnesty for all past offences, but that the rebels, instead of concord preferred sedition, and instead of peace and plenty chose war and want.[62]

At last, on the eighth day of the month of Ab,[63] the four new banks were completed and Titus ordered the battering-rams set up against the western wall of the Temple. But for the previous six days the largest and most powerful of the siege-engines had been incessantly battering the wall without making any impression; the enormous size, closeness and firm adhesion of the stones had resisted all its efforts. Other troops, too, during the same time had endeavored to undermine the foundation of the northern gate but succeeded no further than in extricating a few front stones. Therefore, despairing of making any further attempts with engines and wall-breakers against this massive enclosure and seeing that his endeavors to spare a foreign temple led only to the slaughter of many of his own soldiers, Titus commanded that the gates of the outer court be set on fire.[64]

In the meantime Ananus of Emmaus, the cruelest of Simon's executioners,[65] and Archelaus, the son of Magadatus,

[61] Bell. Jud., VI. iii. 4.
[62] Bell. Jud., VI. iii. 5.
[63] About the 27th of August.—Thackeray.
[64] Bell. Jud., VI. iv. 1.
[65] He was employed also as the executioner of Matthias, son of Boethus, who persuaded the people to admit Simon into Jerusalem (Bell. Jud., V. xiii. 1.).

deserted to the Romans. Titus, having heard of their cruelty to their countrymen, was going to put them to death, but his good faith,—his promise of security to deserters,—overcame his resentments and he let them go, though he did not give them the same privileges that he afforded to others.

On the following day, the ninth of Ab, while the gates were still burning, Titus assembled his generals to advise him on what action to take in regards to the Temple. Some of these maintained that it would be best to act in accordance with the laws of war and demolish it. Others were of the opinion that if the rebels desisted from using it as a fortress it should be saved, but if they did use it for purposes of warfare it should be burnt. Titus, however, declared that even if they did fight therefrom, they ought not to avenge themselves on things instead of men, and that in any case he was not in favor of burning down so vast a work to the detriment of the Romans, as it would be an ornament to the Empire if it continued. Impressed by so lofty an idea, Tiberius Alexander, the Quartermaster-General, Sextus Cerealis, the commander of the fifth legion, and Fronto Eternius, the leader of the two Alexandrian legions, came over to his view. Accordingly, dissolving the assembly, Titus gave orders to his troops to extinguish the gates and clear the entrances for his legions; [66] while he himself retired to watch the proceedings from Antonia,[67] determined, on the following day, at dawn, to storm the Temple with his entire army.

"But God," bewails Josephus, "had long since condemned it to the fire; and now that fatal day has come." For upon Titus' retiring the insurgents attacked the Romans and an engagement ensued between those who guarded the Sanctuary and the troops who were quenching the fire which was burning in the inner court of the Temple; but the Romans put the Zealot guards to flight, pursuing them right up to the holy house itself. At this moment, one of the soldiers, without

[66] Bell. Jud., VI. iv. 3.
[67] Bell. Jud., VI. iv. 4.

orders, snatched some of the burning timbers, and, mounting on the shoulders of one of his comrades, threw them through the low door which gave access on the north side into the Temple's vault room, and set it on fire. This occurred on the tenth day of Ab, the very same day on which the Temple had formerly been burnt by the king of Babylon.[68]

When this conflagration was reported to Titus, he rushed to the scene to stop it from spreading. Behind him came all his generals; while after them followed the excited soldiery who had long been eager for the Temple treasures which they deemed inexhaustible. Both by shouting and signals Titus ordered his troops to quench the flames, but in the carnage which raged between them and the crowds of defenseless people who had collected around the sacred chambers, his orders were not listened to. As they reached nearer to the Sanctuary they pretended they did not even hear his orders, but on the contrary, shouted to those who were before them to throw in more firebrands. The insurgents by this time could no longer offer resistance; they were everywhere slain and everywhere beaten. Around the altar lay dead bodies heaped one upon another; on the steps leading to it flowed a stream of blood, and the bodies of the victims killed above slid down upon them at the bottom.[69]

As Titus found it impossible to restrain his soldiers and the fire was gaining more and more, he entered with his generals and surveyed the Holy Place of the Temple. The splendor filled him with wonder; and as the fire had not yet penetrated the Holy of Holies he made every effort to save it; he even directed Liberalius, a centurion of his bodyguard, to club any one of his troops who disobeyed his orders. But their respect for Titus and their fear for the officer gave way to their insatiable hope for plunder. Seeing that everything

[68] This corresponds with the date given in Jeremiah, iii. 12f. In 2 Kings, xxv. 8, however, the day is mentioned as the 7th; while the Rabbinical tradition (Mishna, Taanith, iv. 6, and Taanith, 29a-b.) places both burnings on the 9th of Ab.

[69] Bell. Jud., VI. iv. 6.

around them was made of gold, and anticipating that everything within was full of money, they threw in even more firebrands, till the whole noble structure went up in flames beyond redemption.[70]

Deeply as one must mourn the loss of this most admirable edifice that had ever been seen or heard of, both for its curious construction and its magnitude, and also for the vast wealth bestowed upon it, as well as for the glorious reputation it had for its holiness; yet we may comfort ourselves with the thought that it was Fate that decreed it so to be, which is inevitable both as to living beings and as to works of art or places. And one may well wonder at the accuracy of Destiny, for she waited until the very month and the very day on which in bygone times the Temple was burnt by the Babylonians. The number of years from its first foundation by King Solomon to its present destruction, which took place in the second year of the reign of Vespasian, amounted to one thousand and one hundred and thirty years seven months and fifteen days; and from its rebuilding by Haggai in the second year of the reign of Cyrus, till its destruction under Vespasian, to six hundred and thirty-nine years and forty-five days.[71]

And now the Romans, judging it unnecessary to spare the buildings surrounding the Holy House, set them all on fire, excepting the eastern and southern cloisters with their gates. They also burnt down the treasury chamber in which there were vast amounts of money, costly garments, and other valuables,—the plunder which the Zealots had laid up. They then came to the one remaining cloister of the outer court on which several thousand women and children had taken refuge. But before Titus had known of it or given any orders concerning their disposal, the soldiers, carried away by hate and fury, set fire to the cloister from underneath, with the result that many were killed throwing themselves down out of the flames, while the rest lost their lives in the fire. These

[70] Bell. Jud., VI. iv. 7.
[71] Bell. Jud., VI. iv. 8.

innocent victims owed their destruction to a false prophet who on that day had made a public proclamation that God commanded them to go up on the colonnade and there await miraculous signs of their deliverance. Numerous indeed, were such prophets at the time who, suborned by the Zealots, deluded the wretched people into believing that they bore messages from God, in order to check their desertions.[72]

But there was a star resembling a sword which stood over the city, and a comet which continued a whole year. And again, before the rebellion, when foreign Jews flocked to Jerusalem for the Passover, on the eighth of the month of Nisan, at the ninth hour of the night (3 A.M.), so great a light shone around the altar and the Holies, that it appeared to be daylight; and this lasted for half an hour. During the same festival also, a cow that had been brought to be sacrificed gave birth to a lamb in the midst of the Temple; moreover, the eastern gate of the inner court, which was of brass and very heavy, and which when closed or opened required twenty men to move, was seen at midnight to open of its own accord. Besides these, a few days after the festival, on the one-and-twentieth day of the month of Iyar, before the setting of the sun, chariots and soldiers in their armor were seen running through the clouds and blockading the city; and at the feast of Pentecost, the priests, on entering the inner court, as was their custom to perform their ministrations, reported a quaking followed by a voice, as of a great multitude, saying, "Let us remove from here."

But presaging even more clearly the doom of Jerusalem, were the wild outcries of Jeshua, the son of Ananus. Four years before the war began, when Jerusalem was enjoying peace and prosperity, this man who had come from the country to the city to celebrate the feast of the Tabernacles, as he was standing in the Temple, suddenly began to cry out, "A voice from the east, a voice from the west, a voice from the four winds, a voice against Jerusalem and the Holy House,

[72] Bell. Jud., VI. v. 2.

a voice against the bridegrooms and the brides, a voice against the whole nation." This cry he continued unceasingly, running day by day through the streets of Jerusalem, crying more loudly and lamentably on Sabbaths and holidays than on other days, but never getting hoarse or weary. Neither threats nor punishments could make him desist, or wring from him a groan or complaint, or, indeed, induce him to utter any other words than those which composed his dirge over the city. During the whole period up to the beginning of the war he neither went near nor spoke to any of the citizens, but daily repeated his lament, "Woe, woe to Jerusalem!" Neither did he curse those who beat him, nor bless those who offered him food, but to all men that same melancholy ditty was his one reply. At the beginning of the siege, however, as he was running along crying, "Woe to the city!" a stone hurled from one of the Roman engines struck him and killed him on the spot.[73]

While the Temple was still burning, and the Romans plundered, burnt, and massacred indiscriminately, John of Gischala and his Zealots effected their escape through the Tyropeon bridge into the Upper City.[74] This, however, did not lessen the joy of the soldiers, for the amount of the plunder which they had obtained was so vast that throughout Syria the standard of gold was depreciated to half its former value.[75] Among some priests who during the confla-

[73] In addition to Josephus (Bell. Jud., VI. v. 3), Tacitus (Hist., v. 13) and Suetonius (Vesp., 4), the Talmud abounds with presages and omens indicating the destruction of Jerusalem. One of these (Yoma, fo. 39) reads: "Forty years before the destruction, they (the gates of the Temple) suddenly, of a night, flew open of their own accord, and could not be closed until R. Jochanan ben Zakkai addressed them, and exclaimed, 'Temple, Temple! what use is it that thou showest thyself frightened? I know that thy end will be destruction, for long ago Zechariah the son of Iddo prophesied against thee, and said, Open thy gates, O Lebanon, that fire may consume thy cedars.' "—Zechariah, xi. 1-2.

[74] Bell. Jud., VI. v. 1-2.

[75] Bell. Jud., VI. vi. 1.

gration took refuge on top of the wall, which was four meters broad,[76] there was a boy who, parched with thirst, confessed his condition to the Roman guards, begging them for their pledge of security should he come down for water. Commiserating his young age and the distress he was in, they promised him protection. But no sooner did he drink and fill his vessel which he had brought with him, than he raced back to his comrades. The guards, failing to catch him, cursed his perfidy. The reply which the boy made was, "I have not broken the agreement, for the security I had given me was not in order to my staying with you, but only in order to my coming down safely, and taking up some water, both of which I have performed, and thereupon think myself to have been faithful to my engagement." Such cunning, especially in so young a child, astonished the Romans whom he had outwitted. Five days later the priests were starved into surrender; they entreated for their lives, but Titus told them that the hour for mercy had passed, and that it behooved priests to perish with their Temple, and so ordered them executed.[77]

And now, beaten on all sides, and everywhere surrounded, John and Simon begged for a conference with Titus. Anxious to save the last section of the city, Titus, having appointed an interpreter, took up a position on the eastern end of the bridge which connected the Temple Mount with the Upper City, and himself began the discussion:

> *"Well, sirs, are you at last satiated with the miseries of your country:—you who without the least notion of either our power or your own wickedness have like madmen brought your people, your city and your Temple to destruction; you who ever since Pompey conquered you never ceased rebelling, and have now made open war with the Romans? Have you depended on your multi-*

[76] Bell. Jud., VI. I.
[77] Bell. Jud., VI. vi. I.

tude? Have you relied on the loyalty of your allies? And what nation beyond the limits of our empire would choose to assist you against the Romans? Are your bodies stronger than ours? Yet you know that even the Germans are our slaves. On the strength of your walls? But what could be a greater obstacle than the ocean by which the Britons are encompassed who yet do homage to the Roman arms? On your courage of soul and in the sagacity of your generals? Nay, indeed, you cannot but know that the very Carthagenians have been defeated by us. It can therefore be nothing else but the Roman kindness which has excited you against us....

"To begin with, we allowed you to possess this land and to set over it kings of your own blood; then we maintained the laws of your forefathers and permitted you to live, either among yourselves or in your dealing with others, as pleased you; above all, we permitted you to collect that tribute which is paid to God, with such other gifts as are dictated by Him. Nor have we called those who carried those donations to account, nor prohibited them; till at length you became richer than ourselves, even when you were our enemies; and you made preparations for war against us with our money....

"When my father came to this country he had no design to punish you for what you have done under Cestius.[78] *Had he come to overthrow your nation, his duty surely was to run to your fountain-head and lay waste this city immediately; whereas he went and burnt Galilee to afford you time for repentance. But by you this humanity was taken for weakness, and upon our mildness you nourished your impudence. When Nero died you acted like the wickedest of scoundrels. Emboldened by our civil dissensions you abused your opportunities by preparing for war. Nor were you ashamed to raise disturbances against those, now made emperors,*

[78] For these events see, Bell. Jud., III. xviii. 9f.

whose mildness as generals you had experienced. Thus, when the government was devolved upon us, when throughout the empire was perfect tranquillity, and even foreign nations sent embassies to congratulate us, once again you were in arms. You sent ambassadors to your friends beyond the Euphrates, fostering rebellion; new walls were built by you round your city, seditions arose, one tyrant contending against the other, and a civil war broke out among you; such indeed as became none other but men as wicked as you are.

"I then came to this city with sad injunctions from my reluctant father. When I heard the people were disposed to peace, I rejoiced at it. I urged you to stop those proceedings before I began this war. I spared you even after you had fought against me for a long time. I gave you my pledge of security to deserters, and kept my faith with them when they fled to me. It was unwillingly that I brought my engines against your walls. I always prohibited my soldiers, when they were set upon your slaughter, from severity against you. After every victory I persuaded you to peace, as if I had been myself conquered. When I came near your Temple, I again departed from the laws of war, and appealed to you to preserve your holy house for yourselves. I allowed you a quiet exit out of it, and a pledge for your security, or, if you so wished, an opportunity to fight in another place. Yet have you scorned all my proposals, and have set fire to your Temple with your own hands.

"And now, you vile wretches, you desire to treat with me by word of mouth. What do you desire to save comparable to what is lost? What protection do you think you deserve now that your Temple is destroyed? Even now you stand in your armor, and in this your utmost extremity you cannot bring yourselves so much as to pretend to be supplicant. O, miserable creatures! What do you depend on? Are not your people dead,

your Temple gone, your city at my mercy and are not your own very lives in my hands? And do you still deem it glorious to die? However, I will not imitate your madness. If you throw down your arms, and surrender your bodies to me, I grant you your lives; and I will act like a lenient master of a family; what cannot be healed shall be punished, and the rest I will preserve for my own use (?)."[79]

The reply which John and Simon gave to Titus was that they could not accept his offer, having sworn never to lay down their arms. They offered, however, to surrender the town on the condition that they be permitted to pass through the wall, with their arms, and make their way unmolested to the desert (probably to the desert of Arabia, or other countries on the south and east, beyond the limits of the Roman empire, with the intention of resuming the conflict from that basis at a more favorable opportunity, as is evident from the Sibylline poet, xii. 107, and Bell. Jud., VII. x. 1; xi. 1).

Indignant that these men, whom he already regarded as his captives, should make their own terms as if they were the conquerors, Titus withdrew all his offers of security, proclaiming that hereafter the tyrants must fight for their salvation as best they could, for all his actions henceforth would be governed by the laws of war. He then ordered his soldiers to burn the city, permitting them also to plunder it, and then rest for the remainder of the day. On the next day they set fire to the archives, the Acra, the Council House, and the district called Ophel. The lanes were also burnt, together with those houses that were packed with the bodies of those who died from the famine.[80]

Finding it impossible to attack the Upper City, without raising embankments, owing to the steep nature of the local-

[79] Bell. Jud., VI. vi. 2.
[80] Bell. Jud., VI. vi. 3.

ity, Titus, on the twentieth of the month of Ab,[81] distributed that work among his forces. The conveyance of timber was very difficult, since all the trees within the distance of a hundred furlongs had been cut down for the former earthworks. The banks now erected by the legions were on the west side of the city, opposite Herod's new palace; while the whole body of the auxiliary troops threw up embankments on the east, at the Xystus, whence they reached to the bridge and the tower which Simon, when at war with John, had built as a citadel for himself.[82]

While these earthworks were going up, John and Simon were celebrating the failure of their negotiations with Titus, by murdering eight thousand of the people and stealing their money. They also took two Roman prisoners. One of them they slaughtered on the spot, and dragged his body through the city, as if in the person of this trooper they were avenging themselves on all the Romans. The other, pretending to have something to say to Simon, was brought before him, but having nothing to tell him, was handed over to one Ardala to be put to death. Ardala bound his hands behind his back and bandaged his eyes, to be killed in sight of the Romans; but as the officer was drawing his sword, the soldier contrived to escape and return to his ranks.[83] During these days also, Simon's Idumean allies met secretly to deliberate about surrendering themselves to Titus, and sent five men to beseech his protection. Hesitating for a while, Titus consented and sent them back to bring the others. But as the Idumeans were preparing to march out, Simon detected the plot, and after executing the five emissaries, he imprisoned their commanders and put under increased vigilance the rest of the Idumeans. The guards, however, were now powerless to prevent desertion; for although many of the Idumeans were slain in their attempt, a far larger number of them escaped to the Romans.

[81] September the 8th.—Thackeray.
[82] Bell. Jud., VI. viii. 1.
[83] Bell. Jud., VI. viii. 1.

Titus received them all, regardless of his former proclamation.[84]

During the same interval also, a priest named Jeshua ben Thebuthus, in exchange for a pardon from Titus, surrendered from a secret compartment in the Temple, two candelabras, similar to those which stood in the Holy of Holies, along with shew-bread tables, mixing bowls, and vials, all made of solid gold and very heavy; he also handed over the holy purple hangings, the high-priests' vestments, the crown of gold set with precious stones, and many other articles of public worship. Another priest named Pinnehas, disclosed the tunics and girdles worn by the priests, and received his pardon from Titus.[85]

On the seventh day of Elul,[86] after eighteen days of labor, the earthworks against the Upper City were completed; and no sooner did the battering-rams begin to work, than the western wall and some of the towers succumbed to their pounding. The erstwhile proud oppressors, John and Simon, always prompt to kill, but now trembling villains unwilling to die, offered no resistance. Famished, deserted by their comrades and no longer able to secure a pardon, they fled into the subterranean caverns under Shiloah. The Romans, now masters of the wall, poured through the lanes with drawn swords, and massacred all whom they met without discrimination and without mercy.[87]

On the following day, when Titus came to examine the ruins, and saw the butchery that had been carried on during his absence, he stopped it; and after liberating all whom the tyrants had imprisoned in the fortresses, he gave orders that none but those who were in arms and offered resistance should be killed, and that all others should be kept for judgment. The frenzied troops, however, acting contrary to these specific

[84] Bell. Jud., VI. viii. 2.

[85] Bell. Jud., VI. viii. 3. For what became of these spoils of the Temple which escaped the fire, see Bell. Jud., VII. v. 5.

[86] About the 25th of September.

[87] Bell. Jud., VI. viii. 4-5.

From steel engraving by J. L. Gerôme (N. Y. Public Library).

The Wailing Wall.

orders, slew the aged and the weak and preserved only those who were of serviceable age, whom they penned into the innermost part of the temple-site for adjudication. Titus then appointed the general, Fronto Eternius, to determine the fate of each one according to his merits.

Fronto now crucified all who were recognized as insurgents, which was easy, since the victims became informers against each other. He then selected the tallest and handsomest from among the youths above seventeen years of age and reserved them for the triumphal march in Rome, while the others of them he sent to the Egyptian lead mines. Not knowing what to do with so great a multitude of prisoners, many of whom were either still liable to be put to death or ravished from hunger, and knowing also that the country was now devastated, Titus presented them to his various provinces to be destroyed in the arenas by either sword or wild beasts. Those under seventeen years of age he sold into slavery. During the interval spent by Fronto over this tribunal, eleven thousand of the prisoners died of starvation, either due to the hatred of the Romans who denied them food, or through their own refusal of it when it was given to them, but mostly because corn ran short even for the Romans' own sustenance.[88]

A search was now instituted for those who had taken refuge in the underground crevices. Those who were found alive were immediately executed. There were many whom John and Simon had incarcerated in these tunnels when their above-ground detention houses were filled; these the Romans brought up and freed. Over two thousand dead were also found, some who died by their own hands, others by one another's hands, but chiefly from starvation. From the horrible stench of these bodies came forth John of Gischala,—he who drowned the country in blood; the demon who stood behind the hand of the Roman who threw the firebrand into the Temple,—now haunted by the ghosts of his innumerable victims, cowardly imploring the Romans for that mercy

[88] Bell. Jud., VI. ix. 1-2.

which he himself had often so proudly refused to others. Titus gave him life imprisonment.[89]

And now, as there were no more people left for slaughter or plunder,—for the maddened soldiers would never have spared them so long as there remained any,—Titus ordered the entire city and the Temple ruins razed to the ground, excepting only three, the strongest and finest of the towers, Hippicus, Phasael, and Mariamne, and so much of the wall as enclosed the Upper City on the west side: [90] the latter to afford a camp for the garrison that was to remain there as guard. And this was the end to which the mad Zealots brought Jerusalem, the splendid city of world renown.[91]

During the course of its destruction, Titus persuaded Josephus repeatedly to take whatever he wanted from the ruins of his native city. "But now," the record reads, "that all was destroyed, I thought nothing to be of any value as a comfort under my calamities, and requested him that my relatives might have their liberty: I also had the holy books by Titus' concession. Not long after I asked him for the life of my brother and fifty friends and was not denied. When also I went to the Temple (site, or Fronto's detention camp), by permission of Titus, where there were a great many captive women and children, I got all those whom I remembered as friends and acquaintances to be set free and restored to their properties; being in number one hundred and ninety.[92] And when I was sent with Cerealis to a village called Theoca to find out whether it was fit for a camp, and saw among many crucified captives three whom I remembered as former

[89] Bell. Jud., VI. ix. 3-4.

[90] (a) "Upper City" in this instance seems to be an error in copying. "Temple site" is probably correct. (b) The Tower of Phasael, under the erroneous name of "David's Tower," is still to be seen.

[91] Bell. Jud., VII. i. 1.

[92] These were evidently from among the thousands of prisoners consigned by Titus to Fronto, and held on the temple-site for judgment.

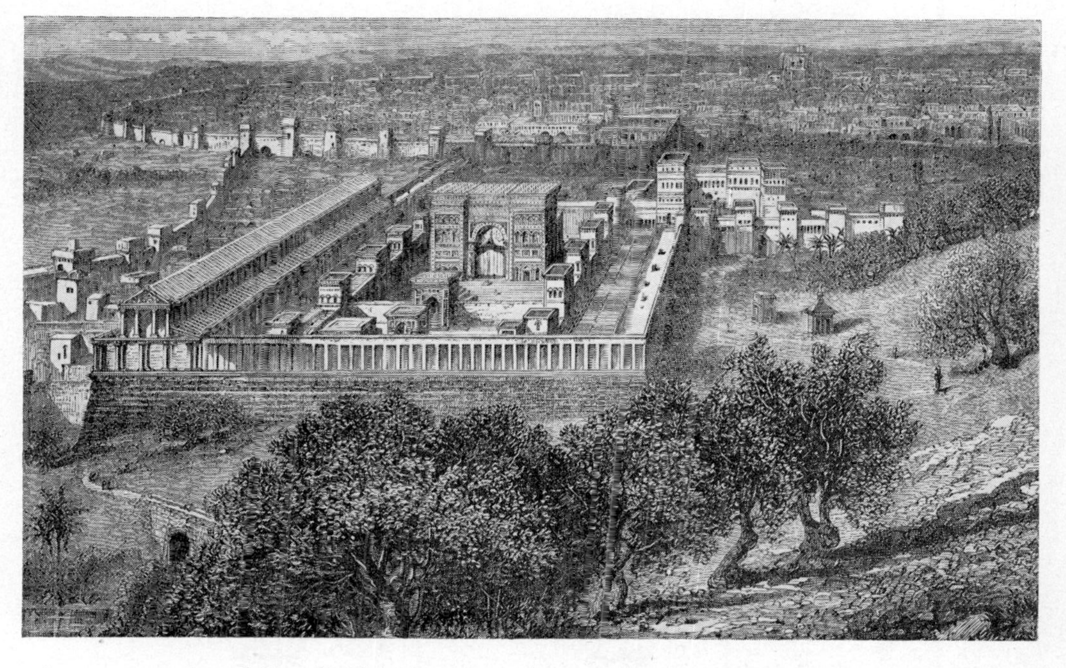

A reconstruction of Herod's Temple at Jerusalem. (Reproduced from Abbott's Dictionary of Religious Knowledge.)

acquaintances, and went with tears in my eyes to Titus and told him about them, he immediately ordered them taken off and the greatest care given:—two of them died under the physician's hands, while the third recovered."[93]

The total number of those who were taken prisoners during the entire war, 66-73 CE., amounted to ninety-seven thousand; and of those who perished during the five months' siege of Jerusalem alone amounted to eleven hundred thousand. The great number of those who perished during the siege was possible, since most of the victims were not natives, but pilgrims who had come to celebrate the Passover and were suddenly cooped in, as in a prison, when Titus on his return from Alexandria surrounded the city with his legions (Bell. Jud., VI. ix. 3-4; compare with V. iii. 1, and xiii. 7). According to Archbishop Usher (1581-1656) who follows Justus Lipsius (1547-1606), who again follows Josephus, the number of Jews who were destroyed during the seven years from Gessius Florus to the Destruction, 64-70, in Judea and the neighboring countries, amounted to 1,337,490 (Whiston, in note to Bell Jud., VI. ix. 3).

[93] Vita, 75.

CHAPTER X

The CONCLUSION *of the* WAR, 71-73 CE.

LEAVING behind the Tenth Legion as a garrison in Jerusalem, Titus with the rest of his army descended to Caesarea-on-the-Sea, there to deposit the bulk of his spoils, and to consign his captives to safe-keeping; for the winter season prevented him from sailing for Italy.[1]

He then marched to Caesarea-Philippi, where many of the prisoners were thrown to the wild beasts or compelled to engage one another in gladiatorial combats. While Titus was thus celebrating in this non-Jewish city, information reached him from Terentius Rufus, the commander of the guard at Jerusalem, that the missing arch-bandit, Simon bar Giora, had been captured under very peculiar circumstances:—While the Romans besieged the Upper City, Simon with some stone cutters were digging an underground passage of escape. They had all the necessary tools, and were well provided with food. Through the cretacious strata, for some distance, their work continued undisturbed, but on coming upon rock they were unable to accomplish their purpose; with provisions also failing, Simon was compelled to emerge. Imagining that he could cheat the sentinels, he disguised himself as a ghost who had

[1] Bell. Jud., VII. i. 2-3.

arisen from the dead, expecting by this means to scare them off and thus escape. The guards were indeed aghast when they first saw him,—dressed in the customary Jewish white grave-clothes, augmented by a royal purple mantle,—but on discovering who he was they bound him, and called for their commander, who dispatched the news to Titus. On receiving this message, Titus instructed Rufus to send Simon forthwith to Caesarea-on-the-Sea, while he himself returned to his base to receive him. Here Titus ordered him held as the principal sacrifice to Jupiter after the triumphal procession which he was to celebrate at Rome.[2]

At Caesarea-on-the-Sea also, Titus, on the 24th of October, celebrated the eighteenth birthday of his brother Domitian by destroying in different Roman ways two thousand five hundred rebel captives. Going then to Berytus, where he remained for a longer time, on the 17th of November he celebrated the sixty-first birthday of his father by destroying a still greater number of John's and Simon's supporters; and though the destruction of these victims was accomplished by the medium of wild beasts, enforced gladiatorial contests, and by flame, Josephus tells us that "to the Romans it all seemed too light a punishment for the crimes they had committed."[3] From Berytus, Titus proceeded to Antioch. When the Greeks of this city were informed that Titus was coming, they were ostensibly so happy over it that they were too impatient to remain within their walls, but advanced to a distance of thirty furlongs to meet him. But when they saw him approaching they accompanied their hypocritical acclamations with a petition for the expulsion of the Jews from their city. But Titus, without paying them any attention, and without even giving them an answer, diverted from his course, and without making his intended stop at Antioch, continued his march to Zeugma, where, as a result of his conquest of Judea, a deputation from the king of

[2] Bell. Jud., VII. ii. 1-2.
[3] Bell. Jud., VIII. iii. 1-2.

Parthia awaited him with a golden crown. Having accepted this, and feasted the King's messengers, Titus, returning, stopped at Antioch. When on this occasion the Antiochians invited him to their theater, he graciously consented. But when again they entreated him to expel the Jews from their city, his stern reply was: "How can this be done, since their own country to which they would be banished is destroyed." Failing in this, they petitioned him at least to cancel their privileges of citizenship; but this again Titus refused, and permitting the Jews of Antioch to continue in the enjoyment of their privileges exactly as before, he departed for Egypt.

On his way, passing through Jerusalem, Josephus joined his retinue, and marched with him to Alexandria, where they were to commence their journey for Rome. On his arrival at Alexandria with his two legions which had accompanied him, Titus dismissed them to their homes, the Fifth to Moesia (now Bulgaria), and the Fifteenth to Panonia (now Austria). As for John and Simon, and the seven hundred prisoners whom Fronto Eternius had especially selected, Titus gave orders that they should at once be conveyed to Italy, wishing to produce them at the Triumph. And now Titus and Josephus sailed for Rome, arriving there "somewhere about the middle of June" (71 CE.).[4]

That Josephus did not accompany Titus through Syria after the destruction of Jerusalem, but remained in the neighborhood of its ruins, cultivating his farm till Titus, coming southwards from Antioch, invited him to join him, is indicated by the facts recorded (*Vita*, 76) *as follows: "When Titus had quelled the insurrection in Judea, and conjectured that the land which I held at Jerusalem would bring me no profit because a garrison was to be quartered there, he gave me another piece of*

[4] Bell. Jud., VIII. v. 1-3. The date "middle of June," is given by Schuerer, who follows Chambalu.

ground in the plain"—thus providing Josephus with comfort and a means of existence;—"and when he was going away to Rome, he took me with him on board," etc.

It will be noticed, too, that nowhere in the works of Josephus, or of any other authority, is there any indication that Jewish citizens other than insurgents or incorrigibles, except those who were crucified in view of the besieged rebels, "to strike terror into them in the hope that this would hasten their surrender,"—which was quite in order, considering the barbarous age in which he lived,—or for lack of corn or other means of maintaining them, were put to death by Titus. As further proof that Titus never thirsted for innocent blood during the war, or sought to avenge himself on the Jews after the war, aside from the many others which we met with in the course of our history, is the fact that even immediately after the war, when Titus was at Antioch, he entertained no hatred against, but rather compassion for the persecuted race (Bell. Jud., VII. *v.* 2); *and that, under most perilous circumstances. Another such instance is the fact that when Catullus, the Roman governor of Cyrene, brought Jonathan and his followers to Rome to press a false accusation against Josephus as the sender of arms and money for the promotion of the Cyrenean insurrection, Vespasian, through the intervention of Titus, burnt only Jonathan, who was the fomenter of the rebellion, and sharply reprimanded Catullus, but never punished Jonathan's innocent dupes* (Bell. Jud., VII. *xi.* 3). *All history bears witness to the softness and almost feminine gentleness of his disposition, and even in the horrors of the siege of Jerusalem he deserved the character thus ascribed to him. The efforts which Titus made to save Jerusalem and the Temple were an exception to the general rule of destruction which had been carried out against Carthage, Syracuse, Corinth and other capitals.*

History also tells us that "Titus took from no man, he gave to all profusely"; he made it a point of never sending a suitor away unsatisfied. "No man," he said, in answer to a prudential remonstrance, "ought to leave the prince's presence disappointed." One evening at the dinner table, remembering that he had made no present to anyone since the morning, he exclaimed, "I have lost a day." (Suet. l. c.). We may thus account for the preeminent favor he enjoyed with his countrymen, which they declared by calling him "the Delight of the human race" (Suet., Titus, l.).

Educated in the imperial court, Titus was thoroughly trained in all elegant accomplishments: he could speak Greek fluently, and could compose verses; he was proficient in music; he could write shorthand, and could imitate handwriting so skilfully that he used to say that he might have been a most successful forger (Suet., Titus 3). He was very handsome (Tacitus, Hist. ii. 1, v. 1), with a fine, commanding expression (Piny's Preface), of a vigorous frame, and well trained in all exercises of a soldier. (See also Sil. Ital., iii., 603). The career of this prince was very short however, for on the 13th of September, 81, after a reign of two years and two months, he died, not yet having quite completed his fortieth year. (Various conflicting reports of the cause and manner of his death are given by Suetonius, Dion, Plutarch, Victor, Eusebius and others, and are collected by Reimar in a note to Dion, lxvi., 26).

Nothing, however, could equal the splendor of the Triumph which Vespasian and Titus celebrated in honor of their Judean achievements. Previous notice having been given of the day appointed for this pompous solemnity, not a soul of the immense citizenry remained at home, but everybody went forth to gain a position where it was possible to stand, leaving only such a passage as was necessary for those whom they were to gaze upon as they marched by.[5] Long before the break of day the military under their commanders had already lined up before the imperial palace; and as soon as the sun rose, Vespasian and Titus came out with laurels and dressed in the traditional purple robes, and proceeded to the Octavian Walks; for it was there that the senate, the judiciary, and those of the equestrian order were awaiting them. A tribunal had been erected, with chairs of ivory placed for them upon it. Shouts of joy rose from the troops as the emperors took their seats. Vespasian, having acknowledged their acclamations, gave them a signal of silence; then, covering his head with his cloak, recited the customary prayer, Titus joining him in the adoration. Then, after a pause for breakfast, the procession began.[6]

Silver and gold and ivory in mighty quantities, fashioned in all manner of forms, streamed like a river. Tapestries of the purest purple, or embroidered in Babylonian art, were borne along. Transparent gems, some set in crowns of gold, some in other designs, swept by in such profusion, as to correct one's supposition that any of them was a rarity. The images of the gods were also carried, being remarkable as much for their hugeness as for their art; nor was any of these of any other but very costly material. Animals of many species were led along, all adorned with appropriate ornaments. The numerous attendants conducting each group of animals were dressed in purple garments, all over interwoven with gold. Even among the seven hundred Zealot captives none was unadorned, while the variety and beauty of their garments concealed from view any unsightliness arising from wounds.

[5] Bell. Jud., VII. v. 3.
[6] Bell. Jud., VII. v. 4.

Nothing, too, in the procession was more astonishing than the pageants that were borne along, many of them three or four stories high. On tapestries bedecking these stages, various representations of the war were shown. Here was to be seen a prosperous country devastated, there entire squadrons of enemies slain; here a party in flight, there taken into captivity, and walls of enormous height and strength demolished and fortifications captured. Whole cities were seen destroyed, temples set on fire, houses pulled down over the heads of their owners, and rivers of fire flowing through a country no longer cultivated or peopled, but blazing far away into the long and dreary distance. On each of these pageants was shown the commander of the city that was captured and the manner in which he was taken. A number of ships, commemorating the battle of Lake Tiberias, also followed.

Conspicuously standing out among the general plunder were the spoils taken from the Temple of Jerusalem. These consisted of the golden table, many talents in weight, the seven-branched candlestick, which was also made of gold, a copy of the Law, and other articles. After these spoils followed the images of victory, all made of either ivory or solid gold. Behind them drove Vespasian, followed by Titus; while besides them rode Domitian on a charger that was in itself a marvel.[7]

The procession ended at the temple of Jupiter Capitolinus, where it halted until the execution of the enemy's general was announced. This general was Simon bar Giora, who had just marched among the captives; with a halter around his neck he was dragged to the Tarpeian Rock, abutting the Forum, scourged as he went, and there hurled over its precipice as a sacrifice to the gods. When the announcement was made that Simon was no more, and the prayers customary in such solemnities had been duly offered, the emperors withdrew to their palace.[8] John of Gischala was taken to the dungeon

[7] Bell. Jud., VII. v. 5.
[8] Bell. Jud., VII. v. 6.

The Tarpeian Rock.

where he languished for the rest of his contemptible life.[9] With the triumphal ceremonies concluded, Vespasian decided to build a Temple of Peace, which was completed with such speed and beauty as surpassed all human conception. Into this shrine were brought all the rarities which until then had been scattered over every part of the empire; here, too, Vespasian laid up the golden vessels which were taken from the Temple of Jerusalem, but the Law and the purple hangings of the Holy of Holies he ordered to be deposited and kept in the imperial palace.[10]

To commemorate the great victory coins were struck upon which Judea was represented as a sorrowing woman under a palm tree, standing with bound hands, or seated upon the ground, with the inscriptions "Judea Capta" or "Judea Devicta."

[9] Bell. Jud., VI. ix. 4, near end.
[10] Bell. Jud., VII. vi. 1.

On an arch which was later erected to Titus, and which is still standing, the candelabrum and the utensils of the Temple are plainly visible.

At the departure of Titus from Alexandria, however, the whole of Judea was not yet subdued. The south-Palestinian fortresses of Herodium, Machaerus, and Masada, were still in the hands of the insurgents. The reduction of these strongholds was left to Lucilius Bassus. Herodium surrendered immediately, but Machaerus, east of the Dead Sea, required a much longer time. Machaerus stood on the summit of a rocky hill so high as to make its reduction very difficult. But in addition it was also entrenched on all sides within ravines of a depth not easy to traverse and utterly impossible to bank up.[11] Yet, after many fierce conflicts, even this stronghold capitulated before it was taken by storm.[12]

With these affairs settled, Bassus hastened to a forest called Jardes, where a large number of insurgents who had formerly fled from Jerusalem and now from Machaerus had been hiding. As he arrived at the place and began to surround it, in order to prevent the fugitives from escaping, they attempted in a body to break through the encircling cavalry, but were met with stubborn resistance. A protracted contest followed; but in the end, while the casualties among the Romans were twelve dead and a few wounded, not one of the bandits survived the battle.[13]

After the conquest of Jardes, however, Bassus died and Flavius Silva who succeeded him marched against the southernmost fortress of Masada, the only stronghold which still held out. In this fortress the Sicarii, under the leadership of Eleazar ben Jair, had established themselves at the beginning of the war, and had continued to maintain their position. This Eleazar was a descendant of the bandit leader, Judas of Galilee, who in 6 CE., when Quirinius was sent as censor

[11] Bell. Jud., VII. vi. 2f.
[12] Bell. Jud., VII. vi. 4.
[13] Bell. Jud., VII. vi. 5.

to Judea, compelled the people to rebel against taxation, plundering or destroying the properties of those who complied with the Roman mandate.[14]

Masada, like many other fortresses in Palestine, stood on a high rock surrounded on all sides by deep ravines, the sides of which one could scarcely clamber, excepting in two places where the rock subsided, permitting passage, though not without difficulty. The city was enclosed by a wall, nearly a mile in circumference, eighteen feet high, and twelve feet broad, upon which stood thirty-seven lofty towers. Besides this wall, Masada had also a strong palace with four towers, built by Herod the Great, and which was connected by an underground tunnel with the fortress. Within the city there were numerous large rock-hewn reservoirs full of water,[15] and supplies of corn, wine, oil, pulse and dates, enough to last for many years. There were also arms, sufficient for ten thousand men, besides great stores of unwrought iron, brass and lead.[16]

Silva, having surrounded the city, in order to prevent any of the Sicarii from escaping, seized a point called the White Cliff, which was the only one capable of supporting earthworks; and there ordered his troops to throw up earth to a height of three hundred feet. This embankment, however, was found not sufficiently high for the use of engines; a platform of enormous stones, seventy-five feet high by as many wide, was constructed on top of it, and on this the battering-ram was brought to bear against the wall. Having further provided an enormous tower entirely encased in iron, from which the Romans, by volleys of darts and stones from their lighter engines, drove the defenders to retirement, Silva, after long resistance, succeeded in effecting a breach in the enclosure.

But the Sicarii had meanwhile erected another wall be-

[14] Bell. Jud., VII. viii. 1.
[15] Bell. Jud., VII. viii. 3.
[16] Bell. Jud., VII. viii. 4.

hind it, which was not so likely to crumble under shock as the former, for it was made pliable and designed to deaden the blows of the huge battering-ram. Great wooden beams were laid parallel with each other in two separate rows a wall's breadth apart, the intervening space being filled with earth. To prevent the soil from spilling through, this double wall was bound together by other beams laid transversely; and though this construction appeared to be real masonry, it was more shock-proof, for the more violently it was battered the more compact it became, by the yielding of the material which settled down and solidified under the concussion. When Silva saw this, and thinking it easier to destroy the structure by burning, he ordered his men to throw lighted torches upon it. Being chiefly made of wood, it speedily blazed up, and the whole became a vast wall of fire. The Romans then, stationing a strong watch before it, to prevent the Sicarii from escaping, withdrew to their camp for the assault on the next morning.[17]

But Eleazar was not the man either to think of fleeing or to permit others to do so. Realizing that the situation was hopeless, he assembled his men and, in a long oration which Josephus, following the example of other historians of his time, puts into the mouth of his character,[18] induced them to set the city on fire, kill their wives and children, and then themselves, rather than give themselves up to the Romans. The time has come, Eleazar reminds his comrades, when they must prove their lofty ideals by their actions.[19] Introducing the doctrine of the immortality of the soul, he directs their attention to the felicity it enjoys when it separates from the body at death:

[17] Bell. Jud., VII. viii. 2, at the beginning, and sec. 5.

[18] This example had been set by Thucydides, as he himself (i. 22) confesses. Julius Caesar in his Gallic War almost invariably reports his own speeches in "oratio indirecta" (see Weber, "Josephus und Vespasian," p. 219, and Thackeray, "Six Lectures," pp. 41ff.).

[19] Bell. Jud., VII. viii. 6.

"...Let sleep furnish you with a most convincing proof of what I say—sleep, in which the soul, undistracted by the body, while enjoying in perfect independence the most delightful repose, holds converse with God by right of kinship, ranges the universe and foretells many things which are to come. Why then should we fear death who welcome the repose of sleep? And is it not surely foolish, while pursuing liberty in this life, to grudge ourselves that which is eternal?[20]

"We, therefore, who have been raised in a discipline of our own, ought to become an example to others of readiness to die. If, however, we must have support in this matter, let us look at the Indians[21] *who bear life as a burden. Reluctantly they endure the period of earthly existence, as some necessary service due to nature, but hasten to release their souls from their bodies; and though no calamity impels nor drives them from the scene, from sheer longing for the immortal state, they announce to their comrades that they are about to depart. Nor is there anyone who would hinder them, but all felicitate them and give them commissions to their loved ones; so certain and absolutely sincere is their belief in the intercourse which their souls hold with one another.*

[20] This recalls Socrates' speech to the Athenians upon their verdict: "... A night of unbroken rest, untroubled by dreams, ... if death is like that, surely it is no evil. ... But if death is a migration into some land where all dead have gone before us, ... it is as well, for there we would find ... Minos and Rhadamanthus, Aeacus and Triptolemus (reputed judges of the dead in Hades), and all the sons of the gods who behaved rightly in life. We would find and converse with Orpheus and Hesiod and Homer. Would this be ill, my friends? ... It would be a pleasure to meet there Palamedes and Ajax, and compare their experiences. ..."

[21] Clearchus, in his works on Education, traced the descent of the Indian gymnosophists from the Magi, and Diogenes Laertius (Proem. 9), who is our authority, adds, "Some assert that the Jews also are descended from the Magi." Jews and Brahmans are also associated by Megasthenes (Clem., Strom., i. 15). For this latter I am indebted to Dr. Thackeray's note to verse 179 in his I Apion.

Then, after listening to these behests they commit their bodies to the fire,[22] *so that the soul may be parted from the body in the utmost purity, and expire amidst hymns of praise. Indeed, their dearest ones escort them to their death more readily than do the rest of mankind their fellow-citizens when starting on a very long journey; for themselves they weep, but them they count happy as now receiving immortal rank. Are we not, then, ashamed of being more mean-spirited than Indians, and of bringing, by our faint-heartedness, shameful reproach upon our country's laws, which are the envy of all mankind?*

"Yet, even had we from the first been schooled in the opposite doctrine and taught that man's highest blessing is life and that death is a calamity, still the crisis is one that calls upon us to bear it with a stout heart, since it is by God's will and of necessity that we are to die.... While our hands are free and can grasp the sword, let them render an honorable service. Unslaved by the enemy let us die, as free men with our children and wives let us quit this life together! This our laws demand,[23] *this our wives and children entreat."*[24]

He would have proceeded in his exhortation, but was cut short by his hearers, vying with each other in eagerness to begin their destruction at once. They quickly piled up their stores and set them on fire. Then, having chosen by lot ten men to slay the rest, they laid themselves down on the ground, each beside his wife and children, and offered their throats to the executioners. The ten, having slaughtered all, applied the same rule of the lot among themselves, that he on whom

[22] Calanus was the name of a gymnosophist who followed Alexander the Great, and burnt himself to death in the presence of his army (Plutarch, Alex., 65 etc.).

[23] The Law contains no such injunction.

[24] Bell. Jud., VII. viii. 7. (Thackeray's translation, with some changes.)

the first lot fell should cut the throats of the nine others; the last man, having first assured himself that there was no more work to do, drove a dagger into his own body. They died in the belief that not a soul of them had been left alive; but one old woman, and another, a relative of Eleazar, with five children escaped by concealing themselves in an underground cavern while the rest were busying themselves with the slaughter. Nine hundred and sixty perished; and the tragedy occurred on the fifteenth day of the month of Nisan.[25]

On the next morning when the Romans reappeared before the city, seeing none of the rebels and that all was solitude and silence, they were at a loss at what had happened. They shouted, as if to awaken them to action; the shouts were heard by the two women and the children, who, coming out from their hiding place, reported the speech and the occurrences which followed it.[26] When the fortress was thus taken, Silva left a garrison in the city and himself departed with his army to Caesarea. Thus, with the fall of Masada the war in Palestine ended.[27]

But the war against the Zealots and the Sicarii did not end with the fall of this last fortress. Some of these assassins fled to Egypt and Cyrenaica, where, not content with their escape, they again began their revolutionary disturbances and the murdering of those who opposed their sedition. The Jews of Alexandria, realizing that their safety was menaced, met in council and determined to put down these dangerous enemies to their peace. Six hundred were caught immediately on the spot, and all of those who fled into the interior of the country and the Egyptian Thebes were soon also arrested and brought back.[28] When Lupus, the governor of Alexandria,

[25] Bell. Jud., VII. ix. 1.

[26] Bell. Jud., VII. ix. 2.

[27] According to Thackeray (Bell. Jud., VII. ix. 1), who follows Schuerer, who again follows Niese's reckoning, the date of this occurrence was May the second, 73 CE.

[28] Bell. Jud., VII. x. 1.

reported this commotion to the emperor, Vespasian, fearing that Egypt might become a new center of revolt, ordered the beautiful Temple of Onias at Memphis, in the district of Heliopolis, to be closed.[29] Lupus carried out his master's orders; but when soon after he died, his successor Paulinus completely stripped the edifice of its treasures, threatening the priests with severe punishment if they failed to surrender them all, and prohibited worshippers from approaching the precinct for ever. The duration of this Temple from its erection to its closure was two hundred and forty-three years.[30]

Bas-relief of the Arch of Titus, showing the spoils of the Temple of Jerusalem, the seven-branched candlesticks, etc.

The frenzy of these fanatics spread like a disease as far as Cyrenaica. The last of these degenerates, having previously endangered the peace of this province, had almost involved in his own fate the few Jews who had escaped the ruin of their country. A certain weaver of Cyrene, named Jonathan,

[29] Bell. Jud., VII. x. 2.
[30] Bell. Jud., VII. x. 4.

collected a multitude of the poorer class about him, and promising to show them miraculous portents and apparitions led them in armor into the Lybian Desert. The more prudent of the Judeans denounced their deluded brethren to Catullus, the local governor, who seized them, and ordered many executed. Jonathan, however, who had evaded the pursuing cavalry for some time, when captured, revenged himself on the informers by accusing many of them of being his accomplices.[31] Catullus listened with greedy ears to his charges, and even suggested names of such as could plausibly be implicated, in order that he too might be thought to have won a Jewish war. On such evidences, after slaying one Alexander, with whom he had formerly had a quarrel, and his wife Berenice, Catullus caused the wealthy Jews to be massacred; which he thought he could safely do, because he confiscated their properties and added them to the emperor's revenues.[32]

To prevent any Jews outside of his jurisdiction from exposing his treachery and criminality, he persuaded Jonathan to bring a charge of sedition against the most reputable Jews both at Alexandria and at Rome. One of those thus incriminated was Josephus, the author of this history. Catullus embarked for Rome, bringing Jonathan and his companions along with him in chains, expecting that his accusations, with himself alone as witness, would be amply sufficient for their condemnation. But Vespasian, having his suspicions about the affair, ordered a strict investigation of the facts. Discovering that the charges against Jonathan's dupes were false, Vespasian ordered them freed; but Jonathan himself was first tortured and then burnt alive.[33] Catullus suffered nothing worse than a severe reprimand; but not long after he lost his reason, continually crying that he saw the ghosts of those whom he had murdered standing before him. His malady continued to

[31] Bell. Jud., VII. xi. 1.
[32] Bell. Jud., VII. xi. 2.
[33] Bell. Jud., VII. xi. 3.

grow worse until ulcers of the stomach put an end to his accursed life.[34]

At this point Josephus concludes the History of the greatest war, not only of the Jews, but of all that up to his time had ever broken out in the entire history of nations. Leaving the style of its rendition to the judgment of his readers, he asserts that throughout its composition, Truth was his single aim.[35]

Concerning the death of Josephus there is no exact record. His own Biography (Vita, 65) implies that it occurred "when Vespasian, Titus and Agrippa were no longer among us." Vespasian died in the year 79, Titus in 81, and Agrippa, according to Photius (Biblioth., cod. 33), in the third year of Trajan, or 100 CE. Josephus, therefore, would have died later than this latter date. The accuracy of the statement of Photius has, however, been called in question, and Niese (Hist. Zeitschrift, bd. lxxvi. 193ff.) identifying Epaphroditus, the patron of the historian, with the freedman of Nero, conjectures that Josephus was involved in the ruin of his patron (Suet., Domit., 14), falling a victim to the suspicions of Domitian about the year 95 CE.

Suetonius (Domit., xv. and xvii; compare Dion Cassius, lxvii. and xii.) informs us that Flavius Clemens, a cousin of Domitian, was put to death, and that his wife Domitilla, also a relative, was exiled to the Island of Pandataria, the emperor having heard of their leaning toward Judaism. Tacitus (Agric. xliv.) tells us: "Executions not only took place from time to time and at long intervals, but they occurred in continuous successions"; and Dion (lxvii. 14) says: "Proselytes were despoiled of their property, sent to exile or condemned to death."

From all these, and the fact that among the emperors of whom Josephus speaks in his Vita (65) as dead, Domitian,

[34] Bell. Jud., VII. xi. 4.

[35] Bell. Jud., VII. xi. 5; compare with first section of Preface to War.

who succeeded them, is not named; and also that he never even once mentions the names of Nerva and Trajan, it is most obvious that during the reign of Domitian, Josephus also endeavored to win over proselytes. He must have been a friend of Clemens, as Josephus lived in one of the Flavian palaces presented to him by Vespasian (Vita, 76). When Domitian sentenced Clemens and other converts to Judaism, it is possible that Josephus was accused for having led them astray. Three books, "Concerning our Jewish Opinion about God and His Essence," which he promised to write, "if God will permit me" (Antiq., XX. xi. 3), remained unwritten as the thread of his life was probably cut short by Domitian before his own death in the year 96 CE.

Eusebius (Hist. Eccl., iii. 9) and Jerome (De Vir. illustr., xiii.) tell us that Josephus was honored with a statue at Rome, and that his works were placed in the Palatine library.

Coin of Eleazar.

Coin of Simon ben Giora.

CHAPTER XI

The CRITICS *of* JOSEPHUS

"The false pen of the scribes worketh for falsehood."
(JER. VIII. 8.)

IN the Christian Church from the earliest times, due to a disputed passage in the Antiquities (XVIII. iii. 3), concerning the actions and character of Jesus the Nazarene, the works of Josephus have acquired an immense popularity. Repudiated by the Jews, he was adopted by the Christians as one of themselves. His history of Herod was an excellent commentary of the Gospels; and his account of the siege of Jerusalem, "one of the bases of Christian apologetics, Christ having foretold in His eschatological discourse the very events there narrated." The passage in which Jesus is expressly designated as the Messiah foretold by the prophets, and made use of during many centuries to sustain the Christian apology, runs as follows:

"About this time arises Jesus, a wise man, if indeed He should be called a man. For He was a doer of marvellous deeds, a teacher of men who receive the truth with pleasure; and He won over to Himself many Jews and

many also of the Greeks. He was the Christ. And when Pilate had sentenced Him to be crucified on the evidence of our leaders, those who had loved Him at first did not desert Him, for He appeared to them alive again the third day as the divine prophets had foretold this and ten thousand other wonders concerning Him. And even now the tribe of Christians, named after Him, is not extinct."

For twelve hundred years, from the time of Eusebius (260-340 CE.), who first quoted this passage,[1] till the sixteenth century, its genuineness was never questioned. And in fact, such a testimony coming from a Jew was extremely welcomed and treasured by the early Fathers. Indeed, it contributed not a little to exalt the reputation of Josephus in the Christian Church; the bare estimation of what was said in his favor up to the tenth century alone, occupies more than thirteen folio pages in Havercamp's edition of Josephus (Vol. vii.).

The writings of Josephus have been very frequently mentioned and cited by ancient writers, almost from the date of their appearance, and onward in regular succession. Suetonius (Vesp., 5) enumerates the many omens and presages which kindled the ambition of Vespasian, or had served to prepare him for the high fortune. Among these he mentions the responses he obtained from an oracle of Mount Carmel, assuring him that the highest thought which his ambition might entertain, should be realized. Suetonius was a contemporary of Josephus—surviving him a few years—and he might probably have received this and other facts connected with Jewish affairs from Josephus.

A few years later than Suetonius, Justin Martyr (about 147 CE.) in his Exhortation to the Greeks, appeals to the evidence of the two Jewish writers, Josephus and Philo, as well known to those whom he addresses. And in his Dial. cum

[1] Eusebius, Hist. Eccl., i. 11; and Demonstr. Evang., iii. 5.

Trypho (p. 230), upbraiding the Jews, he tells them, "You know that Jesus was risen from the dead and ascended into heaven, as the prophecies did foretell was to happen." Irenaeus (about 120-200), by his mode of citing Josephus seems to indicate that already his works had become generally known. Theophilus, bishop of Antioch (about 170), less than eighty years after the death of Josephus, having referred to the testimony of Manetho and Menander, mentions also Josephus as the composer of a history of the Jewish war with the Romans.

Clement of Alexandria (150-215), in the course of an exposition of Daniel's prophecy of the "seventy weeks" (Strom., i), cites Josephus. Tertullian (160-220), a contemporary of Clement, in his Apology addressed to the heathens, mentions Josephus; but the terms in which he does so are important, as showing the light in which he was viewed at so early a time. A writer so well informed as Tertullian, after enumerating the writers,—Oriental and Greek,—whose writings might be adduced in support of what he had affirmed, adds, "and he who approves, or reproves those, Judaeus Josephus the fervent defender of Jewish antiquity." Dion Cassius (early part of 3rd century) frequently cites Josephus. Minutius Felix, the Christian apologist, in the course of his confutation of heathenism, finds occasion to appeal to the writings of Josephus.

Origen (185-254) often quotes Josephus; and Porphyry, the adversary of Christianity, writing a few years later, in his treatise De Abstinentia, iv. 11, refers very distinctly to Josephus' writings, designating them in their order. Thus, at the close of the third century, the writings of Josephus were well known to the learned world, and were customarily cited as the most authentic sources of information relating to Jewish affairs.

From this era onward, the references to Josephus, especially by the Christian Fathers, are very frequent. Jerome (ab. 340-418), who in his De Viris Illustr. makes Josephus most expressly acknowledge that "Christ was slain by the Pharisees on account of the greatness of his miracles" and that "Jerusalem was destroyed on account of the slaughter of James the Apostle," again, in his Epist. ad Marcel., cites Josephus, designating him as "Vernaculus Judaeorum." In his Epist. ad Eustochium he further names him "The Grecian Livius"; in his catalog of Ecclesiastical writers the works of Josephus are generously enumerated, and in his De Vir. Illustr., xiii., he says that, "Such was his reputation, that a statue was erected to his honor."

Pelusiata and Sozomenos of the fifth century, Cassiodorus and Evagrius of the sixth, and numberless others through the rest of the centuries prior to the Renaissance extolled him to the skies. The opinion of Scalliger (1540-1609), the most learned man of his age, was that "Josephus was the most diligent and the greatest lover of truth of all writers." Scalliger also affirmed that, "It is safer to believe him, not only as to the affairs of the Jews, but also as to those which are foreign to them, than all the Greek and Latin writers before him."[2]

In the sixteenth century, however, with the Revival of Letters and Learning, which led to a remarkable interest in the study of classical Greek, the genuineness of the Christian passage in the eighteenth book of the Antiquities was questioned. First, it was seen, aside from not being Josephian in either style or character, that, where it is placed, the Testimonium is both anachronous and wholly irrelevant. It is preceded by an account of rioting under Pilate, who introduces the standards with the emperor's images into Jerusalem and threatens the Jewish objectors with death if they do not desist. This is known to have occurred in 26 C.E. In the following section is the account of another disturbance, when he seizes the Temple's sacred money, ostensibly for the building of a viaduct. This happened in the year 36, after which Pilate was recalled by the Syrian legate and sent to the Em-

[2] Scalliger, De Emend. Temp., Preface, p. 17.

peror on charges of cruelty and of causing sedition (Antiq., XVIII. iii. 2). And now, with Pilate having been succeeded by Marcellus as the Roman Procurator of Judea, comes the Christ passage saying, "At this time arises Jesus," etc., which took place in the year 30 under Pilate; and is itself followed by a story of shameful practices by the priests of the goddess Isis which led to the destruction of her temple and the punishment of those who introduced new rites into Rome,—a story which had nothing to do with the subject which Josephus has in hand.

Secondly, it was observed that since the Testimonium which was cited for the first time by Eusebius (260-340), had been unknown to his predecessors Justin (103-164), Tertullian (150-230), and to Origen (185-254), it must, consequently, either have crept into the text within the latter's century, or been forged by the pious charlatan Eusebius himself.[3] In the third instance it was asked, how could Josephus, who in all his works had so passionately defended Judaism, have acknowledged Jesus as the Christ? But the aptitude of the early Church Fathers for interspersing historical manuscripts with Christian references had by the sixteenth century become too well known; and the evidence of the fraud was sufficiently self-supporting without recourse to their pious propensities for comprobation.

In view of these facts, a reaction was sure to follow. It is easily understood, however, that the relinquishment of the interpolation, which for twelve centuries had supplied the papists with a convenient weapon for the persecution and

[3] For an idea of this man's mentality, one needs only take a glance at his Eccles. Hist., Bk. i. chapt. 7, where he explains the genealogical discrepancies between Matthew and Luke; or his description of the martyrdom of Polycarp, in iv. 15; or the silly story concerning the martyrs mentioned by Justin, in iv. 17; or the stories concerning Blandina, Sanctus, and the others who were "in eager desire for martyrdom," in v. 1; or the other stupid lies he hands down to us as history in his Book of Martyrs, "for the benefit of posterity."

forced conversion of Jews, could not be adjudged at once; a controversy of pro and con was carried on incessantly for three hundred years. In the seventeenth century the popularity of Josephus was yet so high as to induce Rembrandt to name one of his Jewish portraits after him. In the eighteenth century, most homes in England still possessed two books, a Bible and a Josephus. In the nineteenth century, a final battle over the authenticity of this passage was opened, a battle which ran into the twentieth century, and it was not until our own time that both Josephus and the Testimonium were completely rejected. And since in his writings, completed only sixty years after the Crucifixion, he disregarded no single event, whether petty or of major importance,—omitted no passing revolt, no temporary tumults, no warranted or unwarranted executions of any social or political interest,—especially of those from Herod the Great to the destruction of Jerusalem, the Gentile aversion of Josephus is all the deeper, not alone due to his failure to mention the "Messiah," but also to his complete silence on such an event as the life of Jesus and his terrible death under Pilate.

Far bitterer in their virulence against Josephus, however, are his own people. For whereas by the Christians he was rejected only with the rejection of the Testimonium, by the Jews he was repudiated since his very own time and, supposedly, for considerably graver reasons. Their first suspicion against him arose when he returned the plunder of the Dabaritta robbers to Agrippa's officials,[4] and again when he refused to allow John of Gischala to carry off the corn which the Romans had collected as taxes and stored away in several Galilean villages.[5] Again, not long after, he was accused by a band of robbers of treason, for having gathered up the remains of Herod's palace at Tiberias after they had plundered and burnt it, and hand them over to Agrippa's

[4] Bell. Jud., II. xxi. 3f; Vita, 26-27.
[5] Vita, 13f.

officers.[6] Josephus' persistent efforts, such as these and many others, to pacify his province and to secure peace before the inevitable catastrophe which he foresaw, were continually looked upon as harboring designs for betraying the country to the Romans; and thus charged with aiding the enemy, John demanded of the Sanhedrin at Jerusalem that they remove "the traitor" from office.[7]

For his refusal to destroy himself in the cave of Jotapata, and for his surrender to the Romans, he was branded as a coward and a renegade;[8] and later in Jerusalem when, by order of Titus, he engaged, often at the greatest risk of his life, in negotiating with the Zealots for an honorable surrender,[9] he was once struck by a stone so as to be rendered unconscious.[10] And lastly, for his description of these degenerates as the most worthless and criminal of human beings,—robbers and rebels cast off by God and justly punished by the Romans,—he was for ever condemned by the later Jews, who have never lost an opportunity to abuse him. Thus, denounced by the Christians for his silence, he is belittled and maligned by the Jews for his disclosures.

"The events of the war," says Jost (Judenthum, i. p. 445), "are narrated by the vain, self-seeking, and treacherous Josephus with horrible callousness; with him the lovers of liberty are all outlaws and robbers, whose downfall and cruel treatment he describes with obvious approval while himself enjoying the comforts of his ill-begotten reward. By his worthless history he has provided for himself eternal curses." Thus bitter is the contempt against Josephus by a writer who, since Josephus himself, was the first Jew who had ever written the history of his people in any other language than Hebrew.

So determined is Jost in his onslaught against Josephus,

[6] Vita, 12-13.
[7] Bell. Jud., II. xxi. 7; Vita, 38-44.
[8] Bell. Jud., III. viii. 1-8.
[9] Bell. Jud., V. iii. 3, vi. 2, vii. 4, ix. 2-4, xiii. 3; VI. ii. 1-3, vii. 2; Vita, 75.
[10] Bell. Jud., V. xiii. 3.

that in the sixth book of his Jewish History (Anhang, pp. 55-73) he fills nineteen closely printed pages to justify his infinitude of unwarranted imputations and charges against him. And though he savagely assails Josephus (idem, p. 66) as a prevaricator, he himself exercises the most excessive abuses of terms in reversing the order of facts, misinterpreting and misquoting the text which lies before him. The violent assault of Isaac Marcus Jost (1793-1860) on the personal character of Josephus and on the trustworthiness of his works, which served to pervert and warp the minds of young clergymen, was hailed as an excellent precedent by future theologians, both Jewish and Christian, for the riddance of an old and troublesome thorn from the flesh of their respective faiths; and who, since Jost, have with remarkable harmony been incapable in their literature of recognizing in Josephus anything but improbity, servility, selfishness, and treason.

During a discourse a few years ago,[11] the learned Professor Salo Baron, having first referred to Jost as a pedagog, linguist, publicist and journalist, an English grammarian and a Shakespearean glossographer, portrays the polymath as follows:

> (*Page* 12) *"In general, Jost's philosophy of history is very simple; he is not even a theologian like most of the other Jewish historians of the 19th century. It is perhaps one of his essential weaknesses that, treating a subject like the history of the Jewish people, he had no definite view as to what this Jewish people really was. Personally almost an agnostic, a man who boasted of not having gone to a synagogue for more than twenty years, because, as he said, 'he did not go to theater,' he could hardly feel deep sympathy with Jewry as a purely religious group.*[12]

[11] At a public meeting of the American Academy for Jewish Research, at New York.

[12] As his authority for this, Prof. Baron gives H. Zirndorf's "Isaak Markus Jost und seine Freunde" (Cincinnati, 1886).

(Page 14) "*In his first volume he devotes a large chapter of more than* 100 *pages to Palestine, its topographical, hydrographic and climatic conditions ... (and) there is hardly any connection between his long introduction and the other chapters of his book. If occasionally he attempts to explain a certain phenomenon by the influence of nature, he does little more than betray his complete naïveté.*

(Page 17) "*Occasionally Jost does attempt to sketch the profile of an important historical personality, but even when he tries his utmost, as in the case of Herod, his characters are too conventional to be true, too lame and ordinary to be stirring.*

(Page 18) "*To be sure, Jost's mind was not of the type best fitted to deal with the complicated and obscure problem of Jewish intellectual history, particularly at a time when the sources were so widely scattered and so little investigated. Being of a rather sceptical and rationalistic trend of mind, he could hardly grasp the vital forces in any purely religious movement; for him ... religions were often created by individuals in pursuit of worldly ends.... He was not a great original thinker, and all the philosophy he knew was under the predominant influence of Kantian or post-Kantian systems.*

(Page 19) "*Towards that element of Jewish thought which seemed to lie closest to his comprehension, namely the Law, he was far from sympathetic. This otherwise quiet and cool-headed man loses his temper when he speaks of the Talmud and its laws. He has not quite the fervor of the French iconoclast of the* 18*th century, but he is ready to denounce the Talmud as the source of many evils throughout Jewish history.*

(Page 31) "*In a series of violent denunciations, Luzzato goes as far as to call Jost the 'hater of God and enemy of the Jews.'*"

A description in detail of the character, or rather mentality, of every writer of every land and language and their criticisms on Josephus, would require a large set of volumes; because no ancient historian can be named who has been at once so hotly assailed, so warmly defended, and as repeatedly commented upon as he. But of the few of his severest critics, since Jost, most familiar to us, whom we shall now discuss, it will be seen that, precisely as in his own case, a certain twist exists in the psychological constitution of almost every one of these individuals, which evidently accounts for their incapability of estimating truth.

The first of these is the French-Jewish half-apostate Joseph Salvador. For a student of Jewish history, to read this man's work, "The History of the Roman Domination in Judea, and the Destruction of Jerusalem" (Paris, 1842), would be repugnant, due to his shameless perversion of facts.

As if the example set by his predecessor Jost was too tame for him, Salvador (Vol. ii. c. 8f.) improves upon it by taxing Josephus with deliberate treason against Judea, maintaining that he accepted the command of Galilee only to paralyze the defense and to ruin the cause of his country. Concerning John of Gischala, on the other hand, he says, "He had with him the whole popular party of Galilee, and all the Zealots, every man of whom had sworn to die or destroy every particle of territory which might produce an income for Caesar. Most of the principal cities of Galilee were impatiently awaiting to march under his orders."

Again (p. 78), referring to John, after having generously paraded his "great popularity," he adduces proof of the "nobility" of this scoundrel, and of the nature of the friends he had: "Since his youth," says he, "a deep affection existed between him and the son of a personality not less celebrated in the history of the Christians than in Jewish tradition. This friend was Simon, the son of Gamaliel, the teacher from whom the Apostle Paul had received his first instruction during his youth." Such is his admiration of this bandit, notwithstanding his betrayal of his own Peace Party which elevated him to position of president, and in spite of the fact that he misappropriated funds from the nation's treasury. Such are his encomiums upon John,—the perjurer who had broken faith with Josephus at Tiberias, with Titus on the surrender of his home town Gischala, with the people of Jerusalem whom he later murdered indiscriminately, with his own personal old friend and benefactor, Simon ben Gamaliel, whom he probably also murdered, and lastly with God, when he broke his oath not to surrender to the Romans, but instead, when his day was over, begged them for his life and for mercy. All these facts are passed over by Salvador in silence.

As for Simon bar Giora, here is what he says:—(p. 116) "The means by which he created an army, the plan of the campaign which he adopted against the legions of Vespasian before he shut himself up in the Jewish capital, his vigorous conduct and his 'beautiful' death are equaled only by the history of the Gallic hero, Vercingetorix, the son of Celtillus."

Resuming his abuses of Josephus, as if annoyed, he goes on: (p. 176) "Having retained for six months, against the will of the Committee, the post of Commander-in-Chief in the province most abounding in energetic men, Josephus did not hesitate to write to this same Council the following words, which under other circumstances might have been looked upon as the jeering expression of a talented hoaxer: 'If you want to treat with the Romans let me know it immediately; if you persist in continuing the war, send me sufficient forces to fight them.'" The fall of Jerusalem and the destruction of the Temple are explained by Salvador with similar gerrymandering, as "a necessary stage in the spread among the peoples" of what he calls the Christian form of Judaism. To the beautiful Berenice, the sister of Agrippa II, and to "Contemporary Women," he devotes no less than twenty-four pages of his distasteful history.

Joseph Salvador was born at Montpellier, France, in 1796; his father was a pious Jew, while his mother was a devout Catholic. His father gave him a good Jewish education, his mother taught him in her own religion, and in 1816 he graduated at the university of his native town as a doctor of medicine. Very early, however, he abandoned the medical career, to devote himself entirely to literature, for which purpose he went to Paris, where he remained the rest of his life.

Though claiming to be a staunch Jew and a member of a Jewish synagogue, Salvador maintained that Judaism died with the fall of Jerusalem. But in order to assure his salvation, he worshipped both in the synagogue and in the church; and while fasting on Yom Kippur, he never failed to attend the Catholic Mass. His brother Benjamin married a Huguenot; his sister Sophie's husband was a Jewish lawyer.

According to family tradition, Salvador's paternal ancestors were descendants of the Maccabees, the saviors of Israel, —the name "Salvador" meaning "savior,"—who emigrated from Africa to Spain in the ninth century, and fled from the latter country to escape the Inquisition, in the fifteenth century, finding a refuge in France. In 1873 Salvador died at Versailles. At his own request he was buried in the Protestant cemetery of Le Vigan, near Montpellier, in his brother's family vault, the rabbi of Nimes officiating.

Some three years after the publication of Salvador's History there appeared, what at the time was regarded as an important source of information, the "Cyclopaedia of Biblical Literature," by the Rev. John Kitto. Under the title "Josephus," the essence of his very long and severe criticism is in many instances very similar to that of Jost and Salvador. "The worst stain on Josephus' character," this cleric tells us, "is his desertion of his country in the hour of her sorest need," and flares up because, "while Judea Captiva wept under her desolate palm-tree, he could live in splendor in the house assigned to him by her conquerors, enjoy a share of their booty, and boast of their patronage; while his countrymen were dead, or enslaved, this 'nescio quis Arabarches' (taken from Juvenal, i. 130) could bear to see his own triumphal statue set up among their oppressors, and could sit as a congratulating guest, offering homage and adoring cringes, whilst the triumphal pageant for Judea ravaged, and Jerusalem burnt, filled the hours of a long summer's day ere it unfolded its pomps before him."

> "*(How peculiarly Kitto's) heart has learned to glow*
> *For others' good, and melt at others' woe!"*
>
> (From Alexander Pope's "Homer's Odyssey," Bk. 18. 1. 279.)

John Kitto was born at Plymouth, England, in 1804. His father was a poor mason and a drunkard, who could afford him only three years' schooling; and so, in his twelfth year he began to earn his own living as a barber's apprentice, but was soon dismissed for theft. In 1817 he joined his father at his trade; but when stepping from the top of a ladder to the roof of a house, he lost his footing, and fell a distance of thirty-five feet into the court beneath. By this fall he was severely injured bodily, and totally and permanently deprived of his hearing. On recovering his strength, he resorted to various expedients to gain a few pennies whereby he might buy books; for reading was his passion. His pitiable condition —pinched with hunger, shivering in rags, and walking about with exposed and bleeding feet,—led to his being put in the Plymouth workhouse, where he remained from 1819 to 1823. At this time he attracted the attention of the famous scientist Harvey, and also of other educated persons who were interested in the articles he wrote for the Plymouth Weekly Journal; and through them obtained the post of sub-librarian of the Plymouth Public Library. From this position he passed, in 1824, into the service of a Mr. Groves, a dentist at Exeter. Through Mr. Groves, again, he was engaged by the Church Missionary Association as printer's apprentice. By this time he had acquired some knowledge of Latin and Greek, and now began to study Persian; his first book, "Essays and Letters," also appeared at this time (1825). But Kitto was too much given to literature to become an efficient printer, and was consequently dismissed by the Association. In 1833, after spending some years in Malta, and later as a missionary in Bagdad, he obtained employment as a literary hack with the Penny Magazine. During the same year, too, he married. In 1838 he published his Pictorial Bible. By now he had at last found his place, and produced in succession numerous works, among which was the "Cyclopaedia of Biblical Literature," which was edited under his personal supervision, containing the biography of Josephus—an article which has nothing to do with either the Bible, Bible science, or any literature concerning Bible times. In 1850, owing to a paralytic stroke, which totally incapacitated him, he was put on the civil list, and received a grant of a hundred pounds a year, "on account of his meritorious work." He had been all his life subject to severe headaches, for some years also, due to a derangement in the vocal organs, unable to speak a word; but in 1851 he manifested decided indications of cerebral debility, and on the 9th of August, 1854, he died.

Our next critic is the Protestant theologian Heinrich Ewald, once adjudged one of the most learned Oriental and Scriptural scholars of his time. But his "History of Israel," first (1847) in five volumes, and later increased to seven and again to eight, which in its own day was considered a standard work, has, due to its content of countless inaccuracies, purposeful misstatements, stupid dogmatisms and ridiculous propagandism for the conversion of Jews, with the appearance of other historical works, especially those of Graetz in 1853, Raphall in 1855, and Milman in 1875, been entirely relegated to oblivion. So great an influence as a scholar and Biblicist was he, that Graetz, an even poorer exegete than himself, writes of him (Vol. V. p. 695) that, whereas both the rationalists and orthodox Christian theologians failed to arrive at a correct understanding of the sacred Scripture of the Jews, Ewald, "a man of childlike mind, was the first to raise the veil, to comprehend the language of the Prophets and Psalmists, and to reveal the ancient history of the Jewish people in its true light." What Graetz, however, in his own ineptitude, failed to notice in the ambiguous and tricky phraseology of Ewald's History is, as a later and finer scholar (Stanley's "History, etc." Preface to third volume) describes him, that though for him, ostensibly, "the people of Israel was truly 'the people of God,' and its history the history of a true religion, . . . singularly enough, Ewald had only contempt for that people whom as the originators of the Old and the New Testament he glorified." (An incident in Ewald's life, related by Dean Stanley, deserves mention here. While an Oxford student, Stanley visited Ewald at an inn in Dresden. During the conversation the "great scholar" Ewald, grasping a small copy of the Greek Testament, said, "In this little book is contained all the wisdom of the world.")

"The great rebellion against the power of Rome on the part of the Judeans," so the "great" Ewald begins the most important (8th) volume of his History (p. 1), "had at length been put down; the Sanctuary and Jerusalem had been laid in ruins, the people of the ancient religion . . . had been suddenly and basely degraded. . . . But (p. 3), inasmuch as Christ had some forty years previously appeared in the Community of the nation, and as He had shown most clearly for those and all times what was the nature of the true and perfect religion, the first and great question of the age was what would be the attitude of the members of this nation to Him and to His requirements. The answer to that question, however, had been most plainly given in a twofold form before the unquenchable conflagration had broken out,—first, by all that took place at Christ's crucifixion, and, secondly, by all that followed in the course of the next three decades."

(Page 26) "As the disciples had for thirty or forty years always looked with the most intense expectation for the fulfilment of all His predictions,[13] and as the parent Church had fled from Jerusalem in the year 66,[14] because it was convinced that the prophecies which Christ had left to His disciples with reference to such an end of things had then been accomplished, so they undoubtedly perceived with agitated astonishment that a great part of the predictions of the Lord was now fulfilled with the destruction of Jerusalem and the Temple, and could the more believingly await the fulfilment of the rest." Such is what "the great" Ewald hands to us as a History of Israel.

Naturally, in a Jewish history written by a learned bigot of this stamp, which neither in appearance nor in nature has any relationship with its name, for an impartial reader to expect an instructive account concerning any fact would be most preposterous. As an illustration of its worthlessness, a few passages from the text of Josephus are placed here side by side with their parallels in the seventh volume of Ewald's History to prove how, in order to gratify the sensibilities of those whom by his sacrimonious revelations he hoped to apostize, he distorts or reverses events of the Jewish war and facts concerning the principal persons who took part in it, that he may thereby render such history, over which he fancies they feel humbled, more flattering:

EWALD	JOSEPHUS
Page 533: "Josephus represents the average degree of culture to which a . . . moderate priest of those times could attain.	His "Contra Apionem" redundantly proves the contrary.
Idem: "Two priests, Joazar and Judas, were joined with him, but since they found it very difficult	Vita, 12: "Now, as soon as I arrived in Galilee, I wrote to the Sanhedrin at Jerusalem about them and asked for their instructions what to do. They

[13] He here refers to Matt., xxiv. 34-35.

[14] In accordance with Eusebius (Eccl. Hist., III. v. 2-3), and he alone, who says that the Christians had left the city in consequence of a divine admonition and migrated to the city of Pella, in Perea.

EWALD	JOSEPHUS
to get in Galilee the tithes which fell to them in Judea, they soon desired to go back to Jerusalem.	advised me to remain at my post and take care of Galilee, retaining my colleagues, if they were willing to stay. My colleagues, however, having amassed great riches from tithes which they received as priestly dues, decided to return home.
P. 537: "But Josephus was in this matter also very compliant, and as he desired to be gracious to John of Gischala he had not only allowed him to confiscate and carry away the imperial corn,—that is, corn that was still lying in the villages of Galilee forming the Roman land-taxes,—but also to sell to Judeans of Caesarea-Philippi at a great profit the oil of Galilee, as not having passed through heathen hands.	Bell. Jud., II. xxi. 1: "There arose a treacherous person, a man of Gischala whose name was John. His character was that of a very cunning and very knavish person, beyond the ordinary rate of other men.—Vita, 13: "He desired me to give him authority to carry off that corn which belonged to Caesar and lay in the villages of Upper Galilee, professing a desire to expend the proceeds on the repair of the walls of his native town. Detecting his ultimate design and present intentions, I declined his request; as the authority entrusted to me by the Jerusalem authorities extended to that district, I intended to reserve the corn either for the Romans (in case of an accommodation) or for my own use (in case of war). Unsuccessful with me, he returned to my colleagues, who were blind to coming events and quite open to bribes. So he bribed them and they delivered the corn to him. Then John introduced another trick. He stated that the Jewish inhabitants of Caesarea-Philippi, having by the king's order been shut up by Modius, his viceroy, and having no pure oil (as required by the Jewish dietary laws), had sent a request to him to see that they were supplied with this commodity. . . . John's motive in making this assertion, however, was not piety, but profiteering of the most barefaced description; for he knew that at Caesarea two pints were sold for one drachma (20¢), whereas at Gischala eighty

EWALD	JOSEPHUS
	pints could be had for four drachmas. So he sent off all the oil in the place, having obtained my authority to do so; which yet I did not grant him voluntarily, but only out of fear of being stoned to death if I withheld it.
P. 560-1: "The first thing was that the popular feeling in Jerusalem veered round soon and plainly in favor of the Zealots. . . . All of a sudden the cry was raised that they—'an Antipas, a Levi and a Sapha'—were friends of the Romans in disguise, and they were thrown into the prison . . . and put to death. This John himself, however, was regarded as an assassin employed by men in higher position, and there were many who sanctioned the murder; at all events, it went by unpunished. (Note his syntactic trickery.)	Bell. Jud., IV. iii. 1-5: "The head of the fanatical party, or as they called themselves, the Zealots, was John of Gischala. After he had escaped the hands of Titus by flight, he went with his followers to Jerusalem and sought to win over the people to himself and to rekindle in their breasts a determination to continue the war in a bolder and more resolute spirit. He readily succeeded in gaining over the youths to his side. And since now on all hands the war loving rabble from the country poured into the city, the party of the Zealots was soon in the ascendancy. They next proceeded to set aside those who were suspected of friendship for the Romans. Several of the most distinguished men, among them Antipas, who belonged to the family of Herod, were put under arrest and then murdered in prison. —Schuerer's abridgement.
Idem: "But now when everything was to become more rational, 'it' was proposed to choose a high-priest by lot from all the numerous members of all the families of a priestly house. . . . They actually chose by lot from the first priestly house Phannias, the son of Samuel, from the village of Aphtha, a plain man, who had first to be instructed in the functions of the high-priest."	Idem, 6-8: "Hereupon they called for one of the pontifical tribes, called Eniachim and cast lots for a high-priest. . . . By chance the lot fell to an individual named Phannias, son of Samuel of the village of Aphtha, a man who not only was not descended from high-priests, but was such a clown that he scarcely knew what the high-priesthood meant. At any rate they dragged their unwilling victim out of the country and dressed him up for his assumed part, as on a stage, put the sacred vestments upon him, and instructed him how to act in keeping with the occasion."—Thackeray's translation.

As another deluding piece of information Dr. Ewald (p. 563) tells us that, "Josephus was deeply despised on account of his treachery," whereas (p. 567) "The habits of John of Gischala were always those of a genuinely cultivated and scholarly man, a lover of art (!!) and not one of those people who indulged in fasting and other gloomy habits." Professor Ewald evidently arrived at this conclusion concerning John on account of the fact that he neither observed dietary laws, nor esteemed the sanctity of the Sabbath, nor that of an oath.

As further evidence of Prof. Ewald's complete untrustworthiness are the following examples:

EWALD	JOSEPHUS
Page 568: "Simon was not learned or wily like John, but he surpassed him in physical strength and bravery. . . . The Sicarii in Masada at first mistrusted him, and permitted him with the 'rich ladies' whom he had taken as hostages, to dwell in the lower part of the fortress only.	Bell. Jud., IV. ix. 3: "There was a certain Simon, son of Giora (Gher, or one converted to Judaism), and a native of Gerasa, a youth less cunning than John but his superior in physical power and effrontery who . . . had joined the brigands at Masada. At first they regarded him with suspicion, and permitted him and 'his following of women' access only to the lower part of the fortress (Thackeray's translation).
P. 580-1: "And as the leaders had collected within the walls far too small a quantity of corn for such a mass of people, famine soon arose.	Bell. Jud., V. i. 4: "In their mutual hatred of one another they destroyed the immense store of grain which had been gathered up in the city, lest their rivals should not profit by it (Schuerer's abridgment), . . . which would have been sufficient for a siege of many years.
P. 609: "Titus ordered the aged and the weak to be at once put to death."	Bell. Jud., VI ix. 2: "Titus issued orders to kill only those who were found in arms and offered resistance and make prisoners of the rest. But the troops, contrary to these specific orders, slew the aged and the weak, and only those of serviceable age did they shut up in the Women's Court."

In the same History (vol. vii. p. 466-7), Prof. Ewald further states that during the great fire at Rome the Jews instigated Nero against "Simon called Peter" and the Christians. But though the burning of Rome in the year 64 and its imputation to the Christians living there at the time are recorded by both Tacitus (Ann., xv. 44) and Suetonius (Nero, xvi. and xxxviii.), no mention is made by either of the Jews in this connection. Tacitus states: "In order to relieve himself from the infamy of being believed to have ordered the conflagration, and to suppress that rumor, that Nero falsely charged with guilt and punished with the most cruel tortures the persons commonly called Christians." Suetonius (Nero, xxxviii.) does not even go as far, but speaking independently of the two incidents states, that because he was "disgusted with the old buildings and the narrow winding streets he set the city on fire." He (in Nero, xvi.) does not attribute the persecution of the Christians to the burning, but because they were looked upon as "a sort of people who held a new and malicious superstition." Now, as to whether the Apostle Peter was martyred or executed or neither, is not a subject for our discussion; but the legend that he was in Rome, especially during the time of Nero, though strenuously upheld by the Roman, has long ago been exploded by all other Christian Churches.[15] Ewald, however, will use any patristic fabrication as an authority for convenience.

The reverend Ewald (p. 590) further says that "the Romans went on fortifying their three camps from the fourteenth of April," etc., but both to add color and to moralize his statement, he particularly points out that the day on which Titus commenced the re-enforcement of these encampments occurred exactly on "the day on which thirty-seven years previously Christ had been crucified," as if such an

[15] This subject is expertly treated in Smith's Dictionary of the Bible, Vol. iii. p. 2453f.

interval,—thirty-seven years,—had ever synchronized with any other space of time between two similarly important events. And (p. 581 and again p. 597) in his attempt to prove the infallibility of retribution, he directs our attention to the fact that, "God had not during the war provided water for the Jews but had done so abundantly for their enemies." With such morals this foolish missionary fills the eight volumes of his "History of Israel."

To portray Josephus in the blackest possible colors, and thereby also to ingratiate himself with his audience, he designates him throughout as "the Josephus of many crimes," "the old deserter," "the time server," "the traitor who speaks so much and so willingly of himself," and as he who "has not read the Old Testament even carefully enough"; whereas John of Gischala he depicts as "the astute and learned John." Simon bar Giora is termed "the brave young hero Simon, the second chief hero of the entire war," and the Zealots are represented as "the pious," "the learned," "the priestly," "the faithful," "the exclusive," "the Zealots of God," and as "the Zealots of the Law."

For his perversion of history, later scholars have severely criticized Ewald. Even Dean Keim, professor of historical theology at the University of Zurich, described as a "great critical scholar," a man "singularly candid and moderate," and of a "tender and lovable disposition,"[16] was compelled to remonstrate against this rabid anti-Semite in disguise, for his "reversing the order of facts," "exaggerating," "distorting," and for "asserting what is not justified by history."

Heinrich Ewald was born in Gottingen in 1803. In 1820 he entered the University of Gottingen, where the well-known Jew-hater Eichhorn was then teaching; but Ewald denied having been much influenced by him. In 1824 he

[16] Such is Prof. Samuel Macauley Jackson's opinion of him in the Schaff-Herzog Encyclopedia of Religious Knowledge.

began to teach theology at Gottingen, where in 1827 he was made professor. In 1837 he was expelled from his post, with six other trouble-making professors, for political pamphleteering. In 1838 he received an appointment at Tubingen, but soon came into a bitter feud with F. C. Bauer and the Tubingen school. After "laboring" (?) ten years in Tubingen, he was recalled to Gottingen, no longer as a professor of theology but only as a "teacher" in that subject, where he continued until 1866, when for his violent attack upon the government he was again expelled from the university, though he was still allowed his salary. This privilege, however, was withdrawn in 1868, on account of his insulting utterances against the king and against the people. In 1874 he was imprisoned for libel against Bismarck.

Ewald was a solitary man. He was married twice; but all his life he stood aloof from his fellows. Of an ill-tempered disposition, he had no intimate friends; and was in ever-increasing measure intolerant of any opinion which contradicted his own. In his later years his self-conceit became so insolent, that he dared to advise the Courts and the Church consistories, and to address the Pope and the prelates in Germany on Roman tenets. In 1875, due to an attack of heart-disease, his turbulent life ended.

Our next authority is a man to whom the Jewish theological student never fails to turn for the edification of his historical attainments,—the most inimitable, the most indisputable, and the most renowned of all Jewish historiographers, Heinrich Graetz. So supreme is he, that not to know him is, in some quarters, conclusive proof of ignorance. One reason for the immense popularity of his "History of the Jews" among his co-religionists, that it has held first rank as an authority, and that it has been translated from its original German into four languages, English, French, Russian and Hebrew,—a very rare occurrence in Jewish literature,—is its extraordinary pro-Jewish treatment. Another reason is its elegant diction; its beautiful phraseology, vividity, and a remarkable abstinence, in all its five volumes, from long, high-sounding terms. But, as if endeavoring to exonerate Graetz from blame for his innumerable groundless assertions and misrepresentations, Dr. Gotthard Deutsch[17] attempts to explain that "the impossibility of mastering all the details made him inaccurate in many instances." Considering, however, that several Christian theologians have mastered all the Hebraic details necessary for their far more difficult Jewish works more expertly and accurately, the incapability on the part of Graetz rather than "the impossibility" of overcoming such particulars is too evident for us to accept Dr. Deutsch's apology.[18]

Typical of Graetz is the introductory statement in his first volume, where he says: "On a bright morning in spring nomadic tribes penetrated into Palestine; whereas the Bible, which is his only source, states neither that it was in the spring nor that it was a bright morning."[19] That Graetz was either destitute of such fairness as is necessary for an historian, or possessed of a certain constitutional incapacity or some intellectual vacuum, which led him to misconstrue and misconjecture the text which lay before him, is evident throughout his entire work.

As illustrative not only of how unhistorical his History is and of how little attention he pays to his authorities, but also of how generally irresponsible and inconsistent he is, even with himself, are the following excerpts from his second volume, where he treats of the Maccabean period and describes the Jewish War:

[17] In the Jewish Encyclopaedia, under "Graetz."

[18] Schuerer's "History of the Jewish People," for example, which is far more than equal in size to that of Graetz's, is regarded not only as a literary masterpiece from every point of view, but also as an indispensable authority to theological students, Jewish or Christian, both young and old.

[19] Quoted from the Jewish Encyclopaedia, under "Graetz."

Vol. ii. p. 250-1: "When the rising in Judea was reported at the court of Rome, Nero was too busy to attend to such trifles; he had to play the zither, to perform on the stage, to indulge in orgies, and to devise murder.	Vol. ii. p. 284: "The news of the rising in Judea came upon him like a thunderbolt.... Nero trembled, for the revolution in Judea might be the precursor of grave events.
Idem, p. 257: "King Agrippa, who from motives of self-interest, was in favor of peace..."	Idem, p. 278: "To Agrippa himself the revolt was not quite unwelcome, for he hoped to reap some benefit from it."

The mode of Queen Mariamne's execution is nowhere recorded. In the Antiquities (XV. vii. 4 end), however, Josephus says, "she was led to execution"; whereas, according to the Bellum (I. xxii. 5), "she was put to death." Therefore Graetz, to be "accurate," executes her in two ways as follows:

Vol. ii. p. 104: Mariamne was led to the scaffold."	Vol. ii. p. 105: Mariamne was delivered up to the axe of the executioner."

Inconsistencies due to carelessness are the following:

GRAETZ	JOSEPHUS
Vol. ii. p. 30: "Consequent upon the life of celibacy which the Essenes adopted, the loss made by death in their ranks could not naturally be replaced. To avoid dwindling away entirely, they had recourse to the expedient of enrolling novices and making proselytes.	Bell. Jud., II. viii. 2: "They adopt other men's children, . . . (though) they do not condemn wedlock and the propagation thereby of the race. (Sec. 3:) "There is yet another order of Essenes, which, while at one with the rest in its mode of life, differs from them in its view on marriage, . . . they have no intercourse with their wives during pregnancy, thus showing that their motive in marrying is not self-indulgence but procreation of children.
Idem, p. 90: "Malich (the king of the Nabatheans) was forced to become the vassal of the Judean king (Herod)."	Bell. Jud., I. xix. 6: "Herod gained such a reputation with them (i.e., the Arabs), that they chose him for their Protector. (Antiq., XV. v. 5:) "They stood amazed at Herod's warlike spirit, ... and made him ruler of their nation."

GRAETZ	JOSEPHUS
Idem, p. 92: "Herod invited Aristobulus to Jericho, and bade his followers dispatch the youth whilst he was disporting in the bath.	Antiq., XV. iii. 3: "Herod was invited to Jericho, where, at his instigation, his servants drowned Aristobulus while swimming in one of the fish ponds, of which there were large ones about the house.

Referring to Justus of Tiberias, Graetz (Vol. ii. p. 166) speaks of him as having "related to the very smallest minutiae everything which took place under Pilate"; whereas Photius (820-891), who was the last man known to have seen the lost work of Justus, (Biblioth., Cod. 33) says, "He was very brief in expression, and passed over much that was necessary."

An example of Graetz's insufficient familiarity also with the Talmud (in spite of his world-wide fame as a profound Talmudic scholar), is the following, (Vol. ii. p. 238) where he says: "Frivolity in the women and licentiousness in the men were so completely the order of the day that the most eminent teacher of morality of that time (i.e., before the destruction of Jerusalem), Jochanan ben Zakkai, found himself obliged to abolish the ritual hitherto used in cases of adultery."

Now, in the first place, that R. Jochanan ben Zakkai was not a teacher of morality but a teacher of the Law, and that his period of activity was not before, but entirely "after the Temple was destroyed," are clearly shown in the Talmud, tracts Sukka, iii. 12, Rosh Hashana, iv. 1, 3-4, Rosh Hashana, 31b, Menachoth, x. 5, and Sota, 40b, where several legal enactments or customs are altered. Secondly, while the edict discussed here by Graetz for the doing away with the drinking of the water of bitterness in cases of suspected adultery is truly recorded in the Mishna (Sota, ix. 9), it was determined upon at Jabne, not before but after the Destruction, or, in other words, not as a necessity due to its great frequency before the final catastrophe, but as infeasible and impracticable in the Dispersion. Nine other innovations (enumerated in Rosh Hashana, 31b, and Sota, 40a) introduced by R. Jochanan, were adopted for the same reason,—to replace such rituals as were inapplicable or incompatible under foreign circumstances.

A great practice with Graetz, apparently, was that of direct copying, or of paraphrasing the work of his predecessors. Examples of such transcriptions are the following:

SALVADOR	GRAETZ
Vol. ii. p. 118-119: "Neron parcourait les pays des Grecs. Il était en Achaie, lorsqu' après avoir appris successivement l'insurrection de Juifs, les premiers avantages qu'elle avait obtenus, les préparatifs de guerre de Jerusalem on lui annonça la mort de Cestius Gallus. . . . Il étalait aux yeux de la Grece entière ses talens privés de conducteur de chars, de comédien, de versificateur, de joueur d'instrumens, de chanteur. . . . Au nombre des personnages qui l'avaient suivi dans son voyage en Grèce, on distinguait Flavius Vespasian. Ce general . . . etait en pleine disgrace. Toutfois, comme la nécessité se faisait sentir de mettre a la tête de la guerre de Judée un homme d'un mérite éprouvé, Vespasian fut choisi.	Vol. ii. p. 284: "The Emperor Nero was courting popular favor in Greece, by appearing in the arena as singer, player, and charioteer. Whilst engaged in these engrossing pursuits, there came upon him like a thunderbolt the news of the rising in Judea and the defeat of the Roman army under Cestius. . . . The emperor was then apprised of the death of his general Cestius. . . .[20] Nero selected as his successor Flavius Vespasian . . . who was known to be one of the ablest generals of his time. . . . Vespasian was not in the emperor's favor at that time, and Nero would have given some other general his post, but the emperor had no choice, for the ability of Vespasian was unquestionable, and Judea required a strong hand.
Idem, p. 463: "Simon revétit une tunique blanche, mit par dessus un manteau pourpre attache avec une agraffe, de manière à se cacher le visage. Il sorti de sa retraite et marcha vers le temple. Les gardes romaine, etonnées, l'arrêtèrent et lui	Idem, p. 313: "In a white robe, covered with a purple mantle, he suddenly appeared before the Roman sentinels who were reposing among the ruins of the Temple. They gazed at him with terror. He merely addressed them with the following

SALVADOR	GRAETZ
dèmanderent son nom. Il répondit de la conduire à leur commandant.	words: 'Take me to your general.'
Idem, p. 466: "Les médailles représentent une femme pleurant sous un palmier.... On y lit pour exergue: 'Judea devicta', 'Judea capta', la Judée vaincue, la Judée captive.	Idem, p. 314: "Coins were struck, upon which Judea was variously represented as a sorrowing woman under a palm tree.... The coins bore the inscriptions, 'the Conquered' or 'the Captive Judea' (Judea devicta, Judea capta).
Idem: "L'arc-de-triomph de Vespasian et de Titus est un des monumens de Rome les mieux conserves. On y voit encore le chandelier a sept branches, la table d'or, les ornemens sacredoteaux."	Idem: "Later on, a beautiful arch was erected to Titus, which is still standing, and upon which the carved reliefs of the... seven-branched candlestick, the golden table,... and vessels of the Temple are plainly visible."

To belie the writings of Josephus, to besmear his name and his character and to belittle his lifelong assiduity, is a most sacred task of many modern theologians. Thus, Dr. Graetz (p. 268), following the examples set by his predecessors, Jost, Salvador and Ewald, quivers with rage at the callosity of "the historian friendly to Rome, who could not sufficiently darken the rebellion of the Judeans." By his conduct, (p. 276) he asserts, "he has materially contributed to the fall of the Judean nation." Naming Josephus (p. 281) "a demon of discord, to whose lot had fallen the task of promoting a spirit of harmony amongst the people," he charges him with having brought civil war upon Galilee, contempt upon the Sanhedrin, disunion amongst the patriots, and, like the three before him, finally (p. 283) comes to the conclusion that "he 'must bear eternal opprobrium' of having unmanned and broken the one strong bulwark of Judea, the

[20] That Cestius died at this time is recorded by Tacitus (Hist., v. 10), but no record exists that his death was reported to Nero, who in any case would not have appointed as generalissimo in Judea a defeated general.

vigorous and warlike Galilee, through indecision, egotism, and above all, his extraordinary duplicity."

To be fair with Graetz, however, it can hardly be said that his excessive partiality, his knock-kneed deductions, his intense hatred of Josephus or showy coquetting of his enemies, as the occasion may require, and his artful dodging of important historical facts, as his over-righteous reasoning often dictated to him, are due to his deliberate intention to misrepresent or his cold indifference to truth. But to gain an entrance into the hearts of his brethren-in-faith, and that he might also display a most glorious past of his race before those outside of his faith,—which obviously was his most fervent desire,—a History without such distortions seemed to him impossible.

But however deep the corruption of the Herodian high-priests and of that age in general, and whatever the degeneracy of the Jewish war leaders, there is nothing in the history of the Jewish people for a Jew to smother or to pour balm into, or to feel humbled for. It is true the Jews have had their Ecclesiarchs, Zealots, Sicarii, and other scoundrels who in the name of religion have plundered estates, devastated territories, destroyed whole cities and exterminated entire communities. But so also have other nations had Crusaders, Inquisitors, Massacrers, and other assassins whose unutterable crimes, atrocities and rape committed under the banner of the Cross are well recorded. Such are the facts which should have recurred to the talented mind of Dr. Graetz before he determined upon his unhistorical History and an unnecessary Apology for Judaism.

Heinrich Hirsch Graetz was born October 31st, 1817, in Xions, a village of 775 inhabitants of the province of Posen, in Prussia, where his father, Jacob, had a small butcher-shop. At thirteen, having received his elementary instruction in reading, writing, reckoning, and in translating the Bible, he was sent to Wollstein, a town with a population of 2258 souls, distinguished for "the enlightened spirit pervading it and the active encouragement accorded to students in their desire for culture," where relations of more comfortable circumstances undertook to further the boy's education. There, according to his biographer, at the age of fourteen, he began a work on the calender in the Hebrew language, entitled "Cheshbon Hoeisim," which he finished a year later. A great thirst for learning now took possession of young Graetz; he became interested in History, and soon after, Latin, French, and the ancient masterpieces attracted his attention. In each instance he was his own instructor.

Having read Lessing, Mendelssohn, Schiller and other German classics, he made Fénelon, Voltaire, Rousseau, Racine and Victor Hugo his favorite French authors. Though Latin gave him the most trouble, he mastered Nepos, Curtius, Ovid, and Virgil,—all these without neglecting his Talmudic studies, much to the surprise of his Rabbi, Samuel Munk.

For November 1835, the following entry was found in his diary:

> *"By the various contradictory ideas that perplexed my brain—heathen, Jewish, and Christian, Epicurean, Kabbalistic, Maimonidian, and Platonic—my faith was made so insecure that, when a notion concerning God, eternity, or the like, assailed me, I wished myself into the abyss of the nether world."* [21a]

But another entry of some time later, says:

> *"Like furies such thoughts tugged at my heart-strings, when, as often happened, they arose, suggested by my poverty as well as by certain classes of books. Only the clear, star-studded sky, upon which my eyes were wont to rest with delight on Saturday evenings,*

renewed the blessed comforting consciousness in me: Yes, there is a God beyond the starry canopy."[21b]

However, not long after, Graetz began to resent the Jewish religious practices, the multiplicity of ceremonies and the graceless Hebraic mannerisms; attributing these conditions to the Talmud, and consequently, after four years and a half of his sojourn in Wollstein, he resolved to quit the village, as an unfit place to live in; the death of an uncle who was his main supporter, some conflicts with his relatives and companions, and also a disappointing love affair, contributed to his decision, and Graetz, not yet nineteen, decided to go to Prague.

At the Austrian frontier, however, he was forbidden to enter because he had not the ten florins in his possession which all travelers must show to the immigration officials to gain admission into the country. Graetz, therefore, turned back to his parents who were now living at Zerkow; and to some more Latin, and Biblical and Talmudic studies. But here again, irritated at the pettiness of his environment, he abused the rabbi, annoyed the worshipers, and on the eve of the Day of Atonement he horrified his parents by refusing to perform the ritual of Kapores. At about this time too, Graetz began to study Greek, and also investigated the New Testament. The impression its first reading made upon him, he describes as follows: "Despite the many absurdities and in consistencies, the mildness of Jesus fascinated me; at the same time, its disorder so repelled me that I was completely confounded."

In 1837 Graetz went to Oldenburg, where the District Rabbi, Shimshon Rephoel Hirsch, a man of modern culture, had undertaken to provide the young man with board and lodging in his own house, while his father was to furnish his clothing. Hirsch took a fatherly interest in the learned *bocher,* while the duties he assigned to him were those of

[21a] and [21b]. As quoted by his biographer, Dr. Philipp Bloch.

Assistant District Rabbi. Accompanying the Rabbi on his daily tours, they discussed Biblical and Talmudic subjects, while at home he helped his master on the preparation of a book entitled "Horeb," and when the Rabbi had to go to a resort for his health, he authorized Graetz to adjudicate Shaaleth. But wherever he was and whatever the circumstances, Graetz never neglected his studies. While with Hirsch, he learned English, and finding some Syriac literature in the rabbi's library, he began to study that language. In the third year of his stay in Oldenburg, however, "*his relations with the mistress of the house were disturbed by slight discords, such as can not fail to arise in long-continued, familiar intercourse, and tend now to strengthen, now to abridge intimacy.*" And so, together with concern about his career, and a desire to see his parents, who had meantime removed from Zerkow to Kosten, a somewhat larger town, Graetz, in 1840, departed from Oldenburg.

At Kosten, in order to secure means for a university course, Graetz, near the end of the same year, contracted a position as Rabbi in Ostrovo, a small town inhabited mostly by Jews. But here again, the unaesthetic life and habits of the Ghetto annoyed him, and after one year and a half, having at the same time run into trouble "*in a manner not altogether pleasant,*" Graetz, with the little money he had saved, departed for the University of Breslau.

In 1845 he obtained his doctorate. But though his graduation thesis, "Gnosticism and Judaism," and additional publications, had won him the highest respect among theologians and scholars, his instability, surliness, and passion for meddling in all congregational politics hindered him from securing a position for over five years. In 1850, however, an offer was made to him by the Jewish Community of Lundenburg, a small town near Vienna, to take charge of their Cheder. Graetz, now thirty-three years of age, embraced the offer joyfully; and the deal, ratified on September 12th, was to begin one month later. Hurriedly he returned home to solemnize his marriage with his love, a lady, obviously of exceptionally noble qualities, who for several years had stood by him, trusted him, and loyally waited for his eventual settlement.

Once more, however, "*the atmosphere of the narrow, undisciplined Ghetto life*" of the small Austrian community "*began to oppress him*" and weigh on his mind. A falling out with the Lundenburg rabbi, "*a narrow-minded Talmudist,*" ... "*unceasing intrigues,*" ... "*malicious denunciations,*" ... *and* "*serious humiliations*" also contributing to his annoyances, Graetz, in 1852, resigned his position at Lundenburg and set out for Berlin.

In Berlin, at last, Graetz found his haven—no Ghetto mannerisms nor Talmudic practices, but sufficient *Schachermacherei* and mixing to compensate him for all his past vexations. Arriving at the Capital in September, he was cordially received by a Dr. Michael Sachs, who in turn introduced him to a Dr. Veit, who undertook to publish his "History of the Talmudic Period." As a frequent visitor at Sachs' house, he also met Leopold Zunz. On the following February (1853), a railroad director and journalist, Joseph Lehman, asked Graetz whether he would be "disposed to become a member of the faculty of a rabbinical seminary, which was yet to be planned, organized, and authorized by the government,—a procedure requiring eighteen months' time. Graetz, with a wife and child, who as yet were unprovided with bread, accepted the honor and consented to wait. When in the autumn of 1854 this institution came into existence, he and a Jacob Bernay became its "regularly appointed teachers," under Z. Frankel as its "Director."

The duration of this engagement, how he fared in it, or in what manner it terminated, is somewhat obscure. The story concerning this subject, as given by his biographer and disciple, Dr. Philipp Bloch, who, judging by his understanding of nautics, may at some time have been a skipper, is rather difficult to define. Disposing of the matter in maritime figures, he tells us that, "while in his position as a teacher at the Seminary, his vessel had floated into deep, navigable waters, that he could venture to ply the oars with full force, unfurl all his sails, and, favored by wind and weather and propelled by a buoyant courage peculiar to his sanguine nature, steer straight for the destination whither impulse drew him."

Within the meantime, however, parts of Graetz's "History of the Jews" began to appear from the press in regular succession. The first part published was the history from the Downfall of the Jewish State to the Completion of the Talmud, represented in the pages 321 to 635 of the second volume of the American edition. In 1856 appeared the history from the death of Judas Maccabeus to the Downfall of the Jewish State, represented in Vol. i. pp. 487-531 to Vol. ii. pp. 1-320. From this time on, the rest of the History continued in annual sections, and it was not until 1876, it appears, that the entire work was completed. But the fault-finding with his hermeneutics among Talmudists, scholars and young theologians alike, was so vigorous that the slightly strained relations which existed between him and his old friend and benefactor, Rabbi Shimshon Rephoel Hirsch, broke off forever. An attack made on his History by a young anti-Semite, Heinrich von Treitschke, became so alarming that it necessitated the talent of the highly esteemed Jewish writer, H. B. Oppenheim, to dispose of its author as "a man without tact and fanatically one-sided, whose great learning has been rendered useless by the absurdity of his practical deductions."[22] On the other hand, in 1869 the Prussian government made him an honorary professor of the Breslau University, and in 1888 the free-thinking Spanish Academy of Madrid bestowed upon him honorary membership of its Association; probably in recognition of his treatment of the nation's history of the Inquisition.

[22] After the outbreak of the World War, Treitschke was himself attacked as one of its spiritual instigators.

In addition to his "History of the Jews," Graetz published numberless other Biblical and philosophical works; his literary activity continued almost to his very end. Early rising, late retiring, and frugal living were the habits of his life. He was of sinewy constitution, never ailing even in his declining years. Very unexpectedly, however, in July 1891 his heart began to fail him, and on the seventh of September he passed away.

Such was his life; such his "History"; such the man who sits in judgment of Josephus.

Through the examples set by such resourceful and practiced predecessors as Jost, Salvador, Ewald, and Graetz, the belying and garbling of offensive historical records, either for the edification of religion or in pretense of deep piety, became, for a certain class of clerics, not only a more desirable and simpler task than the writing of the truth, but also an established custom. Consequently, since Graetz, religious literature, disguised under every denomination—Roman, Christian, Jewish, or Josephian "Histories"—has sprung up from all directions in such profusion that religious histories became repulsive to one's nostrils and truth began to issue under different names.

Among the innumerable works, still belonging to the old category, one of those standing out most conspicuously is Dr. Morris J. Raphall's "Post-Biblical History of the Jews," published in 1855-6,—simultaneously with Graetz's History for the same period, which had been completed for some years before it went to press. On examining his chapter commencing with "The Roman Occupation of Judea" (Vol. ii. p. 194) it will be found that, while at times he follows the basic text of Josephus, it never forms his chief authority for that period, except when that text is neutral or helpful to his own ends; and that he steadfastly avoids Josephus unless the Scripture, the Talmud, or some other favorite authority confirms[23] or assists him to maintain a necessary point,[24]—even when such evidence conflicts with what ordinarily would be regarded as a more reliable reference.[25] Of far greater merit as authorities, he esteems, in addition to Jost, Salvador, Ewald, and Graetz, the military manual of "Monsieur Chevalier Folard," whose system of column formation has been ridiculed by outstanding tacticians, and John Gillies' "History of Greece," which is reputed to have been written from a "strongly anti-social and anti-democratic standpoint." In addition to these, the Gospels, the Ante- and Post-Nicean Fathers, the Apocrypha, several Encyclopaedias, some French Revolutionary histories, and only a few of the ancient Greek and Latin writings, besides, of course, the Talmud and Midrashim, form the bulk of his literature in the preparation of his "Post-Biblical History of the Jews."

Thus, though showing a deep enthusiasm and great ambition, his work, due to its shallowness and aridity, is neither instructive nor entertaining. His personal indifference to truth and his avidity for the sensational and romantic cannot be better demonstrated than by the few instances given here wherein, to make his point, he not only ignores his only authority, Josephus, but, at times, clashes also with his favorite Talmud. One of these is the following:

RAPHALL	JOSEPHUS	THE TALMUD
Vol. ii. p. 442: "The chiefs of the Zealots saw how necessary it was to conciliate their powerful allies (the Idumeans). Besides, it appeared quite practicable to establish a tribunal altogether dependent on	Bell. Jud., IV. v. 4: "Having now come to loathe indiscriminate massacre, the Zealots instituted mock trials and courts of justice. . . . So they issued a peremptory summons to seventy leading citizens to appear in the	Shabboth, xva; Rosh Hashana, xxxia; Sanhedrin, xiia; Aboda Zara, viiib: "Forty years before the destruction of the Temple, the Sanhedrin removed from the Lishkath Hagazis, and after that it held its sittings in the

[23] For instances see, his Vol. ii. pp. 60, 469, 484, etc.
[24] Idem, 137, 401, 471 note 30, etc.
[25] Idem, 263, 272, 277, etc.

RAPHALL	JOSEPHUS	THE TALMUD
the dominant faction. . . . A Sanhedrin of seventy-two citizens of Jerusalem was appointed; the Lishkath Hagazis,[26] so long deserted, 'was once more occupied' as a Supreme Court of Justice. . . . The judges who were to occupy the seats of Simon ben Shetach,[27] of Sameas,[28] and of Ananus,[29] had been elected from the lower order of the middle class."	Temple, assigning to them, as in a play, the role, without the authority, of judges; the Zealots then (in this first session) accused Zacharias of betraying the state to the Romans. . . . They adduced no evidence or proof in support of the charge, but declared that they were fully convinced of his guilt and claimed this as sufficiently establishing the fact. . . . Two of them then set upon Zacharias and slew him in the midst of the Temple."	Chanujoth (or merchants' shops)." (This record in the Talmud was made not less than a hundred years after the Destruction; and no mention is made in any of these four nor in any other tract, where the Lishkath Hagazis is spoken of, that "it was once more occupied.")

In comparing these versions we notice, first, that while Josephus gives the number of judges as seventy, Raphall, having followed the Talmud, Sebachim, i. 3 and Jadajim, iii. 5 and iv. 2, gives their number as seventy-two. Had he followed the tracts of Sanhedrin, i. 1, 6 and Shebuoth, i. 2, it would have been seventy-one. Secondly, whereas Josephus says, "They instituted courts," and speaks of "Courts of Justice," in the plural, Rabbi Raphall prefers to designate the judiciary by the more colorful and impressive name Lishkath Hagazis, in accordance with Shabboth, xva, Rosh Hashana, xxxia, Sanhedrin, xiia, and Abode Zara, viiib, though the

[26] The "Hall built of hewn stones," where the Sanhedrin formerly sat.

[27] He was a brother of the Maccabean Queen, Alexandra.

[28] A successor of Simon.

[29] Of the high-priestly family of the same name. During the siege of Jerusalem he was murdered by the Zealots.

singular is inconsistent with history. For, had he followed Taanith, i. 6, Baba Mezia, viii. 6, Aboda Zara, i. 4, and Tohoroth, vi. 3, where the suspended Court House is recorded as having been superseded by "merchants' stalls,"—in the plural,—he would indeed have arrived at a welcome agreement with the Talmud, but it would at the same time, on the one hand, have brought him also into a disagreeable harmony with Josephus and, on the other, with the Gospels of Matthew, xxi. 12, and John, ii. 14, where these oxen, sheep and dove-dealers' and money changers' booths are mentioned. And, thirdly, for his statement that the Lishkath Hagazis "was once more occupied," his own rabbinical imagination is his only authority, for no record exists to verify the occurrence.

And, having already thoroughly remodeled the history of and exonerated the later Maccabeans from the stigma of their miserable conduct, and then represented the reign of Herod, not according to Josephus, or rather Nicolas of Damascus, but according to Appian of Alexandria, a lawyer who wrote eighty years later, and utterly distorted every event which took place under Herod and his descendants, he commences his description of the Siege of Jerusalem in the same spirit of insincerity.

Following the set formula of his predecessors, Dr. Raphall (ii. 419) enters this history with the report to the Emperor of Cestius Gallus' defeat [30] and death,[31] while he was at Achaia. Like them also, he embodies into the report the fact that when Nero received the bad tidings he was in the act of exhibiting his talents as a charioteer, musician and versifier, which, though not mentioned by Josephus, is recorded by Tacitus and Suetonius.[32] Then, introducing Vespasian, on the one hand (p. 422) he says, "Notwithstanding the avarice

[30] Bell. Jud., II. xx. 1.

[31] Tacitus, Hist., v. 10.

[32] Compare Tacitus, Annal., xiv. 14-17, with Suetonius, Nero, xx-xxii, and Vesp., iv.

which formed the great reproach of his character as emperor, and contrary to the general practice of Roman governors, who, after administering the affairs of a province during a few years, came back with immense wealth, Vespasian returned from Africa so poor that not only was he obliged to mortgage a portion of his small patrimony to his elder brother, Flavius Sabinus, but also to carry on a traffic in beasts of burden, which ... by no means raised him in public estimation." But a few pages later (p. 426), forgetting what he had previously said concerning the Flavian's integrity, he tells us, "Vespasian, profiting by the calamitous experience of Cestius Gallus, determined to reduce the whole country before he attacked Jerusalem, ... as he was in no hurry to terminate the war which would be sure to enrich him." Concerning Josephus, in one place (p. 424), he says, "Beyond one body of eight thousand men, Josephus raised no troops." But a few pages later (p. 428), again forgetting what he had said before, he also tells us that, "Forty thousand (of his garrison) were slaughtered (by the Romans)."

The extreme difficulty in following his history of the war comprehensively is due, aside from his frequent inconsistencies, also to numberless unassociated interferences which break up the narrative. The final death-struggle at Jerusalem, also, is distorted beyond recognition; and having told us altogether very little about any fact, he disposes of the last three books of Josephus' "History of the War"—containing the most important and most interesting events of the war—in the last three pages of his own work, and then concludes with, "It is not our intention to enter into any detail of the military defense of Jerusalem, the high character of which we have already described in the words of that truly competent judge, 'the Chevalier Folard(!).'" And this is Dr. Raphall's "Post-Biblical History of the Jews."

The custom among a certain class of scholars of perverting the history of Josephus and his time, had by now become a favorite pastime. For, in addition to diversion, such writing carries with it not only a most convenient opportunity for the exhibition of a knowledge of ancient languages, of proficiency in Talmud,—pretended or real,—and of learning in general, but at the same time also offers a circumstance where one can vent any amount of pious passion with the least fear of unfavorable criticism or reproach. Consequently, the volumes of vulgarity, religious propagandism, and abuse directed against Josephus became so numerous that no library would or could any longer accommodate all. For the names of a small part of such works alone,—including Rabbi Jacob Hamburger's Encyclopaedia, wherein he, though not even familiar with the subject, had the courage to include an article on Josephus, giving the number of parts of "Against Apion" as "Three Books,"—and a small comment upon each, several separate volumes would be necessary.

An extensive criticism directly against Josephus which appeared after that of Dr. Raphall in his History, is that of Dr. Alfred Edersheim in the Smith Dictionary of Christian Biography. To avoid the unnecessary reading of repetitious trash, suffice it to say that in twenty closely printed pages, in which he performs the parts of analyst, prosecutor, judge and preacher, there is no form of accusation or condemnation of Josephus that he omits. And although in his "Jewish Social Life," where he proscribes for the "city which had crucified the Lord" only one alternative, "either the judgment of Sodom, or the mercy of the Gospels and the healing of the Cross," he refers to Josephus as a trustworthy authority, in the Dictionary every conceivable charge is laid at his feet.

Edersheim was born in Vienna, of Jewish parents, in 1825, and educated at the university of that city. For financial reasons, in 1842 he accepted a tutorship in Pesth, Hungary, under the wealthy Scotch Presbyterian clergyman John Duncan, who converted him to Christianity. In 1843, when Duncan returned to Scotland, Edersheim went along with him, and after studying divinity in Edinburgh, he was in

1846 ordained to the Presbyterian ministry, and soon afterwards received an appointment to the Free Church of Aberdeen as a missionary to the Jews. After serving as such for twelve years he became "select" preacher to the University of Oxford, and finally Vicar of Loders, Bridport, under the name of "Rev. Dr. Edersheim." In 1889 he died.

The habit of imitating historical literature continued with little variation for the rest of the last and well into the present century. So much so had this practice become an established custom, that entire paragraphs and pages were copied bodily or paraphrased from preceding writers. Of minor instances alone, one finds the proverb, "*A chacun selon ses oeuvres*," first expressed by Salvador, is repeated by Merivale (Vol. vi. p. 435, note 2), and again quoted by Bentwich ("Josephus," p. 71).[33] Shakespeare's precept, "nothing extenuate, nor set down in malice" (taken from Othello, v. 2, near end), first quoted by Raphall (Vol. i. p. 18), is used again by Bentwich ("Josephus," Preface, p. 6), and again also by Foakes-Jackson ("Josephus and the Jews," Introduction, p. xvi.). "He who carried furthest servility and national abnegation received the prize," first said by Graetz (Vol. ii. p. 236), is copied by Frederick Huidekoper ("Judaism in Rome," p. 32), though placed in quotation marks, but without extending recognition to the author. A likening of the Jewish Rebellion to the French Revolution, first noted by Raphall (Vol. ii. p. 435), has also been represented by Merivale ("Rom. Hist.," Vol. vi. p. 447), Schuerer (Div. I. Vol. ii. p. 227), and Bentwich ("Josephus," p. 62). The reference to Titus' Arch, "*Il est à souhaiter, pour l'honeur des Juifs, que cette anecdotte soi vraie: les longs resouvenirs conviennent aux long malheurs*," first expressed by Madame de Staël ("Corinne," chapt. 4), is quoted in the original French by Merivale (Rom. Hist., Vol. vi. p. 472, note 3), and again,

[33] In the case of Bentwich alone, it is duly acknowledged as having first been commented by Salvador.

translated into English, by Duruy-Mahaffy ("Hist. of Rome," Vol. v. p. 132, note 1). These are only a few of the very many such examples.

With the commencement of our own third decade, however, the conventional practice of imitating previous writers, —who through excessively bad faith had fallen into disrepute with the more modern and observing reader,—has at last been abandoned, and a more up-to-date and seemlier mode of attacking the odious "reprobate" (Josephus) was adopted. Not that in the innovation ampler veracity was sought for or intended, because unadulterated truth was never the maxim of pious writers, but solely as an expedient which under the changed circumstances they hoped would more effectively serve their ends.

The new idea originated with an obscure German professor, Richard Laqueur, whose "Judische Historiker Flavius Josephus" appeared in 1920, in the city of Giesen. Disregarding texts, nullifying recorded facts and ignoring their authorities, but based chiefly on personal assumptions, his work is one of the most preposterous and misleading histories on antiquity ever written. In the Preface of his volume the author tells us that in its preparation he spent "ten years of arduous labor," which not even his "four years' service in the World War, fighting for the Fatherland" had interrupted. For this assiduity, if we may trust him,—for the size of his book, the little and careless research and poor literary quality do not reveal such "arduous labor"—he deserves our most unstinted commendation. But judging this man by the churlishness, vindictiveness and cold malice displayed throughout his pages,[34] it seems that not even among the Furies could be found his equal; and of all Jewish histories since Jost, indeed, none is more perverse than his. Though assuming to be the

[34] Even his admirer, Dr. Thackeray (Six Lectures, p. 20), inadvertently admits that "he carried the process of denigration too far."

acme of exegesis, and pretending to supply all the missing links in the history of Josephus, his work is in fact nothing but a catalog of baseless speculations, absurd theories and stupid suppositions,[35] plus unbounded venom of the most pernicious virulence.

Yet, notwithstanding its bigotry, venality and untrustworthiness, some scholars, who should have used their talents for better causes, have hastily adopted this man's work, not only as their model for composition, but also raised him as their chief authority and informant for all their subsequent publications. The explanation for this anomalous procedure lies not alone in the fact that by so elevating Laqueur they have made it possible for themselves to play off his many fantastical anti-Josephian ideas, but also in the ease wherewith they could shift the stigma of their own indulgence in such colorful theories from themselves back to him, whose name they affix as reference to their quotations. Moreover, not only has it taught the newer and more effective mode of operation, but has also ushered in a most convenient fashion of lying by proxy.

Most conspicuous among men of learning who have thus graciously volunteered to serve as his inferiors are two friends and collaborators, Dr. Henry St. John Thackeray, an Anglican theologian, and Dr. Robert Eisler, the Jewish Orientalist. Both pre-eminent for their own exegetical attainments, yet, because of the new color and magic which his speculations furnish to their stories, they have condescended to yield the palm and bow to him as his disciples. For what other reason could there really be for these two scholiasts, who have de-

[35] One of Laqueur's inventions (pp. 126f., 255) is that Josephus was commissioned by Vespasian and Titus to write the history of the war from a Roman point of view, for propagandist purposes,—to strengthen the Flavian dynasty. Another of his fancies (pp. 274ff.) is, that when Josephus' fame as an author was endangered by the criticism of Justus of Tiberias, he made overtures to the Christians at Rome by inserting the Christ Testimonium in his Jewish Antiquities to insure their preservation.

voted their lives to Josephian research and study, to seek and make use of the support of a less-than-mediocre Laqueur on a subject in which they themselves, indeed, have no superior? And so, thus reanimated by these novel ideas, as also by the attendant immunity from ridicule for advancing them, they resumed the antiquated campaign against Josephus with greater effrontery than ever.

Thus, in Thackeray's Introduction to the first volume[36] of his translation of Josephus (1926) alone, there are seven references to Laqueur; in the Introduction to his second volume[37] (1927), six; and in his "Six Lectures on Josephus the Man and the Historian," not less than twenty such citations. Naturally, as a token of good-fellowship also, the Appendix to his third volume of Josephus[38] contains at least fifty complimentary obeisances or recognitions in honor of his "dear friend, Dr. Eisler," and not less than thirty other such courtesies are extended to him in the "Six Lectures" (1929),—all of which are generously reciprocated by his Jewish comrade in his "Messiah Jesus," translated into English in 1930.

In the Preface to the "Six Lectures," written by Dr. George Foot Moore, Dr. Moore tells us that "Dr. Thackeray's judgment of the character of Josephus, as a man, is not flattering, but fairly recognizes the difficulties of a situation into which he had come not wholly by his own fault; ... (that) his estimate of him as an historian is more favorable than that of many scholars; ... (and that) in both aspects he should be assessed by the actualities of his own time, not by the ideals of another age." This moderation towards Josephus, in estimating his character and the extenuation of his literary shortcomings, in view of his adverse circumstances, as pledged by Dr. Moore are, indeed, humane obligations and in conformity with modern standards of thinking. But whether

[36] This volume contains the Vita, and the thesis Against Apion.
[37] Books I-III of the Bellum.
[38] Books IV-VII of the Bellum.

Dr. Thackeray is equal to such advanced sentiments, we shall judge by the tales he himself tells us.

The first half of his First Lecture is a carefully planned and cleverly worded prolog in which Dr. Thackeray,—as if preparing, not for an estimation, but for the prosecution, or rather persecution, of Josephus,—makes every effort to win the graces of his Jewish audience, and, by the way, also to accommodate every opinion. In this task, in direct opposition to Dr. Moore's assurances, he enters with the statement that his subject is Josephus, the Man and the Historian, "rather than the age in which he lived." Josephus then (p. 10) is called to the Bar in connection with the much discussed discrepancies between his two records on the subject of his appointment to Galilee which, says Dr. Thackeray, "make it exceedingly difficult to reconstruct the history and to discover his real aims and policy." For in the Bellum, Josephus states that he was sent to that province as a General, whereas in the Vita, he recounts that he was commissioned to pacify the revolutionaries of Galilee and to "wait and see what action the Romans would take."[39]

And now, since neither account contains individually a fully detailed outline of all the instructions which Josephus had received from his superiors, or of each single minute duty assigned to him (though on several other occasions he mentions various additional commands which they gave him), Dr. Thackeray detects a so-called short measure, and describes it as a delusive inconsistency, serious enough to befuddle him. Evidently, in order not to mystify him, Josephus should at each separate occasion have given, not only a full list of his entire investiture and specified particularly every responsibility imposed upon him, but also the mule he was riding on, the wagon-loads which followed him, the beasts of burden which probably also formed a part of his equipment, and the size of the war-chest the Sanhedrin had supplied him with on his departure for Galilee.

[39] Compare, Bell. Jud., II. xx. 4-5, with Vita, 7.

Dr. Thackeray's next concern (p. 11) is, "where (has) Josephus actually acquired his knowledge of Roman methods and tactics?" and (p. 12) after considerable garbling and suppressing of several offending historical facts, without so far having shown any cause or warrant for such a conclusion, remarks, "If we attempt to fathom the policy and motives of Josephus at this period, we can only say that he was playing a double, waiting game." To substantiate this (p. 13), he adduces as an instance the reply which Josephus gave John of Gischala on his request for permission to seize the imperial granaries in the villages of Upper Galilee (viz., "I intend to keep the corn either for the Romans or for my own use."—Vita, 13), to which our fair judge, Prof. Thackeray, adds, "No wonder such a general was suspected of harboring designs of betraying the country to the enemy."

The remainder of Josephus' campaign in Galilee before the arrival of the Romans, his military operations after Vespasian's invasion of his territory, his entrenchment and the siege at Jotapata, his retreat into the cave, his negotiations with the forty deserters which he found there, and his capture by the Flavian conquerors,—all of which are discussed in the First Lecture,—are, as might be expected, "estimated" with the same prejudice and injustice as have been his preliminary "problems." And (p. 15) when he arrives at Josephus' prediction that Vespasian would shortly become emperor, which is attributed also to R. Jochanan ben Zakkai, Dr. Thackeray has the courage to state before a Jewish patronage, which especially brought him here from England specifically to deliver these paid lectures, that the Rabbis (of post-Mishnaic times) "have not scrupled to transfer the honor of the prophecy (which had come true) to their more popular hero." [40] Likewise daring are his "estimates" of Josephus as "a reporter and interpreter," of his liberation from bondage, of his departure with Vespasian for Alexandria and his return with

[40] On this see, Aboth derabbi Nathan, iv. 5.

Titus back to Jerusalem, and of his mediations with the Zealots at the walls of the Holy City.

About Josephus' thirty or more years' residence in Rome, Dr. Thackeray, in the same First Lecture (p. 15) says, he has "little to 'record,'" except that he was "the client of the Flavians" and, as he learned from Prof. Laqueur, that he was "commissioned to write the history of their triumphs." But in his Second Lecture (p. 27), referring to the same history, he tells us that it was "a manifesto intended as a warning to the East of the futility of further opposition." Commenting on Josephus' domestic life, he remarks that, "as is not surprising in an egoist of his character, it has had its matrimonial troubles," having been married "at least three times, being deserted by one wife, and divorcing another." According to our records on this subject,[41] however, the facts as given by Dr. Thackeray are maliciously misinterpreted and misleading.

In closing this Lecture, Dr. Thackeray (p. 19), after calling his readers' attention to his "Concordantial Lexicon to Josephus, which is now on the way to publication" (a business important enough as to require, in the course of his following five Lectures, two additional reminders), finally concludes that Josephus is "not wholly amiable, still less an heroic character, and (that) as a writer he lacks some of the essential qualifications of the great historian, ... an egoist self-interested time-server and flatterer of his Roman patrons." And (p. 20) as if not content with this much alone, he adds to his own findings, in the manner of a spokesman, also those of Prof. Laqueur, which accuse him of being "a rebel against authority, ... (who) set himself up as a despot, (one who) put himself at the head of the rebels and then, by his self-surrender at Jotapata, betrayed them; ... the original organizer of the revolt, ... (who) was largely responsible for the ultimate fall of Jerusalem." But a moment later (p. 21), however, to gain favor also with those whose opinions differ from

[41] Compare Vita, 75-76, with Whiston's note to sec. 75.

his own, he reverses the statements which he had just made for himself and for Dr. Laqueur, and says, "Looking at his character as a whole, I do not think that a lack of patriotism can be reckoned among his faults. His lamentations in his works over his country's fate, his oral exhortations which he puts into the mouth of others, were sincere." And here, while, on the one hand, setting down Josephus as "a pacifist without the strength of character to control the militants," on the other, he asks, "Who, indeed, could have controlled those hot-heads? and who could say how the course of history might have been changed had his counsels prevailed?" Again (p. 20) he first said, "The narrative in the Jewish War is a distorted version of the events, written under Roman direction and patronage," while in his Second Lecture (p. 49) he observes that "'after all reservations have been made,' the narrative in its main outlines must be accepted as trustworthy," after having just said (in the same Lecture, p. 46) also that "Josephus lacks the sober impartiality of Thucydides and, with all his reiterated protestations of zeal for truth, shows from time to time, '*when his statements are subject to control,*' a lax sense of the full meaning of the word":—thus agreeing with every opinion.

On reviewing this Lecture, what most attracts one's attention, is its thoroughgoing ambiguity. Aside from its elasticity of language and the violation of Dr. Moore's pledge to assess Josephus "not by the ideals of another age," Dr. Thackeray's evasion of much of the history in connection with Josephus' campaign in Galilee, which he knew would pique his listeners, but instead, enlarging upon unhistorical matter which he knew they would welcome, reflects on his own unreliability rather than on Josephus' guilt. Neither does his whole-hearted accord with the Zealots in "suspecting Josephus of harboring designs of betraying the country to the enemy," to the great delight of his audience, earn for him any greater commendation.

That all Dr. Thackeray's criticisms about Josephus,

whether his own, or "according to Laqueur," are unworthy of consideration, and that his intentions never were to adjudicate, but to berate and deride him, can readily be seen not alone from the mock trial he had received in the present Lecture, but too frequently also from his comments in his translation of Josephus' writings.

The next four Lectures, resembling the "balaams," or worthless paragraphs which are used by publishers to fill space in newspaper columns, are even more polymeric and barren. Conducing to no enlightenment and devoid of any raison d'être, they are executed, precisely as Dr. Moore (Preface, p. vii.) discreetly says, "with cautious reserve"; and so equivocally are they phrased or worded as to becloud even the most attentive reader. In addition to these objectionable features, the author's incessant repetitions of such "problems" as he had already dealt with, for which, to avoid the appearance of copying himself, he only varies the expression, makes the reading of these intervening four Lectures most tiresome.

The Sixth, or last Lecture, however, is, from Thackeray's point of view, it seems, the most important of all. Subtitled "Josephus and Christianity," it is devoted entirely to the restoration, or rather part-rehabilitation, of the well-known Testimonium on the Founder of Christianity, as found in the eighteenth book of the Antiquities. Elaborately he commences this discourse "with hesitation and misgiving," and is "reluctant," so he says, "to enter the arena." He has "little that is new to contribute to the discussion"; and solemnly desiring also "to avoid the Slavonic evidence discovered in recent years," he confines himself "mainly to the old and well-worn passages in the Antiquities," proposing to "touch but lightly on that new and untried ground."

In spite of all this timidity, however, his preliminaries to this small task alone consist of "observations on three points:—(1) the opportunities Josephus had for obtaining correct information on the 'subject,' (2) the conditions under which he wrote as affording reason for reticence, and (3) the liability of his work to Christian interpolation."

Discussing his first point he says: "Of the main facts of the life and death of Jesus, Josephus cannot have been ignorant," for, as the Apostle Paul said, "this thing hath not been done in a corner."[42]..."Such information as he may have gained in his earlier Palestinian period, being derived wholly from hearsay report, is likely to have been garbled and imperfect," but during his residence in Rome, "documents were available, which would be known to any Christian informants with whom he may have come into contact." Moreover, he asserts that, when the Antiquities appeared (in the year 93 or 95), the Gospels of Mark and Luke were, "*According to credible tradition,*" also in circulation, and to these Josephus could have resorted for enlightenment. And as further proof that Josephus was fully conversant with the New Doctrine and that the disputed reference in the Antiquities was really his own, he adduces Tacitus, whom he represents as having been "simultaneously at work," as one of the "earliest external writers to allude to Christ," and as having "drawn his information on Christianity from the Testimony." And all Dr. Thackeray offers in support of such glaring assertions, are "sufficient grounds, '*in my opinion*'" and the "*belief of some authorities.*" For these and more such reasons (p. 127-8), he contends that, "no allusion to Christianity can be pronounced an interpolation on the sole ground that it approximates to a Christian creed."

Even more inconceivable than these assertions based on "credible tradition," "sufficient grounds," and "the belief of some authorities," is his declaration that Tacitus, as also Luke, was "simultaneously at work" at the time when the Antiquities was written.[43] For, in his Third Lecture, to serve a

[42] Acts, xxvi. 26.

[43] The Antiquities, it will be remembered, was published in the year 93 or 95; Domitian reigned from 81 to 96 CE.

different purpose, he makes Laqueur and Teufel say for him that, "in the time of Domitian, whose hand lay heavy on all intellectual life, the only course possible without risk of outlawry was the one followed by Juvenal, Tacitus and Pliny—namely silence,"... and that "it was only the weak and servile who ventured to write, such as [a] Martial and [a] Josephus."

Having thus, in discussing his "first point" invaded his "second" and "third" also, and consequently depleted the material necessary under those headings, all he now offers in fulfilment of his remaining enumerations are some more theories, analyses, and a generous amount of repetitions. And so, with all his "hesitations" and "misgivings" conquered, and his diffusive "preliminaries" disposed of, he finally arrives at the issue to which his Sixth Lecture is chiefly devoted.

Definitely to prove the authenticity of the Testimonium, Dr. Thackeray (p. 131) commences with an analysis of the two other, similarly debated passages in the Antiquities. One of these (XVIII. v. 2) is in reference to John "the Baptist," the other (XX. ix. 1) to James "the brother of Jesus." Of John, Josephus says, "He was a good man; he commanded the Jews to exercise virtue, both as to righteousness towards one another and piety towards God, and so come to baptism; for the washing would be acceptable to Him, if they made use of it, not in order to rid themselves of some sins only, but for the purification of the body." In regards to this, we do not intend to discuss whether John preached "baptism" to Jews, as was necessary with those who entered a course of repentance (Shibboleth Halleket, 145a), or to non-Jews who wished to embrace Judaism, in which case, according to the Talmud (Yebamoth, 46a-b, and 22a), it was, and yet is, a precircumcisional requirement. But, the important point, aside from the fact that Josephus, in the first place, does not in this passage mention the name of Jesus and, secondly, that John himself does not connect his "baptism" with the Christian movement, the truth, as recognized by at least two most outstanding authorities, is that the so-called baptism spoken of in the Antiquities is not the ritual described in the Gospels (Matt., iii. 11, and elsewhere), but the well-known Tebileh, or immersion ordained in the Bible.[44] As for the second account (XX. ix. 1), wherein James, "the brother of Jesus," with some of his companions are put to death as "breakers of the Law," and where the "Messiah" is indeed alluded to, Jesus is not recognized as such, but referred to only as he "who is called the Christ." But whereas Josephus clearly connects neither the "Baptist" nor the brother of Jesus with the Messianic movement, in the Gospels, which, as should be expected, carry far greater weight with the Christian critic, both are intimately associated with it. Therefore, since these two supplementary accounts in the Antiquities are accepted as authentic, Dr. Thackeray, after a very long and elaborate analysis of the John and James passages, concludes that the Testimonium, or at least part of it, is also authentic.

He thus introduces it, and (p. 136) reads it; "it is brief enough to repeat," he says, "familiar as it will be to you." After reciting it, he recounts its acceptance and veneration by the Christians from the time of Eusebius to the sixteenth century, of its gradual depreciation since the Renaissance, and how it was rejected as an interpolation recently. He names some modern churchmen who still believe it authentic, and other scholars to whom he refers as "redoubtable antagonists." When it comes to himself, however, he first says, "I hesitate to express an opinion," though immediately following, under Dr. Eisler's influence, volunteers three statements in succession: two in agreement with each other, sandwiching a conflicting one between them. In the first of these (p. 137-8), led by Dr. Eisler, he abandons a "former belief that the entire Testimonium is a Christian interpolation"; in the second, that "not only is the style of its language Josephus' own, but that even its expression is not such as a Christian would

[44] About this subject see, Klausner's "Jesus," p. 246-7, and Schechter's "Judaism," p. 109-10.

have used";[45] in the third he returns to his original "belief," saying, "If the whole is not authentic, there is at least a Josephian nucleus in it."

To prove these statements, which are actually contradicting each other, he subjects the Testimonium to another "analysis," which in character is as meretricious as his "estimates" of Josephus in all his past criticisms; for neither is he sufficiently capable of recognizing the meritorious features of his victim, nor would his heavenly-minded listeners tolerate any estimate of him, excepting one consisting of abuse and derision. In this effort, however, in spite of all his learning, he is completely disappointing. For his constant intermingling of Eisler's theories or Eusebius' fabrications, of Biblical and secular quotations or references, of questions which he himself asks and also answers, and of unlimited other irrelevant material, render his reasonings not only extremely tedious, but entirely impossible to follow. So great is the confusion, that in most instances his "analysis" resembles more an Inquisitorial prosecution than a scientific discussion.

He commences (p. 138) the "*analysis*" with "*some details*" which he "*must endeavor briefly to summarize,*" but again goes on with "*internal evidence under three heads,*" and "*the external*" which "*are the two items most damaging to the counsel for the defense.*" How much he enlightens us under all these "heads" and "items," one can conjecture by his introduction of a counsel into the argument, at the conclusion of which (p. 141), after daubing Josephus "a patchwork writer," he extends his gratitude to his "friend Dr. Eisler, who with great generosity has permitted me to avail myself of the results of his researches, which will be fully set out in his forthcoming work ('The Messiah Jesus')." At this point (p. 142), evidently realizing the monotony and emptiness of his own efforts, Dr. Thackeray beseeches further "indulgence"; for, says he, "it is only through such details that

[45] Due to its difficult wording, this statement is loosely quoted.

we can hope to reach the truth in a matter of considerable importance."

In his desperate struggle to prove the much debated Testimonium authentic, he omits no conceivable expedient or aid which he could with any sort of propriety employ; and to accomplish his task he shuns no form of labor. His constant hunting for clues, his continuous reconnoitering and scanning, his practice of ducking and of dodging his responsibility by assigning his reflections to others, his disjoining of one part of his quarry and uniting it with another, entirely unrelated with it, and his never-ending experiments, however, make his inquiry so perplexing and bookish as to render its imperceptibility and obliviousness most welcome. The few clearer and more concrete of his allegations which follow will illustrate in only a small measure his procedure in his stupendous "analysis" of the Christian passage:

"What has recently converted me to Dr. Eisler's view is the very opening of our Passage,[46]... the three little words,—'Now there lived.'" That this phrase is "thoroughly characteristic of Josephus," he attempts (p. 142) to prove by his supposition that Josephus had, "without variation," used it on six other occasions. To this phrase he now adds the next three words, "a certain Jesus," because, he says, "they are found in some MSS. of Eusebius." Now, as the places where he found the phrase "Now there lived" on six other occasions "without variation," he indicates in footnotes, (1) Antiq., XVIII. ix. 1, (2) idem, XX. vi. 1, (3) idem, XX. viii. 7, (4) Bell. Jud., I. xxxiii. 2, (5) idem, I. iv. 7, and (6) idem, IV. iii. 13,—in each instance at the opening of the section. On examining these texts, however, we find that while in his second reference alone the wording is similar, in the fifth it resembles no more than chalk to cheese, and that his remaining four references cannot claim even so little resemblance.

As for the next phrase, "a wise man," Dr. Thackeray, on

[46] The Testimonium has been quoted in full at the beginning of the present Chapter.

the one hand (p. 144), concedes that "Josephus might conceivably have been prepared to assign Him a place on the roll of Jewish sages," but, in the same breath, he also accepts Dr. Eisler's suggestion as plausible, viz., that "the censor has been at work, and by a slight change produced 'sophos' (=a philosopher) out of 'sophistis' (=a sophist)." The next phrase, "If one may call Him a man," says he, has "a ring of insincerity" to which one should "mentally supply,... 'whom His followers call Son of God.'" In the next clause, "a doer of marvelous deeds," Dr. Thackeray finds, "there is no need for any change," but here Dr. Eisler detects an asterisk which he says denotes that Jesus was "a poet." In the clause "a teacher of men who receive the truth with pleasure," Dr. Thackeray observes that the phrase within it, "receive with pleasure," has "an evil connotation"; so much so, that he justifies Eusebius for altering the undignified word "pleasure" into "reverence." And here, as if Dr. Thackeray had been particularly veracious himself, he adds, "But what is truth in Josephus' estimation?" Resuming with the clause, "these and ten thousand other wonderful things concerning Him," he finds the hyperbole within it, "ten thousand other things,... thoroughly Josephian," except that the exaggeration, "ten thousand," is an expression of ridicule. And so on, this most remarkable analysis continues to the last phrase of the Passage. And (p. 148), as he completes his experiment, he proudly exclaims, "That is the solution of the problem to which, after much wavering in the past, I have, thanks to the expert guidance and acute insight of my friend Dr. Eisler, been led," declaring that through his "'benevolent aid,' the text as equilibrated by himself is in keeping with what a Jew like Josephus may be expected to have written." At this point, after a few more similar allusions, supplemented also by three separate and most flattering announcements of "the masterly forthcoming work ('The Messiah Jesus') of the leading living authority, my friend Dr. Eisler," Dr. Thackeray (p. 153) finishes his Sixth Lecture.

Such are the evidences, such the trial, because Josephus 'forgot' to say something about Jesus, or, more likely, did not know anything about him.

As for Dr. Eisler himself, it can truthfully be said that, among all Josephian commentators, past or present, no one has ever equaled or even approached him for erudition. To call him "a leading living authority," which, without explaining the immense range of his various fields, may equally denote only some Grand Mogul, a Houdini, or even a Mezzofanti, does not do full justice to a wizard of so many lores. A single glance at his spectacular "Messiah Jesus" will prove the immense profundity of this man's learning. But whether his trustworthiness is commensurate with his cultural eminence, is a matter which will be decided by his own testimony. Moreover, whether his evidence is of any value at all, even if well-intentioned and sincere, must be considered also by its rationality; for quite frequently his direction is so grotesque, inconsistent and impossible, as to make him appear completely irrational. Dr. H. John Chapman, reverently commenting on his work, in the *Dublin Review* of January, 1932, says that, "if Dr. Eisler's results are absurd, it is because his methods are crazy."

The full title of the book is, "The Messiah Jesus and John the Baptist according to Flavius Josephus' recently rediscovered 'Capture of Jerusalem' and other Jewish and Christian sources, by Rober Eisler, Ph.D., with forty plates, including reproductions of the inedited Russian, Rumanian, and Hebrew MSS. and kindred documents." That he was able to spread out a discussion concerning Jesus "the Messiah" and John "the Baptist" to the extent of 1100, or even 650 large and closely printed pages, of which the English abridgment of his original German edition consists, out of the meager contents of Josephus' "Capture of Jerusalem" (—a Slavonic version of the Jewish War), and other very scanty and dubious sources bearing upon the subject, is not to be wondered at, in view of the dropsical name the book bears. But the fact that, whereas the book assumes to be a treatise on Jesus and John, it chiefly is a polemic against Josephus, is an even greater crux for criticism. For, while Jesus and John very frequently disappear from the scene altogether, there is scarcely a page in the book wherein Josephus is not the topic.

In the Preface Dr. Eisler announces that his work "is fundamentally different in method, scope, and outlook from any Life of Christ or any other book dealing with Christian origins, or any History of the Jewish People in the time of Jesus that I know of." For it claims to show:

"First. That there once existed a rich fund of historical tradition about the Messiah Jesus both among the Jews and the non-Christian Greeks and Romans.

"Second. That this precious material was deliberately destroyed, or falsified, by a system of rigid censorship officially authorized ever since the time of Constantine I, and reinstituted in the reign of Theodosius II and Valentinian III (477 AD.).

"Third. That in spite of the tireless efforts of ecclesiastical revisers, enough has been preserved in certain out-of-the-way corners of the world, among Jews and heretics as well as in quotations occurring in Christian polemic and apologetic literature, to allow us to reconstruct with sufficient clarity and plausibility, and even with a certain amount of picturesque detail, the fundamental features of Jesus' personality and his mission, particularly as they appeared to his enemies.

"Fourth. That through a careful comparison of this mercilessly cold, detached, and unsympathetic pen-portrait of the man Jesus with the naïvely idealizing presentation of the Kyrios Christos by the writers of the early and later Christian Church, it is possible to come quite close to the historical truth about the Nasoraean prophet-king and about his elder relative, the schismatic high priest of the Jews, Johanan 'The Hidden One,' better known as the Baptist.

"It is thus my claim that a history of the Christian origins ... can be written which will chronologically coincide with the history of the Jews and the Romans from 4 BC. to 135 AD. —that is, from the first appearance of Johanan to the downfall of Bar-Kokheba."

Now, in the first instance, that there once existed this profusion of Christian tradition about Jesus, and that this material was deliberately destroyed, or falsified, are facts too well known to require new proofs for verification. Secondly, that in spite of the tireless efforts of the early Fathers, enough of this tradition has been preserved to allow us to reconstruct the fundamental features of Jesus' personality and mission, is a fact which every student of ecclesiastical history also knows. Thirdly, that by comparing these evidences it is possible to reconstruct the history of this extremely important period, has likewise more than sufficiently been proven. But that Dr. Eisler, in using a tremendous amount of this enlightening material, as he really did, has sincerely endeavored to come "close to the historical truth" in regards to John "the Baptist," Jesus, Josephus, or in fact concerning any subject on which he treats in his otherwise remarkable work is, as we shall see, far less convincing.

He then continues:—"In face of the prevalent scepticism and the Neo-Marchionite subjectivism of certain critics, who claim for themselves the right to disregard any evidence in the Gospels which conflicts with their own preconceived picture of Jesus, the present work represents a radical departure. For I claim no such right. I refuse to reject from among documentary materials this or that statement as unworthy of Jesus' personality and his mission. On the contrary, I humbly and honestly accept whatever I find in the sources, duly weighing the evidence when there is conflict or contradiction, unless indeed the trustworthiness of a given source is disproved by facts quite independent of any judgment of values."

He further sincerely believes that "nothing in this book can give offense to a true Christian,... (though) it may cause somewhat of a startling shock to those whom Bernard Shaw has pertinently called...defenders of an idolatrous or iconolatrous worship of Christ,[47]...who are only concerned with the traditional pictures and statues of Jesus and the pretty stories attached to him." With this accomplished, he adds diverse lessons on how one should read his book, then expresses his gratitude, among others, to Dr. Thackeray, who "was able to accept certain essential results" of his analysis, and, after misapplying a misinterpreted verse from Paul's Epistle to the Hebrews (xii. 1), he finally closes his prolog with, "Now let us run the gauntlet and be flogged along the line." We thus have his program, and presumedly also his aims: he even offers not only a long lesson on how to follow him in general, but also special sets of detailed instructions on how and why certain sections of his work should be read and others avoided, for both "expert skippers" and "for those who would probably prefer a less cumbersome book."

Before entering upon the study of his work, however, we might ask why, after proposing to present facts which are, or which Dr. Eisler believes to be, of an indisputable nature, and feeling certain that none of his assertions therein can give offense to a true Christian,—if he took upon himself to be sincere, and to follow his sources with unreserved simplicity, scrupulously and impartially, why does he anticipate having to "run the gauntlet and be flogged along the line?" Secondly, why in discussing an historical truth, based upon "mercilessly cold, detached and unsympathetic" proofs, does he find it necessary to provide both general and special directions for the different intellectual capacities in such a manner that every individual might see his representations from only his own point of view? And above all, we might here also ask, why in a work represented as a discussion on Jesus "the

[47] In the Preface to Shaw's "Androcles and the Lion."

Messiah" and John "the Baptist," are Josephus and his writings the main subject?

In addition to these questionable features, too, so unmethodical and chaotic is its arrangement, that an intelligible study of any topic in the book, in spite of its author's remarkable cleverness and great learning, is not only "cumbersome" but utterly impossible. If by some chance there were any at all who might have benefited by this classic, it surely cannot have been others than his colleague, Dr. Thackeray, who to his "great pleasure was able to accept certain results" from it, and perhaps also his other friend, Prof. Laqueur. For the present writer to say that he too was able to gain by any of its enlightenments, he must confess that such was not his good fortune. In order to acquire, or rather to be able to convey some conception of Dr. Eisler's excogitations, his only choice was to avail himself of what are generally accepted as reliable criticisms on his work; and what seemed to him the shortest and best, is a synopsis of it by the eminent exegetical critic, Dr. Chapman, which follows:

> *"According to Dr. Eisler, Jesus was an itinerant carpenter or smith, who lived mostly like a Bedouin in the desert with Rechabites, and was called a 'Nazoraean' (not a native of Nazareth) or 'secret one,' just as the Mandaeans, a sect of fire-worshippers of Persia, were perhaps called Nazoraia, Keepers of Secrets; his followers were Cainites, bearing the sign of Cain* (*Gen., iv.* 15). *His teaching was that all the Jews should flee the Roman domination by living in the desert on Manna from heaven* (*as exemplified in Matt., vi.* 25-34, *and Luke, xii.* 22-31). *In the year* 21 *his followers, after leading him in triumph into Jerusalem, gained his assent to the storming of the Temple, which they carried together with the adjoining fortress* (*Antonia*). *The wrecking of the temple-banks and the expulsion of the cattle-dealers, however, antagonized the Chief Priests, and they sent*

information to Pilate, who was at Caesarea; the latter arrived swiftly by forced marches and recaptured his palace and the Temple; he slew multitudes of the insurgents and crucified their leader between two of his principal lieutenants. His followers were unable to discover his corpse, but, having caught a glimpse of his twin brother Thomas, who, like Jesus, was a crooked hunchback, only 4 feet and seven inches in height, of terrible appearance, which struck all who approached him with horror, they concluded that he was not really dead; and thereupon proceeded to found a world-wide religion and the Catholic Church.

"John the Baptist is described as a 'lycanthropic scarecrow,' living in the desert; that he was born some thirty years before the Christian era, and lived until 35 CE. *His chief exploit was to be the inspirer and chaplain of the army of rebels who stormed and partially burnt the Temple after the death of Herod the Great in 6* BCE.*, on the occasion of Archelaus."*

Such are Dr. Eisler's portraits of, and conclusions bearing upon Jesus and John, not only due to his crack-brained interpretation of sources,[48] but also because from among the entire inexhaustible fund of historical tradition concerning them, whether Jewish, Christian or heathen, which has either passed or escaped censorship, he has made use of or acknowledged only such as would supply bottom to his extravagances.

Of Josephus' integrity and objectivity likewise, Dr. Eisler's estimate is as low as is conceivably possible. In a section (p. 22) where his veracity is the subject, commencing with his genealogy, he says: "This Joseph, later on called Flavius Josephus, claimed to belong to an old priestly family and to be descended ... from the royal stock of the Hasmoneans."

[48] Such as Tacitus, Annal., xv. 44; Plinius' Letter xcvii; Celsus' argument (partly treated upon in our Second Chapter); Eusebius, and others.

To prove that this claim is false, Dr. Eisler directs our attention to his supposition that the only evidences which Josephus had in support of that birthright are the genealogical records in the Archives at Jerusalem, "which at the time of his writing had already been committed to the flames." But how this homo multarum literarum hopes to foist such a castrated piece of enlightenment, a statement so demonstrably deceptive, upon an informed reader, is unimaginable. For, though the genealogical as all other documents in the Archives at Jerusalem had at the time of his writing, indeed, already been "committed to the flames," those were not at all the ones the text Josephus refers to. But in giving his lineage, Josephus (Vita, sec. 1) says: "I cite as I find it recorded in the 'Public Registers,'" which, after the destruction of Jerusalem, could easily have existed not only among the Jewish communities of Jabne, Gophna, and many other resettlements within Palestine, but also in Alexandria, Antioch and Rome, and even in Euphratean Jewish centers. And how can one say that Josephus did not cherish a record of his family tree among his other personal memoranda?

In another section (p. 25), he asserts that Josephus' claim to have been the Commander-in-chief of Galilee is also false. "What is certain, however," he tells us, "is that the ambitious young man did his best to foment the rebellion," and that "he misused his position to enrich himself by engaging in war-profiteering of the most scandalous character." As proof of this, he cites "the scandalous speculations in Galilean, ritually pure oil," the historical facts of which are so familiar to us as of an entirely different nature. Enlarging upon this he adds: "Although he consistently represents himself as the commander of his troops, it has now become clear through the comparison of the earliest draft of his history with the later editions (all, of course, conveniently chronologized in turn by Laqueur, Thackeray and himself) that his position was somewhere between that of an army-chaplain and that of an army clerk." In a much later section, (p. 185) however, forgetting what he had here said, he makes Josephus "a secretary in attendance on Joazar and Judas," who in fact are the two priests appointed as his subordinates. Another aromatic piece of evidence (p. 211) is that Josephus, from 60 to 64 CE., was "officially connected with the Sanhedrin." As proof of this he points to a passage wherein Josephus calls the chancelleries of Jerusalem "the sinews of state." That passage (Bell. Jud., II. xvii. 6) reads: "The keepers of the Record Office having fled, the rebels set fire to the building. After consuming the sinews of the city in flames, they advanced against their foes." Now, that this passage makes Josephus "officially connected with the Sanhedrin," is an assertion which only an astigmatic mind can make.

The extent to which this burlesque and mockery is carried by these modern Eusebiuses can be conjectured also by the following example: In the Vita (sec. 26ff.), Josephus, in connection with the Dabaritta affair, recounts that, on seeing his life endangered, he "changed his raiment for one of black," whereas in the Bellum (II. xxi. 3), where the incident is repeated, the account reads, he "rushed out with raiment rent and ashes sprinkled on his head." On this variation, Dr. Eisler (p. 196) remarks: "In one he tears his garment according to the Jewish custom, in another he puts on a black garment in sign of mourning, as the pagans do." It may seem rude to question Dr. Eisler's mastery in matters of this nature, but for some reason of his own he must have allowed the fact to fade from his memory that both rending of clothes and wearing of mourning garments, in cases of general grief or affliction, were in those days common not with Jews alone, but, under various circumstances, also with other nations. Though there is no law in the Jewish Canon distinctly permitting or forbidding one to tear his garment when his life is in danger, except the Scriptural law which forbids a high-priest to defile himself under any circumstances,[49] there are several injunctions concerning the subject,

[49] Lev. x. 6, xxi. 10-11.

including one requiring ordinary priests to rend their clothes, though only as a part of, or in connection with, funeral obsequies.[50] There is also the well-known Mishnaic rite of Kerieh,[51] obligatory to both male and female, in case of death of a near relative, in addition to numerous instances in the Scriptures[52] where individuals expressed their different sorrows in this particular manner. Thus, when the armies of Israel were driven before their enemies, "Joshua rent his clothes, and fell upon his face before the ark of the Lord."[53] Job, after his misfortunes, "arose and rent his mantle,"[54] and his friends "rent everyone his mantle."[55] "When Mordechai perceived all that was done, he rent his clothes, and put on sackcloth with ashes."[56] The rending of clothes in cases of calamity as being common also among the pagans, is mentioned by Herodotus[57] of the Persians and Scythians, and the Apocrypha[58] mentions the Assyrians. Even in the Arabian Nights are frequent allusions to rending of clothes.

Not less, again, than pagan was the donning of sad-colored garments, in cases of general calamity, also a Jewish custom. Thus, when "our Sanctuary ... (has been) laid waste, and the Gentiles have profaned it,[59]... Mattathias and his sons ... put on sackcloth and mourned very sore."[60] When Judith was praying to God to assist her against the enemies of the Sanctuary, she "fell upon her face and put ashes upon her head, and ... adjusted (?) the sackcloth wherewith she was

[50] Lev., xxi. 1-3; Ezek., xliv. 25.

[51] As described in Moed Kat., iii. 7; Shabb., xiii. 3.

[52] Gen., xxxvii.. 29, 34, xliv. 13; 2 Chron., xxxiv. 27; Isaiah, xxxvi. 32; Jer., xxxvi. 24 (where the absence of the form is noted), xli. 5: etc.

[53] Joshua, vii. 6.

[54] Job, i. 20, ii. 8.

[55] Job, ii. 12-13.

[56] Esther, iv. 1.

[57] Herodotus' History, ii. 66, iv. 71, viii. 99, ix. 24.

[58] Judith, xiv. 19.

[59] I Macc., ii. 12.

[60] I Macc., ii. 14.

covered."[61] Esther, when in fear, "laid away her glorious dress and put on the garments of anguish and mourning, and instead of fragrant ointments she covered her head with ashes."[62] Even "Joachim the high-priest and all the priests that stood before the Lord, and they who ministered unto the Lord, exceedingly afraid ... and troubled about the fate of Jerusalem and the Temple, had their loins girt and the altar covered with sackcloth."[63]

In the Bellum (III. vii. 28) Josephus, among other expedients which he used to repel the Romans, describes how he poured molten lead upon the besiegers. Commenting on this, Dr. Eisler (p. 198) says: "If one remembers that a single quart of lead weighs more than twenty-eight pounds, that no lead is found in Palestine and must therefore have been proportionately dear, and, lastly, that Jotapata can have had neither leaden water pipes laid on the houses nor leaden gutters, it is inconceivable that even ten quarts of lead could have been collected in the whole town."

Had Dr. Eisler, however, troubled himself more for the sake of historical accuracy and less with flattering a sanctimonious palate, he would have discovered that much the contrary was the truth. For, to begin with, that lead had always been extensively used in Palestine, he would have learned by the many allusions to it in the Scriptures. That it was common in Judea is shown by the expression in Ecclesiasticus (xlvii. 18), where the writer, having in view the description of Solomon's wealth in I Kings (x. 27), says, "Thou didst multiply silver and lead." Lead was one of the spoils of the Midianites which the children of Israel brought with them to the plains of Moab, after their return from the slaughter of the tribe (—Numb., xxxi. 22). The ships of Tarshish supplied the markets of Tyre with lead (—Ex., xxvii. 12). Its

[61] Judith, ix. 1.
[62] Apocr. Esther, xiv. 1-2.
[63] Judith, iii., and iv; especially iii. 8 to iv. 2, also iv. 11 and 14-15.

heaviness to which allusion is made in Ex., xv. 10, and Ecclus., xxii. 14, caused it be used for weights (—Zech., v. 7; compare Prov., xvi. 11). This fact may perhaps also explain its substitution for ordinary stones in the passages of Ecclesiasticus just mentioned. And not only in Palestine was this metal so common, but also in Egypt, on its southern boundary, where the stones of buildings were found fastened together with it (—Layard's "Nimroud and Babylon," p. 357). To the lead mines of Egypt, Fronto, after the desolation of the Holy Land, sent his prisoners (—Bell. Jud., VI. ix. 2). Eleazar had enormous supplies of lead in the fortress of Masada (—Bell. Jud., VII. viii. 4), and Dr. Eisler's assertion that "no lead is found in Palestine," and that "it is inconceivable that even ten quarts of lead could have been collected" for the fortress of Jotapata, is only in keeping with the rest of his evidences and criticisms in his Messiah Jesus,—one of the costliest, vastest, most elaborate, and also most unedifying books ever written against Josephus.

Altogether different and kindlier, however, is the attitude toward Josephus of Rabbi Kalman Schulman, one of the most outstanding Hebraic luminaries of the nineteenth century. He was born at Bykhov, Russia, in 1819, and died in Wilna in his eightieth year. At an early age he was sent to Cheder, but not till two years after his marriage did he enter the Yeshivah at Volozhin. The six years spent by him in study there caused him an infection of the eyes, to cure which he migrated to Wilna. There he went to the Klaus of Elijah Gaon for the study of Talmud, but his extreme poverty caused him to divorce his wife. In 1843 he enrolled in the Yeshivah of Rabbi Israel Ginsberg, from whom he received his rabbinical diploma.

Schulman first became known as a writer through a petition addressed by him to Sir Moses Montefiore in 1846 in behalf of those Jews who had resided within the limit of fifty versts from the German and Austrian boundary-lines, and who by special law of the Russian government had been driven from their homes. The beauty and clearness of his diction made such an impression on Loewe, the friend and secretary of Sir Moses, that he expressed a great desire to become acquainted with the author. Through him Schulman was introduced to the poet Isaac Baer Levinsohn and other Progressivists in Wilna. From this time forward his literary activity was redoubled. His first publication was a funeral oration delivered on the occasion of the death of Rabbi Ginsberg, and printed under the title "Kol Bokim." This was followed in 1848 by "Safah Berurah," "Harisut Beter," "Toledoth Yosef," a biography of Josephus, "Milhamot ha-Yehudim," "Dibre Yeme ha-Yehudim," "Halikot Kedem," and other historical and biographical works. Among all his publications, however, "Toledoth Yosef" is one of the best. The Preface to this book, entitled "To the memory of Josephus," so well expresses my own sentiments that I have seen fit to reproduce it here with an English translation.

אל נשמת המחבר

יוסף בן מתתיהו ! הה , לשמך ולזִכרך יכלה שְׁאֵרי ולבבי ! אותך אֲשַׁוֶה וַאֲדַמֶה לירמיהו בן חלקיהו נְבִיא האמת והצדק , כי הֲלִיכות תולדות ימי חייך עם תולדות ימי חייו נִשְׁתָּווּ : כמוהו ראית עֳנִי בת עַמך בשבט עֶברתו—כמוהו יָעצת צדק לאחיך בני ארצך לשמוע ולהקשיב בקול מַלְכָּם אשר הִמליך אֵל מלך עולָם עליהם , כי אלהים מושיב מלכים לַכִּסֵא , והוא נתֵן מהוד הדר מלכותו עליהם — כמוהו אהבת את בני עַמך אהבה בְלִי מְצָרים , וכמוהו רדפוך המה בלי הָשָׂךְ על רָדפך טובם וְאָשרם וַיִתנוך לְבֹגֵד וְנוֹפֵל אל צורריהם ומַחריבי ארצם — כמוהו נשאת קִינים והגה והי על מַשְׂאות עיר האלהים ועל שִׁממות מִקדש ה׳ ועל בית ישראל כי נפלו בחרב—כמוהו מצאת חן בעיני המושל אשר לכד את

ירושלים בחרבו הקשה—כמוהו היית חטֶר מגזע אהרן קדוש ה׳
וְכֹהֵן לְאֵל עליון , וכמוהו הלכת בגולה עם שְׁבִי ירושלים
וגלות יהודה והפגעת בם בעת רעה ובעת צרה את האויב—.
ובלעדי כל התכונות היקרות האלה , גדול עוד שמך
בגבורה , כי היית גם כהן משוח גבור מלחמה ושר צבא
יהודה בארץ הגליל ; וברוח אמיץ נלחמת מלחמות בני עַמך
בְמִבצר יודפת וַתַּעַשׂ גבורות נוראות ונפלאות , וַתַּעַשׂ לך
שֵׁם גדול בגבורים עד היום הזה . גם היית עוד סופר מהיר
וּמַזכּיר נאמן מאין כמוך , וספָרֶיךָ היקרים והנאמנים מצאו
חן גם בעיני טיטוס , וישׂמח עליהם כמוצא שלל רב , ויתן
להם מקום בראש סִפרי החכמה אשר בבית אוצר ספָריו .
ועל כל אלה נַעלית מאד כי נִמְנֵית בלַהקת התנאים הקדושים
תופשי התורה , ושמך נזכר במסכת אבות בשֵׁם רבי יוסי
הכֹּהֵן*) , ועוד במקומות רבים במשנה ובתלמוד יִזָּכֵר על
טוב שִׁמְךָ**) , וזכרך לברכה עד דור אחרון על עפר יקום .
(הליכות קדם בדברים נוספים) .

---

*) כן דעת הרב ר׳ עמנואל אבוהב בספרו ויכוח הדת הנקרא בשם נאָמאָלאָגיא . **) עיין בבית האוצר להרב ר׳ ח. לעווינזאהן נ״י .

To the Soul of Josephus

"Yosef ben Mattathias, woe! My heart and my soul go out to thy name and to thy memory. I compare thee to Jeremiah the son of Hilkiah, the prophet of truth and justice; because the process of recording thy life and the process of recording his life are the same. Like him thou hast seen the sorrows of thy people. Like him thou hast advised thy brethren of thy country to listen and to obey the voice of their king, whom the Almighty God hath made to rule; because God maketh kings to sit on their thrones; and He giveth them the glory of His Kingdom. Like him thou hast loved the sons of thy people with an unbounded love, and like him they pursue thee forever; because thou hast pursued only their welfare, they made thee a traitor and calumniated thee as one who went over to their enemies and made waste of their country. Like him thou hast lamented for the ruins of the City of God, the desolation of the Temple of God and the House of Israel which fell under the sword. Like him thou hast found grace in the eyes of the ruler who conquered Jerusalem with his mighty sword. Like him thou wast a twig of the root of Aaron, the holy man of God and the high-priest of God Almighty. Like him didst thou go into exile together with the shackled prisoners of Jerusalem and those from Judea; and together with them, like him, thou hast met the enemy under most trying circumstances. Besides thy noble qualities as a man, thou wast also like him an anointed priest, and a hero during your command of the Judean army in the Land of Galilee. With a strong spirit thou hast fought the battles of thy people in the fortress of Jotapata. Thou hast shown great fortitude and skill, and hast made for thee a name among the heroes to this day. Thou wast an excellent writer and a truthful recorder; and thy fine and outspoken books found grace in the eyes of Titus; and he was very happy with them and gave them a place on the top of all scientific and wise books in his own library. And above all thou wast among the holy Tannaim, the Keeper of the Torah; and thy name was mentioned in the tractate Aboth as Rabbi Jose ha-Cohen,[64] as also in many places in the Mishna and the Talmud is thy name spoken of (or alluded to) commendably.[65] Thy blessed memory will remain until the last generation that will spring up on earth."

[64] (a) The Jewish Encyclopedia places this in Challah, iv. 11; Prof. Bentwich (Josephus, p. 249) has it in Moed Katan, 23a. (b) See also the opinion of Rabbi Emanuel Abohab in his book of religious disputations, entitled "Nomologia."

[65] Derek Erez Rabba, v. So also in the Compendium of Rabbi Isaac Baer Levinson. Dr. Bentwich (idem), however, prefers to have it that "The Talmud has no reference to Josephus, for the surmise that he is the Philosopher visited by the four sages who journeyed from Palestine to Rome is no more than a vague possibility. Nor has the supposed identification with Joseph ha-Cohen that is mentioned in the Midrash anything more solid to uphold it."

BIBLIOGRAPHY

THE OLD AND THE NEW TESTAMENTS; THE APOCRYPHA.

JOSEPHUS: Whiston's and Thackeray's translations of,

PHILO JUDAEUS: De Legatione ad Cajum, and Versus Flaccum (Bohn's ed.).

TACITUS: Annals, and History (Bohn's ed.).

SUETONIUS: The Lives of the Twelve Caesars (Bohn's ed.).

PLINY THE ELDER: Natural History.

PLINY THE YOUNGER: The Letters of,

ORIGEN: Fragments from the Writings of, mostly through Rufinus and Eusebius.

EUSEBIUS: Ecclesiastical History, and his Life of Constantine.

EMIL SCHUERER: The Jewish People in the Time of Jesus (especially for Talmudic references).

HENRY HART MILMAN: History of the Jews; and History of Christianity.

HEINRICH GRAETZ: History of the Jews, Vols. II. VI. (1891-1898).

GEORGE BARTON: Jesus of Nazareth; and A History of the Hebrew People.

THOMAS BROWN: The History of the Destruction of the City and Temple of Jerusalem, Albany, N. Y., 1825.

DA COSTA: Israel and the Gentiles, London, 1850.

THEODOR MOMMSEN: Provinces of the Roman Empire.

GEORGE ADAM SMITH: Jerusalem from the Earliest Times, Edinburgh, 1907.

F. RUPERT: The Church and the Synagogue, Paris, 18[illegible]9.

LEWIS B. PATTON: Jerusalem in Bible Times, London, 1908.

CHARLES MERIVALE: History of the Romans Under the Empire, Vols. VI. VII.

KUENEN: The Religion of Israel to the Fall of the Jewish State, London, 1874.

MORRIS J. RAPHALL: Post-Biblical History of the Jews.

FREDERICK HUIDEKOPER: Judaism at Rome—B.C. 76 to A.D. 140.

R. SMITH: The Prophets of Israel, N. Y., 1882.

W. D. MORRISON: The Jews Under Roman Rule.

E. H. PALMER: History of the Jewish Nation, London, 1874.

EDWIN BEAN: Jerusalem Under the High-Priest, London, 1912.

DURUY-MAHAFFY: History of Rome and the Roman People, Vols. IV-VI.

WILLIAM HALE: The History of the Jews, London, 1851.

SAMUEL SHARPE: The History of the Hebrew Nation and its Literature.

JAMES STEVENSON RIGGS: History of the Jewish People (Scribner's, 1905).

SOLOMON SCHECHTER: Studies in Judaism (Second Series).

MARGOLIS and MARKS: History of the Jewish People.

JULIUS WELLHAUSEN: Israel.

JOHN WORCESTER: The Jewish Sacrifices.

WILLIS MASON WEST: Ancient History.

ARTHUR PENRHYN STANLEY: The Jewish Church (Scribner's, 1876).

HENRY STEBBING: Essay on Josephus.

SOLOMON ZEITLIN: Josephus on Jesus.

NORMAN BENTWICH: Josephus.

F. J. FOAKES-JACKSON: Josephus and the Jews.

HENRY ST. JOHN THACKERAY: Josephus, the Man and the Historian.

H. GUTTMAN: Josephus.

B. BRUENE: Josephus und seine Verhaeltnise zum Judenthum.

HANS DRUENE: Untersuchungen ueber Josephus.

JOSEPH SALVADOR: Histoire de la Domination Romaine en Judee.

GEORGE ROUTLEDGE: Judaism and the Beginning of Christianity, London, 1923.

J. W. LIGHTLEY: Jewish Sects and Parties in the Time of Jesus, London, 1925.

THOMAS ROBINSON: The Evangelists and the Mishna, London, 1859.

G. WILDON PIERITZ: The Gospels from the Rabbinical Point of View, London, 1873.

J. ESTLIN CARPENTER: Life in Palestine When Jesus Lived, London, 1915.

A. EDERSHEIM: Sketches of Jewish Social Life in the Days of Christ.

A. EDERSHEIM: "Josephus" (in Smith's Dict. of Christ. Biogr.).

EDMOND STAPFER: Palestine in the Time of Christ.

A. HAUSRATH: The Time of Jesus.

G. HOBEN: The Virgin Birth (Chicago, 1903).

A. KNOWLING: Our Lord's Virgin Birth (3rd ed., London, 1907).

A. NEWMAN: Saint Athanasius (New York, 1911).

W. THORBURN: A Critical Examination of the Evidences for the Doctrine of the Virgin Birth (London, 1908).

MARTIN ZEIDEL: In the Time of Jesus.

THEODORE KEIM: The History of Jesus of Nazara, Vol. I.

BERNARD PICK: The Followers of Jesus in the Talmud, Newark, N. J., 1910.

FRED. C. CONYBEARE: The Historical Christ, London, 1914.

STEPHEN LIBERTY: The Political Relations of Christ's Ministry, London, 1916.

SIMON GREENLEAF: An Examination of the Testimony of the Four Evangelists, Boston, 1846.

JOSEPH WHELESS: Forgery in Christianity.

JOSEPH KLAUSNER: Jesus of Nazareth.

ERNEST RENAN: The Life of Jesus (Engl. transl., Brentano's ed., 1863).

ROBERT EISLER: The Messiah Jesus, John the Baptist, etc.

CONRAD HENRY MOEHLMAN: The Christian-Jewish Tragedy.

M. M. LEMANN: Jesus Before the Sanhedrin (Nashville, 1887).

MAX RADIN: The Trial of Jesus of Nazareth.

RABBI A. P. DRUCKER: The Trial of Jesus (Bloch, New York, 1907).

EDWARD HOLTON JAMES: The Trial Before Pilate (Concord, N. H., 1909).

GIOVANNI ROSADI: The Trial of Jesus (Engl. transl., N. Y. ——).

RICHARD W. HUSBAND: The Prosecution of Jesus (Princeton, 1916).

THOMA LEWIN: The Siege of Jerusalem by Titus.

Jew. Quart'ly Review, on Josephus, 1928 and 1931.

Dublin Review, on Josephus, London, 1926.

Quest, on Josephus, London, 1926 and 1927.

J. HENRY MIDDLETON: Topography and Archeology of Rome.

ENCYCLOPAEDIAS: Jewish; Catholic; Smith's Biblical; Schaff-Herzog; Abbot and Conant; Hamburger's; Kitto's; the "Extra Volume of Hasting's Dictionary of the Bible"; Hasting's Dictionary of the Apostolic Church.

Maps:

Henry Kiepert's Atlas Antiquus; Sidney E. Morse's Geographic Bible Atlas.

Note: Throughout this book, in all footnotes where reference is made to a work only by mention of its author, the reference is always to that volume of the writer which is specified in the Bibliography.

Index

A

B

C

D

E

F

I

J

O

P

Q

R

S

T

U

V

W

Z